The Mathematics of Financial Models

Founded in 1807, John Wiley & Sons is the oldest independent publishing company in the United States. With offices in North America, Europe, Australia and Asia, Wiley is globally committed to developing and marketing print and electronic products and services for our customers' professional and personal knowledge and understanding.

The Wiley Finance series contains books written specifically for finance and investment professionals as well as sophisticated individual investors and their financial advisors. Book topics range from portfolio management to e-commerce, risk management, financial engineering, valuation and financial instrument analysis, as well as much more.

For a list of available titles, visit our Website at www.WileyFinance.com.

The Mathematics of Financial Models

Solving Real-World Problems with Quantitative Methods

KANNOO RAVINDRAN

WILEY

Cover image: © Getty Images
Cover design: Wiley

Published by John Wiley & Sons, Inc., Hoboken, New Jersey.
Published simultaneously in Canada.

Library of Congress Cataloging-in-Publication Data:

ISBN 978-1-118-00461-6 (Hardcover)
ISBN 978-1-118-22185-3 (ePDF)
ISBN 978-1-118-23552-2 (ePub)

10 9 8 7 6 5 4 3 2 1

Contents

Preface

The purpose of this book is to give the reader a better appreciation and insight into the use of quantitative tools to solve real-world problems when there is a notion of cost (or money) involved. Examples of such problems exist in abundance in practice (e.g., budgeting, management of financial risks, valuation of financial instruments, optimizing the efficiency of operations, extension or termination of a contract, etc.) where one is interested in either minimizing the cost or maximizing the profit/revenue associated with a business decision. Despite the vast number of examples where quantitative methods are applied to solve practical problems in finance, due to time constraints, I can only discuss a limited number of them. As such, it is imperative for the reader to realize that the examples in this book are by no means exhaustive and it is my sincere desire to discuss more examples spanning across different industries in future editions of the book.

To discuss the application of quantitative methods in this book, I have organized the book into four sections. The first section focuses on problems associated with the construction of zero curves, discounting, and future valuing. The second section discusses problems associated with valuing both vanilla and exotic options. The third section focuses on estimation and the calibration of parameters used in pricing/hedging models, and the last section mentions hedging strategies, real options, and variable annuities.

To discuss these topics, instead of getting into details regarding the use of the underlying models, I provide sufficient background necessary to ensure that the reader is able to philosophically understand the problem that needs to be solved. Once this is done, I apply the relevant quantitative methods and underlying models to solve the problems, while keeping details on the quantitative methods used as supplemental materials on the website.

Though I have assumed that readers will have some general understanding of basic finance, derivatives, first-year calculus, and probability, this book is appropriate for any student, academic, and practitioner (which includes everyone from an end user to a market maker and anyone from a back-office function to a front-office function). More precisely, for readers who are quantitatively biased, this book provides the necessary practical examples and information so that nuances associated with the practicality of the problem can be better understood in order to better appreciate the use of quantitative tools to solve such problems in practice. For a reader who is less quantitatively inclined, the book presents tools that the reader can understand and apply to problems in practice without having to understand the proofs and theorems.

Acknowledgments

The quality of this book would definitely not have been possible without the feedback and suggestions of various practitioners—all of whom I have worked with and highly respect. I appreciate the time that they took from their tight schedules to comment on drafts of this manuscript and the online material. These people include Jacques Boudreau, Simon Chan, Pin Chung, Kirk Evans, Dan Heyer, Stefan Jaschke, and Gudmundur Magnusson. I am also very grateful to Dan, who contributed to a few sections of the materials on the website. Despite the valuable feedback, due to time constraints, I could only selectively incorporate some of the comments. As a consequence, I am totally responsible for any lack of clarity or depth in the material and any typos (or errors) that are still present.

Finally, I would like to thank the staff at Wiley Finance for being professional and patient with me throughout this project, despite unforeseen holdups on my end.

CHAPTER 1

Setting the Stage

Since the seminal Black-Scholes and Merton papers in 1973, the derivatives market has exploded by leaps and bounds. Derivatives are now being traded in esoteric asset classes like weather, mortality, credit, and real estate—just to name a few. While reasons for this development can be attributed to a myriad of factors, including taxes, market inefficiencies, creativity in product development, advances in financial modeling, investor sophistication, and so on, it is undeniable that the single biggest motivation for the existence of the current state of affairs in the derivatives market is the existence of sophisticated market participants. This, fueled by a flurry of publications on risk-quantification techniques, led investment banks in the late 1970s and early 1980s to employ mathematicians, physicists, and engineers with PhDs as their in-house rocket scientists or *quants* or eggheads. Thus began the migration of academics to the lucrative world of finance (who, at that time, were struggling to find decent university positions in their respective fields of mathematics, physics, and engineering). As a consequence, the field of financial economics grew exponentially in mathematical complexity, with practitioners beginning to question the assumptions underlying the Black-Scholes model in the hope of building a more realistic model that would give them a better competitive advantage.

After the 1987 stock market crash and a series of highly publicized derivatives-based bankruptcies in the 1990s, the use of the derivatives as useful risk-management tools has been constantly questioned and criticized. Even the legendary investor Warren Buffett labeled derivatives as the financial weapons of mass destruction. The irony of this undeserving bad press is that many of these losses could have easily happened even when trading cash instruments, since the primary reason for the bulk of these financial disasters has been the lack of proper controls and corporate governance.[1] Despite many of these unfounded criticisms, the derivatives markets has and will continue to flourish as financial markets become more globalized and bankers are constantly looking at innovative ways to strip and repackage risks to provide more effective, efficient, and customized solutions to the hedging-and-speculating clientele.

Given the above backdrop, it is not surprising to see quantitative tools deployed by derivatives practitioners finding their way (over the years) to the quantification of nonfinancial risks, as risk managers try to better understand the interdependence between financial market risks and nonfinancial market risks. The consequence of trying to better quantify and understand this risk interdependence is the ability to optimize the way resources are manipulated and deployed (or allocated) so as to maximize the value to the firm. This also explains the popularity of the growing discipline of Real Options[2] in which quantitative tools borrowed from the financial engineering world are integrated with those from other disciplines (e.g., engineering, actuarial science, manufacturing, or airline operations management) to create an integrated platform that can be used to better assess the impact of the operations' management on financial market risks, which, in turn, impacts the costs and ways the operations are run.

WHY IS THIS BOOK DIFFERENT?

There are many good technical books written on derivatives-related topics. With the exception of a few, many of them assume a certain level of mathematical familiarity and maturity with stochastic calculus—thereby making the materials almost nonaccessible or in comprehensible to practitioners (or wannabe practitioners) coming fresh out from an MBA or an undergraduate program, or who are eager to roll up their sleeves to learn such tools themselves. On the other hand, the books that provide a good foundation on derivatives (with very little emphasis on stochastic calculus), do not go far enough to provide the mathematical tools that are often necessary to

[1]There have been numerous examples of such incidences during the past few decades. One example of such an incident occurred in 2008 when Jerome Kerviel (Société Générale) hid his losses of USD$7 billion. As a consequence of being found guilty, Jerome was handed down a five-year prison sentence in addition to a permanent ban from working in the financial services industry. Another example is Bruno Iksil (also known as the London Whale) from JP Morgan. In this 2012 incident, JP Morgan lost about USD$7 billion.

[2]Myers in 1977 used the methods advocated by Black-Scholes and Merton (in their 1973 papers) to quantify corporate liabilities.

solve the practical problems encountered by a risk manager, analyst, or an operations manager.

The quantitative tools required by a risk practitioner are unique compared to the tools required by practitioners in other disciplines; these tools heavily borrow from and combine fields of pure mathematics, applied mathematics, probability, statistics, computer science, and so on—very much akin to the operations research field. As a consequence, any beginner without a good grasp of the tools can easily get lost in this quantitative maze. Based on my extensive risk-modelling experience across different businesses, I have found that while it is good for any aspiring professional to understand the mathematical rigor motivating these tools,[3] it is more important for someone to be able to understand the tools that are available, the strengths and weaknesses (limitations) of such tools, know how to apply the tools effectively, and fully comprehend what the risks are—all the while being able to ask the right questions without losing sight of common sense. As a consequence, given the power of personal computers and the ready availability of good quantitative commercial software packages like Microsoft Excel, @RISK, Matlab, and so on, it suffices for practitioners to understand the heuristics associated with the applications of these tools and how these tools can be adapted and customized for the needs of solving the particular problem.

Since this book is targeted to practitioners (and wannabe practitioners), I have kept the contents of this book to the discussion of practical issues and how quantitative tools are used to solve these problems, while leaving the review of such quantitative tools to the website accompanying this book. I have also had the luxury of using parts of this book to teach undergraduate and graduate students in business and financial engineering programs, as well as professionals on quantitative and modeling techniques. Given the number of students that I have taught over the decades with versions of this material, I think it is fairly safe to say that for readers to extract maximum value from this book they should have some level of familiarity with basic derivatives and financial concepts, undergraduate calculus, probability, and statistics. Although this book should be useful to any practitioner on a stand-alone basis, it can easily complement many of the widely used textbooks on derivatives, finance, and operations research.

ROAD MAP OF THE BOOK

To reiterate: The objective of this book is to illustrate the use of quantitative methods and techniques in business, finance, and operations management.

[3]Examples of this would be the study of measure theory and diffusion processes using stochastic calculus.

Despite the fact that there are numerous practical examples of how these methods are applied to solve real-world problems, due to time constraints I was unfortunately only able to find the time to discuss a few of such examples in this edition of the book.[4]

The book can be intuitively and broadly partitioned into the following four sections:

- First Section: Comprising Chapter 2, this section focuses on the basic building block of finance that is associated with the present valuing and future valuing of cash flows. More precisely, Chapter 2 discusses examples of market instruments and the use of these instruments to construct a zero (or discount) curve that can be used for present or future value cash flows.
- Second Section: Comprising Chapters 3, 4, and 5, this section focuses on the valuation of financial derivatives. The section starts by discussing the valuation of simple financial options with and without early exercise in Chapter 3. Given the predominant use of simulations in nearly all types of analysis that are carried out today, and the age of cheap computer hardware, it is important for any practitioner to have a good working knowledge of implementing simulations (despite them not being highly efficient!). Chapter 4 introduces the reader to simulations and walks the reader through various issues encountered when using simulations to solve a problem. It concludes with examples of applications of the simulation method in practice. The final chapter of this section uses the ideas discussed in Chapters 3 and 4 to value complex path-dependent options.
- Third Section: Comprising Chapters 6 and 7, this section focuses on the estimation of parameters in a model and the risks arising from the mis-estimation of these parameters. Chapter 6 kicks off this section by discussing the estimation of the parameters in trading models. As any trader would appreciate, the bulk of trading that is done using models revolves around the view on the correctness of the model parameters. Chapter 7 discusses ways of managing such risks and, more importantly, quantifying the effectiveness of hedging strategies used to manage the risks before implementing them.
- Fourth Section: The last section of the book discusses further applications of quantitative methods as they relate to specific industry

[4]It is my desire to add to these examples in subsequent editions of the book so as to eventually end up with a compendium of examples spanning across industries.

problems—taking into consideration the nuances of appropriate business specifics. Starting with Chapter 8 on the valuation of variable annuities (an investment-based insurance product), the section concludes with the chapter on real options.

As mentioned earlier, the use of quantitative methods in daily business and financial affairs is becoming increasingly prevalent. Thus, the more one gets comfortable with the use and manipulation of the software (e.g., Microsoft Excel, @RISK, Matlab), one's ability to quantify the risks, value decisions, consumer behavior, revenues, profits, and so on using appropriate techniques and models becomes better and easier.

In writing this book, I cannot reiterate enough that these examples are far from exhaustive. As such, I welcome readers to submit suggestions (or examples) they want to be discussed in future editions of the book.

REFERENCES

Black, F., and M. Scholes. 1973. "The Pricing of Options and Corporate Liabilities." *Journal of Political Economy* 81:673–659.

Buffett, Warren. 2002. *Berkshire Hathaway Annual Report.*

Merton, R. C. 1973. "Theory of Rational Option Pricing." *Bell Journal of Economics and Management Science* 4:141–83.

Myers, S. C. 1977. "Determinants of Corporate Borrowing." *Journal of Financial Economics* 5:147–130.

CHAPTER 2

Building Zero Curves

One important task that financial practitioners face daily is the need to present value (or discount) a cash flow that is going to be paid (or received) some time in the future. While it is straightforward to do this if a discount rate for the respective cash flow is known, in practice this is far from truth as:

- Instruments have varying definitions and settlement criteria associated with the rates that are used for trading the respective instruments.[1]
- Instruments that trade in the marketplace are usually not zero coupon bonds—hence making it difficult to extract the exact discount rates.
- The maturity (or coupon) date of instruments typically does not mirror the dates of the cash flows that need to be discounted.

Given the above, it is important for any practitioner to have a consistent and objective process that can be used to discount any future cash flow. To help with this, I will focus my discussion in this chapter on the use of liquid market instruments to construct a curve of zero rates[2] so as

[1]For example, swaps are traded using swap rates, bonds are traded using yields-to-maturity (or bond prices), and Treasury bills are traded using quoted prices (which are actually yields). This naturally leads one to the following two important questions:

1. Which rate is the right one to use?
2. How does one find the relative value of one instrument vis-a-vis another?

[2]A zero rate is an interest rate applied to a specific time to present (future) value cash flow from (to) that time, where all zero rates are expressed as continuously compounded rates. Thus, if the one-, two-, and three-year zero rates are 2, 3, and 5 percent respectively, then receiving a dollar one, two, and three years from now is equivalent to receiving $e^{-1*0.02} = 0.9802$, $e^{-2*0.03} = 0.9418$, and $e^{-3*0.05} = 0.8607$

to be able to discount cash flows from varying maturities. Starting with an overview on how various interest-bearing instruments are valued and traded, the chapter goes on to discuss the construction of the zero curve using a linear function assumption. The chapter concludes with the use of a cubic polynomial to construct the zero-rate curve following which a discussion on the difference in the types of zero curves produced using these methods is given.

MARKET INSTRUMENTS

There are many instruments that are traded in the financial markets. Since the concept of calculating the present value of cash flow involves the use of interest rates, I will restrict my discussion to interest-bearing instruments. As this comprises a very broad universe of instruments, for the purposes of illustration, I will focus on treasury bills, treasury bonds, euro-dollar futures, and swaps.

Treasury Bills

Treasury bills (or T-bills) are short-term debt instruments that are issued by the U.S. Treasury. With maturities of less than a year, these zero-coupon bonds are usually issued with maturities of 1, 3, 6, and 12 months. While 12-month T-bills are auctioned monthly, T-bills of other maturities are auctioned weekly.[3] As stated in the T-bill settlement calculation put out by the U.S. Treasury, the formula used to convert a discount yield into a settlement price is given by the expression

$$DY = \frac{100 - Price}{100} * \frac{360}{T} \tag{2.1}$$

respectively today. These numbers are also sometimes called zero-coupon discount factors or discount factors for short. Each zero rate is uniquely associated with a maturity date (or term), and the collection of all these zero rates across varying maturities is called a zero-rate curve or zero-rate term structure or zero curve. Since a zero rate is used to present a future dollar—the quality of the counterparty paying this dollar would affect the magnitude of this present value. Hence the present value of a dollar received from a AAA entity for a given maturity would *never* be greater than the present value of a dollar received from a BBB entity for the same maturity. This difference in present values is simply due to the value of the AAA/BBB credit spread as perceived by the market participants.

[3]For more details associated with Treasury bills, go to www.treasurydirect.gov/indiv/research/indepth/tbills/res_tbill.htm.

TABLE 2.1 Calculating the Cash Price of a Treasury Bill

	A	B	C
1	Quoted Price (%)	5.00%	
2	Time to Maturity (days)	30	
3	Cash Price	99.5833333	=100-(B1*B2*100/360)

where *DY* represents the discount yield (or quoted price[4]), Price represents the cash (or settlement) price associated with the Treasury bill, and *T* represents the number of calendar days from today to the maturity date.[5] Table 2.1 shows the use of equation (2.1) when $DY = 0.05$ and $T = 30$ days.

As can be seen from Table 2.1, when the quoted price is 5 percent, the cash price paid for this T-bill is USD99.5833 so as to receive USD100 in 30 days.

Treasury Notes

Treasury notes (or T-notes) are debt instruments that are issued by the U.S. Treasury. With maturities of more than a year but no more than 10 years, these semi-annual coupon bonds are usually issued with maturities of 2, 3, 5, 7, and 10 years and the next business-day settlement. While a 10-year T-note is auctioned only in the months of February, May, August, and November, the T-notes of other maturities are auctioned monthly.[6] The formula that is used to compute the accrued interest between coupon dates is of the form

$$AI = 100 * \frac{d}{N} * \frac{C}{2} \tag{2.2}$$

where *AI* represents the accrued interest owed to the owner of the note since the last coupon date, *d* represents the number of calendar days from the last coupon date to the settlement date, *N* represents the number of calendar days

[4]Quoted price is the terminology that is used to refer to a traded price (i.e., the price seen on a trading screen) although in this instance the quoted price refers to the yield and not the price.

[5]For the purposes of settlement, *T* is calculated from the day the transaction is settled–which is one business day following the trade date.

[6]The 10-year T-note is also auctioned as a reopening in the other months of the year, where the definition of reopening means that the already issued (i.e., existing) 10-year T-notes are reissued with the same maturity dates, coupon sizes, and coupon dates but with different issue dates. The reader is referred to the link www.treasurydirect.gov/instit/marketables/tnotes/tnotes.htm for details.

between the last and next coupon dates, and c represents the annual coupon rate associated with the bond.[7] Since bonds are traded interchangeably using both prices and yields-to-maturity (or yields), it is important for any practitioner to understand the following interplay between these two forms of representations:

- The prices on which bonds are traded (quoted) are called *clean prices,* because they do not include the accrued interest that must be paid to the seller of the bond in order to compensate the seller for holding the bond from the last coupon date to the settlement date.
- The yields on which bonds are traded are calculated using *dirty prices* that are obtained by adding the bond clean prices to their accrued interests [which are computed using equation (2.2)].
- The relationship that connects a bond yield to a bond price takes the form

$$QP_{Bond} + \left(100 * \frac{d}{N} * \frac{C}{2}\right) = \frac{100 + \dfrac{100 * C}{2}}{(1 + \frac{y}{2})^{x+n-1}} + \sum_{i=1}^{n-1} \frac{\dfrac{100 * C}{2}}{(1 + \frac{y}{2})^{x+i-1}} \quad (2.3)$$

where QP_{Bond} represents the quoted price, $d/N/C$ are as given in equation (2.2), n denotes the number of periods taken to receive the last coupon, y denotes the yield-to-maturity of the bond, and x denotes the stub period between the settlement date and the next coupon date which is given by the formula

$$x = \frac{\text{Number of days between settlement date and next coupon date}}{\text{Number of days between last coupon date and next coupon date}}$$

The Microsoft Excel function "=Price()" gives the clean price of a bond and can be used to value the type of bonds discussed above by using a basis of 1.[8] Microsoft Excel also has a function, "=Accrint()", that provides the

[7]This is sometimes also called the A/A or Actual/Actual day-count convention, where the Actual in the numerator refers to the actual number of days between the last coupon date and settlement date, while the Actual in the denominator refers to the number of calendar days between the last and next coupon dates. Other conventions that are sometimes used are A/360 (or Actual/360), A/365 (or Actual/365), 30/360, and so on.

[8]The last argument of the "=Price()" function is called the basis, which can either be 0, 1, 2, 3, or 4, where each value refers to a different type of day-count convention. The interested reader is referred to Microsoft Excel for further details.

TABLE 2.2A Calculating Bond Yield from Bond Price

	A	B	C
1	Quoted Price (Clean Price)	$98.85	
2	Bond Maturity Date	2-Sep-14	
3	Current Date (Settlement Date)	10-Jun-12	
4	Coupon Rate (Annual)	8%	
5	Yield to Maturity (Guess)	8.57%	
6	Quoted Price–Guess Price	$0.00	=B1-PRICE(B3,B2,B4,B5,100,2,1)

accrued interest a bond buyer has to pay in addition to the bond's clean price.[9]

Table 2.2a shows how Microsoft Excel's "=Price()" function can be used to obtain the yield-to-maturity of a bond from its quoted price.

As can be seen from Table 2.2a, a guess on the yield-to-maturity is initially done and then iterated in a manner to make the result in cell B6 zero. One can alternatively obtain the solution in cell B5 using another Microsoft Excel function—"=Yield()"—with the appropriate arguments. In practice, it is not uncommon for a portfolio to contain millions of bonds, bonds with uneven coupon sizes, or infrequent coupon dates. As a consequence, due to the lack of efficiency and standardization between the bonds, it is impractical to use Microsoft Excel functions to compute bond prices and yields. In such instances, practitioners resort to the use of numerical methods (e.g., Newton's Method).

To illustrate the use of Newton's Method to compute bond yields, I will redo the example in Table 2.2a. In order to do this, one needs to first rewrite equation (2.3) as follows:

$$f(y) = QP_{Bond} + \left(100 * \frac{d}{N} * \frac{C}{2}\right) - \frac{100 + \dfrac{100 * C}{2}}{(1 + \frac{y}{2})^{x+n-1}} - \sum_{i=1}^{n-1} \frac{\dfrac{100 * C}{2}}{(1 + \frac{y}{2})^{x+i-1}} \tag{2.4a}$$

In doing so, the required yield of the bond is simply the solution of the equation $f(y) = 0$.

[9]It is important for the reader to realize that as long as the price is known (whether it is a clean or dirty price), the yield-to-maturity of a bond can be manually calculated by varying the yield input until the price is matched.

By Newton's method, the solution to the equation $f(y) = 0$ can be obtained by recursively solving

$$y_n = y_{n-1} - \frac{f(y_{n-1})}{\frac{df(y_{n-1})}{dy_{n-1}}} \tag{2.4b}$$

for $n = 1, 2, 3, \ldots$, where y_0 is the initial guess. $\frac{df(y)}{dy}$ in equation (2.4b) can be obtained by differentiating equation (2.4a) with respect to y and shown to give rise to equation (2.4c)

$$\frac{df(y)}{dy} = \frac{(x+n-1) * (100 + \frac{100 * C}{2})}{2 * (1 + \frac{y}{2})^{x+n}} + \frac{1}{4} \sum_{i=1}^{n-1} \frac{(x+i-1) * 100 * C}{(1 + \frac{y}{2})^{x+i}} \tag{2.4c}$$

Table 2.2b shows the implementation of Newton's method using equations (2.4a), (2.4b), and (2.4c) to obtain the required bond yield.

As can be seen from Table 2.2b, one is able to converge to the bond yield obtained in Table 2.2a using Newton's method in 3 iterations.

Treasury Bonds

Treasury bonds, like the T-notes, are also debt instruments that are issued by the U.S. Treasury. With a maturity of more than 10 years, these semi-annual coupon bonds are auctioned in the months of February, May, August, and November, although they are reopened during the other months of the year. The computations associated with accrued interest, yield-to-maturity, quoted price, settlement, and so on are identical to those used for T-notes.

Eurodollar Futures

Eurodollars refer to U.S. dollar deposits in a U.S. or a foreign bank that is domiciled outside the United States.[10] A Eurodollar futures contract is

[10]The origin of these types of deposits goes back to the Cold War. More precisely, before the Cold War, it was customary to make deposits in the country of the denominated currency (e.g., to make a U.S.-dollar-denominated deposit one would need to deposit U.S. dollars in a bank that is domiciled in the United States and to make a yen-denominated deposit one would need to deposit yen in a bank that is domiciled

TABLE 2.2B Calculating Bond Yield Using Newton's Method

	A	B	C	D	E	F	G
1	Quoted Price (Clean Price)	$98.85					
2	Bond Maturity Date	2-Sep-14					
3	Current Date (Settlement Date)	10-Jun-12					
4	Coupon Rate (Annual)	8%					
5	Yield to Maturity Initial Guess (y_0)	0.03					
6	Most Recent Coupon Date Before	2-Mar-12					
7	Next Coupon Date	2-Sep-12	=EDATE(B6,6)				
8	# calendar days between coupons	182.5					
9	d (yrs)	0.5479	=(B3- B6)/B8				
10	N (yrs)	1.0082	=(B7- B6)/B9				
11	x (yrs)	0.4603	=(B7- B3)/B10				
12	n	5					
13	AI	2.1739	=100*B9*B4/(B10*2)				
14	i	0	1	2	3	4	5
15	y_i	3.000%	8.176%	8.557%	8.559%	8.559%	8.559%
16	PV(principal & 5th coupon pymt)	97.3180	86.9813	86.2730	86.2696	86.2696	
17	PV(4th coupon)	3.7991	3.4822	3.4602	3.4601	3.4601	
18	PV(3rd coupon)	3.8561	3.6245	3.6082	3.6081	3.6081	
19	PV(2nd coupon)	3.9140	3.7727	3.7626	3.7626	3.7626	
20	PV(1st coupon)	3.9727	3.9269	3.9236	3.9236	3.9236	
21	dPV(principal & 5th coupon pymt)/dy	213.8250	186.3621	184.5061	184.4970	184.4970	
22	dPV(4th coupon)/dy	6.4759	5.7881	5.7409	5.7407	5.7407	
23	dPV(3rd coupon)/dy	4.6735	4.2836	4.2565	4.2564	4.2564	
24	dPV(2nd coupon)/dy	2.8155	2.6464	2.6345	2.6344	2.6344	
25	dPV(1st coupon)/dy	0.9007	0.8682	0.8659	0.8659	0.8659	
26	f(y)	−11.8360	−0.7637	−0.0037	0.0000	0.0000	
27	df(y)/dy	228.6906	199.9484	198.0039	197.9944	197.9944	

CALCULATED USING CURRENT DATE AND BOND MATURITY DATE

Y_0

$Y_1 = Y_0 - f(Y_0)/[df(Y_0)/d(Y_0)]$

a futures contract on a 3-month Eurodollar deposit. The last trading day associated with a Eurodollar futures contract tends to be two business days (at 1100 hours London time) prior to the third Wednesday of the months of March, June, September, and December of the first 10 years. In addition to this, the four nearest serial months (which are not in the March quarterly cycle) are also included as expiry dates.[11]

in Japan). During the Cold War, the former Soviet Union bloc nations had to use U.S. dollars to do their import and export. Due to the fear of getting their assets frozen, the Soviet Union invested its U.S. dollars in a British bank (which was owned by the Soviet Union) that had a British charter, which in turn made the deposit into a U.S. bank that was domiciled in the United States—thereby creating the first-known transaction of a Eurodollar deposit.

[11]For further details on the contract specifications associated with the Eurodollar futures contract, see www.cmegroup.com/trading/interest-rates/stir/eurodollar_contract_specifications.html.

Given how a Eurodollar futures contract is constructed, the Eurodollar futures interest rate is defined to be $100 - QP$, where QP represents the quoted Eurodollar futures price. Furthermore, the contract or settlement price associated with this QP is given by the expression $10,000 * [100 - 0.25 * (100 - QP)]$. Thus, a QP of 99.25 gives rise to a Eurodollar futures interest rate[12] of 0.075 percent and a contract price of USD998,125 where each contract results in a maturity value of USD1,000,000.

Since Eurodollar futures contracts provide a market expectation where the underlying 3-month LIBOR rates will be in the future, practitioners use them as a proxy for 3-month forward rate agreements[13] with some adjustments. To do this, practitioners use the approximation[14]

$$Forward\ rate = Futures\ rate - \frac{1}{2}\sigma^2 t_1 t_2 \tag{2.5}$$

to correct the futures rate, where the *futures rate* represents the rate of a 3-month Eurodollar futures contract rate maturing at time t_1 that is continuously compounded, $t_2 - t_1 \approx 0.25$, σ represents the standard deviation of the change in the interest rate, and *forward rate* represents the continuously compounded forward rate for a 3-month LIBOR setting on t_1 and settling on t_2. The reader is referred to Hull (2012) for further details. Table 2.3 shows how these calculations are implemented in practice.

Swaps

Since the first interest rate swap transaction between World Bank and IBM in 1991, interest rate swaps have grown to be one of the most widely traded derivatives contracts on the over-the-counter (OTC) markets. In its simplest form, a swap basically is a financial instrument that allows two parties to exchange floating interest rate payments for fixed rate ones over a fixed

---

[12]This can be obtained by simply computing the quantity $(100 - QP)\,\%$.

[13]Forward rate agreements (FRAs) are also considered as single period swaps, which are essentially bilateral financial contracts trading in the over-the-counter market in which one party agrees to exchange the interest payments linked to the then-prevailing 3-month LIBOR for those linked to a prespecified forward rate.

[14]There are two reasons for the need of the correction in equation (2.5). The first stems from the fact that in a forward rate contract there is no concept of marked-to-market compared to a Eurodollar futures contract in which the positions are marked-to-market daily until the contract matures at time t_1. The second stems from the fact that, unlike a forward contract where the parties only settle up at time t_2, in a Eurodollar futures contract, assuming it is held to expiry date, the parties settle up at time t_1.

TABLE 2.3 Calculating Continuously Compounded Forward Rates from a Eurodollar Futures Price

	A	B	C
1	Quoted Futures Price	$94.00	
2	Implied Futures Rate	6.000%	=(100-B1)/100
3	Time to Futures Contract Maturity	8	
4	Time to Settlement of Underlying LIBOR Contract	8.25	
5	Standard Deviation of Short Rate	1.20%	
6	Continuously Compounded Futures Rate	5.955%	=LN(1+(B2*(B4-B3)))/(B4-B3)
7	Convexity Adjustment	0.475200%	=0.5*B5*B5*B3*B4
8	Continuously Compounded Forward Rate	5.480245%	=B7-B6

period of time based on a predefined notional amount.[15] This type of swap is also called a simple, fixed-floating swap. See Ravindran (1997) for further details on this type of a swap and variations on this theme.

Unlike the instruments discussed earlier, pricing an interest rate swap requires a zero-rate curve as an input. Suppose that a discount factor associated with a given time t_i is denoted by D_{t,t_i} (where the current time is t, the zero-rate is assumed to be given for time t_i and $t_i > t$) and $D_{t,t} = 1$ (since the present value of a dollar today is simply a dollar), and that one is interested in pricing[16] an n-period swap where the floating rates are reset n times during the life of the swap at times $t_1, t_2, \ldots, t_n$ and $t \leq t_1 < t_2 < \ldots < t_n$. Assume further that the cash flows arising from the settlement of the floating and fixed interest rates are done so at times $t_2, t_3, \ldots, t_{n+1}$ where $t \leq t_1 <$

[15]To illustrate, consider an example of a two-year, semiannually reset interest rate swap on a notional of USD100MM. In this instance, one party pays interest payments using the floating rate of 6-month LIBOR that are reset once every 6 months (at 0-month, 6-month, 12-month, and 18-month time) and receives interest payments once every 6 months (on the dates when the floating-rate payments are settled at the 6-month, 12-month, 18-month, and 24-month periods) that are based on a fixed rate (called the swap rate). As a consequence, there will be four cash-flow exchange dates at 6 months, 12 months, 18 months, and 24 months. On each cash-flow date the interests arising from both the floating and fixed interest rates would be netted off. The party resulting in a negative cash flow position would end up writing a check to its counterparty. Thus, a swap rate can be intuitively thought of as a blending of the market's expectation on how the future 6-month floating rates will unfold. Furthermore, it may be of interest to the reader to note that a single-period swap (i.e., $n = 1$) is equivalent to a forward rate agreement.

[16]Pricing a fixed-floating interest rate swap is analogous to finding a fixed rate associated with the swap, so the practice of exchanging interest-rate payments based on a floating-rate LIBOR for those based on a fixed swap rate would require no upfront exchange of cash flows.

TABLE 2.4 Calculating Swap Rates from a Zero Curve

	A	B	C	D
1	Time (t_1)	Discount Factors (D_i)	$(t_{i+1} - t_i) * D_{i+1}$	
2	0.0000	1		
3	0.5050	0.975066115	0.492408388	=(A3-A2)*B3
4	1.0000	0.946485148	0.468510148	=(A4-A3)*B4
5	1.5020	0.91382152	0.458738403	=(A5-A4)*B5
6	2.0030	0.860514339	0.431117684	=(A6-A5)*B6
7		Swap Rate	7.537%	=(B2-B6)/SUM(C3:C6)

$t_2 < \ldots < t_{n+1}$. Then the fixed rate of the swap can be shown to be given by the following formula.[17]

$$\frac{D_{t,t_1} - D_{t,t_{n+1}}}{\sum_{i=1}^{n}(t_{i+1} - t_i)D_{t,t_{i+1}}} \tag{2.6}$$

An application of equation (2.6) is given in Table 2.4.

LINEAR INTERPOLATION

In the previous section, I discussed the quoting, pricing, and settling of some commonly traded interest-rate instruments. In addition, I also discussed how a zero curve can be used as an input to value a fixed-floating interest rate swap. Given this backdrop, I will now focus on the construction of a zero curve using observed, tradeable prices and rates.

Although a zero rate associated with a specific maturity can be used to determine the present value of a cash flow happening on the maturity date, the purpose of a zero curve is to:

- Reproduce the prices/rates of the instruments that are used to construct the zero curve.
- Interpolate and extrapolate relevant zero rates that can be used to determine the present value of cash flows linked to maturities that do not coincide with those used for the zero rate curve calibration.

The process of building a zero curve using a collection of liquid tradeable interest-rate instruments is called *zero-curve construction*. It starts with the shortest instrument maturity and then gradually builds the curve out (or

[17]This is discussed in detail in the Appendix of this chapter.

TABLE 2.5 Market Information

	A	B	C
1	Instruments	Quoted Prices/Rates	Maturities (years)
2	Overnight Rate	0.10%	0.0000
3	1-month Eurodollar futures	99.850	0.0833
4	2-month Eurodollar futures	99.700	0.1677
5	3-month Eurodollar futures	99.500	0.2500
6	6-month Eurodollar futures	99.000	0.5000
7	12-month Eurodollar futures	98.800	1.0000
8	2-year semiannual reset swap	2.00%	
9	5-year semiannual reset swap	3.00%	

bootstraps[18]) over longer maturities. In this section, I discuss the process of zero-curve building, assuming that

- Liquid instruments used to build the zero curve are given.
- Linear method is used to interpolate between two given zero rates.
- Zero rates beyond the longest available instrument maturity are extrapolated horizontally.

Using the market data given in Table 2.5 and assuming that the zero rates are extrapolated horizontally beyond the 5-year maturity (as this is the longest maturity associated with the given market information), I will now discuss the construction of a zero curve using a four-step process for terms less than five years.

Assuming that $r_{t,u}$ represents the zero rate associated with a maturity time u when the current time is t (where $u > t$), one can obtain the appropriate zero rates by going through the following four steps.

Step 1: Convert Eurodollar Futures Prices to Forward Rates

From the discussion on Eurodollar futures, one can convert the 1-, 2-, 3-, 6-, and 12-month quoted Eurodollar futures prices into implied 3-month futures rates (as in Table 2.6), which can be converted to implied 3-month forward rates.

[18]The term bootstrap is used to reflect the fact that in putting on a pair of boots and tightening up the laces, one has to start from the bottom-most end of the holes (which the lace has to go through) and then tighten the lace across each hole to eventually arrive at the topmost end of the holes.

TABLE 2.6 Extracting Futures Rates from Eurodollar Prices

	A	B	C	D	E
1	Instruments	Quoted Prices/Rates	Maturities (years)	Continuously Compounded Implied Futures Rate	
2	Overnight Rate	0.10%	0.0000		
3	1-month Eurodollar futures	99.850	0.0833	0.150%	=LN(1+(((100-B3)/100)*(C3-C2)))/(C3-C2)
4	2-month Eurodollar futures	99.700	0.1677	0.300%	=LN(1+(((100-B4)/100)*(C4-C3)))/(C4-C3)
5	3-month Eurodollar futures	99.500	0.2500	0.500%	=LN(1+(((100-B5)/100)*(C5-C4)))/(C5-C4)
6	6-month Eurodollar futures	99.000	0.5000	0.999%	=LN(1+(((100-B6)/100)*(C6-C5)))/(C6-C5)
7	12-month Eurodollar futures	98.800	1.0000	1.196%	=LN(1+(((100-B7)/100)*(C7-C6)))/(C7-C6)
8	2-year semiannual reset swap	2.00%			
9	5-year semiannual reset swap	3.00%			

By using equation (2.5) and assuming a short-rate standard deviation of 1.2 percent, one gets the continuously compounded 3-month forward rates as shown in Table 2.7.

Step 2: Calibrate Zero Rates for First Year

From Table 2.7, the reader should observe that since the continuously compounded overnight rate is 0.1 percent, I have trivially assumed that the zero rate is 0.1 percent at time 0 (i.e., $r_{0,0} = 0.1\%$).

To obtain the other zero rates, it is first important to understand the relationship between zero rates and continuously compounded forward rates. More precisely, if $r_{t,u}$ and $r_{t,w}$ represent the respective zero rates for maturities u and w (obtained from the zero curve at current time t) respectively where $t < u < w$, then the continuously compounded forward rate applied from time u to w is given by the expression

$$\frac{[r_{t,w} * (w - t)] - [r_{t,u} * (u - t)]}{w - u} \tag{2.7}$$

Since the continuously compounded 3-month forward rate at time 0.0833 years is 0.15 percent, if $r_{0,0.0833}$ and $r_{0,0.3333}$ represent the continuously compounded zero rates at times 0.0833 years and 0.3333 years respectively, then using equation (2.7) one gets

$$\frac{(r_{0,0.3333} * 0.3333) - (r_{0,0.0833} * 0.0833)}{0.3333 - 0.0833} = 0.0015 \tag{2.8a}$$

Additionally because of the linear interpolation assumption, it follows that

$$\frac{r_{0,0.3333} - r_{0,0.0833}}{0.3333 - 0.0833} = \frac{r_{0,0.0833} - r_{0,0}}{0.0833 - 0} = \frac{r_{0,0.0833} - 0.001}{0.0833} \tag{2.8b}$$

Solving equations (2.8a) and (2.8b), one has $r_{0,0.0833} = 0.11\%$ and $r_{0,0.3333} = 0.14\%$. Putting all these together, one can arrive at the zero rates given in Table 2.8.

Continuing to build the zero curve for longer maturities, one now needs to get $r_{0,0.1667}$ (zero rate at time 0.1667 years) and $r_{0,0.4167}$ (zero rate at time

TABLE 2.7 Extracting Continuously Compounded Forward Rates from Futures Rates

	A	B	C	D	E
1	Instruments	Quoted Prices/Rates	Continuously Compounded Implied Futures Rate	Continuously Compounded Forward Rate	
2	Overnight Rate	0.10%			
3	1-month Eurodollar futures	99.850	0.150%	0.150%	=C6-(0.5*0.012*0.012*(1/12)*(0.25+(1/12)))
4	2-month Eurodollar futures	99.700	0.300%	0.299%	=C7-(0.5*0.012*0.012*(1/12)*(0.25+(1/12)))
5	3-month Eurodollar futures	99.500	0.500%	0.499%	=86-(0.5*0.012*0.012*(1/12)*(0.25+(1/12)))
6	6-month Eurodollar futures	99.000	0.999%	0.996%	=C9-(0.5*0.012*0.012*(1/12)*(0.25+(1/12)))
7	12-month Eurodollar futures	98.800	1.196%	1.187%	=C10-(0.5*0.012*0.012*(1/12)*(0.25+(1/12)))
8	2-year semiannual reset swap	2.00%			
9	5-year semiannual reset swap	3.00%			

TABLE 2.8 Zero Rates Obtained Using the First Eurodollar Futures Contract

	A	B
1	Time (years)	Zero Rates
2	0	0.1000%
3	0.0833	0.1100%
4	0.3333	0.1400%

TABLE 2.9 Zero Rates Obtained Using the First Two Eurodollar Futures Contracts

	A	B
1	Time (years)	Zero Rates
2	0	0.100%
3	0.0833	0.110%
4	0.1667	0.120%
5	0.3333	0.140%
6	0.4167	0.228%

0.4167 years) so as to match up with the 3-month forward rate starting 2 months from now. Using equation (2.7) one gets

$$\frac{(r_{0,0.4167} * 0.4167) - (r_{0,0.1667} * 0.1667)}{0.4167 - 0.1677} = 0.00299 \qquad (2.8c)$$

Since $r_{0,0.1667}$ can be linearly interpolated using the zero rates $r_{0,0.0833}$ and $r_{0,0.3333}$, it readily follows that $r_{0,0.1667} = 0.0012$. Using this value, in equation (2.8c), it is easy to see that $r_{0,0.4167} = 0.00228$.

Putting this together with Table 2.8, one can arrive at Table 2.9.

Repeating this for all the subsequent times, one can arrive at Table 2.10.[19]

Using Table 2.10, the zero rates in the time interval (0, 0.0833) or (0.0833, 0.1677) or (0.1617, 0.2500) or (0.2500, 0.3333) or (0.3333, 0.4167) or (0.4167, 0.5000) or (0.5000, 0.7500) or (0.7500, 1.0000) or

[19]Throughout this example I have assumed that the tenor underlying the forward rates is the same as that for the Eurodollar futures contract and is 0.25 years.

TABLE 2.10 Zero Rates Obtained Using All Eurodollar Futures Contracts

	A	B
1	Time (years)	Zero Rates
2	0	0.100%
3	0.0833	0.110%
4	0.1667	0.120%
5	0.2500	0.130%
6	0.3333	0.140%
7	0.4167	0.228%
8	0.5000	0.305%
9	0.7500	0.535%
10	1.0000	0.644%
11	1.2500	0.752%

(1.0000, 1.2500) can be easily obtained using linear interpolation. For example, to compute $r_{0,0.3}$, the zero rate at 0.3 years, one has to use the rates at times 0.2500 and 0.3333 to linearly interpolate and obtain

$$r_{0,0.3} = 0.13\% + \frac{(0.14\% - 0.13\%) * (0.3000 - 0.2500)}{0.3333 - 0.2500} = 0.136\%$$

Step 3: Calibrate to Obtain Zero Rates for First Two Years

To value a 2-year swap, one has to resort to using the formula given in equation (2.6). To do this, one would need the discount factors at times 6, 12, 18, and 24 months (or equivalently the zero rates $r_{0,0.5}$, $r_{0,1}$, $r_{0,1.5}$, and $r_{0,2}$). Since one can easily read off the zero rates $r_{0,0.5}$ and $r_{0,1}$ from Table 2.10, it remains to only find the zero rates $r_{0,1.5}$ and $r_{0,2}$.

Given that the maturities in Table 2.10 go out to only 1.25 years, one has to first guess the zero rate $r_{0,2}$ and then linearly interpolate the value of $r_{0,1.5}$ (using the values $r_{0,1.25}$ and $r_{0,2}$) so as to ensure that the 2-year swap rate is matched.

To do this, first observe that the discount factors associated for times 1.5 years and 2 years are given by the expressions $D_{0,1.5} = e^{-1.5*r_{0,1.5}}$ and $D_{0,2} = e^{-2*r_{0,2}}$ respectively. Putting all these together into equation (2.6) to value a 2-year, fixed-floating interest rate swap, one has

$$\frac{1 - D_{0,2}}{0.5 * (D_{0,0.5} + D_{0,1} + D_{0,1.5} + D_{0,2})} = 0.02$$

TABLE 2.11 Zero Rates for First Two Years

	A	B
1	Time (years)	Zero Rates
2	0	0.100%
3	0.0833	0.110%
4	0.1667	0.120%
5	0.2500	0.130%
6	0.3333	0.140%
7	0.4167	0.228%
8	0.5000	0.305%
9	0.7500	0.535%
10	1.0000	0.644%
11	1.2500	0.752%
12	1.5000	1.171%
13	2.0000	2.007%

where $D_{0,0.5} = e^{-0.5 * r_{0,0.5}}$ and $D_{0,1} = e^{-1 * r_{0,1}}$ refer to the discount factors for times 0.5 years and 1 year, respectively. Using the linear interpolation of the zero-rate curve in the time interval (1.25,2) yields,

$$\frac{r_{0,2} - r_{0,1.5}}{2 - 1.5} = \frac{r_{0,1.5} - r_{0,1.25}}{1.5 - 1.25}$$

Putting all these together, one can arrive at Table 2.11.

Step 4: Calibrate to Obtain Zero Rates for First Five Years

Applying a similar idea to step 3, one can arrive at Table 2.12.

The information in Table 2.12 can be alternatively represented as in Figure 2.1.

Given the constructed zero-rate curve in Figure 2.1, one can easily read off zero rates for any maturity. Although the methodology discussed provides a reader with a good idea on how linear interpolation can be used to bootstrap a zero curve using market information, in practice the reader has to bear in mind some of the following subtleties associated with this method:

- Instead of linearly interpolating and bootstrapping zero rates, one can alternatively linearly interpolate and bootstrap discount factors or natural logarithm of discount factors or forward rates. Doing this can possibly yield a completely different zero curve—in the process arriving at different values when discounting cash flows. As a consequence, for the purposes of consistency, it is imperative for one to do what market

TABLE 2.12 Zero Rate Term Structure

	A	B
1	Time (years)	Zero Rates
2	0.0000	0.100%
3	0.0833	0.110%
4	0.1667	0.120%
5	0.2500	0.130%
6	0.3333	0.140%
7	0.4167	0.228%
8	0.5000	0.305%
9	0.7500	0.535%
10	1.0000	0.644%
11	1.2500	0.752%
12	1.5000	1.171%
13	2.0000	2.007%
14	2.5000	2.178%
15	3.0000	2.348%
16	3.5000	2.518%
17	4.0000	2.688%
18	4.5000	2.858%
19	5.0000	3.028%

practitioners generally do as opposed to doing something that is theoretically correct. The reader is referred to Van Deventer, Imai, and Mesler (2005) for further details.

- In the discussion presented, I used only the overnight rate, Eurodollar futures, and the swap rates to construct the zero curve. The reason for

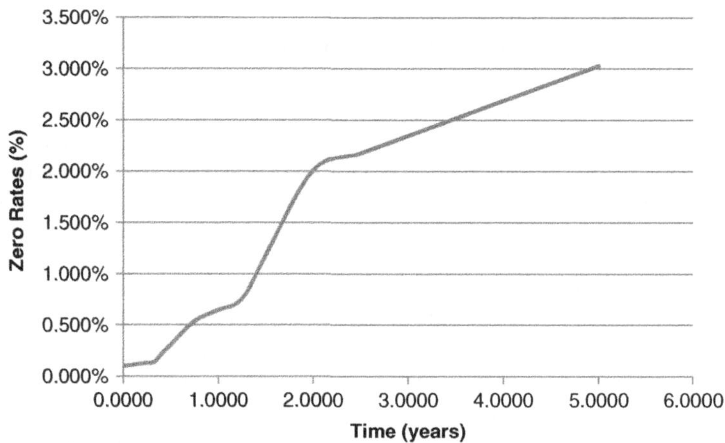

FIGURE 2.1 Term Structure of Zero Rates for the First Five Years

this stems from the fact that I wanted to construct a zero rate curve using the LIBOR (or rates at which investment banks can borrow and lend from each other). To similarly build a zero-government curve (or any other curve of a different credit rating), one has to use the appropriate liquid financial instruments with the appropriate credit ratings.

- In my discussion thus far, I did not pay any heed to the settlement process associated with the underlying financial instruments (i.e., take into consideration the time lag between transaction and settlement). In practice, this needs to be factored so as to ensure that instruments priced using the constructed zero-rate curve reproduce the market (or traded) prices of the instruments with appropriate settlement conventions.
- To construct a zero-rate curve to value instruments using LIBOR, I used instruments directly linked to LIBOR. In the beginning of this chapter, I made reference to the fact that in constructing a zero-rate curve, it is imperative for one to be able to use liquid instruments that sometimes are the derivatives of the underlying instruments that would have been, theoretically, the correct choice of instruments to use. In such an instance, market makers would use related instruments including the appropriate spreads to ensure that appropriate liquid-market instruments are used.[20]

CUBIC SPLINING

In the previous section, I discussed how linear interpolation is used to construct a zero-rate curve. As can be seen from Figure 2.1, using linear interpolation gives rise to kinks on instrument maturity dates—an unwelcome property for the following reasons:

- Forward rate curves that are derived from kinky zero-rate curves are very often discontinuous at the knot points. This in turn makes some of the interest rate models unusable.
- Sophisticated interest rate term structure models cannot be reliably calibrated using market-based instruments.
- Valuing a coupon-bearing instrument using a linear interpolation vis-à-vis a method that does not allow for kinks (e.g., cubic interpolation) could potentially yield significantly different results.

[20]Fueled by the market crash of 2008 and the Dodd-Frank Act, the market practice has been trending toward using a floating rate that is supported by more collateralization, such as the Overnight Indexed Swap (OIS) rate. As a consequence, interest rate swaps whose floating rates are indexed to the OIS rates instead of LIBOR are becoming more popular. See, for example, Smith (2012).

As a consequence of the above, practitioners resort to the use of cubic polynomials to construct a zero-rate curve. More precisely, using the concept of cubic splining, practitioners use market information to construct a smoother zero-rate curve so as to be able to get more accurate prices for nonliquid, market-based instruments. In this section, I will revisit the linear interpolation example and show how the zero-rate curve can be constructed using cubic splining.

Splining over One Time Interval

To apply the cubic splining method, first assume that one wants to fit a cubic polynomial in the time interval (0, 0.3333), using the information of the overnight rate and the 1-month continuously compounded 3-month forward rate.

In Step 2 of the previous section, I had assumed that the zero rate at time 0.0833 years can be linearly interpolated using the overnight rate and the guessed zero rate at time 0.3333 years as shown in equation (2.8b). In this section, I will assume that one is interested in fitting the cubic function $a_0 + b_0 t + c_0 t^2 + d_0 t^3$ in the time interval $(t_0, t_{0.3333})$ where $t_0 = 0$, $t_{0.3333} = 0.3333$. As in the linear interpolation, one has to first guess a zero rate for $t_{0.3333}$ and then apply the cubically splined zero curve to ensure the reproduction of the continuously compounded forward rate.

Letting the appropriate zero rates at times $t_0, t_{0.3333}$ be given by $r_{0,0}, r_{0,0.3333}$ respectively (where $r_{0,0} = 0.001$ and $r_{0,0.3333}$ is the guessed rate) and making the substitution into the cubic function, one gets

$$a_0 = r_{0,0} \tag{2.9a}$$

$$a_0 + b_0 t_{0.3333} + c_0 t_{0.3333}^2 + d_0 t_{0.3333}^3 = r_{0,0.3333} \tag{2.9b}$$

One can now solve equations (2.9a) and (2.9b) with the aid of $t_{0.3333}, r_{0,0}, r_{0,0.3333}$ (which are either known or can be guessed) and easily compute a_0. Since equation (2.9b) now reduces to an equation in three unknowns, b_0, c_0, and d_0, to compute the value of these unknowns one would need another two equations.

To get the remaining two equations, one can assume that the zero rate curve is instantaneously linear at times 0 and 0.3333 which would imply that the second derivative at times 0 and 0.3333 are both 0. Since the second derivative of $a_0 + b_0 t + c_0 t^2 + d_0 t^3$ is $2c_0 + 6d_0 t$, using the appropriate substitutions at times 0 and 0.3333 one gets

$$c_0 = 0 \tag{2.9c}$$

$$c_0 + 3d_0 t_{0.3333} = 0 \tag{2.9d}$$

From equations (2.9a), (2.9b), (2.9c), and (2.9d), one can easily arrive at the results

$$a_0 = r_{0,0} = 0.001,$$

$$b_0 = \frac{r_{0,0.3333} - r_{0,0}}{t_{0.3333}} = \frac{r_{0,0.3333} - 0.001}{0.3333}$$

$$c_0 = d_0 = 0$$

Putting this together, one gets the function

$$0.001 + \frac{r_{0,0.3333} - 0.001}{0.3333}t \tag{2.10}$$

for $0 = t_0 \leq t \leq t_{0.3333} = 0.3333$.

Using equation (2.10), one can easily interpolate the value of the zero rate at time 0.0833 years and arrive at the value $0.001 + \frac{r_{0,0.3333} - 0.001}{0.3333}(0.0833)$. Since the market price of the 1-month Eurodollar futures contract implied a continuously compounded forward rate of 0.0015, one would need equation (2.8a) to hold. Making the substitution for $r_{0,0.0833}$ in equation (2.8a), one can arrive at

$$\frac{1}{0.3333 - 0.0833}\left\{(r_{0,0.3333} * 0.3333) - \left[\left[0.001 + \frac{r_{0,0.3333} - 0.001}{0.3333}(0.0833)\right] * 0.0833\right]\right\} = 0.0015 \tag{2.11}$$

Solving equation (2.11) for $r_{0,0.3333}$, one gets $r_{0,0.3333} = 0.0014$. Using equation (2.10), one can also show that $r_{0,0.0833} = 0.0011$—which matches the numbers in Table 2.8.

Splining over Two Time Intervals

To draw a comparison to Table 2.9, one would need to fit a cubic polynomial in each of the time intervals (0, 0.3333) and (0.3333, 0.4167) using the overnight rate, the 1-month, and 2-month Eurodollar futures contract prices.

As a consequence, one is interested in fitting a function $a_0 + b_0t + c_0t^2 + d_0t^3$ in the time interval $(t_0, t_{0.3333})$ and the function $a_1 + b_1t + c_1t^2 + d_1t^3$ in the interval $(t_{0.3333}, t_{0.4167})$ where $t_0 = 0$, $t_{0.3333} = 0.3333$, $t_{0.4167} = 0.4167$. As before, one has to simultaneously guess at the zero rates for $t_{0.3333}$ and $t_{0.4167}$ and then apply the cubically splined zero curve to ensure the reproduction of the market rates for the overnight, 1-month, and 2-month instruments.

Letting the appropriate zero rates at times $t_0, t_{0.3333}, t_{0.4167}$ be given by $r_{0,0}, r_{0,0.3333}, r_{0,0.4167}$ respectively and making the substitution into the cubic function, one gets

$$a_0 = r_{0,0} \tag{2.12a}$$

$$a_0 + b_0 t_{0.3333} + c_0 t_{0.3333}^2 + d_0 t_{0.3333}^3 = r_{0,0.3333} \tag{2.12b}$$

$$a_1 + b_1 t_{0.3333} + c_1 t_{0.3333}^2 + d_1 t_{0.3333}^3 = r_{0,0.3333} \tag{2.12c}$$

$$a_1 + b_1 t_{0.4167} + c_1 t_{0.4167}^2 + d_1 t_{0.4167}^3 = r_{0,0.4167} \tag{2.12d}$$

where both $r_{0,0.3333}$ and $r_{0,0.4167}$ are guessed zero rates that are used so their interpolated cubic spline values can reproduce the given market rates.

Since equations (2.12a) to (2.12d) have eight unknowns and only four equations, one needs another four equations to solve for the unknown variables. To do this, I will assume[21] that the cubic functions are continuous in their first and second derivatives at the time node $t_{0.3333}$ so as to arrive at the equations

$$(b_0 - b_1) + 2(c_0 - c_1) t_{0.3333} + 3(d_0 - d_1) t_{0.3333}^2 = 0 \tag{2.12e}$$

$$(c_0 - c_1) + 3(d_0 - d_1) t_{0.3333} = 0 \tag{2.12f}$$

To get the remaining two equations, I will assume, as before, that the zero-rate curve is instantaneously linear at times 0 and 0.4167, which would imply that the second derivatives at times 0 and 0.4167 are both 0. Doing this yields

$$c_0 = 0 \tag{2.12g}$$

$$c_1 + (3 d_1 t_{0.4167}) = 0 \tag{2.12h}$$

To solve equations (2.12a) to (2.12h), one can rewrite these equations using matrix notation to obtain $MX = Y$, where

$$X = [a_0, b_0, c_0, d_0, a_1, b_1, c_1, d_1]^T$$

$$Y = [r_{0,0}, r_{0,0.3333}, r_{0,0.3333}, r_{0,0.4167}, 0, 0, 0, 0]^T$$

and, M is an 8×8 matrix that takes the form as shown in Figure 2.2.

[21]Doing this allows one to ensure that at the connecting note (i.e., at time $t_{0.3333}$) the 2 cubic functions $a_0 + b_0 t_{0.3333} + c_0 t_{0.3333}^2 + d_0 t_{0.3333}^3$ and $a_1 + b_1 t_{0.3333} + c_1 t_{0.3333}^2 + d_1 t_{0.3333}^3$ are continuous. As a consequence, the kinks which were present when simply connecting the linear pieces (in the linear interpolation method) will no longer exist.

$$
\begin{bmatrix}
1 & 0 & 0 & 0 & 0 & 0 & 0 & 0 \\
1 & t_{0.3333} & t_{0.3333}^2 & t_{0.3333}^3 & 0 & 0 & 0 & 0 \\
0 & 0 & 0 & 0 & 1 & t_{0.3333} & t_{0.3333}^2 & t_{0.3333}^3 \\
0 & 0 & 0 & 0 & 1 & t_{0.4167} & t_{0.4167}^2 & t_{0.4167}^3 \\
0 & 1 & 2t_{0.3333} & 3t_{0.3333}^2 & 0 & -1 & -2t_{0.3333} & -3t_{0.3333}^2 \\
0 & 0 & 1 & 3t_{0.3333} & 0 & 0 & -1 & -3t_{0.3333} \\
0 & 0 & 1 & 0 & 0 & 0 & 0 & 0 \\
0 & 0 & 0 & 0 & 0 & 0 & 1 & 3t_{0.4167}
\end{bmatrix}
$$

FIGURE 2.2 The Form of the 8 × 8 Matrix

The system of equations can now be solved for $a_0, b_0, c_0, d_0, a_1, b_1, c_1, d_1$ when the zero rates $r_{0,0.3333}$ and $r_{0,0.4167}$ are known (and in this case they are guessed). To get the exact values of these rates (and hence unique solutions to the system of equations), one would need two additional equations in $r_{0,0.3333}$ and $r_{0,0.4167}$. These equations can be obtained by realizing that the zero rates in the intervals (0, 0.3333) can be interpolated using the function $a_0 + b_0t + c_0t^2 + d_0t^3$ while those in the interval (0.3333, 0.4167) can be interpolated using the function $a_1 + b_1t + c_1t^2 + d_1t^3$. As consequence, it readily follows that

$$a_0 + b_0t_{0.0833} + c_0t_{0.0833}^2 + d_0t_{0.0833}^3 = r_{0,0.0833} \tag{2.12i}$$

$$a_0 + b_0t_{0.1667} + c_0t_{0.1667}^2 + d_0t_{0.1667}^3 = r_{0,0.1667} \tag{2.12j}$$

Since equations (2.12i) and (2.12j) are not a function of $r_{0,0.3333}$ and $r_{0,0.4167}$ one needs two more equations (one connecting $r_{0,0.0833}$ with $r_{0,0.3333}$ and the other connecting $r_{0,0.1667}$ with $r_{0,0.4167}$). Drawing on the relationship between zero rates and forward rates in equation (2.7), one can easily arrive at

$$\frac{(r_{0.3333} * 0.3333) - (r_{0.0833} * 0.0833)}{0.3333 - 0.0833} = 0.0015 \tag{2.13a}$$

$$\frac{(r_{0.4167} * 0.4167) - (r_{0.1667} * 0.1667)}{0.4167 - 0.1667} = 0.00299 \tag{2.13b}$$

where $t_{0.0833} = 0.0833, t_{0.1667} = 0.1667$ and the corresponding zero rates at these times are given by $r_{0,0.0833}$ and $r_{0,0.1667}$ respectively.

Putting all the pieces together allows one to arrive at cubic polynomial coefficients as given in Table 2.13.

Using the values in Table 2.13, it is easy to arrive at the zero rates as shown in Table 2.14.

TABLE 2.13 Splining Coefficients When Fitting over Two Time Intervals

	A	B
1	Coefficients	Values
2	a_0	0.0010000
3	b_0	−0.0023004
4	c_0	0.0000000
5	d_0	0.0296136
6	a_1	0.0064840
7	b_1	−0.0516564
8	c_1	0.1480680
9	d_1	−0.1184544

TABLE 2.14 Zero Rates Obtained Using First Two Eurodollar Futures Contract and Splining

	A	B
1	Time (years)	Zero Rates
2	0	0.100%
3	0.0833	0.083%
4	0.1667	0.075%
5	0.3333	0.133%
6	0.4167	0.210%

By comparing the results of Table 2.9 with Table 2.14, the reader will see a slight difference in the zero rates that is caused by the use of different fitting functions.

Splining over Four Time Intervals[22]

To draw a comparison with Table 2.10, one has to go through the splining process over the time intervals (0, 0.3333), (0.3333, 0.4167), (0.41677,

[22]It is more accurate to spline over the five time intervals (0,0.3333), (0.3333,0.4167), (0.4167,0.5000), (0.5000,0.7500), and, (0.7500,1.2500). Since "0.5000" refers to both the settlement time for the 3-month Eurodollar futures contract and the maturity time of the 6-month Eurodollar futures contract, for the purposes of keeping my example simple and easy to follow, I collapsed the time intervals (0.4167,0.5000) and (0.5000,0.7500) to the interval (0.4167,0.7500). As a consequence, one only needs to do the splining over the time intervals (0,0.3333), (0.3333,0.4167), (0.4167,0.7500), and, (0.7500,1.2500). The reader would be

0.7500) and (0.7500, 1.2500). As before, one has to first assume that one is interested in fitting a function $a_0 + b_0 t + c_0 t^2 + d_0 t^3$ in the time interval $(t_0, t_{0.3333})$, $a_1 + b_1 t + c_1 t^2 + d_1 t^3$ in the time interval $(t_{0.3333}, t_{0.4167})$, $a_2 + b_2 t + c_2 t^2 + d_2 t^3$ in the time interval $\left(t_{0.4167}, t_{0.75}\right)$, and $a_3 + b_3 t + c_3 t^2 + d_3 t^3$ in the time interval $(t_{0.75}, t_{1.25})$ where $t_0 = 0$, $t_{0.3333} = 0.3333$, $t_{0.4167} = 0.4167$, $t_{0.75} = 0.75$, and $t_{1.25} = 1.25$. Again, one has to simultaneously guess at the zero rates for times $t_{0.3333}$, $t_{0.4167}$, $t_{0.75}$, and $t_{1.25}$ and then apply the cubically splined zero curve to ensure the reproduction of the market rates for the overnight, 1-month, 2-month, 3-month, 6-month, and 12-month instruments.

Letting the appropriate zero rates at times $t_0, t_{0.3333}, t_{0.4167}, t_{0.75}, t_{1.25}$ be $r_{0,0}, r_{0,0.3333}, r_{0,0.4167}, r_{0,0.75}, r_{0,1.25}$ respectively, one gets

$$a_0 = r_{0,0} \quad (2.14a)$$

$$a_0 + b_0 t_{0.3333} + c_0 t_{0.3333}^2 + d_0 t_{0.3333}^3 = r_{0,0.3333} \quad (2.14b)$$

$$a_1 + b_1 t_{0.3333} + c_1 t_{0.3333}^2 + d_1 t_{0.3333}^3 = r_{0,0.3333} \quad (2.14c)$$

$$a_1 + b_1 t_{0.4167} + c_1 t_{0.4167}^2 + d_1 t_{0.4167}^3 = r_{0,0.4167} \quad (2.14d)$$

$$a_2 + b_2 t_{0.4167} + c_2 t_{0.4167}^2 + d_2 t_{0.4167}^3 = r_{0,0.4167} \quad (2.14e)$$

$$a_2 + b_2 t_{0.75} + c_2 t_{0.75}^2 + d_2 t_{0.75}^3 = r_{0,0.75} \quad (2.14f)$$

$$a_3 + b_3 t_{0.75} + c_3 t_{0.75}^2 + d_3 t_{0.75}^3 = r_{0,0.75} \quad (2.14g)$$

$$a_3 + b_3 t_{1.25} + c_3 t_{1.25}^2 + d_3 t_{1.25}^3 = r_{0,1.25} \quad (2.14h)$$

where $r_{0,0.3333}$, $r_{0,0.4167}$, $r_{0,0.75}$, and $r_{0,1.25}$ are guessed zero rates used to reproduce the given market rates by using interpolated cubic spline values.

Since equations (2.14a) to (2.14h) have 16 unknowns and only 8 equations, one would need another 8 independent equations with these unknowns so as to arrive at unique solutions for the cubic polynomial coefficients. Using reasoning similar to that used to fit cubic splines over two time intervals, one can arrive at the following equations

$$(b_0 - b_1) + 2(c_0 - c_1) t_{0.3333} + 3(d_0 - d_1) t_{0.3333}^2 = 0 \quad (2.14i)$$

$$(c_0 - c_1) + 3(d_0 - d_1) t_{0.3333} = 0 \quad (2.14j)$$

$$(b_1 - b_2) + 2(c_1 - c_2) t_{0.4167} + 3(d_1 - d_2) t_{0.4167}^2 = 0 \quad (2.14k)$$

$$(c_1 - c_2) + 3(d_1 - d_2) t_{0.4167} = 0 \quad (2.14l)$$

---

interested to note that in splining over the actual 5 intervals, one would arrive at a zero curve that is not that different from that obtained when splining over 4 time intervals. The reader is left to see this as an exercise.

$$(b_2 - b_3) + 2(c_2 - c_3)t_{0.75} + 3(d_2 - d_3)t_{0.75}^2 = 0 \quad (2.14m)$$
$$(c_2 - c_3) + 3(d_2 - d_3)t_{0.75} = 0 \quad (2.14n)$$
$$c_0 = 0 \quad (2.14o)$$
$$c_3 + (3d_3t_{1.25}) = 0 \quad (2.14p)$$

To solve these equations, using matrix notation, one can rewrite them as $MX = Y$, where

$$X = [a_0, b_0, c_0, d_0, a_1, b_1, c_1, d_1, a_2, b_2, c_2, d_2, a_3, b_3, c_3, d_3]^T$$
$$Y = [r_{0,0}, r_{0,0.3333}, r_{0,0.3333}, r_{0,0.4167}, r_{0,0.4167}, r_{0,0.75}, r_{0,0.75}, r_{0,1.25}, 0, 0, 0, 0, 0, 0, 0, 0]^T$$

and, M is the 16×16 matrix which is given in Figure 2.3.

Since the system of equations can be easily solved for a_i, b_i, c_i, d_i(for $i = 0, 1, 2, 3$) once $r_{0,0.3333}, r_{0,0.4167}, r_{0,0.75}, r_{0,1.25}$ are known, one now needs to determine the values of these rates. Using the fact that zero rates in the intervals (0, 0.3333), (0.3333, 0.4167), (0.4167, 0.75), and (0.75, 1.25) can be interpolated using the cubic splines

$$a_0 + b_0t + c_0t^2 + d_0t^3 \text{ for } t_0 \le t \le t_{0.3333}$$
$$a_1 + b_1t + c_1t^2 + d_1t^3 \text{ for } t_{0.3333} \le t \le t_{0.4167}$$
$$a_2 + b_2t + c_2t^2 + d_2t^3 \text{ for } t_{0.4167} \le t \le t_{0.75}$$
$$a_3 + b_3t + c_3t^2 + d_3t^3 \text{ for } t_{0.75} \le t \le t_{1.25}$$

one can easily arrive at equations (2.14q) to (2.14u).

$$a_0 + b_0t_{0.0833} + c_0t_{0.0833}^2 + d_0t_{0.0833}^3 = r_{0,0.0833} \quad (2.14q)$$
$$a_0 + b_0t_{0.1667} + c_0t_{0.1667}^2 + d_0t_{0.1667}^3 = r_{0,0.1667} \quad (2.14r)$$
$$a_0 + b_0t_{0.25} + c_0t_{0.25}^2 + d_0t_{0.25}^3 = r_{0,0.25} \quad (2.14s)$$
$$a_2 + b_2t_{0.5} + c_2t_{0.5}^2 + d_2t_{0.5}^3 = r_{0,0.5} \quad (2.14t)$$
$$a_3 + b_3t_1 + c_3t_1^2 + d_3t_1^3 = r_{0,1} \quad (2.14u)$$

Using the relationship between spot and forward rates, it can be seen that

$$\frac{(r_{0.3333} * 0.3333) - (r_{0.0833} * 0.0833)}{0.3333 - 0.0833} = 0.0015 \quad (2.15a)$$
$$\frac{(r_{0.4167} * 0.4167) - (r_{0.1667} * 0.1667)}{0.4167 - 0.1667} = 0.00299 \quad (2.15b)$$

$$
\begin{bmatrix}
1 & 0 & 0 & 0 & 0 & 0 & 0 & 0 & 0 & 0 & 0 & 0 & 0 & 0 & 0 & 0 \\
1 & t_{0.3333} & t_{0.3333}^2 & t_{0.3333}^3 & 0 & 0 & 0 & 0 & 0 & 0 & 0 & 0 & 0 & 0 & 0 & 0 \\
0 & 0 & 0 & 0 & 1 & t_{0.3333} & t_{0.3333}^2 & t_{0.3333}^3 & 0 & 0 & 0 & 0 & 0 & 0 & 0 & 0 \\
0 & 0 & 0 & 0 & 1 & t_{0.4167} & t_{0.4167}^2 & t_{0.4167}^3 & 0 & 0 & 0 & 0 & 0 & 0 & 0 & 0 \\
0 & 0 & 0 & 0 & 0 & 0 & 0 & 0 & 1 & t_{0.4167} & t_{0.4167}^2 & t_{0.4167}^3 & 0 & 0 & 0 & 0 \\
0 & 0 & 0 & 0 & 0 & 0 & 0 & 0 & 1 & t_{0.75} & t_{0.75}^2 & t_{0.75}^3 & 0 & 0 & 0 & 0 \\
0 & 0 & 0 & 0 & 0 & 0 & 0 & 0 & 0 & 0 & 0 & 0 & 1 & t_{0.75} & t_{0.75}^2 & t_{0.75}^3 \\
0 & 0 & 0 & 0 & 0 & 0 & 0 & 0 & 0 & 0 & 0 & 0 & 1 & t_{1.25} & t_{1.25}^2 & t_{1.25}^3 \\
0 & 1 & 2t_{0.3333} & 3t_{0.3333}^2 & 0 & -1 & -2t_{0.3333} & -3t_{0.3333}^2 & 0 & 0 & 0 & 0 & 0 & 0 & 0 & 0 \\
0 & 0 & 1 & 3t_{0.3333} & 0 & 0 & -1 & -3t_{0.3333} & 0 & 0 & 0 & 0 & 0 & 0 & 0 & 0 \\
0 & 0 & 0 & 0 & 0 & 1 & 2t_{0.4167} & 3t_{0.4167}^2 & 0 & -1 & -2t_{0.4167} & -3t_{0.4167}^2 & 0 & 0 & 0 & 0 \\
0 & 0 & 0 & 0 & 0 & 0 & 1 & 3t_{0.4167} & 0 & 0 & -1 & -3t_{0.4167} & 0 & 0 & 0 & 0 \\
0 & 0 & 0 & 0 & 0 & 0 & 0 & 0 & 0 & 1 & 2t_{0.75} & 3t_{0.75}^2 & 0 & -1 & -2t_{0.75} & -3t_{0.75}^2 \\
0 & 0 & 0 & 0 & 0 & 0 & 0 & 0 & 0 & 0 & 1 & 3t_{0.75} & 0 & 0 & -1 & -3t_{0.75} \\
0 & 0 & 1 & 0 & 0 & 0 & 0 & 0 & 0 & 0 & 0 & 0 & 0 & 0 & 0 & 0 \\
0 & 0 & 0 & 0 & 0 & 0 & 0 & 0 & 0 & 0 & 0 & 0 & 0 & 0 & 1 & 3t_{1.25}
\end{bmatrix}
$$

FIGURE 2.3 The Form of the 16×16 Matrix

$$\frac{(r_{0.5} * 0.5) - (r_{0.25} * 0.25)}{0.5 - 0.25} = 0.00499 \quad (2.15c)$$

$$\frac{(r_{0.75} * 0.75) - (r_{0.5} * 0.5)}{0.75 - 0.5} = 0.00996 \quad (2.15d)$$

$$\frac{(r_{1.25} * 1.25) - (r_1 * 1)}{1.25 - 1} = 0.01187 \quad (2.15e)$$

where

$$t_{0.0833} = 0.0833, t_{0.1667} = 0.1667, t_{0.25} = 0.25, t_{0.5} = 0.5, t_1 = 1$$

and the corresponding zero rates at these times are given by $r_{0,0.0833}$, $r_{0,0.1667}$, $r_{0,0.25}$, $r_{0,0.5}$, and $r_{0,1}$ respectively.

Solving equations (2.14a) to (2.14u) subject to equations (2.15a) to (2.15e) yields the cubic polynomial coefficients as given in Table 2.15.

TABLE 2.15 Splining Coefficients When Fitting over Four Time Intervals

	A	B
1	Coefficients	Values
2	a_0	0.001000
3	b_0	–0.002282
4	c_0	0.000000
5	d_0	0.029449
6	a_1	0.006210
7	b_1	–0.049173
8	c_1	0.140673
9	d_1	–0.111224
10	a_2	–0.001112
11	b_2	0.003543
12	c_2	0.014155
13	d_2	–0.010009
14	a_3	–0.007687
15	b_3	0.029844
16	c_3	–0.020914
17	d_3	0.005577

TABLE 2.16 Zero Rates Obtained Using All Eurodollar Futures Contract and Splining

	A	B
1	Time (years)	Zero Rates
2	0.0000	0.1000%
3	0.0833	0.0827%
4	0.1667	0.0756%
5	0.2500	0.0890%
6	0.3333	0.1330%
7	0.4167	0.2098%
8	0.5000	0.2947%
9	0.7500	0.5285%
10	1.0000	0.6820%
11	1.2500	0.7833%

Using Table 2.15, one easily obtains the zero rates as presented in Table 2.16.

Splining over All Time Intervals

To draw a comparison with Table 2.12, one has to go through the process over the time intervals (0, 0.3333), (0.3333, 0.4167), (0.4167, 0.7500), (0.7500, 1.2500), (1.2500, 2.0000), and (2.0000, 5.0000). As before, I will assume that one is interested in fitting a function $a_i + b_i t + c_i t^2 + d_i t^3$ (for $i = 0, 1, 2, 3, 4, 5$) in the time intervals $(t_0, t_{0.3333})$, $(t_{0.3333}, t_{0.4167})$, $(t_{0.4167}, t_{0.75})$, $(t_{0.75}, t_{1.25})$, $(t_{1.25}, t_2)$, and (t_2, t_5) respectively, where $t_0 = 0$, $t_{0.3333} = 0.3333$, $t_{0.4167} = 0.4167$, $t_{0.75} = 0.75$, $t_{1.25} = 1.25$, $t_2 = 2$, and $t_5 = 5$. As before, one has to simultaneously guess at the zero rates for $t_{0.3333}$, $t_{0.4167}$, $t_{0.75}$, $t_{1.25}$, t_2, and t_5 and then apply the cubically splined zero curve to ensure that one is able to reproduce the market rates for the overnight, 1-month, 2-month, 3-month, 6-month, 12-month, 24-month, and 60-month instruments. By letting the appropriate zero rates at times $t_0, t_{0.3333}, t_{0.4167}, t_{0.75}, t_{1.25}, t_2, t_5$ be given by $r_{0,0}, r_{0,0.3333}, r_{0,0.4167}, r_{0,0.75}, r_{0,1.25}, r_{0,2}, r_{0,5}$ respectively, one gets

$$a_0 = r_{0,0} \qquad (2.16a)$$

$$a_0 + b_0 t_{0.3333} + c_0 t_{0.3333}^2 + d_0 t_{0.3333}^3 = r_{0,0.3333} \qquad (2.16b)$$

$$a_1 + b_1 t_{0.3333} + c_1 t_{0.3333}^2 + d_1 t_{0.3333}^3 = r_{0,0.3333} \qquad (2.16c)$$

$$a_1 + b_1 t_{0.4167} + c_1 t_{0.4167}^2 + d_1 t_{0.4167}^3 = r_{0,0.4167} \qquad (2.16d)$$

$$a_2 + b_2 t_{0.4167} + c_2 t_{0.4167}^2 + d_2 t_{0.4167}^3 = r_{0,0.4167} \qquad (2.16e)$$

$$a_2 + b_2 t_{0.75} + c_2 t_{0.75}^2 + d_2 t_{0.75}^3 = r_{0,0.75} \tag{2.16f}$$

$$a_3 + b_3 t_{0.75} + c_3 t_{0.75}^2 + d_3 t_{0.75}^3 = r_{0,0.75} \tag{2.16g}$$

$$a_3 + b_3 t_{1.25} + c_3 t_{1.25}^2 + d_3 t_{1.25}^3 = r_{0,1.25} \tag{2.16h}$$

$$a_4 + b_4 t_{1.25} + c_4 t_{1.25}^2 + d_4 t_{1.25}^3 = r_{0,1.25} \tag{2.16i}$$

$$a_4 + b_4 t_2 + c_4 t_2^2 + d_4 t_2^3 = r_{0,2} \tag{2.16j}$$

$$a_5 + b_5 t_2 + c_5 t_2^2 + d_5 t_2^3 = r_{0,2} \tag{2.16k}$$

$$a_5 + b_5 t_5 + c_5 t_5^2 + d_5 t_5^3 = r_{0,5} \tag{2.16l}$$

$$(b_0 - b_1) + 2\left(c_0 - c_1\right) t_{0.3333} + 3\left(d_0 - d_1\right) t_{0.3333}^2 = 0 \tag{2.16m}$$

$$\left(c_0 - c_1\right) + 3\left(d_0 - d_1\right) t_{0.3333} = 0 \tag{2.16n}$$

$$(b_1 - b_2) + 2(c_1 - c_2) t_{0.4167} + 3\left(d_1 - d_2\right) t_{0.4167}^2 = 0 \tag{2.16o}$$

$$(c_1 - c_2) + 3\left(d_1 - d_2\right) t_{0.4167} = 0 \tag{2.16p}$$

$$(b_2 - b_3) + 2\left(c_2 - c_3\right) t_{0.75} + 3\left(d_2 - d_3\right) t_{0.75}^2 = 0 \tag{2.16q}$$

$$\left(c_2 - c_3\right) + 3\left(d_2 - d_3\right) t_{0.75} = 0 \tag{2.16r}$$

$$(b_3 - b_4) + 2\left(c_3 - c_4\right) t_{1.25} + 3\left(d_3 - d_4\right) t_{1.25}^2 = 0 \tag{2.16s}$$

$$\left(c_3 - c_4\right) + 3\left(d_3 - d_4\right) t_{1.25} = 0 \tag{2.16t}$$

$$(b_4 - b_5) + 2\left(c_4 - c_5\right) t_2 + 3\left(d_4 - d_5\right) t_2^2 = 0 \tag{2.16u}$$

$$\left(c_4 - c_5\right) + 3\left(d_4 - d_5\right) t_2 = 0 \tag{2.16v}$$

$$c_0 = 0 \tag{2.16w}$$

$$c_5 + (3 d_5 t_5) = 0 \tag{2.16x}$$

where $r_{0,0.3333}$, $r_{0,0.4167}$, $r_{0,0.75}$, $r_{0,1.25}$, $r_{0,2}$, and $r_{0,5}$ are guessed zero rates.

As before, to solve these equations, one has to use the matrix notation to rewrite equations (2.16a) to (2.16x) as $MX = Y$, where

$$X = [a_0, b_0, c_0, d_0, a_1, b_1, c_1, d_1, a_2, b_2, c_2, d_2, \ldots, a_5, b_5, c_5, d_5]^T$$

$$Y = [r_{0,0}, r_{0,0.3333}, r_{0,0.3333}, r_{0,0.4167}, r_{0,0.4167}, r_{0,0.75}, r_{0,0.75}, r_{0,1.25}, r_{0,1.25}, r_{0,2}, r_{0,2}, r_{0,5}, 0, 0, \ldots, 0]^T$$

and, M is given by the (24×24) matrix as shown in Figure 2.4.

Since the system of equations can be solved for a_i, b_i, c_i, d_i (for $i = 0, 1, 2, 3, 4, 5$) once the guessed zero rates are known, it remains for one to determine these guessed zero rates. Using the fact that zero rates in the

$$
\begin{bmatrix}
1 & 0 & 0 & 0 & 0 & 0 & 0 & 0 & 0 & 0 & 0 & 0 & 0 & 0 & 0 & 0 & 0 & 0 & 0 & 0 & 0 & 0 & 0 & 0 \\
1 & t_{0.3333} & t_{0.3333}^{2} & t_{0.3333}^{3} & 0 & 0 & 0 & 0 & 0 & 0 & 0 & 0 & 0 & 0 & 0 & 0 & 0 & 0 & 0 & 0 & 0 & 0 & 0 & 0 \\
0 & 0 & 0 & 0 & 1 & t_{0.3333} & t_{0.3333}^{2} & t_{0.3333}^{3} & 0 & 0 & 0 & 0 & 0 & 0 & 0 & 0 & 0 & 0 & 0 & 0 & 0 & 0 & 0 & 0 \\
0 & 0 & 0 & 0 & 1 & t_{0.4167} & t_{0.4167}^{2} & t_{0.4167}^{3} & 0 & 0 & 0 & 0 & 0 & 0 & 0 & 0 & 0 & 0 & 0 & 0 & 0 & 0 & 0 & 0 \\
0 & 0 & 0 & 0 & 0 & 0 & 0 & 0 & 1 & t_{0.4167} & t_{0.4167}^{2} & t_{0.4167}^{3} & 0 & 0 & 0 & 0 & 0 & 0 & 0 & 0 & 0 & 0 & 0 & 0 \\
0 & 0 & 0 & 0 & 0 & 0 & 0 & 0 & 1 & t_{0.75} & t_{0.75}^{2} & t_{0.75}^{3} & 0 & 0 & 0 & 0 & 0 & 0 & 0 & 0 & 0 & 0 & 0 & 0 \\
0 & 0 & 0 & 0 & 0 & 0 & 0 & 0 & 0 & 0 & 0 & 0 & 1 & t_{0.75} & t_{0.75}^{2} & t_{0.75}^{3} & 0 & 0 & 0 & 0 & 0 & 0 & 0 & 0 \\
0 & 0 & 0 & 0 & 0 & 0 & 0 & 0 & 0 & 0 & 0 & 0 & 1 & t_{1.25} & t_{1.25}^{2} & t_{1.25}^{3} & 0 & 0 & 0 & 0 & 0 & 0 & 0 & 0 \\
0 & 0 & 0 & 0 & 0 & 0 & 0 & 0 & 0 & 0 & 0 & 0 & 0 & 0 & 0 & 0 & 1 & t_{1.25} & t_{1.25}^{2} & t_{1.25}^{3} & 0 & 0 & 0 & 0 \\
0 & 0 & 0 & 0 & 0 & 0 & 0 & 0 & 0 & 0 & 0 & 0 & 0 & 0 & 0 & 0 & 1 & t_{2} & t_{2}^{2} & t_{2}^{3} & 0 & 0 & 0 & 0 \\
0 & 0 & 0 & 0 & 0 & 0 & 0 & 0 & 0 & 0 & 0 & 0 & 0 & 0 & 0 & 0 & 0 & 0 & 0 & 0 & 1 & t_{2} & t_{2}^{2} & t_{2}^{3} \\
0 & 0 & 0 & 0 & 0 & 0 & 0 & 0 & 0 & 0 & 0 & 0 & 0 & 0 & 0 & 0 & 0 & 0 & 0 & 0 & 1 & t_{5} & t_{5}^{2} & t_{5}^{3} \\
0 & 1 & 2t_{0.3333} & 3t_{0.3333}^{2} & 0 & -1 & -2t_{0.3333} & -3t_{0.3333}^{2} & 0 & 0 & 0 & 0 & 0 & 0 & 0 & 0 & 0 & 0 & 0 & 0 & 0 & 0 & 0 & 0 \\
0 & 0 & 1 & 3t_{0.3333} & 0 & 0 & -1 & -3t_{0.3333} & 0 & 0 & 0 & 0 & 0 & 0 & 0 & 0 & 0 & 0 & 0 & 0 & 0 & 0 & 0 & 0 \\
0 & 0 & 0 & 0 & 0 & 1 & 2t_{0.4167} & 3t_{0.4167}^{2} & 0 & -1 & -2t_{0.4167} & -3t_{0.4167}^{2} & 0 & 0 & 0 & 0 & 0 & 0 & 0 & 0 & 0 & 0 & 0 & 0 \\
0 & 0 & 0 & 0 & 0 & 0 & 1 & 3t_{0.4167} & 0 & 0 & -1 & -3t_{0.4167} & 0 & 0 & 0 & 0 & 0 & 0 & 0 & 0 & 0 & 0 & 0 & 0 \\
0 & 0 & 0 & 0 & 0 & 0 & 0 & 0 & 0 & 1 & 2t_{0.75} & 3t_{0.75}^{2} & 0 & -1 & -2t_{0.75} & -3t_{0.75}^{2} & 0 & 0 & 0 & 0 & 0 & 0 & 0 & 0 \\
0 & 0 & 0 & 0 & 0 & 0 & 0 & 0 & 0 & 0 & 1 & 3t_{0.75} & 0 & 0 & -1 & -3t_{0.75} & 0 & 0 & 0 & 0 & 0 & 0 & 0 & 0 \\
0 & 0 & 0 & 0 & 0 & 0 & 0 & 0 & 0 & 0 & 0 & 0 & 0 & 1 & 2t_{1.25} & 3t_{1.25}^{2} & 0 & -1 & -2t_{1.25} & -3t_{1.25}^{2} & 0 & 0 & 0 & 0 \\
0 & 0 & 0 & 0 & 0 & 0 & 0 & 0 & 0 & 0 & 0 & 0 & 0 & 0 & 1 & 3t_{1.25} & 0 & 0 & -1 & -3t_{1.25} & 0 & 0 & 0 & 0 \\
0 & 0 & 0 & 0 & 0 & 0 & 0 & 0 & 0 & 0 & 0 & 0 & 0 & 0 & 0 & 0 & 0 & 1 & 2t_{2} & 3t_{2}^{2} & 0 & -1 & -2t_{2} & -3t_{2}^{2} \\
0 & 0 & 0 & 0 & 0 & 0 & 0 & 0 & 0 & 0 & 0 & 0 & 0 & 0 & 0 & 0 & 0 & 0 & 1 & 3t_{2} & 0 & 0 & -1 & -3t_{2} \\
0 & 0 & 1 & 0 & 0 & 0 & 0 & 0 & 0 & 0 & 0 & 0 & 0 & 0 & 0 & 0 & 0 & 0 & 0 & 0 & 0 & 0 & 0 & 0 \\
0 & 0 & 0 & 0 & 0 & 0 & 0 & 0 & 0 & 0 & 0 & 0 & 0 & 0 & 0 & 0 & 0 & 0 & 0 & 0 & 0 & 0 & 1 & 3t_{5}
\end{bmatrix}
$$

FIGURE 2.4 The Form of the 24 × 24 Matrix

intervals (0, 0.3333), (0.3333, 0.4167), (0.4167, 0.75), (0.75, 1.25), (1.25, 2), and (2, 5) can be interpolated using the cubic splines

$$a_0 + b_0 t + c_0 t^2 + d_0 t^3 \text{ for } t_0 \le t \le t_{0.3333}$$
$$a_1 + b_1 t + c_1 t^2 + d_1 t^3 \text{ for } t_{0.3333} \le t \le t_{0.4167}$$
$$a_2 + b_2 t + c_2 t^2 + d_2 t^3 \text{ for } t_{0.4167} \le t \le t_{0.75}$$
$$a_3 + b_3 t + c_3 t^2 + d_3 t^3 \text{ for } t_{0.75} \le t \le t_{1.25}$$
$$a_4 + b_4 t + c_4 t^2 + d_4 t^3 \text{ for } t_{1.25} \le t \le t_2$$
$$a_5 + b_5 t + c_5 t^2 + d_5 t^3 \text{ for } t_2 \le t \le t_5$$

one can arrive at the following

$$a_0 + b_0 t_k + c_0 t_k^2 + d_0 t_k^3 = r_k$$

(for $k = 0.0833, 0.1667, 0.25, 0.5, 1, 1.5, 2.5, 3, 3.5, 4, 4.5$)

Using the spot and forward rate relationship in equation (2.7), it can be seen that

$$\frac{(r_{0,0.3333} * 0.3333) - (r_{0,0.0833} * 0.0833)}{0.3333 - 0.0833} = 0.0015 \tag{2.17a}$$

$$\frac{(r_{0,0.4167} * 0.4167) - (r_{0,0.1667} * 0.1667)}{0.4167 - 0.1667} = 0.00299 \tag{2.17b}$$

$$\frac{(r_{0,0.5} * 0.5) - (r_{0,0.25} * 0.25)}{0.5 - 0.25} = 0.00499 \tag{2.17c}$$

$$\frac{(r_{0,0.75} * 0.75) - (r_{0,0.5} * 0.5)}{0.75 - 0.25} = 0.00996 \tag{2.17d}$$

$$\frac{(r_{0,1.25} * 1.25) - (r_{0,1} * 1)}{1.25 - 1} = 0.01187 \tag{2.17e}$$

Using the swap pricing formula given in equation (2.6), one can also get

$$\frac{1 - D_{0,2}}{0.5(D_{0,0.5} + D_{0,1} + D_{0,1.5} + D_{0,2})} = 0.02 \tag{2.17f}$$

$$\frac{1 - D_{0,5}}{0.5(D_{0,0.5} + D_{0,1} + D_{0,1.5} + D_{0,2} + D_{0,2.5} + D_{0,3} + D_{0,3.5} + D_{0,4} + D_{0,4.5} + D_{0,5})} = 0.03 \tag{2.17g}$$

where the discount factor associated with time t_i is given by the expression $D_{0,t_i} = e^{-r_{0,t_i} t_i}$.

TABLE 2.17 Splining Coefficients for the Entire Fit

	A	B
1	Coefficients	Values
2	a_0	0.0010000
3	b_0	–0.0022419
4	c_0	0.0000000
5	d_0	0.0290874
6	a_1	0.0056071
7	b_1	–0.0437057
8	c_1	0.1243912
9	d_1	–0.0953038
10	a_2	0.0003465
11	b_2	–0.0058298
12	c_2	0.0334892
13	d_2	–0.0225821
14	a_3	–0.0200372
15	b_3	0.0757053
16	c_3	–0.0752243
17	d_3	0.0257349
18	a_4	0.0553137
19	b_4	–0.1051369
20	c_4	0.0694495
21	d_4	–0.0128447
22	a_5	–0.0542164
23	b_5	0.0591582
24	c_5	–0.0126981
25	d_5	0.0008465

Solving equations (2.16a) to (2.16x)—subject to equations (2.17a) to (2.17g)—yields the numbers in Table 2.17.

With the values in Table 2.17, one can then obtain the zero rates shown in Table 2.18.

The information in Table 2.12 and Table 2.18 can be alternatively represented as in Figure 2.5.

As can be seen from Figure 2.5, the zero curve obtained using a cubic-splining approach has a much smoother fit (by the nature of the construction)—in the process helping one avoid kinks in a zero rate term structure. As mentioned, when calculating the present value of instruments

TABLE 2.18 Splined Zero Rate Term Structure

	A	B
1	Time (years)	Zero Rates
2	0.00000	0.00100
3	0.08333	0.00083
4	0.16667	0.00076
5	0.25000	0.00089
6	0.33333	0.00133
7	0.41667	0.00210
8	0.50000	0.00298
9	0.75000	0.00528
10	1.00000	0.00618
11	1.25000	0.00732
12	1.50000	0.01052
13	2.00000	0.02008
14	2.50000	0.02754
15	3.00000	0.03183
16	3.50000	0.03358
17	4.00000	0.03343
18	4.50000	0.03200
19	5.00000	0.02994

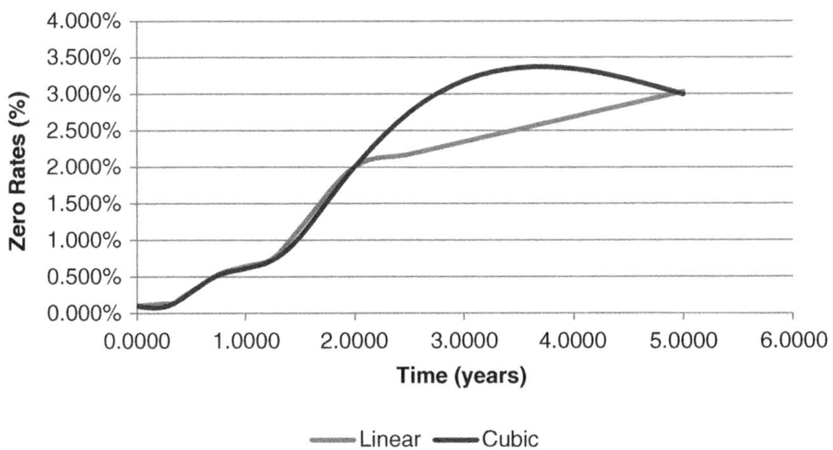

FIGURE 2.5 Comparison of Zero Curves Obtained Using Linear Interpolation and Cubic Splining Methods

with cash flows lying in the two- to five-year bucket, one can expect a big discrepancy arising from the use of the two methods. Valuing a four-year at-market swap using the linearly interpolated zero curve yields an annual swap rate of 2.67 percent. This same structure, when valued using a zero curve obtained using a cubic splining, yields a value of 3.32 percent, creating a difference of 64 annual basis points. Put another way, this causes a difference of about \$24,340 when the notional size of the swap is \$1,000,000 (a 2.4 percent difference). Clearly, the higher the notional amount of the swap, the higher the present value of this discrepancy.

APPENDIX: FINDING SWAP RATES USING A FLOATING COUPON BOND APPROACH

To do this, I will assume that one is interested in valuing an n-period fixed-floating swap in which the floating rates are set at times $t_1, t_2, \ldots, t_n$ and settled at times $t_2, t_3, \ldots, t_{n+1}$. This interest swap can be represented as shown in Figure 2.6a where N is the notional principal of the swap (based on which interest cashflows are calculated), R is the swap rate that one is trying to determine, and L_i (for $i = 1, 2, \ldots, n$) is the ith Libor (floating rate) that is yet to be set in the future and hence denoted by "?" as the dotted cashflows.

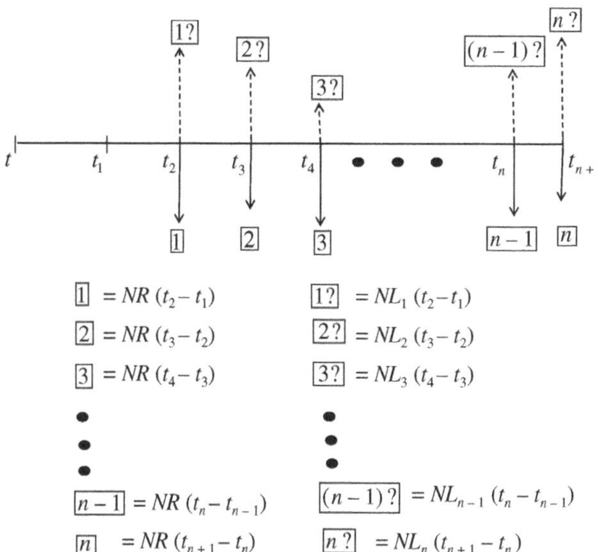

$\boxed{1} = NR\,(t_2 - t_1)$ $\quad\boxed{1?} = NL_1\,(t_2 - t_1)$

$\boxed{2} = NR\,(t_3 - t_2)$ $\quad\boxed{2?} = NL_2\,(t_3 - t_2)$

$\boxed{3} = NR\,(t_4 - t_3)$ $\quad\boxed{3?} = NL_3\,(t_4 - t_3)$

•
•
•

$\boxed{n-1} = NR\,(t_n - t_{n-1})$ $\quad\boxed{(n-1)?} = NL_{n-1}\,(t_n - t_{n-1})$

$\boxed{n} = NR\,(t_{n+1} - t_n)$ $\quad\boxed{n?} = NL_n\,(t_{n+1} - t_n)$

FIGURE 2.6A Cash Flows in a Fixed-Floating Swap

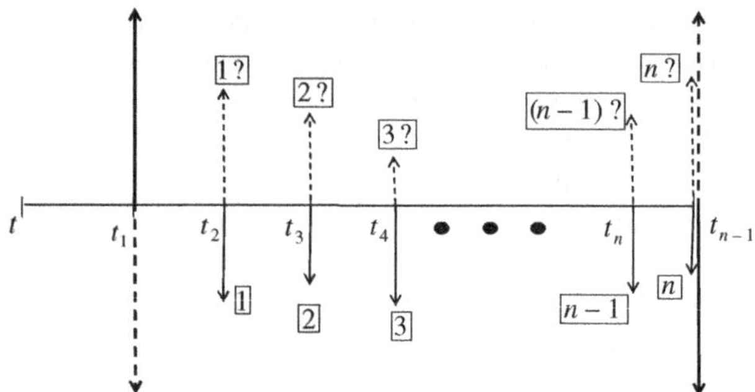

FIGURE 2.6B Cash Flows in a Fixed-Floating Swap with Principals

Adding the notional principals to both the commencement and end of swap, one can then arrive at Figure 2.6b.

The cash flows in Figure 2.6b can now be decomposed into Figures 2.6c and 2.6d.

The value of the floating rate bond in Figure 2.6d is 0 (simply because any bond whose floating rate coupons are ALL based on the then-prevailing market rates simply has no value to the holder of the bond). The consequence of this is the simplification of Figure 2.6a to Figure 2.6c. Given this backdrop, it just remains to observe that for Figure 2.6c to hold true all the present values of the cash flows must net out to 0. More precisely one would need that

$$(N * D_{t,t_1}) = \left(N * SR * (t_2 - t_1) * D_{t,t_2}\right) + \left(N * SR * \left(t_3 - t_2\right)\right) * D_{t,t_3} + \cdots + \left(N * SR * \left(t_{n+1} - t_n\right) * D_{t,t_{n+1}}\right) + (N * D_{t,t_{n+1}}) \quad (2.18)$$

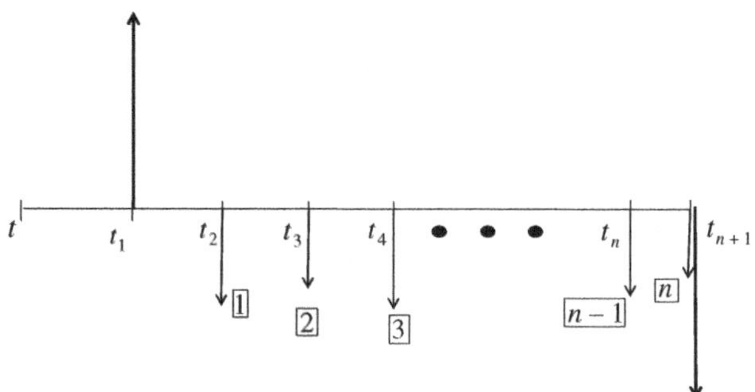

FIGURE 2.6C Cash Flows of a Fixed Rate Bond

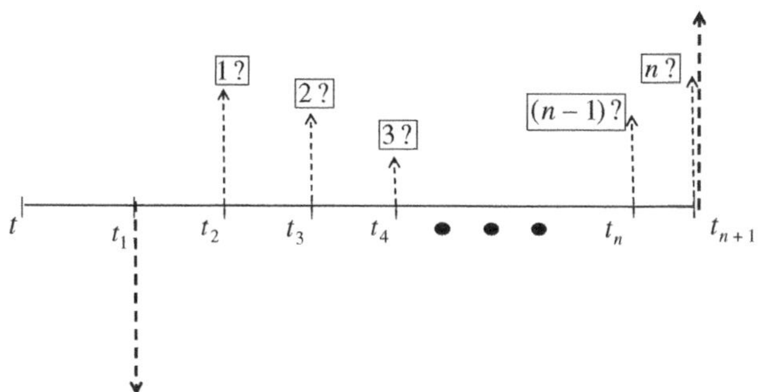

FIGURE 2.6D Cash Flows of a Floating Rate Bond

where N represents the notional principal associated with the swap, SR represents the swap rate that one is trying to determine, and both D_{t,t_i} and t_i (for $i = 1, 2, \ldots, n + 1$) are as defined in equation (2.6).

It easy to see that equation (2.18) can be simplified to obtain equation (2.6).

REFERENCES

Hull, J. C. 2012. *Options, Futures and Other Derivatives*. 8th ed. Upper Saddle River, NJ: Prentice Hall.

Ravindran, K. 1997. *Customized Derivatives: A Step-by-Step Guide to Using Exotic Options, Swaps and Other Customized Derivatives*. New York: McGraw-Hill.

Smith, J. S. 2012. *A Teaching Note on Pricing and Valuing Interest Rate Swaps Using LIBOR and OIS Discounting*. Unpublished manuscript.

Van Deventer, D. R., K. Imai, and M. Mesler. 2005. *Advanced Financial Risk Management*. Hoboken, NJ: Wiley Finance.

CHAPTER 3

Valuing Vanilla Options

Options and options-embedded instruments trade in abundance and diversity on both the over-the-counter (OTC) and exchange-traded markets globally. Since the underlyings of these options span a multitude of asset classes (e.g., equity, commodity, interest rate, and currency—just to name a few), it is not surprising to expect the option landscape to be a very complex one. Despite the complexity of the landscape, all options can be categorized as either vanilla or exotic:

- Vanilla options refer to options that allow owners to transact (i.e., buy or sell) the asset underlying the option for a pre-specified price at a pre-specified time(s) in the future.
- Exotic options refer to options that are not vanilla options (e.g., buy the asset for the average price of the asset realized during the life of the option).

Regardless of the nature of the option (vanilla or exotic), all option owners have the ability to exercise at

- One prespecified time (or option maturity).[1]
- Any time up to and including the option maturity.[2]
- Limited times up to and including the option maturity.[3]

The reader is referred to Hull (2012) or any good introductory finance book for further descriptions of these options. For the ease of discussion,

[1] Such options are called European-style exercise options.

[2] Such options are called American-style exercise options.

[3] Such options are called Mid-Atlantic options, limited exercise options, discrete style exercise options, and so on.

TABLE 3.1 Options Prices (when S&P 500 Value is 1681, $T - t$ = seven days)

	Call		Put	
Strike	Bid	Offer	Bid	Offer
1660	28.20	30.30	0.45	0.65
1665	23.40	25.40	0.70	0.90
1670	18.90	20.60	1.05	1.25
1675	14.60	16.50	1.65	2.05
1680	11.00	12.30	2.60	3.00
1685	7.50	8.40	3.90	4.40
1690	4.70	5.30	6.00	6.30
1695	2.55	3.10	8.50	9.80
1700	1.30	1.65	12.10	13.40
1705	0.55	0.95	15.60	17.70
1710	0.30	0.50	20.20	22.30
1715	0.10	0.25	25.10	27.20

Source: www.cboe.com.

unless otherwise mentioned, I will henceforth restrict my discussion to European-style options.

One of the most common and widely traded European-style options is the one linked to the S&P 500 index that trades under the symbol SPXW on the Chicago Board Options Exchange (CBOE).

Table 3.1 shows a snapshot of the S&P 500 (ticker symbol: SPXW) option chain taken during trading hours. As can be seen from the table, the option chain illustrates the impact of varying strike values on the option premiums. Despite this, it is difficult in practice to trade these options if one cannot ascertain how relatively cheap or expensive one option is to another. As a consequence, to be able to trade the options effectively, it is imperative to be able to price these options using a model that professional traders use in practice.

Since the purpose of this chapter is to discuss the application of quantitative methods to price vanilla options, I start with an example to illustrate the derivation and use of the Black-Scholes formulae to price options on nondividend-paying stocks. I then discuss the pricing of similar options when the underlying assets range in diversity from dividend-paying stocks to equity indices to currency rates to commodity prices to interest rates (in particular, swaps, forward rate agreements, and bonds)—and in the process illustrate how practitioners adapt the basic Black-Scholes model to suit their purposes. The chapter then discusses the valuation of options with early-exercise features before concluding with a risk-management application in practice.

BLACK-SCHOLES FORMULAE

It has been about 40 years since Black-Scholes and Merton published their seminal papers on the valuation of vanilla, European-style stock options based on several simplifying assumptions. Since then, the Black-Scholes model has been modified, extended, and adapted when valuing vanilla and exotic options. Although the authors used diffusion equations to arrive at their famed results, I will in this section use heuristic arguments supported by basic calculus and probability arguments to arrive at the same results.

One of the key assumptions that Black–Scholes made was that the stock-price process of a nondividend-paying stock can be characterized by the equation[4]

$$\frac{dS}{S} = rdt + \sigma dz \tag{3.1}$$

where

- S is the price of the stock.
- r is the annualized continuously compounded risk-free rate.
- σ is the annualized volatility of the stock-price return.
- dz is the random variable drawn from a standard normal probability density function.
- dS is the small change in the stock price over a small time interval dt.

To obtain the formula to price a European-style, vanilla call option, the authors go about solving equation (3.1) subject to the boundary condition $\max[S_T - K, 0]$ (where S_T represents the price of the stock on option maturity and K represents the strike price of the option) and assuming that there is no possibility of a riskless arbitrage in continuous time using Ito's lemma. See Black and Scholes (1973) for details.

To solve equation (3.1) subject to the boundary condition, one first needs to observe that the diffusion equation is equivalent to assuming that future

[4]The intuition behind the use of equation (3.1) stems from the assumption that the continuously compounded returns of the stock are lognormally distributed. See Hull (2012) for further details.

stock price movements follow a geometric Brownian motion distribution. More precisely, ln S_T is assumed to be normally distributed with a mean of $lnS_t + \left(r_{t,T} - \frac{1}{2}\sigma^2_{t,T}\right)(T-t)$ and a variance of $\sigma^2_{t,T}(T-t)$

where

S_t is the price of the stock at time t.
$r_{t,T}$ is the zero rate corresponding to a maturity (T) using zero curve at time t.
$\sigma_{t,T}$ is the spot volatility rate corresponding to a maturity (T) using spot volatility curve at time t.
t is the time today.
T is the time when option matures.

Using the notion of risk-neutral valuation[5] (i.e., the reason for using $r_{t,T}$ as both the stock growth rate and discount rate), the expression to value the option is given by the present value of the expected option payoff $\max[S_T - K, 0]$. Doing this, one gets the expression

$$c_{S_t,K,t,T,r_{t,T},\sigma_{t,T},Spot}(van) = e^{-r_{t,T}(T-t)} E_{S_T}\left[\max\left(S_T - K, 0\right)\right] \qquad (3.2)$$

where $E_{S_T}[\max(S_T - K, 0)]$ in equation (3.2) refers to the expectation of $\max[S_T - K, 0]$ taken with respect to the random variable S_T.[6]

[5]This is merely an artificial assumption made to ensure that no preferences of the option holder are factored into the mathematical derivation of the option pricing, hence not allowing for any arbitrage. The reader is referred to Hull (2012) for a detailed discussion.

[6]Another way of looking at the same problem (which will prove to be immensely valuable when trying to value an exotic option called a pay later option, discussed in Chapter 5) can be done by first writing down the profit (not the payoff!) to the option owner at time T. Doing this yields the option owner a profit of $\max[S_T - K - c_{S_t,K,t,T,r_{t,T},\sigma_{t,T},Spot}(van)e^{r_{t,T}(T-t)}, -c_{S_t,K,t,T,r_{t,T},\sigma_{t,T}Spot}(van)e^{r_{t,T}(T-t)}]$, where $c_{S_t,K,t,T,r_{t,T},\sigma_{t,T},Spot}(van)e^{r_{t,T}(T-t)}$ represents the value of the option premium that is paid at time t and future valued to time T. To ensure that the option is fairly priced, one needs the present value of the expected value of the profit to be 0. More succinctly, one would need that $0 = e^{-r_{t,T}(T-t)}\{E_{S_T}[\max(S_T - K - c_{S_t,K,t,T,r_{t,T},\sigma_{t,T},Spot}(van)e^{r_{t,T}(T-t)}, -c_{S_t,K,t,T,r_{t,T},\sigma_{t,T},Spot}(van)e^{r_{t,T}(T-t)})]\}$. Simplifying this yields the expression $c_{S_t,K,t,T,r_{t,T},\sigma_{t,T},Spot}(van) = e^{-r_{t,T}(T-t)}\{E_{S_T}[\max(S_T - K, 0)]\}$—which is essentially equation (3.2).

Letting $g(S_T)$ represent the probability density function (pdf) of S_T, it readily follows from equation (3.2) that

$$c_{S_t,K,t,T,r_{t,T},\sigma_{t,T},Spot}(van) = e^{-r_{t,T}(T-t)} \int_0^\infty \max(S_T - K, 0)\, g(S_T)\, dS_T$$
$$= e^{-r_{t,T}(T-t)} \int_K^\infty (S_T - K) g(S_T)\, dS_T$$
$$= e^{-r_{t,T}(T-t)} \int_K^\infty S_T g(S_T)\, dS_T$$
$$-e^{-r_{t,T}(T-t)} \int_K^\infty K g(S_T)\, dS_T \qquad (3.3a)$$

Observing that $g(S_T) = \frac{1}{\sigma_S\sqrt{2\pi}S_T} e^{-0.5\left[\frac{\ln S_T - \mu_S}{\sigma_S}\right]^2}$ where $\mu_S = lnS_t + \left(r_{t,T} - \frac{1}{2}\sigma_{t,T}^2\right)(T-t)$ and $\sigma_S = \sigma_{t,T}\sqrt{T-t}$, it readily follows that

$$e^{-r_{t,T}(T-t)} \int_K^\infty S_T g(S_T) dS_T = e^{-r_{t,T}(T-t)} \int_K^\infty S_T \frac{1}{\sigma_S\sqrt{2\pi}S_T} e^{-0.5\left[\frac{\ln S_T - \mu_S}{\sigma_S}\right]^2} dS_T \quad (3.3b)$$

$$e^{-r_{t,T}(T-t)} \int_K^\infty K g(S_T) dS_T = K e^{-r_{t,T}(T-t)} \int_K^\infty \frac{1}{\sigma_S\sqrt{2\pi}S_T} e^{-0.5\left[\frac{\ln S_T - \mu_S}{\sigma_S}\right]^2} dS_T \quad (3.3c)$$

Substituting equations (3.3b) and (3.3c) into equation (3.3a), one can arrive at the famed Black-Scholes equation that is used to value European-style call options on nondividend-paying stocks. More precisely, this takes the form of[7,8]

$$c_{S_t,K,t,T,r_{t,T},\sigma_{t,T},Spot}(van) = S_t N\left(d^1_{S_t,K,t,T,r_{t,T},0,\sigma_{t,T}}\right)$$
$$- K e^{-r_{t,T}(T-t)} N\left(d^2_{S_t,K,t,T,r_{t,T},0,\sigma_{t,T}}\right) \qquad (3.4a)$$

---

[7] $d^2_{S_t,K,t,T,r_{t,T},0,\sigma_{t,T}}$ is sometimes presented in financial textbooks as $d^2_{S_t,K,t,T,r_{t,T},0,\sigma_{t,T}} = d^1_{S_t,K,t,T,r_{t,T},0,\sigma_{t,T}} - \sigma_{t,T}\sqrt{T-t}$.

[8] As an astute reader will realize, $N(a)$ is in fact the cumulative probability function associated with a standard normal probability. So $N(a) = \Pr(Z \leq a)$, where Z represents a normal pdf with a mean of 0 and variance of 1.

where $d^1_{a,b,c,d,e,f,g} = \frac{\ln(a/b)+\left(e-f+\frac{1}{2}g^2\right)(d-c)}{g\sqrt{d-c}}$, $d^2_{a,b,c,d,e,f,g} = \frac{\ln(a/b)+\left(e-f-\frac{1}{2}g^2\right)(d-c)}{g\sqrt{d-c}}$

and $N(a) = \int\limits_{-\infty}^{a} \frac{1}{\sqrt{2\pi}} e^{-0.5z^2}\, dz$.

One can go through a similar exercise to show that a European style put option (where the maturity payoff to the option buyer is of the form $\max[K - S_T, 0]$) can be priced using the expression

$$p_{S_t,K,t,T,r_{t,T},\sigma_{t,T},Spot}(van) = -S_t N\left(-d^1_{S_t,K,t,T,r_{t,T},0,\sigma_{t,T}}\right) + Ke^{-r_{t,T}(T-t)} N\left(-d^2_{S_t,K,t,T,r_{t,T},0,\sigma_{t,T}}\right) \quad (3.4b)$$

Equations (3.4a) and (3.4b) have been implemented in Microsoft Excel so as to value both European-style call and put options on nondividend-paying stocks.

The value of the option given in Table 3.2 is for the case when there is only one stock underlying the option. In practice, when transacting in exchange-traded options, it is imperative for the trader to stipulate the contract size associated with the trade—where each contract size typically[9] has a multiplier of 100. Thus, the actual cost of the transaction is simply the price of the option on one share of the stock multiplied by the contract multiplier for one contract (which is 100 in this case) and the number of contracts. Table 3.3 shows the instance of valuing an option on Baidu stock (stock-trading symbol: BIDU) where each contract has a multiplier of 100. Furthermore, when transacting a similar trade on the OTC market, it suffices to simply stipulate the contract size, as the lot size for each contract is assumed to be one. As a consequence, the trade in Table 3.3 can be done in an OTC market using a contract size of 500.

Another observation that the reader needs to take note of is that most stock options that trade on the exchange tend to be American style in nature vis-à-vis their OTC counterparts. The methodology discussed in Table 3.2 can only be used to value European-style exercise types and not the Bermudan or American-style exercise types. The valuation of early-exercise features in an option is discussed later in this chapter.

[9]Contrary to the common belief, this multiplier is not unique to each stock-ticker symbol. For example, shares of Apple trade under the symbol AAPL on the Nasdaq stock exchange. There are two types of multipliers used when trading options on this stock. One is the usual multiplier of 100, while the other is a multiplier of 10—where each option contract has its own unique ticker symbol that reflects the multiplier, option type, expiry date, and strike price.

TABLE 3.2 Valuing European-Style Options on Nondividend-Paying Stocks

	A	B	C
1	Current Price, S_t ($)	$40.00	
2	Strike Price, K ($)	$40.00	
3	Volatility, σ (%)	20.00%	
4	Risk Free, r (%)	6.00%	
5	Current Time, t (years)	0	
6	Expiry, T (years)	2	
7	d_1	0.565685425	=(LN(B1/B2)+((B4+(0.5*B3*B3))*(B6-B5)))/(B3*SQRT(B6-B5))
8	d_2	0.282842712	=(LN(B1/B2)+((B4-(0.5*B3*B3))*(B6-B5)))/(B3*SQRT(B6-B5))
9	Call	6.879048813	=[(B1*NORMSDIST(B7))-(B2*EXP(-B4*(B6-B5))*NORMSDIST(B8))]
10	Put	2.355866282	=[-(B1*NORMSDIST(-B7))+(B2*EXP(-B4*(B6-B5))*NORMSDIST(-B8))]

TABLE 3.3 Valuing European-Style Options on Nondividend-Paying Stocks in the Presence of Contract Sizes

	A	B	C
1	Current Price, S_t ($)	$100.00	
2	Strike Price, K ($)	$100.00	
3	Volatility, σ (%)	15.00%	
4	Risk Free, r (%)	2.00%	
5	Current Time, t (years)	0	
6	Expiry, T (years)	1	
7	Lot Size/Contract	100	
8	Contract Size	5	
9	d_1	0.208333333	=(LN(B1/B2)+((B4+(0.5*B3*B3))*(B6-B5)))/(B3*SQRT(B6-B5))
10	d_2	0.058333333	=(LN(B1/B2)+((B4-(0.5*B3*B3))*(B6-B5)))/(B3*SQRT(B6-B5))
11	Call	3480.920822	=[(B1*NORMSDIST(B9))-(B2*EXP(-B4*(B6-B5))*NORMSDIST(B10))]*B7*B8
12	Put	2490.854488	=[-(B1*NORMSDIST(-B9))+(B2*EXP(-B4*(B6-B5))*NORMSDIST(-B10))]*B7*B8

ADAPTATIONS OF THE BLACK-SCHOLES FORMULAE

Given the backdrop of the earlier section, it is important for the reader to understand how the original Black-Scholes option pricing formulae has been adapted by traders to price options on various underlyings (e.g., dividend paying stocks, commodity futures, and so on). In this section, I will discuss the assumptions made by practitioners and the models used to value such options in three different instances.

Pricing Options on Dividend-Paying Stocks

In the previous section, I discussed the valuation of European-style options on non-dividend paying stocks. In practice, there are companies that do pay quarterly dividends to their shareholders (e.g., Apple, Microsoft, and Bank of America). Additionally, when valuing options on indices, the issue of valuing options on dividend-paying stocks becomes more pressing, especially if the index is mostly made up of dividend-paying stocks (e.g., S&P 500 Index).

To be able to value options on dividend-paying stocks, I will first assume that dividends are paid continuously (a very reasonable assumption when valuing options on indices but not when valuing options on a single stock[10]). Since a dividend has the effect of decreasing the value of a stock, assuming that a stock pays a continuously compounded dividend rate of q, equation (3.1) takes the form of

$$\frac{dS}{S} = (r - q)dt + \sigma dz \tag{3.5}$$

where

S is the price of the stock.
r is the annualized continuously compounded risk-free rate.
q is the annualized continuously compounded dividend yield.
σ is the annualized volatility of the index return.
dz is the random variable drawn from a standard normal probability density function.
dS is the small change in the stock price over a small time interval dt.

[10]The reason for this stems from the fact that dividends are usually paid no more than four times a year on a given stock (i.e., discrete payment amounts at discrete times).

As earlier, observing that the diffusion equation given by equation (3.5) is equivalent to assuming that ln S_T is assumed to be normally distributed with a mean of

$$\ln S_t + \left(r_{t,T} - q_{t,T} - \frac{1}{2}\sigma_{t,T}^2\right)(T-t) \text{ and a variance of } \sigma_{t,T}^2(T-t)$$

where

S_t is the price of the stock at time t.
$r_{t,T}$ is the zero rate corresponding to a maturity (T) using zero rate curve at time t.
$q_{t,T}$ is the zero-dividend rate corresponding to a maturity (T) using zero dividend curve at time t.
$\sigma_{t,T}$ is the spot-volatility rate corresponding to a maturity (T) using spot volatility curve at time t.
t is the time today.
T is the time when the option matures.

It readily follows that the formula for pricing the call option on a dividend-paying stock can be obtained by taking an approach similar to equation (3.2). As a consequence, one has

$$c_{S_t,K,t,T,r_{t,T},q_{t,T},\sigma_{t,T},Spot}(van) = e^{-r_{t,T}(T-t)}E_{S_T}\left[\max\left(S_T - K, 0\right)\right] \quad (3.6)$$

Equation (3.6) can be simplified to obtain

$$\begin{aligned} c_{S_t,K,t,T,r_{t,T},q_{t,T},\sigma_{t,T},Spot}(van) = {} & S_t e^{-q_{t,T}(T-t)} N\left(d^1_{S_t,K,t,T,r_{t,T},q_{t,T},\sigma_{t,T}}\right) \\ & - K e^{-r_{t,T}(T-t)} N\left(d^2_{S_t,K,t,T,r_{t,T},q_{t,T},\sigma_{t,T}}\right) \quad (3.7a) \end{aligned}$$

where $d^1_{S_t,K,t,T,r_{t,T},q_{t,T},\sigma_{t,T}}$ and $d^2_{S_t,K,t,T,r_{t,T},q_{t,T},\sigma_{t,T}}$ are as defined earlier.

The formula to price a put option on a dividend-paying stock can similarly be shown to be

$$\begin{aligned} p_{S_t,K,t,T,r_{t,T},q_{t,T},\sigma_{t,T},Spot}(van) = {} & -S_t e^{-q_{t,T}(T-t)} N\left(-d^1_{S_t,K,t,T,r_{t,T},q_{t,T},\sigma_{t,T}}\right) \\ & + K e^{-r_{t,T}(T-t)} N\left(-d^2_{S_t,K,t,T,r_{t,T},q_{t,T},\sigma_{t,T}}\right) \quad (3.7b) \end{aligned}$$

Equations (3.7a) and (3.7b) can easily be programmed on the Microsoft Excel spreadsheet as shown in Table 3.4.

TABLE 3.4 Valuing European-Style Options on Dividend-Paying Stocks

	A	B	C
1	Current Price, S_t ($)	$40.00	
2	Strike Price, K ($)	$40.00	
3	Volatility, σ (%)	20.00%	
4	Risk Free, r (%)	6.00%	
5	Dividend Rate, q (%)	2.00%	
6	Current Time, t (years)	0	
7	Expiry, T (years)	2	
8	d^1	0.424264069	=(LN(B1/B2)+((B4-B5+(0.5*B3*B3))*(B7-B6)))/(B3*SQRT(B7-B6))
9	d^2	0.141421356	=(LN(B1/B2)+((B4-B5-(0.5*B3*B3))*(B7-B6)))/(B3*SQRT(B7-B6))
10	Call	5.797289275	=(B1*EXP(-B5*(B7-B6))*NORMSDIST(B8))-(B2*EXP(-B4*(B7-B6))*NORMSDIST(B9))
11	Put	2.842529178	=-(B1*EXP(-B5*(B7-B6))*NORMSDIST(-B8))+(B2*EXP(-B4*(B7-B6))*NORMSDIST(-B9))

Although Table 3.4 shows the valuation of an option on dividend-paying stocks using equations (3.7a) and (3.7b), these equations can also be used to value options on indices and currencies. Since the application of the equations to value index options is straightforward, I will only discuss the adaptation of equations (3.7a) and (3.7b) to value currency options.

Like stock and index options, currency options also trade on both the exchange and OTC markets where the underlying asset could be either a spot currency or currency futures or currency forward rate. For the sake of convenience, I will assume that the underlying is a spot-currency rate. Because currency rates can be quoted in two ways (e.g., USD/EUR and EUR/USD), one has to understand the context in which terms like call and put options are used, since a call option on a currency rate that is written one way (e.g., USD/EUR) is the same as a put option on the same currency rate that is written in a reciprocal manner (e.g., EUR/USD).

Garman and Kohlhagen (1983) observed that currency rate movements are a function of both the domestic risk-free rate and foreign risk-free rate of that currency. They then went on to assume that the foreign risk-free rate can be treated as a continuously compounded dividend rate and modified equation (3.5) to arrive at

$$\frac{dS}{S} = (r - rf)dt + \sigma dz \tag{3.8}$$

where

- S is the currency-exchange rate (expressed as the number of domestic units divided by foreign units).
- r is the annualized continuously compounded domestic risk-free rate.
- rf is the annualized continuously compounded foreign risk-free rate.
- σ is the annualized volatility of spot currency rate returns.
- dz is the random variable drawn from a standard normal probability density function.
- dS is the small change in the exchange rate over a small time interval dt.

Given the similarity of equation (3.8) to equation (3.5), one can easily use equations (3.7a) and (3.7b) to value the currency options by replacing $q_{t,T}$ in the formulae with $rf_{t,T}$. Doing this, one can arrive at the setup laid out in Table 3.5 when the underlying currency rate is the CAD/USD (Canadian dollar/U.S. dollar) pair.

TABLE 3.5 Valuing European-Style Currency Options

	A	B	C
1	Spot Rate, S_t (CAD/USD)	1.3000	
2	Strike Price, K (CAD/USD)	1.3000	
3	Volatility, σ (%)	15.00%	
4	CAD (domestic) Risk Free, r (%)	2.00%	
5	U.S. (foreign) Risk Free, r_f (%)	1.00%	
6	Current Time, t (years)	0	
7	Expiry, T (years)	1	
8	d^1	0.141666667	=(LN(B1/B2)+((B4-B5+(0.5*B3*B3))*(B7-B6)))/(B3*SQRT(B7-B6))
9	d^2	−0.008333333	=(LN(B1/B2)+((B4-B5-(0.5*B3*B3))*(B7-B6)))/(B3*SQRT(B7-B6))
10	Call (CAD/USD)	0.083137733	=(B1*EXP(-B5*(B7-B6))*NORMSDIST(B8))-(B2*EXP(-B4*(B7-B6))*NORMSDIST(B9))
11	Put (CAD/USD)	0.070331225	=-(B1*EXP(-B5*(B7-B6))*NORMSDIST(-B8))+(B2*EXP(-B4*(B7-B6))*NORMSDIST(-B9))

From Table 3.5, it can be seen that the option premiums[11] (given in cells B10 and B11) are denominated in CAD/USD (or domestic/foreign). For this to be converted to a dollar amount, one would need a notional in U.S. dollars so that the premiums paid for the option are denominated in Canadian dollars.[12]

Pricing Options on Futures Contracts

In the option pricing examples discussed thus far, the option holder's payoff at the time of exercise was computed by comparing the value of the stock price (or spot index value or spot currency rate) at the time of exercise with the value of the option strike. Unlike these options, options on futures contracts are settled upon exercise by comparing the value of a futures price (or rate) at the time of exercise to the option strike price.[13]

Futures contracts and options on futures contracts are both extensively traded on the Chicago Mercantile Exchange (CME).[14] Like the options discussed earlier, options on futures also tend to be American-style in nature and usually physically settled (with the underlying futures contract) upon exercise. In the event that the holder of the futures-option contract has no desire to take physical delivery of the underlying futures contract, the holder can either easily unwind the entire futures options position prior to option expiry or transact in the OTC markets (which tend to be cash settled). Although the OTC version of the futures options can have early-exercise features, it is just as easy for one to transact in a European-style option that is cash settled based on the level of the futures contract at the time of the option expiry. As a consequence, I will discuss the valuation of a European-style futures option in this section.

Given the nature of a futures contract, the reader should note that the model that is used to mimic stock-price movements does not lend itself

---

[11]The call (put) option in Table 3.5 refers to the call (put) on USD or put (call) on CAD in the nomenclature of the currency markets. Sometimes this can be further abbreviated as USD call (call on USD) or a USD put (put on USD) and so on.

[12]In the event the premium needs to be paid in USD, one only needs to convert the premium in CAD using the spot rate. In the event the notional is given in CAD, one would need to convert the notional to USD using the strike rate.

[13]It is implicitly assumed that the maturity of the futures contract usually exceeds that of the option contract unlike that for an option on a forward contract (where the maturity of the forward contract is assumed to usually match that of the option contract).

[14]See Chicago Mercentile Exchange (CME) website (www.cmegroup.com) for contract specifications.

naturally to the modeling of movements in a futures price. The reader is referred to Black (1976) for further details relating to the reasons. The consequence of this is the diffusion process:

$$\frac{dF}{F} = \sigma dz \tag{3.9}$$

where

F is the price of the futures.
σ is the annualized volatility of futures price returns.
dz is the random variable drawn from a standard normal probability density function.
dF is the small change in the futures price over a small time interval dt.

As before, one first can observe that the diffusion equation given by equation (3.9) is equivalent to assuming that ln F_T is normally distributed with a mean of $\ln F_t - \frac{1}{2}\sigma_{t,T}^2(T-t)$ and a variance of $\sigma_{t,T}^2(T-t)$ where

F_t is the price of the futures contract at time t.
$\sigma_{t,T}$ is the spot-volatility rate corresponding to a maturity (T) using spot volatility curve at time t.
t is the time today.
T is the time when option matures.

It readily follows that the formula for pricing the call option on a futures contract paying stock is similar to equation (3.6) and takes the form

$$c_{F_t,K,t,T,r_{t,T},\sigma_{t,T},Fut}(van) = e^{-r_{t,T}(T-t)}E_{F_T}\left[\max\left(F_T - K, 0\right)\right] \tag{3.10}$$

Using the distributional assumption for F_T, it can be seen that equation (3.10) can be simplified to obtain

$$\begin{aligned} c_{F_t,K,t,T,r_{t,T},\sigma_{t,T},Fut}(van) = e^{-r_{t,T}(T-t)}\Big[F_t N\left(d^1_{F_t,K,t,T,0,0,\sigma_{t,T}}\right) \\ - KN\left(d^2_{F_t,K,t,T,0,0,\sigma_{t,T}}\right)\Big] \end{aligned} \tag{3.11a}$$

$$\begin{aligned} p_{F_t,K,t,T,r,\sigma,Fut}(van) = e^{-r_{t,T}(T-t)}\Big[-F_t N\left(-d^1_{F_t,K,t,T,0,0,\sigma_{t,T}}\right) \\ + KN\left(-d^2_{F_t,K,t,T,0,0,\sigma_{t,T}}\right)\Big] \end{aligned} \tag{3.11b}$$

Equations (3.11a) and (3.11b) have been implemented on an Excel spreadsheet as shown in Table 3.6.

Table 3.6 shows the valuation of European-style futures options. The setup provided in the table can be customized to allow for the pricing of the European-style options contract on any type futures contract (e.g., Eurodollar futures, oil futures, grain futures, and so on) by incorporating contract sizes, lots per contract size, and other settlement conventions. The reader is referred to the CME website for examples of such applications.

Pricing Options on Forward Contracts

Despite being philosophically similar, unlike futures contracts that only trade on the exchanges (e.g., CME), forward contracts trade on the OTC markets. Although some market participants transact in options on forward contracts in order to exercise into the underlying spot contract, more often than not this is done for mathematical convenience.[15] Given this backdrop, one can use the same diffusion equation given by equation (3.9)

$$\frac{dF}{F} = \sigma dz$$

where

F is the forward rate.
σ is the annualized volatility of forward rate returns.
dz is the random variable drawn from a standard normal probability density function.
dF is the small change in the forward rate over a small time interval dt.

As a consequence, the implementation laid out on Table 3.6 still holds, although adjustments need to be made to take into consideration settlement

[15]To model an interest rate or commodity-spot price at some time in the future, practitioners assume that the future interest rate (or spot price) movements are centered at the current forward rate (or price) that is implied by the market and follows the diffusion process used for modeling futures prices/rates. In addition, one also assumes that the option would mature at the same time as the forward. The purpose of this is to ensure that upon the exercise of the option, the spot-interest rates (or prices) at the time of option expiry are compared with the strike rate—as the forward rates (or prices) converge to the spot rates (or prices) on the day of the forward contract maturity. The reader is again referred to Hull (2012) for details.

TABLE 3.6 Valuing European Style Options on Futures Contracts

	A	B	C
1	Current Price, F_t ($)	$1,200.00	
2	Strike Price, K ($)	$1,200.00	
3	Volatility, σ (%)	25.00%	
4	Risk Free, r (%)	4.00%	
5	Current Time, t (years)	0	
6	Expiry, T (years)	1	
7	d^1	0.125	=(LN(B1/B2)+((0.5*B3*B3)*(B6-B5)))/(B3*SQRT(B6-B5))
8	d^2	–0.125	=(LN(B1/B2)-((0.5*B3*B3)*(B6-B5)))/(B3*SQRT(B6-B5))
9	Call	114.6911067	=((B1*NORMSDIST(B7))-(B2*NORMSDIST(B8)))*EXP(-B4*(B6-B5))
10	Put	114.6911067	=(-(B1*NORMSDIST(-B7))+(B2*NORMSDIST(-B8)))*EXP(-B4*(B6-B5))

mechanisms associated with the underlyings of the options. To help shed more light on this comment, I present three such examples.

Interest Rate Swaptions An interest rate *swaption* (i.e., an option on an interest rate swap) is one example of commonly traded interest rate options in OTC capital markets around the world. Upon exercise of the swaption, the holder has the right to enter into an interest rate swap so as to either receive or pay a fixed rate[16] on the swap. This is akin to the swaption holder taking physical delivery of the underlying swap upon exercise. Because these contracts trade in the OTC market, the holder has the flexibility of receiving the in-the-money payoff in cash instead of taking physical delivery of the underlying swap, provided this mode of settlement is prespecified prior to the maturity of the option. When trading swaptions, practitioners use the terms[17] right-to-pay (RTP) option and right-to-receive (RTR) option. These refer to the right to pay a fixed rate on the swap underlying the option or the right to receive a fixed rate on the swap underlying the option, respectively.

The RTP-option payoff to the owner is slightly different from the payoff associated with the purchase of a futures call option contract. The reason for this stems from the fact that once the RTP option is in the money, the owner of the option exercises into a swap. As a consequence, on option maturity date, the owner of the RTP option on a notional principal of a dollar receives a payoff that is of the form

$$\max[F_T - K, 0] \sum_{i=1}^{n} \tau_i D_{T,T+\tau_1+\ldots+\tau_i}$$

where

F_T is the swap rate on option maturity.
K is the strike rate.
n is the number of cash-flow exchanges in the swap.
τ_i is the tenor (time between the setting of the i floating rate and settling of the cash flows arising from this setting).
$D_{T,T+\tau_1+\ldots+\tau_i}$ is the discount factor that is used to discount the cash flow arising from the settlement of the i floating rate using the zero curve at time T.[18]

[16]This is also the strike rate of the swaption.
[17]The term RTP (RTR) option can be thought of as a call (put) option on interest rate swap.
[18]The term $\sum_{i=1}^{n} \tau_i D_{T,T+\tau_1+\ldots+\tau_i}$ is sometimes known as the swap delta.

The resulting RTP (call) and RTR (put) option-pricing formulae can be simplified, as in equations (3.12a) and (3.12b).

$$c_{F_t,K,t,T,ZRC,\sigma_{t,T},IRS}(van) = \left[F_t N\left(d^1_{F_t,K,t,T,0,0,\sigma_{t,T}}\right) - KN\left(d^2_{F_t,K,t,T,0,0,\sigma_{t,T}}\right)\right] \sum_{i=1}^{n} \tau_i D_{t,T+\tau_1+\ldots+\tau_i} \quad (3.12a)$$

$$p_{F_t,K,t,T,ZRC,\sigma_{t,T},For}(van) = \left[-F_t N\left(-d^1_{F_t,K,t,T,0,0,\sigma_{t,T}}\right) + KN\left(-d^2_{F_t,K,t,T,0,0,\sigma_{t,T}}\right)\right] \sum_{i=1}^{n} \tau_i D_{t,T+\tau_1+\ldots+\tau_i} \quad (3.12b)$$

where

F_t is the forward start swap rate[19] computed using the zero-rate curve at time t (ZRC) for a swap whose first floating rate is set at time T and whose last floating rate is set at time $T + \tau_1 + \tau_2 + \ldots + \tau_{n-1}$.

$D_{t,T+\tau_1+\ldots+\tau_i}$ is the discount factor used to discount the cash flow arising from the setting of the ith floating rate using the zero-rate curve at time t (ZRC).

$\sum_{i=1}^{n} \tau_i D_{t,T+\tau_1+\ldots+\tau_i}$ is assumed to be given.[20]

Table 3.7 shows the implementation of equations (3.12a) and (3.12b) to price options on interest rate swaps.

Interest Rate Caps/Floors In addition to swaptions, caps and floors are another class of interest rate options that get traded quite widely in the OTC markets. Since the terms *cap* and *floor* are used to refer to a collection of caplets and floorlets respectively, the price of a cap (floor) is simply the sum of the prices of *all* the underlying caplets (floorlets). Hence to price a cap or a floor, one needs to know how to price a caplet and a floorlet.

Practitioners use the term caplet (floorlet) to refer to a call (put) option on LIBOR. More precisely, on option maturity the value of the LIBOR (e.g.,

---

[19]This can be in practice calculated using equation (2.6).

[20]This is in practice computed from the same zero rate curve that is used to calculate the forward start swap rate.

TABLE 3.7 Valuing European-Style Swaptions

	A	B	C
1	Current Forward Swap Rate, F_t ($)	3.25%	
2	Strike Price, K ($)	3.50%	
3	Volatility, σ (%)	20.00%	
4	Swap Delta, $\sum t_i D_i$ ($)	2.3	
5	Current Time, t (years)	0	
6	Expiry, T (years)	2	
7	d^1	−0.120589892	=(LN(B1/B2)+((0.5*B3*B3)*(B6-B5)))/(B3*SQRT(B6-B5))
8	d^2	−0.403432604	=(LN(B1/B2)-((0.5*B3*B3)*(B6-B5)))/(B3*SQRT(B6-B5))
9	Call	0.006150736	=((B1*NORMSDIST(B7))-(B2*NORMSDIST(B8)))*B4
10	Put	0.011900736	=(-(B1*NORMSDIST(-B7))+(B2*NORMSDIST(-B8)))*B4

1-month LIBOR, 3-month LIBOR) is compared with a strike rate. As a consequence, the owner of each caplet (floorlet) is essentially purchasing an RTP (RTR) or a call (put) option on a single-period swap (also called a forward rate agreement).

Since one is dealing with single-period swaps, to value a caplet on a notional principal of a dollar, it is straightforward to write down the caplet owner's payoff on the option's maturity date as

$$\max[F_{t_i} - K, 0]\tau_i D_{t_i,t_i+\tau_i}$$

where

F_{t_i} is the value of the LIBOR rate that sets on t_i (option maturity) and settles at time $(t_i + \tau_i)$.
K is the strike rate of caplet.
τ_i is the tenor of the ith floating rate.
$D_{t_i,t_i+\tau_i}$ is the discount factor that is used to discount the cashflow arising from the settling of the ith floating rate using the zero curve at time t_i.

Taking the present value of the expectations allows one to arrive at equations (3.13a) and (3.13b).

$$c_{F_{i,t},K,t,t_i,\tau_i,ZRC,\sigma_{t,t_i},FRA}(van) = \left[F_{i,t}N\left(d^1_{F_{i,t},K,t,t_i,0,0,\sigma_{t,t_i}}\right) - KN\left(d^2_{F_{i,t},K,t,t_i,0,0,\sigma_{t,t_i}}\right)\right]\tau_i D_{t,t_i+\tau_i} \tag{3.12a}$$

$$p_{F_{i,t},K,t,t_i,\tau_i,ZRC,\sigma_{t,t_i},FRA}(van) = \left[-F_{i,t}N\left(-d^1_{F_{i,t},K,t,t_i,0,0,\sigma_{t,t_i}}\right) + KN\left(-d^2_{F_{i,t},K,t,t_i,0,0,\sigma_{t,t_i}}\right)\right]\tau_i D_{t,t_i+\tau_i} \tag{3.12b}$$

where

$F_{i,t}$ is the forward rate applied from time $(t_i, t_i + \tau_i)$ computed using the zero-rate curve at time t (ZRC).
$D_{t,t_i+\tau_i}$ is the discount factor that is used to discount the cash flow arising from the settling of ith floating rate using the zero rate curve at time t (ZRC) and assumed to be given for our purposes.

Table 3.8 shows the implementation of equations (3.12a) and (3.12b) to evaluate both a caplet and a floorlet.

TABLE 3.8 Valuation of Caplet and Floorlet

	A	B	C
1	Current Forward Swap Rate, F_t (%)	3.50%	
2	Strike Price, K (%)	3.25%	
3	Volatility, σ (%)	17.00%	
4	Swap Delta, $t_i D_i$ ($)	0.48	
5	Current Time, t (years)	0	
6	Expiry, T (years)	0.5	
7	d^1	0.676601131	=(LN(B1/B2)+((0.5*B3*B3)*(B6-B5)))/(B3*SQRT(B6-B5))
8	d^2	0.556392978	=(LN(B1/B2)-((0.5*B3*B3)*(B6-B5)))/(B3*SQRT(B6-B5))
9	Call	0.001519213	=((B1*NORMSDIST(B7))-(B2*NORMSDIST(B8)))*B4
10	Put	0.000319213	=(-(B1*NORMSDIST(-B7))+(B2*NORMSDIST(-B8)))*B4

TABLE 3.9 Valuation of Cap and Floor

	A	B	C	D
1		Option 1	Option 2	Option 3
2	Current Forward Swap Rate, F_t (%)	3.20%	3.50%	3.40%
3	Strike Rate, K (%)	3.25%	3.25%	3.25%
4	Volatility, σ (%)	17.00%	19.00%	21.00%
5	Swap Delta, t_iD_i ($)	0.226	0.229	0.227
6	Current Time, t (years)	0	0	0
7	Expiry, T (years)	0.25	0.5	0.75
8	d^1	−0.139902195	0.618777772	0.339030719
9	d^2	−0.224902195	0.484427484	0.157165385
10	Call (caplet)	0.000194676	0.000761481	0.000733809
11	Put (floorlet)	0.000307676	0.000188981	0.000393309
12	Call (Cap)	0.001689965	=SUM(B10:D10)	
13	Put (Floor)	0.000889965	=SUM(B11:D11)	

Table 3.9 shows an example of how three caplets (floorlets) are put together to arrive at the value of a cap (floor).

Bond Options In addition to swaptions and caps/floors, bond options (or bondtions) represent the third class of interest-rate options that get traded quite widely in the OTC markets. Unlike the earlier examples, however, trading bond options can be trickier since bonds get quoted by both price and yield. As a consequence, it becomes imperative to ensure that when a call option on a bond is being transacted, the transaction also contains details whether the underlying is a bond price or a bond yield.[21]

Since most bond options that trade in the OTC market tend to be European-style in nature, where the underlying is bond-yield based,[22] one would need to know how to adapt the models of the earlier examples to price bond options. To do this, one has to tweak the payoffs—just like what was done for swaptions, caps, and floors.

Although there are a few ways of defining an option payoff associated with a bond yield, one common form of representation is that the owner of

---

[21]Given the inverse relationship between a bond price and yield, a call option on a bond price is in fact a put option on the yield of the same bond (with some adjustments made to the notional size of the options).

[22]If the underlying is a bond price instead of a bond yield, there are certain limitations on how much stochasticity a bond price can exhibit. See Hull (2012).

a call option gets \$10,000 for every basis point the option finishes in-the-money—which can be alternatively rewritten as follows:[23,24]

$$\max[BY_T - K, 0] * 10{,}000 * 10{,}000$$

where

BY_T is the value of the bond yield at T (option maturity date).
K is the strike rate of the option.

Taking the relevant expectations and present value yields the following result in equations (3.13a) and (3.13b)

$$c_{FBY_t,K,t,T,ZRC,\sigma_{t,T},Bond}(van) = \left[FBY_t N\left(d^1_{FBY_t,K,t,T,0,0,\sigma_{t,T}}\right) - KN\left(d^2_{FBY_t,K,t,T,0,0,\sigma_{t,T}}\right)\right] * N \qquad (3.13a)$$

$$p_{F_{i,t},K,t,t_i,\tau_i,ZRC,\sigma_{t,T},Bond}(van) = \left[-F_t N\left(-d^1_{FBY_t,K,t,T,0,0,\sigma_{t,T}}\right) + KN\left(-d^2_{FBY_t,K,t,T,0,0,\sigma_{t,T}}\right)\right] * N \qquad (3.13b)$$

where

FBY_t is the forward bond yield[25] of the bond applicable from time T to bond maturity that is computed at time t.

$N = 10{,}000 * 10{,}000 * D_{t,T}$

$D_{t,T}$ is the discount factor used to discount the cash flow arising at time T using the zero-rate curve at time t (ZRC).

Table 3.10 shows the implementation of equations (3.13a) and (3.13b).

[23]The first 10,000 refers to the conversion required to convert the decimal-based yield differential to one that is denominated in basis points. The second 10,000 refers to the dollar payoff associated with each basis point the option finishes in the money.
[24]Bond options are also traded on the CBOE under the trading symbols FVX, TNX, and TYX. Similar to the example, these options are also written on bond yields with each basis point in-the-money providing the option holder \$100 instead of the \$10,000 per the example.
[25]Since the calculation of the forward bond yield is a little complicated, I have included it as an Appendix to this chapter.

TABLE 3.10 Valuation of Bond Options

	A	B	C
1	Current Forward Swap Rate, F_t (%)	3.25%	
2	Strike Yield, K (%)	3.50%	
3	Volatility, σ (%)	20.00%	
4	Discount Factor	0.987	
5	Current Time, t (years)	0	
6	Expiry, T (years)	2	
7	d^1	−0.120589892	=(LN(B1/B2)+((0.5*B3*B3)*(B6-B5)))/(B3*SQRT(B6-B5))
8	d^2	−0.403432604	=(LN(B1/B2)-((0.5*B3*B3)*(B6-B5)))/(B3*SQRT(B6-B5))
9	Call (On Yield)	0.002639468	=((B1*NORMSDIST(B7))-(B2*NORMSDIST(B8)))*B4
10	Put (On Yield)	0.005106968	=(-(B1*NORMSDIST(-B7))+(B2*NORMSDIST(-B8)))*B4

As the reader will note, to convert the values in cells B9 and B10 to a dollar amount to be consistent with the payoff to the owner of the bond options, one still needs to multiply the values in cells B9 and B10 by 10,000 $*$ 10,000.

LIMITATIONS OF THE BLACK-SCHOLES FORMULAE

In the previous sections, I discussed the use of the Black-Scholes model and how it can be adapted to value options on indices, currencies, swaps, and bonds. In all these discussions, one common underlying thread was that the options could only be exercised on the option maturity date. In this section, I will discuss the valuation of early-exercise options restricting my discussion to nondividend-paying stocks.

Valuing options that allow for early exercise can be a tricky proposition since one has to decide at the time of exercise if it is economically better to exercise the option and collect the proceeds or delay the exercise. Given this backdrop, one can expect the valuation of early-exercise features to be more numerically intensive, simply because this amounts to solving a multidimensional integration problem. To see this, note that in valuing European-style options, one calculates the expectation of the option payoff with respect to the stock price on option maturity—which is essentially a single-variate integration problem. When early-exercise features are permitted, one would need to compute the value of the payoffs at the times of exercise (which would imply the need to integrate with respect to the stock prices at such times) resulting in a multivariate integration problem.[26]

Cox, Ross, and Rubinstein (1979) solved the issue of early exercise using an intuitive approach. By breaking down stock price movements over time

[26]To see this, consider the simple example when there is only one exercise time (on option maturity, T). The payoff to the call option holder at this time is $\max[S_T - K, 0]$. Thus to compute the option value, one has to compute $e^{-r_{t,T}(T-t)} \int_0^\infty \max[S_T - K, 0]\, g(S_T|S_t)\, dS_T$, where $g(S_T|S_t)$ represents the conditional density of the stock price at time T given the value of the stock price at time t (which is the standard probability density function for S_T)—a single variate integral. Now suppose that the option holder is also allowed to exercise at time u, where $t < u < T$. Then at time u, the option holder's payoff is $\max[S_u - K, e^{-r_{u,T}(T-u)} \int_0^\infty \max(S_T - K, 0)\, g(S_T|S_u)\, dS_T]$. Thus, the value of the option is given by the expression $e^{-r_{t,u}(u-t)} \int_0^\infty [\max[S_u - K, e^{-r_{u,T}(T-u)} \int_0^\infty \max(S_T - K, 0)\, g(S_T|S_u)\, dS_T] g(S_u|S_t)\, dS_u$ —a bivariate integral. It can be easily inferred that as the number of exercise points increase so does that dimensionality of the integral—making this a computationally intensive proposition.

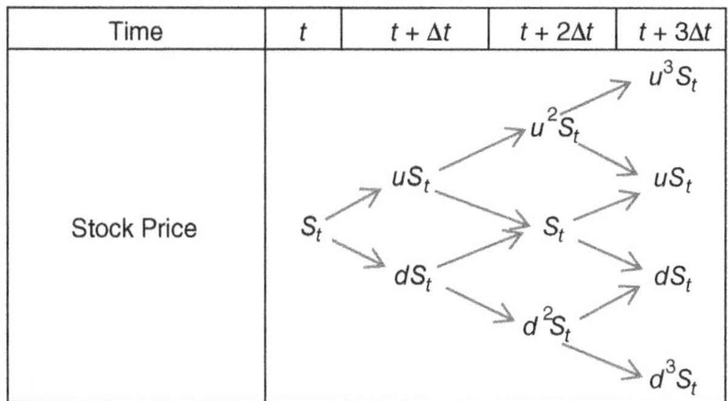

FIGURE 3.1 Illustration of a Stock-Price Tree

into a two-state (up and down) process, and assuming that stock prices recombine (i.e., going up and then coming down is the same as going down and then up), they construct a stock-price tree to value the option. Mathematically they assumed that a stock price at time τ (i.e., S_τ where $t < \tau < T$) can either move up to a level uS_τ with probability p or to a level dS_τ with probability $(1 - p)$ at time $\tau + \Delta t$. By matching the moments of the distribution, they go on to show that

$$u = e^{\sigma_{t,T}\sqrt{\Delta t}} \tag{3.14a}$$

$$d = \frac{1}{u} \tag{3.14b}$$

$$p = \frac{e^{r_{t,T}\Delta t} - d}{u - d} \tag{3.14c}$$

Figure 3.1 shows the generation and the recombination of the stock-price tree for the first three time steps $\Delta t, 2\Delta t$, and $3\Delta t$.

Table 3.11 shows the implementation of the stock-price tree illustrated in Figure 3.1.

The stock price tree can now be used to value the early exercise feature as shown in Table 3.12.

As can be seen in Table 3.12, the payoffs in the option tree at time to maturity (i.e., when time is two years) is simply the payoff associated with holding the option to expiry. Using that as an initial point, the authors use backward induction to work back in time by rolling down the tree. Thus, at the times prior to the option maturity (e.g., when time is 0.66 years), the option holder gets to either exercise (in which case the option pays off) or

TABLE 3.11 Stock Price Tree

	A	B	C	D	E	F	G	H
1	Current Price, S_t ($)	$40.00		Time	0.0000	0.6667	1.3333	2.0000
2	Strike Price, K ($)	$40.00						65.28599
3	Volatility, σ (%)	20.00%					55.4498	
4	Risk Free, r (%)	6.00%				47.09556194		47.09556
5	Current Time, t (years)	0			$40.00		$40.00	
6	Expiry, T (years)	2				$33.97		$33.97
7	N (step size of tree)	3					$28.85	
8	Δt (length of the time interval)	0.666667	=(B6-B5)/B7	Stock Price Tree				$24.51
9	u (upward jump)	1.177389	=EXP(B3*SQRT(B8))					=G3*B9
10	d (downward jump)	0.849337	=1/B9				=F4*B9	
11	p(prob. Upward movement)	0.583669	=(EXP(B4*B8)-B10)/(B9-B10)			=E5*B9		=F4
12					=B1		=E5	
13						=E5*B10		=F6
14							=F6*B10	
15								=G7*B10

TABLE 3.12 Option Price Tree

	A	B	C	D	E	F	G	H
1	Current Price, S_t ($)	$40.00		Time	0.0000	0.6667	1.3333	2.0000
2	Strike Price, K ($)	$40.00						65.28598593
3	Volatility, σ (%)	20.00%					55.44979887	
4	Risk Free, r (%)	6.00%		Stock		47.09556194		47.09556194
5	Current Time, t (years)	0		Price	$40.00		$40.00	
6	Expiry, T (years)	2		Tree		$33.97		$33.97
7	N (step size of tree)	3					$28.85	
8	Δt (length of the time interval)	0.666667						$24.51
9	u (upward jump)	1.177389						$25.29
10	d (downward jump)	0.849337					17.0182213	
11	p(prob. Upward movement)	0.583669				11.13518284		$7.10
12					7.136993502		3.979070429	
13						2.231395006		$0.00
14							0	
15				Option				$0.00
16				Price				=MAX(H2-B2,0)
17				Tree			=MAX(G3-B2,EXP(-B4*B8)*((B11*H16)+((1-B11)*H18)))	
18						=MAX(F4-B2,EXP(-B4*B8)*((B11*G17)+((1-B11)*G19)))		=MAX(H4-B2,0)
19					=EXP(-B4*B8)*((B11*F18)+((1-B11)*F20)))		=MAX(G5-B2,EXP(-B4*B8)*((B11*H18)+((1-B11)*H20)))	
20						=MAX(F6-B2,EXP(-B4*B8)*((B11*G19)+((1-B11)*G21)))		=MAX(H6-B2,0)
21							=MAX(G7-B2,EXP(-B4*B8)*((B11*H20)+((1-B11)*H22)))	
22								=MAX(H8-B2,0)

continue (in which case it would be simply holding the value of the option). At the initial time node (when time is 0 years), no exercise is carried out and hence this is simply the present value of the probability-weighted continuation along the tree (holding value of the option). It should be noted that this binomial tree could also be used to value European-style options by simply forcing the exercise value to be 0 at times 0.66 years and 1.32 years. The final option premium is obtained by making the tree more dense (i.e., $\Delta t \to 0$). The reader is referred to Hull (2012) for details.

To extend the methodology to value the early-exercise features for options on other underlyings, one has to make the appropriate changes in the way the variables $u, d,$ and p are formulated.

APPLICATION IN CURRENCY RISK MANAGEMENT

Thus far, I have presented examples relating to specifically valuing options. In this section I will discuss the use of these techniques to make strategic risk-management decisions.

Assume that a U.S. manufacturing company sells its products in Germany. As a consequence, its operating costs are in U.S. dollars (USD) and its revenue is in Eurodollars (EUR). Using the data in Table 3.13, assume that the manufacturer wants to convert EUR50,000,000 into USD in a month.

Given the backdrop, it is clear that the company is exposed to risks associated with weakening of the EUR (and benefits from the strengthening of the EUR). While it is easy for the company to buy a 1-month put option on EUR to hedge itself right off the bat, before implementing anything it is important for the company to understand the value of implementing such a strategy—which only can be understood by asking the right questions. Here are some questions that the company would need to be able to answer before implementing any kind of hedging strategy.

TABLE 3.13 Currency Hedging Data

Spot (USD/EUR)	1.3100
1 month continuously compounded USD rate	1.0000%
1 month continuously compounded EUR rate	1.2000%
Annualized volatility	13%
Notional to be exchanged in 1 month (millions EUR)	50

Market Based

- What risks is the company exposed to (as in how good or bad can things get as they relate to currency movements)?
- Can the risks be mathematically quantified?
- What short-term and long-term views does the company have on the currency market (or more precisely the impact on USD/EUR)?
- What are the different strategies available to manage the risks (including the pros, cons, and costs associated with the strategies)?
- What are the costs and minimum trade size associated with each strategy?

Operational Based

- How frequently does the EUR need to be converted to USD (e.g., once a month)?
- What flexibility is there on delaying the EUR conversion?
- What is the range of the amount the company expects to be converted every month (e.g., EUR 50 million in the first month, EUR 100 – 130 million in the second month, and so on)?
- What constraints are there on counterparties and instruments used for the transactions?
- What constraints are there on the trading/risk limits?
- What infrastructure does the company have for active versus passive risk management (including the right collection of professionals, systems, etc.)?
- What systems does the company have in place to monitor and mark-to-market their trade positions daily?

Given the above backdrop, I will now address a few of these points.

Risk-Management Strategies—Pros and Cons

To convert the EUR50,000,000 into USD a month from now, the manufacturer has the following four strategies available:[27]

Strategy 1: Use a spot-currency rate with the prevailing spot rate at the end of 1 month.

Strategy 2: Use a 1-month currency forward to lock in a guaranteed exchange rate 1 month from now.

---

[27]In practice one can use more customized options (see Chapter 5) to help with the risk-management program. See Ravindran (1997) for more details on this.

TABLE 3.14 Pros and Cons Associated with Strategies

Strategies	Pros	Cons
1	No upfront cost Unlimited upside	Unlimited downside
2	No upfront cost No downside	No upside
3	No downside	Upfront cost Upside

Strategy 3: Use a 1-month currency option that is struck at the 1-month forward rate.

Strategy 4: Use a combination of (and variation on) the above-mentioned strategies.

Since strategy 4 is a combination of the first three strategies, I will only discuss the pros and cons associated with the first three strategies, which are summarized in Table 3.14.

To understand the summary in Table 3.14, I will first discuss strategy 1. In implementing this strategy, the risk to the manufacturer is that a weaker EUR at the end of one month would result in a lesser USD amount after conversion. On the flip side, a stronger EUR would result in more USD, hence there is both an unlimited upside and downside for the manufacturer.

Strategy 2 involves the implementation of at-the-market currency forwards.[28] With this strategy, the manufacturer effectively locks up a guaranteed exchange rate of 1.3098 USD/EUR[29] associated with conversion of EUR50,000,000. As a consequence, the manufacturer does not have any

---

[28]A currency forward is a guaranteed currency bilateral contract in which one party exchanges the floating currency rate on the contract maturity date for a prespecified fixed currency rate on the maturity of the contract. Both parties of the contract are obligated to fulfill their parts of the contract regardless of the strength (or weakness) of the currency rate on the forward maturity date. See Ravindran (1997).

[29]Since a forward exchange rate contract is a bilateral contract that obligates both parties of the transaction, the payoff to one party of the transaction on maturity date is $S_T - X$ where

T represents the contract maturity date.
S_T represents the exchange rate at time T.
X represents the guaranteed exchange rate (i.e., forward rate) associated with the contract.

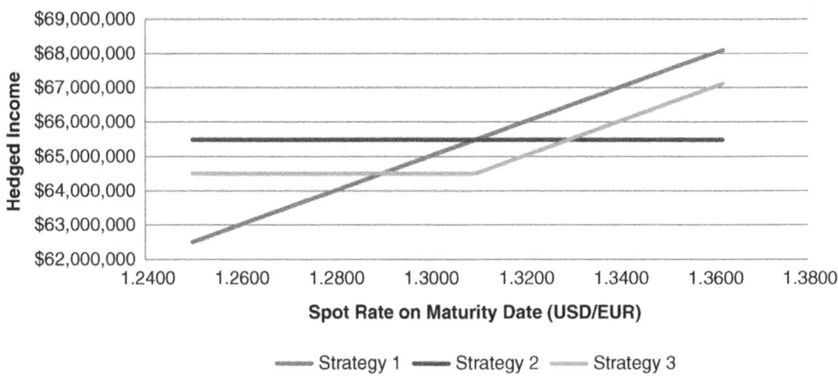

FIGURE 3.2 Net Impact of Risk-Management Strategies

uncertainty associated with the exchange rate, which results in an opportunity cost (not loss) associated with locking up the rate and forgoing any upside on the exchange-rate movements.[30]

In implementing strategy 3, the manufacturer can partake in favorable gains in EUR at the end of the month while being protected against a weakening EUR. Since this is an option-based strategy, the only setback of this strategy is that the manufacturer has to pay an upfront premium of 0.0196 USD/EUR[31] to be protected against unfavorable movements in the exchange rate. It should be noted that the breakeven in purchasing the option is $1.3098 - 0.0196e^{0.1(1/12)} = 1.2902$. This means only if the USD/EUR is less than 1.2902 on its option-maturity date can the manufacturer see some benefit from the purchase of this option after making the appropriate deductions associated with the cost of this protection.

The three strategies discussed above can be graphically represented, as shown in Figure 3.2.

The forward rate is then obtained by observing that X has to satisfy the criteria $E_{S_T}[S_T - X] = 0$ which results in the expression $X = E_{S_T}[S_T] = S_t e^{(r-r_f)(T-t)}$ —using the notation of the currency options example discussed earlier. See Hull (2012).

[30]An at-market forward is a forward contract that does not cost a counterparty of the contract anything to enter into. The reason for this stems from the fact that the forward rate is chosen based on the market conditions so that it translates to a zero cash-flow exchange up front. In practice, it is possible to transact into a forward contract that is based on an off-market rate (in which case cash is typically exchanged at inception of transaction), as this rate is reflective of a rate that requires an exchange of cash at the inception of the contract.

[31]This can be obtained using the currency option calculator in Table 3.5.

As can be seen from the Figure 3.3, one difference between the impacts of strategies 2 and 3 on the bottom line is that the latter protects the manufacturer from the weakening of the EUR since the downside risk is limited. Additionally, when the EUR strengthens, the payoff associated with both the strategies are pretty much the same except that strategy 3 pays off slightly lower than strategy 2 (due to the cost of the insurance paid for strategy 2).

Incorporating Views into Strategies

Suppose now that the manufacturer has a view that EUR will weaken in a month's time to 1.2100 USD/EUR or lower. To monetize his view, he could do one of the following:

Strategy 1A: Use a 1-month currency forward to lock in a guaranteed exchange rate of 1.3098 USD/EUR.
Strategy 2A: Use a 1-month currency option that is struck at 1-month forward (1.3098 USD/EUR).
Strategy 3A: Combination of (and variation on) the above-mentioned strategies.

Given how high the forward rate is relative to the view on the potential exchange rate movement, strategy 1A seems to be the logical choice for managing the risks. Having said that, in addition to implementing strategy 1A, the manufacturer can also sell a call on the EUR (or buy a put on EUR) that is struck at 1.2100 USD/EUR to monetize the view that the EUR will further weaken to lower than 1.2100 USD/EUR.

APPENDIX

Finding a Forward Bond Yield

Letting the current time be t and assuming that the bond yield at a future time T can be modeled using a forward bond yield, one can assume that $\ln(FBY_{T,T})$ is normally distributed with a mean of $\ln\left(FBY_{t,T}\right) - \frac{1}{2}\sigma^2_{t.T}(T-t)$ and variance of $\sigma^2_{t.T}(T-t)$ where

t = current time
T = time in the future
$FBY_{t,T}$ = forward bond yield for a bond starting at time T that is computed at time t (that needs to be determined)

Letting the price of the bond at time T be represented by $FBP_{T,T}(FBY_{T,T})$ so as to reflect the fact that the bond price at time T is a function of its yield-to-maturity at that time, one can use Taylor's expansion to arrive at (ignoring higher order terms)

$$FBP_{T,T}\left(FBY_{T,T}\right) \approx FBP_{T,T}\left(FBY^{*}\right) + \left(FBY_{T,T} - FBY^{*}\right)\frac{dFBP_{T,T}\left(FBY^{*}\right)}{dFBY_{T,T}} + \frac{1}{2}\left(FBY_{T,T} - FBY^{*}\right)^{2}\frac{dFBP^{2}_{T,T}(FBY^{*})}{d^{2}FBY_{T,T}}$$

where FBY^{*} represents the yield corresponding to the forward bond price $FBP_{t,T}$.

Taking expectations of the right-hand side of the equation with respect to $FBY_{T,T}$ using the distributional assumption, one gets

$$\begin{aligned} &FBP_{T,T}\left(FBY^{*}\right) + \left[E\left(FBY_{T,T} - FBY^{*}\right)\right]\frac{dFBP_{T,T}\left(FBY^{*}\right)}{dFBY_{T,T}} + \frac{1}{2}E[\left(FBY_{T,T} - FBY^{*}\right)^{2}]\frac{dFBP^{2}_{T,T}(FBY^{*})}{d^{2}FBY_{T,T}} \\ &= FBP_{T,T}\left(FBY^{*}\right) + \left(FBY_{t,T} - FBY^{*}\right)\frac{dFBP_{T,T}\left(FBY^{*}\right)}{dFBY_{T,T}} \\ &+ \frac{1}{2}[FBY^{2}_{t,T}e^{\sigma^{2}_{t.T}(T-t)} - 2FBY_{t,T}FBY^{*} + (FBY^{*})^{2}]\frac{dFBP^{2}_{T,T}(FBY^{*})}{d^{2}FBY_{T,T}} \end{aligned}$$

Observe now that the expectation of the right-hand side of the equation is also the forward bond price (i.e., $FBP_{t,T}$) and is equal to $FBP_{t,T}(FBY^{*})$. Thus the above equation simplifies to

$$\begin{aligned} 0 &= \left(FBY_{t,T} - FBY^{*}\right)\frac{dFBP_{T,T}\left(FBY^{*}\right)}{dFBY_{T,T}} \\ &+ \frac{1}{2}[FBY^{2}_{t,T}e^{\sigma^{2}_{t.T}(T-t)} - 2FBY_{t,T}FBY^{*} + (FBY^{*})^{2}]\frac{dFBP^{2}_{T,T}(FBY^{*})}{d^{2}FBY_{T,T}} \end{aligned}$$

which results in $FBY_{t,T}$ (the forward bond yield) being the solution of the equation

$$\left[e^{\sigma_{t,T}^2(T-t)}\frac{dFBP_{T,T}^2(FBY^*)}{d^2FBY_{T,T}}\right]FBY_{t,T}^2+2\left[\frac{dFBP_{T,T}(FBY^*)}{dFBY_{T,T}}\right.$$
$$\left.-FBY^*\frac{dFBP_{T,T}^2(FBY^*)}{d^2FBY_{T,T}}\right]FBY_{T,T}$$
$$+\left[(FBY^*)^2\frac{dFBP_{T,T}^2(FBY^*)}{d^2FBY_{T,T}}-2FBY^*\frac{dFBP_{T,T}(FBY^*)}{dFBY_{T,T}}\right]=0$$

REFERENCES

Black, F. 1976. "The Pricing of Commodity Contracts." *Journal of Financial Economics* 3:167–179.

Black, F., and M. Scholes. 1973. "The Pricing of Options and Corporate Liabilities." *Journal of Political Economy* 81:673–659.

Cox, J. C., S. A. Ross, and M. Rubenstein. 1979. "Option Pricing: A Simplified Approach." *Journal of Financial Economics* 7:229–263.

Garman, M. B., and S. W. Kohlhagen. 1983. "Foreign Currency Option Values." *Journal of International Money and Finance* 2:231–237.

Hull, J. C. 2012. *Options, Futures and Other Derivatives*. 8th ed. Upper Saddle River, NJ: Prentice Hall.

Merton, R. C. 1973. "Theory of Rational Option Pricing." *Bell Journal of Economics and Management Science* 4:141–183.

Ravindran, K. 1997. *Customized Derivatives: A Step-by-Step Guide to Using Exotic Options, Swaps and Other Customized Derivatives*. New York: McGraw-Hill.

CHAPTER 4

Simulations

Simulations are used to mimic the behavior of real processes so as to study the effects and/or the results of an experiment under conditions that closely represent realistic situations. In the context of finance, one commonly used tool is Monte Carlo simulations. The origin of Monte Carlo[1] simulations dates back to the 1940s when John Von Neumann, Stanislaw Ulam, and Nicholas Metropolis worked on the Manhattan Project at Los Alamos National Laboratory. Since its inception, Monte Carlo simulations have grown in popularity so much so that the term simulation is synonymous with the words Monte Carlo simulation. Despite its wide use in other fields, it was not until Boyle's 1977 paper that the use of Monte Carlo simulations found its application in finance.

Although not initially popular for about two decades following the publication of Boyle's article, the idea of using simulations to value derivatives began to catch on like a wild fire when the hardware (e.g., fast processing chips) started getting cheaper.

The philosophy underlying the use of simulations to solve any financial problem can be more succinctly reduced to answering the following three questions:

1. How to generate random numbers for a given distribution?
2. How to use simulations to solve the problem at hand?
3. How to reduce the number of simulated paths so as to arrive at the converged result faster (i.e. increase the speed of convergence)?

In this chapter, I will provide the answers to the above questions in the order they are posed. As an astute reader can appreciate, any variate can

[1]The term Monte Carlo was motivated by the casinos in Monte Carlo where Stanislaw Ulam's uncle used to gamble his money away. Due to the need for a code name for a confidential project that Stanislaw Ulam was part of, this moniker was created.

be uniquely transformed using probabilistic and mathematical tricks to a standard uniform variate[2] and vice versa. Hence, starting with a discussion on the generation of a standard uniform number, I proceed to show how a uniform number can be transformed to a variate of any desired probability density function (pdf). I then answer the second question by showing a few examples of how simulations are used in practice. The chapter concludes with a discussion on reducing the noise associated with simulation errors—in the process answering the third question.

UNIFORM NUMBER GENERATION

Given the discussion in the introduction, the need to generate standard uniform numbers should be obvious to the reader. While there are many ways of generating a uniform number, I will discuss three of the more common methods used by practitioners.

Random Sampling

As suggested by the name, there is an element of randomization associated with this method of producing uniform numbers. In practice, uniform numbers are generated randomly using some well-defined system[3] (e.g., computer clock, linear congruential generators, and so on) or some natural phenomena (e.g., the time between each Geiger counter click in the decay of a radioactive substance). Despite the soundness associated with use of a natural phenomenon to produce random numbers, due to the ease of practical implementation, one usually resorts to the use of a well-defined system to generate random numbers.

The generation of a uniform number is a standard feature in many programming languages.[4] Table 4.1 shows the two functions in Microsoft Excel that can be used to generate random numbers.

---

[2]If X has a standard uniform variate, X takes the form $f(x) = \begin{cases} 1 & \textit{if } 0 < x < 1 \\ 0 & \textit{otherwise} \end{cases}$.

[3]The term *well-defined system* is an oxymoron when used to generate random numbers, in that the numbers generated are not truly random (as it has been predetermined by some algorithm). In fact once a certain threshold of generated numbers (also sometimes called periodicity) has been exceeded, these numbers tend to be repeated (and hence defeating the notion of randomness). As a consequence, practitioners are constantly looking for a random number generator with a very high periodicity (and hence a low likelihood of repetition).

[4]For example, in C++, the uniform number can be randomly generated using the function rand() located in stdlib.h (the standard library).

TABLE 4.1 Generation of Random Numbers Using Excel

	A	B	C
1	Uniform random number in interval (0,1)	0.3703	=RAND()
2	Random integers in interval [2,5]	4	=RANDBETWEEN(2,5)

While the first function in Table 4.1 generates a random number in the interval (0,1), the second generates random integers in a prespecified interval. Since the focus of this section is to generate uniform numbers in the interval (0,1), I will restrict my comments to the generation of a standard uniform number. Thus, unless otherwise mentioned, whenever I make reference to a number generator, it is implicitly assumed to be one that generates a uniform number in the interval (0,1).

Table 4.1 shows how easy it is to generate a random uniform number in Microsoft Excel. Furthermore, it is important for one to realize that the numbers generated using the function "=rand()" is based on an algorithm. As a consequence, the generated uniform numbers are in fact pseudo-random. Given this backdrop, it is imperative for the user of these random numbers to know how "good" these pseudo-random number generators are—where the term "good"[5] refers to properties like the uniformity associated with the generated numbers, the speed at which the numbers can be generated, the length of sequence of generated numbers before the sequence gets repeated, and so on.

Like many pseudo-random-number generators, the one in Microsoft Excel also uses a predefined system to generate its random numbers. As can be seen from the Microsoft Support document, the Microsoft Excel function creates this random number by taking the sum of 3 random numbers and then taking the fractional part of the sum. The consequence of this is the ability to generate random numbers with a periodicity of 10^{13} (i.e., 10^{13} numbers need to be generated before the numbers are repeated). This idea was based on 1982/1987 papers by Wichman and Hill. The reader may also be interested to note that these random numbers do pass the Diehard tests (which are a collection of statistical tests put together by Professor George Marsaglia[6] that any good random-number generator should pass).

---

[5]An example of a bad number generator is the ill-famed IBM linear congruential pseudo number-generator RANDU, which is given by the recursive relation $V_{j+1} = 65539 * V_j \, mod(2^{31})$, where V_0 is odd and is usually set to the value 1. (This number can be easily converted into the (0,1) interval by dividing it by 2^{31}). RANDU was widely considered to be a very poorly designed number generator simply because it failed the spectral test (which is a test that can be used to evaluate the randomness associated with linear congruential generators). See also Marsaglia (1968).

[6]http://i.cs.hku.hk/~diehard/.

Stratified Sampling

As suggested by the name, this type of sampling is done on various strata. More precisely, by first dividing the uniform (0,1) interval into n subintervals (or strata) one then samples each stratum. In practice this is done by either taking the midpoint of each stratum's interval (where n is chosen large enough so as to accommodate the number of uniform numbers required) or sampling randomly (using the pseudo-number generators discussed earlier) in each stratum. The motivation for this stems from the desire to have some level of homogeneity within a stratum while having the ability to have enough variation across the strata. This method produces better uniform numbers than those obtained using random sampling. Having said that, using this method to generate variates from multidimensional pdfs can become quite cumbersome—making this an inefficient way of generating multidimensional variates. The reader is referred to Glasserman (2003) for more details.

To generate a uniform number using stratified sampling, one needs to go through the following process:

Step 1: Divide the (0,1) interval into n equal strata $(\frac{i-1}{n}, \frac{i}{n})$ for $i = 1, 2, 3, ..., n$.

Step 2: Generate the required random variates in stratum i from the Uniform $(\frac{i-1}{n}, \frac{i}{n})$ pdf.[7]

I will now discuss the implementation of a stratified sampling method when one is interested in generating two sets of triplets that are uniformly spaced in the (0,1) interval.

Going through the above process, it readily follows from step 1 that one would have three equal strata defined by the intervals $(0, {}^1/_3)$, $({}^1/_3, {}^2/_3)$, and $({}^2/_3, 1)$.

To apply step 2 so as to generate variables that are uniform in each stratum, the reader should first recall from the earlier section that one already is able to generate a random number in the interval (0,1) using the Microsoft Excel function $= rand()$. Hence, a uniform variable in an interval (a, b) can be generated using the relationship "$= a + [(b - a) * rand()]$".[8]

---

[7]If X has a uniform pdf on the interval (a, b), X takes the form $f(x) = \frac{1}{b-a}$ for $a < x < b$.

[8]To see this, observe that if X comes from a uniform pdf on the interval (0,1), $f(x) = 1$ for $0 < x < 1$. If $Y = a + (b - a)X$, $\Pr(Y \leq y) = \Pr(a + (b - a)X \leq y) = \Pr(X \leq \frac{y-a}{b-a}) = \frac{y-a}{b-a}$, for $a < y < b$. From this, it readily follows that the pdf of Y is given by expression $\frac{1}{b-a}$ for $a < y < b$. Hence, Y has a uniform pdf on the interval (a,b).

TABLE 4.2 Generation of Numbers Using Stratified Sampling

	A	B	C
1	Uniform random number 1 (strata 1)	0.17486	=(RAND()*1/3)+0
2	Uniform random number 2 (strata 1)	0.00425	=(RAND()*1/3)+0
3	Uniform random number 1 (strata 2)	0.48757	=(RAND()*1/3)+(1/3)
4	Uniform random number 2 (strata 2)	0.48965	=(RAND()*1/3)+(1/3)
5	Uniform random number 1 (strata 3)	0.74025	=(RAND()*1/3)+(2/3)
6	Uniform random number 2 (strata 3)	0.66827	=(RAND()*1/3)+(2/3)

Table 4.2 shows the implementation of a stratified sampling method to obtain uniform numbers.

As can be seen from Table 4.2, while the first two uniform generated random numbers were drawn from the first stratum $(0, {}^1/_3)$, the second two uniform random numbers are drawn from the second stratum $({}^1/_3, {}^2/_3)$, and the last two numbers are drawn from the last stratum $({}^2/_3, 1)$. Thus the two simulated triplets are (0.1749, 0.4876, 0.7403) and (0.0043, 0.4897, 0.6683).

Latin Hypercube Sampling

McKay, Conover, and Beckman first advocated this sampling method in 1979 to deal with the generation of variables from multivariate distributions. While this method is identical to the stratified sampling method when generating variables from univariate distributions, the process undertaken in this method to generate a multidimensional variate is slightly different from that using a stratified sampling method. In fact, Latin hypercube sampling tends to be a more powerful and efficient method than the stratified sampling method when generating multidimensional variables.

To generate uniform numbers for higher dimensions, one could simply (and blindly) extend the stratified sampling method to higher dimensions. Thus, if one needs to generate a variate from a multidimensional uniform pdf (with dimension d) one can simply divide the (0,1) interval across each dimension into n equal-sized strata and then generate a number in each stratum—resulting in n^d tuplets (where each tuplet is d-dimensional). Clearly as the dimension grows, so does the amount of computational time required to generate such numbers—resulting in an inefficient way of extending the stratified method.

If only n (and not n^d) d-dimensional numbers are required, one can randomly pick a stratum (from the n strata) for each of the d dimensions and then select a random number from each of the selected stratum to end up with a d-dimensional uniform generated number. Once this is done, the process is then repeated over all the remaining strata in each of these dimensions, so as to end up with n d-dimensional numbers—which was what McKay, Conover, and Beckman proposed with their latin hypercube sampling method.

Given the above backdrop, I will now show an application of this method when generating three two-dimensional uniform numbers. As in the stratified sampling method, there would be three equal strata defined by the intervals $(0, {}^1/_3)$, $({}^1/_3, {}^2/_3)$, and $({}^2/_3, 1)$ in both the dimensions. One can randomly pick a stratum in each dimension—ending with a randomly selected stratum pair. Repeating this selection process over the remaining strata two more times, one can arrive at another two pairs of the two-dimensional strata. To get the actual two-dimensional variates, one randomly generates a number from each randomly sampled stratum—eventually ending with three pairs of two-dimensional, uniform numbers. The implementation of this is shown in Table 4.3.

As can be seen from Table 4.3, the 3 simulated pairs are (0.74685, 0.34243), (0.04615, 0.04105), and (0.41683, 0.74714)—where the strata are randomly selected in rows 2 to 4 and 9 to 11. Furthermore, what is presented in Table 4.3 is just one way to implement this in Microsoft Excel although, in practice, there are other, better ways to do this especially when the size of strata selected (n) gets large. The three sampled pairs can be intuitively represented as shown in Table 4.4.

As can be seen in Table 4.4, any selected pair provides the *only* contribution to the stratum inherent in the pair. For example, since one of the selected pair comes from stratum 1 in both the dimensions, there would *not* be any further sampled pair that would contain stratum 1 even as an ordinate of the pair.

In implementing the Latin hypercube method, I have conveniently assumed that the variates generated across each dimension are done independently. In practice, depending on the multivariates that need to be generated, it may be necessary for these variates to have a degree of dependence (something that I have not discussed in my implementation).

The sampling methods described above are just some examples of how practitioners generate uniform numbers. Other methods that are also used in practice include low discrepancy sequences, importance sampling, and randomized Monte Carlo sampling. The interested reader is again referred to Glasserman (2003) for more details.

NON-UNIFORM NUMBER GENERATION

Given the discussion thus far, it is safe to infer that one can easily generate a uniform number in the (0,1) interval. As a next step, I will discuss the

TABLE 4.3 Generation of Random Numbers Using Latin Hypercube Sampling

	A	B	C
1	Selection of Strata (Dimension 1)		
2	First Selection	3	=RANDBETWEEN(1,3)
3	Second Selection	1	=IF(B2=1,RANDBETWEEN(2,3),IF(B2=3,RANDBETWEEN(1,2),IF(RAND()<=0.5,1,3)))
4	Third Selection	2	=6-SUM(B2:B3)
5	Uniform random number (first selected stratum)	0.746850698	=(RAND()*1/3)+((B2-1)/3)
6	Uniform random number (second selected stratum)	0.04614923	=(RAND()*1/3)+((B3-1)/3)
7	Uniform random number (third selected stratum)	0.416835782	=(RAND()*1/3)+((B4-1)/3)
8	Selection of Strata (Dimension 2)		
9	First Selection	2	
10	Second Selection	1	
11	Third Selection	3	
12	Uniform random number (first selected stratum)	0.342435604	
13	Uniform random number (second selected stratum)	0.041051549	
14	Uniform random number (third selected stratum)	0.747135703	

TABLE 4.4 Outcome for One Scenario of Latin Hypercube Sampling

		Dimension 1		
		Stratum 1	Stratum 2	Stratum 3
Dimension 2	Stratum 1	X		
	Stratum 2			X
	Stratum 3		X	

generation of variables from various pdfs. To do this, I will confine my discussion to the following two methods assuming the use of random sampling.[9]

Inverse Transform Method[10]

In this method, one uses the generated uniform number to represent a cumulative probability value. Using the cumulative distribution function associated with the random variable of interest, one converts the cumulative probability value to the appropriate simulated random variable using an analytical transformation.[11] In instances where this is not analytically possible, numerical methods can be used to help solve the problem.

To generate a random variable X from a given pdf $f(x)$, one needs to take the following three-step process:

1. Generate a uniform variable in the interval (0,1).
2. Find the cumulative distribution function $F(x)$ associated with the random variable X.
3. Obtain the required random variable by equating $F(x)$ to the uniform number generated in step 1.

---

[9]While there are more than these two methods that can be used (e.g., the acception–rejection method), for the purposes of my discussion, I only provide an alternative to the inverse transform method so that the reader can see a faster option to the inverse transform method in instances when a relationship can be found between variables that are generable and those that need to be generated.

[10]See Ross (2007) for more details.

[11]To understand the mathematics behind this, suppose that the random variable X has a probability density function $f(x)$ and a cumulative distribution function $F(x) = \Pr(X \leq x)$ where $F(x)$ is a monotonically nondecreasing function that is defined over the same domain. Given any simulated probability, p, in the interval (0,1), one can use $F^{-1}(p)$ to arrive at a unique random variable X.

TABLE 4.5 Generation of Exponential Random Number

	A	B	C
1	Uniform random number	0.333116223	=RAND()
2	Exponential random number, Exp(2)	0.202569748	=-0.5*(LN(1-B1))

Simulating an Exponential Random Variable To simulate an exponential random variable[12] with a rate parameter of 2 (i.e., $f(x) = 2e^{-2x}$ for $x > 0$), one would have to deploy the steps discussed above. Since the first step is trivial, I will only focus on the illustration of steps 2 and 3.

To compute step 2, given the pdf of X, it readily follows that the cumulative distribution function, $F(x) = \Pr(X \leq x)$, is given by the expression

$$\begin{array}{ll} 0 & \text{if } x \leq 0 \\ \int_0^x 2e^{-2u}du = 1 - e^{-2x} & \text{if } x > 0 \end{array}$$

To arrive at step 3, one now has to equate $F(x)$ to the generated uniform random number in step 1 to arrive at $1 - e^{-2x} =$ "$= rand()$" which can be simplified to

$$x = -\frac{1}{2}\ln[1 - \text{“}= rand()\text{”}].$$

Table 4.5 shows the implementation of the generation of an exponential random variable with a known rate parameter.

Simulating a Standard Normal Random Variable In simulating the exponential random variable, one was fortunate enough to find an expression to perform the inversion analytically. In practice, it is often the case that such tractable expressions cannot be easily obtained. As a consequence, one has to resort to the use of numerical methods. In this section, I illustrate an example of one such instance as I discuss the simulation of a standard normal random variable (i.e., $f(x) = \frac{1}{\sqrt{2\pi}}e^{-0.5x^2}$ for $-\infty < x < \infty$).

[12]If X has an exponential pdf with a rate parameter β, X takes the form $f(x) = \beta e^{-\beta x}$ where $x, \beta > 0$.

TABLE 4.6 Generation of Standard Normal Random Number Using Inverse Transform

	A	B	C
1	Uniform random number	0.358807767	=RAND()
2	Normal random number	−0.36164741	=NORMSINV(B1)

To implement step 2, observe that the cumulative distribution function, $F(x) = \Pr(X \leq x)$ is given by the expression

$$F(x) = \frac{1}{\sqrt{2\pi}} \int_{-\infty}^{x} e^{-0,5z^2} dz$$

To implement the final step, one has to equate $F(x)$ to the generated uniform random number to arrive at the equation "$= rand()$" $= F(x) = \frac{1}{\sqrt{2\pi}} \int_{-\infty}^{x} e^{-0,5z^2} dz$. Since this equation cannot be analytically inverted for x, one has to resort to the use of numerical methods. As the Microsoft Excel function "=normsinv(rand())" is able to do this, I will show the implementation of this function in Table 4.6.[13]

Related Distribution Method

As can be seen in the inverse transform method, as long as the functional form of the pdf (from which a random variable needs to be generated) is specified, one can use the method to either analytically or numerically invert the generated uniform number. Sometimes, however, despite the existence of such a pdf, the inverse transform method may not provide the best way to extract the available random numbers. The reason is that when millions of random numbers are needed, the cumulative time taken by Newton's method to converge to the respective solutions can be excessive. In this instance, it is of great value to exploit the functional relationships between easily generable random variables and those that need to be generated—so that the

[13]This can alternatively be done using Newton's method. More precisely, observe that x is a solution of the equation $g(x) = F(x) -$ "$= rand()$" $= 0$. From Newton's method, it readily follows that x can be recursively computed using the relationship $x_n = x_{n-1} - \frac{g(x_{n-1})}{\frac{dg(x_{n-1})}{dx}}$ where $n = 1, 2, 3, \ldots$, x_0 is the initial guess at the solution, and $\frac{dg(x)}{dx} = \frac{1}{\sqrt{2\pi}} e^{-\frac{1}{2}x^2}$. One should further note that $F(x)$ can also be computed for any given value of x using the Microsoft Excel function "=normsdist(x)".

TABLE 4.7 Generation of a Gamma Random Number

	A	B	C
1	Uniform random number 1	0.78624	=RAND()
2	Uniform random number 2	0.24224	=RAND()
3	Exponential random number 1, Exp(3)	0.51430	=-(1/3)*(LN(1-B1))
4	Exponential random number 2, Exp(3)	0.09246	=-(1/3)*(LN(1-B2))
5	Gamma random number, Gamma(2,3)	0.60677	=B3+B4

computational time can be drastically reduced. However, unlike the inverse transform method, it is difficult to identify a series of steps one has to methodically step through to arrive at the required result. Despite this minor drawback, the related distribution method provides a powerful way of generating random variables.

Simulating a Gamma Random Variable To simulate a gamma random variable[14] with a shape parameter of 2 and rate parameter of 3, one first needs to observe that a gamma random variable with a shape parameter α and rate parameter β can be created by adding α independent and identical exponential random variables (each with a rate β).[15] As long as one is able to simulate an exponential variate with rate β, it is straightforward to independently generate another $(\alpha - 1)$ identical random variable and then add them up to arrive at the gamma random variable.[16]

Consider for example the generation of a gamma random variable with shape parameter 2 and rate parameter 3. To do this, one only needs to generate two independent and identical exponential random variables (with a rate of 3). Table 4.7 shows the implementation of generation of the gamma variate.

---

[14]If X has a gamma pdf with a shape parameter α and rate parameter β, X takes the form $f(x) = \frac{\beta^\alpha}{\Gamma(\alpha)} x^{\alpha-1} e^{-\beta x}$ where $x, \alpha, \beta > 0$ and $\Gamma(\alpha) = \int_0^\infty w^{\alpha-1} e^{-w} dw$.

[15]This can be easily seen by noting that the moment-generating function of a gamma pdf (with a shape parameter α and rate parameter β) is the same as the product of α identical moment-generating functions of an exponential pdf (each with a rate β).

[16]The reader should note that this approach works well when α is an integer. In the event that α is not an integer (e.g., 7.3), one can easily decompose such α values into a sum of two components which are integers (i.e., 7) and nonintegral terms lying in the interval (0,1) (i.e., 0.3). The generation of gamma variates when $0 < \alpha < 1$ is, however, a big challenge due to the instability in gamma pdf for values of α in this interval. See for example Devroye (1986).

TABLE 4.8 Generation of a Standard Normal Random Number Using Box-Muller Transformation

	A	B	C
1	Uniform random number 1	0.37819	=RAND()
2	Uniform random number 2	0.19492	=RAND()
3	Normal random number 1	0.47308	=SQRT(-2*LN(B1))*COS(2*PI()*B2)
4	Normal random number 2	1.31184	=SQRT(-2*LN(B1))*SIN(2*PI()*B2)

Simulating a Standard Normal Random Variable Earlier, I discussed the generation of a standard normal variable using the inverse transform method. I will now revisit the same problem using another method. In 1958, Box and Muller showed that by using two independent uniform variates, one can generate two independent standard normal variates by using the transformation[17]

$$Z_1 = \sqrt{-2\ln U_1}Cos(2\pi U_2), \text{ and, } Z_2 = \sqrt{-2\ln U_1}Sin(2\pi U_2)$$

where U_1 and U_2 are the two independent uniform variables.

Table 4.8 illustrates the implementation of the Box-Mulller transformation.

Simulating a Beta Random Variable To simulate a random variable from beta pdf[18] with shape parameters 2 and 3 (i.e., $f(x) = 12x(1-x)^2$ for $0 < x < 1$), the reader has to first observe that if X has a gamma pdf (with shape parameter α and rate parameter β) and Y has an independent gamma pdf (with a shape parameter θ and rate β) then $\frac{X}{X+Y}$ has a Beta pdf with shape parameters α and θ when both X and Y are independent.[19] As a consequence,

[17]To see this, first observe that the joint pdf of U_1 and U_2 is given by the expression $f(u_1, u_2) = 1$ where $0 < u_1, u_2 < 1$. Making the appropriate substitution and taking the Jacobean, one can show that the joint pdf in U_1 and U_2 becomes $f(z_1, z_2) = \frac{1}{\sqrt{2\pi}}e^{-0.5z_1^2}\frac{1}{\sqrt{2\pi}}e^{-0.5z_2^2}$ for $-\infty < z_1, z_2 < \infty$.

[18]If X has a beta pdf with shape parameters α and β, X takes the form $f(x) = \frac{1}{B(\alpha,\beta)}x^{\alpha-1}(1-x)^{\beta-1}$ where $0 < x < 1, \alpha, \beta > 0$ and $B(\alpha, \beta) = \int_0^1 x^{\alpha-1}(1-x)^{\beta-1}dx$.

[19]This can be easily observed by first writing the joint pdf of X and Y and then making the transformation $U = \frac{X}{X+Y}$ and $V = X + Y$ so as to obtain a joint pdf of U and V. To arrive at the desired pdf of U, one needs to integrate out V from the joint pdf of U and V.

TABLE 4.9 Generation of a Beta Random Number

	A	B	C
1	Uniform random number 1	0.81004	0.37721
2	Uniform random number 2	0.65749	0.77369
3	Uniform random number 3		0.60610
4	Exponential random number 1, Exp(1)	1.66093	0.47354
5	Exponential random number 2, Exp(1)	1.07146	1.48583
6	Exponential random number 3, Exp(1)		0.93165
7	Gamma random number	2.73238	2.89102
8	Beta random number, Beta(2,3)	0.48589	=B7/(B7+C7)

Gamma(2,1)   Gamma(3,1)

it suffices for one to be able to generate the two independent gamma variates and then apply the relationship.

In the context of the example, a beta pdf with shape parameters 2 and 3 can be generated using a gamma pdf (with shape parameter 2 and rate parameter 1) and another independent gamma pdf (with shape parameter 3 and rate parameter 1). The implementation of this is given in Table 4.9.[20]

APPLICATIONS OF SIMULATIONS

Thus far, I have only discussed the generation of random variables from any desired pdf. In this section, I will discuss applications of simulations in practice. In doing so, I will address the second question that was posed in the beginning of this chapter. To apply simulations to solve problems in practice, one first needs to identify areas where assumptions are made about the nature of the pdfs being used. If this can be done, then it is a matter of simply applying what has been discussed in the earlier sections of this chapter. The tricky part, however, arises when one cannot find such pdfs. In such an event, trying to apply simulations to solve a problem becomes more an art than science. Whatever the problem, it is imperative for the reader to understand that all formulations require the simulations to be run many times before results can converge to any meaningful number—a reason

[20]While this is true for all values of α and θ, the reader should recall the difficulty associated with generating gamma variates when values of α and θ are not integers.

why the results obtained over each simulated event are averaged over the total number of simulations. One way to obtain a more stable average is to increase the number of simulations, as the greater the number of simulations, the more stable the averaging process. However, doing that is not practical due to the time needed to produce the results. As a consequence, one is led to ask the third question posed in the beginning of this chapter—an issue that is discussed in the next section.

Valuing European-Style Options

In Chapter 3, I discussed the valuation of European-style call and put options using the distributional assumptions for the underlying price/rate movements. To refresh the reader's memory, for a nondividend-paying stock, I assumed that $\ln S_T$ (natural logarithm of the stock price at a future time T) has a normal pdf with a mean of $\ln S_t + (r_{t,T} - \frac{1}{2}\sigma_{t,T}^2)(T-t)$ and a variance of $\sigma_{t,T}^2(T-t)$. By taking the expectation of $\max[S_T - K, 0]$ with respect to S_T and discounting it by $e^{-r_{t,T}(T-t)}$ one was able to arrive at the expression in equation (3.4a) to value a European-style call option on nondividend-paying stocks.

In this example, I revalue the option implemented in Table 3.2 using simulations and show that I can arrive at similar (but not identical) results. To do that, one should first observe that the distributional assumption for S_T can be rewritten as $S_T = S_t e^{(r_{t,T}-\frac{1}{2}\sigma_{t,T}^2)(T-t)} e^{\sigma_{t,T} z \sqrt{T-t}}$, where z is a normal standard variate.[21] Table 4.10 shows the implementation of valuing a European-style call and put option on a nondividend paying stock for one path.

Since basing the option value on one simulated path is not enough, running this over 5,000 paths and then averaging over these 5,000 results yields a call option value of 6.56 and a put option value of 2.41. This compares favorably with the results in Table 3.2 (where the value of the call and put options were shown to be 6.88 and 2.36 respectively).

---

[21]To see this, observe from the distributional assumption of $\ln S_T$ that since $\ln S_T$ has a normal pdf with a mean of $\ln S_t + (r_{t,T} - \frac{1}{2}\sigma_{t,T}^2)(T-t)$ and a variance of $\sigma_{t,T}^2(T-t)$, it readily follows that $\frac{\ln S_T - [\ln S_t + (r_{t,T}-\frac{1}{2}\sigma_{t,T}^2)(T-t)]}{\sigma_{t,T}\sqrt{T-t}}$ has a standard normal pdf. Letting z represent a standard normal variate, one can rearrange the equation $\frac{\ln S_T - [\ln S_t + (r_{t,T}-\frac{1}{2}\sigma_{t,T}^2)(T-t)]}{\sigma_{t,T}\sqrt{T-t}} = z$ to arrive at the required result.

TABLE 4.10 Valuing European-Style Options on Nondividend-Paying Stocks

	A	B	C
1	Current Price, S_t ($)	$40.00	
2	Strike Price, K ($)	$40.00	
3	Volatility, σ (%)	20.00%	
4	Risk Free, r (%)	6.00%	
5	Current Time, t (years)	0	
6	Expiry, T (years)	2	
7	Uniform Random Number	0.68393	=RAND()
8	Standard Normal Random Number	0.47872	=NORMSINV(B7)
9	Stock Price at Maturity, S_t ($)	$49.614	=B1*EXP((B4-(0.5*B3*B3))*(B6-B5))*EXP(B3*B8*SQRT(B6-B5))
10	Call Option Value	$8.527	=MAX(B9-B2,0)*EXP(-B4*(B6-B5))
11	Put Option Value	$–	=MAX(B2-B9,0)*EXP(-B4*(B6-B5))

Simulating a Queue

One of the well-studied areas in operations management is the theory of queues. Queuing problems have been extensively researched and applied in various areas of operations management (e.g., telecommunications, traffic engineering, computing network, and so on) since they were first discussed by Erlang in 1909. The philosophy underlying all queuing problems is based on the fact that there are customers (who arrive according to a prespecified distribution) and servers (who serve according to a prespecified distribution). Using this as a platform, one can then investigate various metrics, ranging from time taken to be served, to the time during which servers are busy, to the number of customers served, and so on. Given the variants on the queuing problems, Kendall, in 1953, suggested a convention that was in the form of *A/B/ k*[22] to help classify basic queuing problems. Over time, this was extended to *A/B/ k/S/N/P*[23] so as to help better classify different types of queuing problems. The interested reader is referred to Ross (2007) or Cooper (1981) for further discussion on queuing.

With the above backdrop, it is not too difficult to see that the simplest variation of the queuing problem happens when there is only one server and both the interarrival-time pdf of the customers and the service-time pdf of the servers are deterministic. In this instance, there are no unknowns, as metrics like waiting time, number of people in queue, time over which the server is busy, and so on can all be exactly determined if they are not already trivially zeroes. The problem gets trickier the moment one departs from these deterministic assumptions. In fact, one of the commonly used assumptions in queuing theory is the M/M/1 queue (where there is one server, interarrival-time pdf of each customer has an exponential pdf with rate λ, and service-time pdf for each customer has an exponential pdf with rate) μ. Since one already knows how to simulate an exponential variate, it only remains for one to put all the pieces together so that quantities of interest can

[22] *A* refers to the distribution of interarrival times examples of which include *M* (exponential pdf), *D* (deterministic pdf), E_n (Erlang pdf with shape parameter n) and, *G* (general pdf). *B* refers to the distribution of service times examples of which include *M* (exponential pdf), *D* (deterministic pdf), E_n (Erlang pdf with shape parameter n), and *G* (general pdf). *k* refers to the number of servers.

[23] *S* refers to the total number of arrivals the queuing system can contain. *N* refers to the size of the population that the arrivals come from. *P* refers to the priority nature of the service examples of which include First In First Out (FIFO) and Last In First Out (LIFO).

be monitored. Suppose, for example, that $\lambda < \mu$[24] and one is interested in quantifying the probability that there is no one in the queue. To do this, one has to keep track of the number of people in the queue, the time of arrival, the time at which the service is completed, and so on. Table 4.11 illustrates the implementation of the queuing system.

As shown in Table 4.11, the commands given for any cell in row 7 all relate to the corresponding cells immediately above in row 6. Furthermore, the reader should also note that the entries in cells C4 and G4 are set to 0 to indicate the start of time, entry in cell D5 is set to 0 to indicate the state of the queuing process when the queue just starts being operational, and that the entry in cell E5 is set trivially to cell C5 (to signify the start of service the moment the first customer walks into the queue). To calculate the probability that there is no one in the queue, one has to first extend the rows further down until one reaches about 5,000 customers. Once this is done, one can now look at Column D and compute the proportion of times the cells in Column D show up 0 see the result to be 0.252.[25]

Estimating Pi

One of the most celebrated constants in the scientific world is the representation for π. Although its origins are in geometry and it simply refers to the ratio of the length of circumference of a circle to the length of diameter of the same circle, it has managed to influence other aspects of life, including entertainment (where it served as a motivation for a character Pi in the bestseller and winner of several Oscar awards, *Life of Pi*). In the context of simulations, my interest in estimating π is to show how this problem can be couched in the form of a simulation problem (where the idea of random variables does not seem to be as transparent as the two earlier examples). To understand how best to use simulations to estimate π, the reader should first note that the area of a circle with unit radius is trivially π. Hence the area of such a circle in first quadrant (i.e., a quarter of the circle) is simply $\frac{\pi}{4}$.

As can be seen in Figure 4.1, if one is allowed to throw a dart randomly onto a square paper of unit length sides, then the proportion of times the dart falls into the shaded region should in the long run be the area of the quarter

---

[24]This assumption is necessary if the server is ever going to catch up with serving all the customers. Otherwise, over the long run, the server would always be busy and hence the probability of there being 0 customers in the queue would be trivially 0.

[25]The asymptotic result for this can be shown to be $1 - \frac{\lambda}{\mu}$ that simplifies to 0.25 for the example in Table 4.11. This is discussed further in Chapter 9.

TABLE 4.11 Simulating an M/M/1 Queue

	A	B	C	D	E	F	G
1	Arrival Rate—λ	6					
2	Service Rate—μ	8					
3	Customer #	Interarrival Time	Chronological Arrival Time	# Currently in System before Arrival	Service Start Time	Service Time	Chronological Service End Time
4			0.00000				0.00000
5	1	0.27988	0.27988	0	0.27988	0.14307	0.42295
6	2	0.13731	0.41719	1	0.42295	0.10576	0.52871
7		=-LN(1-RAND())/B1	=C5+B6	=RANK(C6,($G$4:G5,C6),0)-1	=IF(D6>=1,LARGE($G$4:G5,1),C6)	=-LN(1-RAND())/B2	=E6+F6

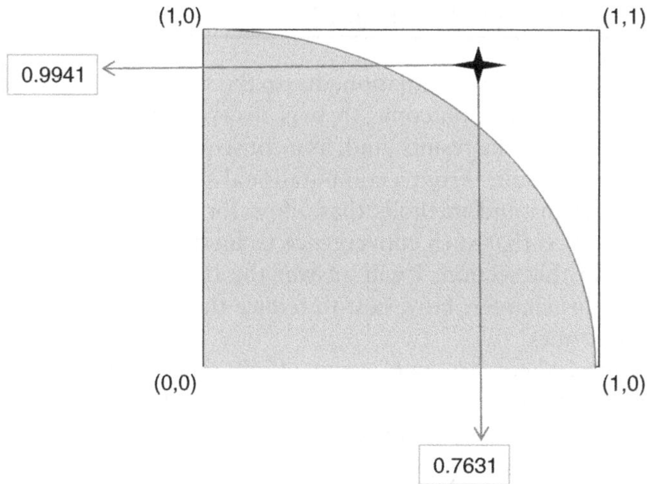

FIGURE 4.1 Inscribing a Square of Unit Length with a Quarter Circle

of a circle with unit radius (i.e., $\frac{\pi}{4}$). To simulate this dart-throwing exercise, one can randomly draw a uniform random variable along the horizontal axis and make another independent draw along the vertical axis. By computing the distance of this random coordinate from the origin, one can determine if the simulated coordinate is in the gray region or out of the gray region. Computing the proportion of times this randomly selected coordinate falls into the gray region and equating it to $\frac{\pi}{4}$, one can estimate π. Table 4.12, shows the implementation of this estimation.

As can be seen from Table 4.12 (cell B1 and B2), the randomly generated coordinate is (0.763, 0.993). This point is illustrated in Figure 4.1. The reader can also see from both Table 4.12 and Figure 4.1, the distance of the simulated coordinate from the origin exceeds 1—resulting in a score of 0. Keeping track of the proportion of times that the value in cell B3 is less than 1 for 5,000 runs gives one a value of 0.784. Equating this to the value of $\frac{\pi}{4}$ gives a value of 3.136 for π.

TABLE 4.12 Simulating Pi

	A	B	C
1	Uniform random number (horizontal)	0.76314	
2	Uniform random number (vertical)	0.99374	
3	Distance from origin	1.25296	=SQRT((B1^2)+(B2^2))

VARIANCE REDUCTION TECHNIQUES

In performing any kind of simulation, due to the variability (or noise) associated with each simulated outcome, there is always going to be an issue relating to the stability of the results (and, as a consequence, the time required to arrive at a stable result). From a computational standpoint one is interested in using algorithms and methods that allow for fast convergence, but the unfortunate part is that such convergence techniques tend to be very problem specific. In this section, I will answer the third question posed in the beginning of this chapter: How best to reduce the variance associated with simulated outcomes?

In practice, there are two ways of obtaining convergence in any simulation-based problem. The first relates to how best to sample the uniform numbers, so that the sampled numbers are well spaced and can adequately capture the distribution from which these variables are generated. This method was discussed in the first section of this chapter when I discussed random, stratified, and Latin hypercube sampling methods. In addition to this, the likes of low-discrepancy sequences, importance-sampling methods, and so on can also be used to effectively reduce sampling errors. Unfortunately, many times, one method does not work best for all the problems. Therefore a practitioner needs to understand how effective each method can be for the problem in hand. To do this, one applies a variety of tests of randomness[26] to compare which of these techniques produces better uniform numbers faster.

Fortunately, in addition to the above, one can do other things to speed up the convergence. This second method focuses on how to best use the simulated variables and use this as a leverage to generate more variables with very little effort—which implies a reduction of the variance of the simulated variables. Given this backdrop, I will now discuss two of the most commonly used approaches.

Antithetic Variable Technique

The philosophy underlying this technique is motivated by the idea that in simulating a path to evaluate the outcome of the experiment, one can simultaneously simulate a parallel path so as to arrive at an additional outcome by simply using the already generated number. To understand this, consider

[26]There are several articles published on how to create and implement randomness tests that can help with the detection of randomness associated with the generated variable, including the Diehard tests. See Marsaglia and Zaman (1995).

two variables Z_1 and Z_2. The variance of the average of $Z_1 + Z_2$ (denoted by $\text{Var}(\frac{1}{2}(Z_1 + Z_2))$ is given by the formula

$$\frac{1}{4}[\text{Var}(Z_1) + \text{Var}(Z_2) + 2\text{Cov}(Z_1, Z_2)]$$

where $\text{Cov}(Z_1, Z_2)$ represents the covariance between Z_1 and Z_2.

Since this covariance is of the form $\text{Corr}(Z_1, Z_2) * \sqrt{\text{Var}(Z_1)} * \sqrt{\text{Var}(Z_2)}$ (where $\text{Corr}(Z_1, Z_2)$ represents the correlation between Z_1 and Z_2), it can be seen that $\text{Var}(Z_1 + Z_2)$ is minimized when $\text{Corr}(Z_1, Z_2) = -1$. Thus, $\text{Var}(Z_1 + Z_2)$ is minimized if both Z_1 and Z_2 are perfectly negatively correlated.

In practice, it is often the case that one is interested in generating values of some function of the random variable (e.g., the value of a derivative on option maturity date) as opposed to simply generating a variable of a pdf. To apply the antithetic variable technique, one first needs to generate variables to arrive at the derivative value f_1. Once that is done, one needs to generate another set (i.e., antithetic) of variables in parallel to obtain a derivative value f_2. Taking the average, one is able to obtain a value of $\frac{f_1+f_2}{2}$. Going through a similar analysis, it can be seen that the variance of $\frac{f_1+f_2}{2}$ is minimized when the correlation between f_1 and f_2 is -1. In particular, as can be seen in Ross (2007), as long as this function is a monotonic function of the variables generated, this is akin to finding negatively correlated random variables.

Given the above backdrop, I will now illustrate this concept with an example. Consider the generation of a European-style call option value discussed earlier, where S_T was generated using the formula $S_t e^{(r_{t,T} - \frac{1}{2}\sigma_{t,T}^2)(T-t)} e^{\sigma_{t,T} z_1 \sqrt{T-t}}$, where $r_{t,T}, \sigma_{t,T}, T$ are all given constants and z_1 represents the normal random variate. To use the antithetic variable technique to generate a derivative value that is perfectly negatively correlated to the initial derivative value, given that the derivative value is a monotonic function of the simulated normal variable, it suffices to generate another normal variable z_2 that is perfectly negatively correlated to z_1 (i.e., $z_2 = -z_1$). Table 4.13 shows the implementation of this idea.

Control Variable Technique

The philosophy underlying the motivation of this technique revolves around the idea that in order to reduce the variance associated with simulating an

TABLE 4.13 Using the Antithetic Method to Value a European-Style Option

	A	B	C
1	Current Price, S_t ($)	$40.00	
2	Strike Price, K ($)	$40.00	
3	Volatility, σ (%)	20.00%	
4	Risk Free, r (%)	6.00%	
5	Current Time, t (years)	0	
6	Expiry, T (years)	2	
7	Uniform Random Number	0.68393	=RAND()
8	Standard Normal Random Number	0.47872	=NORMSINV(B7)
9	Antithetic Normal Random Number	−0.47872	=-B8
10	Stock Price at Maturity, S_t ($)	$49.614	=B1*EXP((B4-(0.5*B3*B3))*(B6-B5))*EXP(B3*B8*SQRT(B6-B5))
11	Antithetic Stock Price at Maturity, S_t ($)	$37.844	=B1*EXP((B4-(0.5*B3*B3))*(B6-B5))*EXP(B3*B9*SQRT(B6-B5))
12	Call Option Value	$4.264	=AVERAGE(MAX(B10-B2,0),MAX(B11-B2,0))*EXP(-B4*(B6-B5))
13	Put Option Value	$0.956	=AVERAGE(MAX(B2-B10,0),MAX(B2-B11,0))*EXP(-B4*(B6-B5))

TABLE 4.14 Using the Control Variate Method to Value a European-Style Option

	A	B	C
1	Current Price, S_t ($)	$40.00	
2	Strike Price, K ($)	$40.00	
3	Volatility, σ (%)	20.00%	
4	Risk Free, r (%)	6.00%	
5	Current Time, t (years)	0	
6	Expiry, T (years)	2	
7	Uniform Random Number	0.68393	=RAND()
8	Standard Normal Random Number	0.47872	=NORMSINV(B7)
9	Stock Price at Maturity, S_T ($)	$49.614	=B1*EXP((B4-(0.5*B3*B3))*(B6-B5))*EXP(B3*B8*SQRT(B6-B5))
10	Call Option Control Variate Term: $S_T - E(S_T)$	$4.515	=B9-B1*EXP(B4*(B6-B5))
11	Call Option Value	$4.523	=[MAX(B9-B2,0)-B10]*EXP(-B4*(B6-B5))
12	Put Option Value	$4.004	=[MAX(B2-B9,0)-(-B10)]*EXP(-B4*(B6-B5))

outcome of an experiment, one should simulate the outcome of an experiment whose analytical solution is known (and as perfectly correlated as possible). To understand this, suppose that one wants to estimate the outcome of the experiment $g(X)$ that is based on the generated variable X.

Since the use of simulation to determine the outcome is equivalent to finding the value of $E[g(X)]$, this method dictates the use of some function $f(X)$ whose expected value $E[f(X)]$ is known. To find the simulated value of $g(X)$ one needs to be able to simulate the value $g(X) - [f(X) - E(f(X))]$. This can be understood by looking at the variance of $g(X) - f(X) + E(f(X))$ and realizing that this is given by the expression $\text{Var}[g(X)] + \text{Var}(f(X)) - 2\text{Cov}(f(X), g(X))$ which is minimized when $g(X)$ and $f(X)$ are perfectly positively correlated. The reader is referred to Ross (2007) for details.

Table 4.14 shows the application of this method, when the stock price itself is used as a control variate (i.e., $f(X) = S_T$ and $E(f(X)) = S_t e^{r(T-t)}$).

REFERENCES

Box, G. E. P., and M. E. Muller. 1958. "A Note on the Generation of Random Normal Deviates." *Annals of Mathematical Statistics* 29:610–611.

Boyle, P. P. 1977. "Options: A Monte Carlo Approach." *Journal of Financial Economics* 4:323–338.

Cooper, R.B. 1981. *Introduction to Queuing Theory*. 2nd ed. New York: Elsevier North/Holland.

Devroye, L. 1986. *Non-Uniform Random Variate Generation*. New York: Springer-Verlag.

Erlang, A. K. 1909. "The Theory of Probabilities and Telephone Conversations." *Nyt Tidsskrift for Matematik B*, 20.

Glasserman, P. 2003. *Monte Carlo Methods in Financial Engineering*. New York: Springer.

Hull, J. C. 2012. *Options, Futures and Other Derivatives*. 8th ed. Upper Saddle River, NJ: Prentice Hall.

Hull, J. C., and A. White. 1990. "Pricing Interest Rate Derivative Securities." *Review of Financial Studies* 3:573–592.

Kendall, D. G. 1953. "Stochastic Processes Occurring in the Theory of Queues and Their Analysis by the Method of the Imbedded Markov Chain." *The Annals of Mathematical Statistics* 24:338–354.

Marsaglia, G. 1968. "Random Numbers Fall Mainly in the Planes." *Proceedings of the National Academy of Sciences* 61:2–28.

Marsaglia, G., and A. Zaman. 1995. "Monkey Tests for Random Number Generators." *Computers in Physics* 8:1–10.

McKay, M. D., W. J. Conover, and R. J. Beckman. 1979. "A Comparison of Three Methods for Selecting Input Variables in the Analysis of output from a Computer Code." *Technometrics* 21:239–245.

Metropolis, N. 1987. "The Beginning of the Monte Carlo Method." *Los Alamos Science Special Issue*, 125–130.

Microsoft Support Documentation. 2011. *Description of the RAND function in Excel.* Article ID: 828795, Revision 7.0. http://support.microsoft.com/kb/828795.

Ross, S. M. 2007. *Introduction to Probability Models.* 9th ed. Boston: Academic Press.

Von Neumann, J. 1951. "Various Techniques Used in Connection with Random Digits." *Applied Mathematics Series* 12, National Bureau of Standards, Washington, DC.

Wichman, B. A., and I. D. Hill. 1982. "Algorithm AS 183: An Efficient and Portable Pseudo-Random Number Generator." *Applied Statistics* 31:188–190.

Wichman, B. A., and I. D. Hill. 1987. "Building a Random-Number Generator." *BYTE* (March): 127–128.

CHAPTER 5

Valuing Exotic Options

In Chapter 3, I presented examples on how vanilla options are priced and how these pricing models are used to analyze various simple risk-management strategies. I also introduced the terminology *exotic options*[1] (i.e., options with in-the-money payoffs that are different from those of the vanilla options). Although examples of exotic options appeared in the late 1980s, the use of exotic options became more prevalent in the early 1990s when practitioners started to better appreciate the power of exotic options to better manage risks or take market view across multiple underlyings and asset classes.

Unlike vanilla European-style options, where one had access to the accurate analytical pricing formulae (examples of which were illustrated and discussed in Chapter 3), due to the complexity of the option payoffs, it is usually difficult to obtain similar analytical expressions for pricing European-style exotic options. As a consequence of this, in the absence of cheap, high-powered computers before the early 1990s, practitioners had to resort to using simplifying assumptions, clever mathematical tricks, and specific numerical algorithms to arrive at reasonable analytical approximations to value these complex, customized options. As mentioned in Chapter 4, it is also precisely this reason why Boyle's 1977 seminal paper on the use of Monte Carlo simulations to value vanilla European-style exotic options did not get the attention it deserved.

---

[1]The origin of exotic options can be traced back to the late 1980s when academicians toyed with the idea of applying the Black-Scholes assumptions to value fancy, nontypical, or nonvanilla payoffs. The consequence of this was a flurry of publications on exotic-option valuation. Despite this, it was not until many years later when hedgers began to better appreciate the path dependency and complexity of their risk exposure and how the theoretically created exotic options could be tweaked to make them more practical—in the process making exotic options more useful.

When computer technology (and hardware) started becoming cheaper, practitioners starting gravitating towards the use of simulations to price these options. This in turn fuelled the creation and trading of even more complex options than what was already trading. As a consequence of this development, the practice of trying to uncover good mathematical approximations started to quickly fall out of favor. It is because of this reason, that I introduced simulations in Chapter 4 and showed how simulations can be used to value vanilla European-style options, among other things.

Since this book is about the use of quantitative methods to solve financial problems, instead of simply valuing exotic options using simulations, I will first attempt to derive accurate analytical pricing formulae (consistent with what was done in Chapter 3).[2] In the event that I am not able to derive such formulae, I will make simplifying assumptions to help me arrive at approximate analytical solutions—consistent with what practitioners did in the past. In instances when such approximations are obtained, I will also use simulations to solve the same problem so as to give the reader a good appreciation for the effectiveness or a lack thereof of these approximations.

For ease of illustration, throughout this chapter I will restrict my discussion to valuing exotic options on indices—and, as such, assume (as in Chapter 3) that index movements are aptly described by equation (3.5)

$$\frac{dS}{S} = (r - q)\,dt + \sigma dz$$

As the reader will recall, the above characterization is equivalent to assuming that $\ln S_T$ is normally distributed with a mean of $S_t + (r_{t,T} - q_{t,T} - \frac{1}{2}\sigma^2_{t,T})(T - t)$, and, variance of $\sigma^2_{t,T}(T - t)$.

VALUING PATH-INDEPENDENT, EUROPEAN-STYLE OPTIONS ON A SINGLE VARIABLE

In this section, I will discuss three examples of widely used exotic options on a single index that are path independent,[3] so as to give the reader a better

[2]The interested reader is referred to Das (1996), Haug (2006), Hull (2012), Nelken (1995), and Ravindran (1997) for extensive discussions on the valuation of exotic options.

[3]Path-independent options refer to options that pay the option owner at the time of exercise a value that is only dependent on the value of the index at the moment of exercise.

appreciation for some of the mathematical techniques used by practitioners to value these options.

Binary Options[4]

One example of a path-independent exotic option is the S&P 500 linked binary option that trades under the symbol BSZ on the Chicago Board Options Exchange (CBOE). The binary call option pays off a bet value of $1 to the option holder if the option finishes in-the-money. Thus, unlike the vanilla call option, this option's payoff can be written as

$$\begin{array}{ll} 1 & \textit{if } S_T \geq K \\ 0 & \textit{otherwise} \end{array}$$

where S_T refers to the S&P 500 index value on option maturity.

To obtain the formula to value this type of a European-style call option, $C_{S_t,K,t,T,r_{t,T},q_{t,T},\sigma_{t,T},Spot}(bin)$, one needs to evaluate the expression

$$C_{S_t,K,t,T,r_{t,T},q_{t,T},\sigma_{t,T},Spot}(bin) = e^{-r_{t,T}(T-t)} E_{S_T} \begin{bmatrix} 1 & \textit{if } S_T \geq K \\ 0 & \textit{otherwise} \end{bmatrix}$$

Doing this yields

$$\begin{aligned} C_{S_t,K,t,T,r_{t,T},q_{t,T},\sigma_{t,T},Spot}(bin) &= e^{-r_{t,T}(T-t)} \int_K^{\infty} g\left(S_T\right) dS_T \\ &= e^{-r_{t,T}(T-t)} N\left(d^2_{S_t,K,t,T,r_{t,T},q_{t,T},\sigma_{t,T}}\right) \end{aligned} \tag{5.1a}$$

The analogous formula for a binary put is given by the expression

$$P_{S_t,K,t,T,r_{t,T},q_{t,T},\sigma_{t,T},Spot}(bin) = e^{-r_{t,T}(T-t)} N\left(-d^2_{S_t,K,t,T,r_{t,T},q_{t,T},\sigma_{t,T}}\right) \tag{5.1b}$$

[4]In addition to being traded on the exchange, binary options are also used by investors to take a view on market directions. Binary options do exist as principal-protected note structures. An example of such a structure is a one-year note that is linked to S&P 500 index value. The purchaser of this note would be guaranteed to receive his/her principal and coupon of (5% $*$ R) at the end of one year (note maturity)—where R refers to the fraction of times the closing S&P index value exceeds 1700 during each trading day in the life of the note. See for example Ravindran (1993b).

TABLE 5.1 Valuation of Binary Options

	A	B	C
1	Current Price, S_t ($)	$40.00	
2	Strike Price, K ($)	$40.00	
3	Volatility, σ (%)	20.00%	
4	Risk Free, r (%)	6.00%	
5	Dividend Rate, q (%)	2.00%	
6	Current Time, t (years)	0	
7	Expiry, T (years)	2	
8	d_2	0.141421356	=(LN(B1/B2)+((B4-B5-(0.5*B3*B3))*(B7-B6)))/(B3*SQRT(B7-B6))
9	Call (Bin)	0.493333048	=EXP(-B4*(B7-B6))*NORMSDIST(B8)
10	Put (Bin)	0.393587389	=EXP(-B4*(B7-B6))*NORMSDIST(-B8))

Table 5.1 shows the implementation of equations (5.1a) and (5.1b).

As can be seen in Table 5.1, the values of the call and put options are given respectively by the values of 0.4933 and 0.3936. In the context of BSZ options, since each contract has a lot size of 100, the value of the BSZ options can be obtained by multiplying the values in cells B10 and B11 by 100. Thus, to execute an order on BSZ options, the trader has to stipulate the number of contracts associated with that trade. This is quite different when compared to the binary option transactions in an OTC market since when trading in OTC markets, the trader has to only stipulate the bet amount (which acts as a total notional amount associated with the trade). Thus if the bet size was USD$1 million, then the quantities in cells B10 and B11 are simply multiplied by USD$1 million to arrive at the respective option premiums.

Pay-Later Options[5]

Another example of an exotic option that trades in the OTC market is called the pay-later option. A pay-later option is essentially a vanilla option in which the option premium is paid at the time of exercise *only* when the option finishes in-the-money (regardless of the amount of in-the-moneyness). Thus, if the option is never exercised (i.e., finishes out-of-the-money), nothing needs to be paid by the purchaser of the option. Based on the description of the profit associated with the purchase of the option, it is straightforward

[5]To see an application of this type of option, consider the purchase of an interest rate cap. If the cap premium turns out to be expensive and the hedger is of the opinion that the cap purchase is not necessary (i.e., the LIBOR on the each of the caplet maturity dates never will exceed the strike rate), as an insurance, the hedger can instead purchase a pay-later cap in which the conditional premium for each caplet is only paid if the caplet goes in-the-money on each caplet expiry date.

to see that the profit profile[6] associated with the purchase of a pay-later call option is given by

$$\begin{array}{ll} S_T - K - C_{S_t,K,t,T,r_{t,T},q_{t,T},\sigma_{t,T},Spot}(PL) & \textit{if } S_T \geq K \\ 0 & \textit{otherwise} \end{array}$$

To obtain the formula to value this type of a call option, one would need to evaluate the expression

$$0 = e^{-r_{t,T}(T-t)} E_{S_T} \begin{bmatrix} S_T - K - C_{S_t,K,t,T,r_{t,T},q_{t,T},\sigma_{t,T},Spot}(PL) & \textit{if } S_T \geq K \\ 0 & \textit{otherwise} \end{bmatrix}$$

and solve for $C_{S_t,K,t,T,r_{t,T},q_{t,T},\sigma_{t,T},Spot}(PL)$. Doing this yields

$$\begin{aligned} C_{S_t,K,t,T,r_{t,T},q_{t,T},\sigma_{t,T},Spot}(PL) &= \frac{\int_K^\infty (S_T - K) g(S_T)\, dS_T}{\int_K^\infty g(S_T)\, dS_T} \\ &= \frac{e^{-r_{t,T}(T-t)} \int_K^\infty (S_T - K) g(S_T)\, dS_T}{e^{-r_{t,T}(T-t)} \int_K^\infty g(S_T)\, dS_T} \\ &= \frac{C_{S_t,K,t,T,r_{t,T},q_{t,T},\sigma_{t,T},Spot}(van)}{e^{-r_{t,T}(T-t)} N\left(d^2_{S_t,K,t,T,r_{t,T},q_{t,T},\sigma_{t,T}}\right)} \end{aligned} \tag{5.2a}$$

The analogous formula for a pay-later put option is given by the expression

$$P_{S_t,K,t,T,r_{t,T},q_{t,T},\sigma_{t,T},Spot}(PL) = \frac{P_{S_t,K,t,T,r_{t,T},q_{t,T},\sigma_{t,T},Spot}(van)}{e^{-r_{t,T}(T-t)} N\left(-d^2_{S_t,K,t,T,r_{t,T},q_{t,T},\sigma_{t,T}}\right)} \tag{5.2b}$$

Table 5.2 shows the implementation of equations (5.2a) and (5.2b).

---

[6]See also Footnote 6 of Chapter 3.

TABLE 5.2 Valuation of Pay-Later Options

	A	B	C
1	Current Price, S_t ($)	$40.00	
2	Strike Price, K ($)	$40.00	
3	Volatility, σ (%)	20.00%	
4	Risk Free, r (%)	6.00%	
5	Dividend Rate, q (%)	2.00%	
6	Current Time, t (years)	0	
7	Expiry, T (years)	2	
8	d_1	0.424264069	=(LN(B1/B2)+((B4-B5+(0.5*B3*B3))*(B7-B6)))/(B3*SQRT(B7-B6))
9	d_2	0.141421356	=B8-(B3*SQRT(B7-B6))
10	Call (Van)	5.797289275	=(B1*EXP(-B5*(B7-B6))*NORMSDIST(B8))-(B2*EXP(-B4*(B7-B6))*NORMSDIST(B9))
11	Put (Van)	2.842529178	=-(B1*EXP(-B5*(B7-B6))*NORMSDIST(-B8))+(B2*EXP(-B4*(B7-B6))*NORMSDIST(-B9))
12	Call (Pay Later)	11.75126885	=B10/(EXP(-B4*(B7-B6))*NORMSDIST(B9))
13	Put (Pay Later)	7.222104307	=B11/(EXP(-B4*(B7-B6))*NORMSDIST(-B9))

From the results in Table 5.2, it can be seen that the pay-later option values are higher than their vanilla counterparts.[7] The reason for this can be easily explained if the reader observes from equations (5.2a) and (5.2b) that the conditional premiums paid for these options are basically the future value of the vanilla options that are conditioned on the probability of exercise. Hence the lower the probability of exercise, the higher this conditional premium.

Nonlinear Payoff Options[8]

Another example of an exotic option that is sometimes quite popular is the nonlinear payoff option. See Ravindran (1997) for details. The purchaser of the nonlinear payoff call option gets on maturity date a payoff of

$$\begin{array}{ll} S_T^\alpha - K & if\ S_T^\alpha \geq K \\ 0 & otherwise \end{array}$$

where $\alpha > 0$.

To derive the formula associated with the nonlinear payoff, one would need to first observe that the formula for the option price, $C_{S_t,K,t,T,r_{t,T},q_{t,T},\sigma_{t,T},Spot,\alpha}$ (NLP), can be obtained by evaluating the expression $e^{-r_{t,T}(T-t)}E_{S_T}[\max(S_T^\alpha - K, 0)]$. Doing this, allows one to get

$$\begin{aligned} C_{S_t,K,t,T,r_{t,T},q_{t,T},\sigma_{t,T},Spot,\alpha}(NLP) &= e^{-r_{t,T}(T-t)} \int_{K^{\frac{1}{\alpha}}}^{\infty} (S_T^\alpha - K)\, g(S_T)\, dS_T \\ &= e^{-r_{t,T}(T-t)} \int_{K^{\frac{1}{\alpha}}}^{\infty} S_T^\alpha g(S_T)\, dS_T \\ &\quad - Ke^{-r_{t,T}(T-t)} \int_{K^{\frac{1}{\alpha}}}^{\infty} g(S_T)\, dS_T \end{aligned}$$

[7]As the astute reader will realize, the pay-later option can easily be replicated by buying a vanilla call option and selling a binary call option (where the size of the bet payoff is the pay-later premium). The reader is referred to Ravindran (1997) for further details.

[8]An example of this type of option was seen in the European and Asian retail markets when currency warrants were issued by banks to give investors a leveraged upside with a limited downside. Another example includes the use of these options to hedge nonlinear exposure to movements in the underlying asset price.

As before, observing that $g(S_T) = \frac{1}{\sigma_S\sqrt{2\pi}S_T} e^{-0.5(\frac{\ln S_T - \mu_S}{\sigma_S})^2}$ where $\mu_S = \ln S_t + (r_{t,T} - q_{t,T} - \frac{1}{2}\sigma^2_{t,T})(T-t)$ and $\sigma_S = \sigma_{t,T}\sqrt{T-t}$, it readily follows that

$$\begin{aligned} &C_{S_t,K,t,T,r_{t,T},q_{t,T},\sigma_{t,T},Spot,\alpha}(NLP) \\ &= e^{-r_{t,T}(T-t)}\left[e^{\mu_S\alpha+\frac{1}{2}\sigma_S^2\alpha^2}N(d_{S_t,K,t,T,r_{t,T},q_{t,T},\sigma_{t,T},\alpha,\alpha}) \right. \\ &\left. - KN(d_{S_t,K,t,T,r_{t,T},q_{t,T},\sigma_{t,T},\alpha,0})\right] \end{aligned} \tag{5.3a}$$

where $d_{S_t,K,t,T,r,q,\sigma,\alpha,\beta} = \frac{\ln\left(\frac{S_t}{K^{1/\alpha}}\right)+\left[r-q+\frac{1}{2}(-1+2\beta)\sigma^2\right](T-t)}{\sigma\sqrt{T-t}}$.

It is easy to show that for the nonlinear payoff put option, the expression simplifies to

$$\begin{aligned} &P_{S_t,K,t,T,r_{t,T},q_{t,T},\sigma_{t,T},Spot,\alpha}(NLP) \\ &= e^{-r_{t,T}(T-t)}\left[- e^{\mu_S\alpha+\frac{1}{2}\sigma_S^2\alpha^2}N(-d_{S_t,K,t,T,r_{t,T},q_{t,T},\sigma_{t,T},\alpha,\alpha}) \right. \\ &\left. + KN(-d_{S_t,K,t,T,r_{t,T},q_{t,T},\sigma_{t,T},\alpha,0})\right] \end{aligned} \tag{5.3b}$$

The pricing formulae in equations (5.3a) and (5.3b) have been implemented in Table 5.3.

As can be seen from Table 5.3, when α is 1, the answers agree with those in Table 3.4. Furthermore, when α is 2, these types of options are also called power options. Although the discussion so far has been restricted to the valuation of European-style, path-independent options, valuing such options with early-exercise features is just an easy extension of what I discussed in Chapter 3 using equations (3.14a), (3.14b), and (3.14c). Succinctly put, to value these options, one only needs to modify the maturity payoffs associated with the options that are being valued—while keeping all the other things similar.

VALUING PATH-DEPENDENT, EUROPEAN-STYLE OPTIONS ON A SINGLE VARIABLE

In the previous section, I discussed three examples of path-independent exotic options. As was seen in these examples, it was relatively straightforward for one to develop analytical expressions to value such options. In

TABLE 5.3 Valuation of Nonlinear-Payoff Options

	A	B	C
1	Current Price, S_t ($)	$40.00	
2	Alpha, α	0.5	
3	Strike Price, K ($)	$40.00	
4	Volatility, σ (%)	20.00%	
5	Risk Free, r (%)	6.00%	
6	Dividend Rate, q (%)	2.00%	
7	Current Time, t (years)	0	
8	Expiry, T (years)	2	
9	mu, μ_s	3.728879454	=LN(B1)+((B5-B6-(0.5*B4*B4))*(B8-B7))
10	sigma, σ_S	0.282842712	=B4*SQRT(B8-B7)
11	$(\alpha\mu_S) + 0.5(\alpha\sigma_S)^2$	3.768879454	=(B2*B9)+(0.5*((B2*B10)^2))
12	$d_{St,K,t,T,r,q,\sigma,\alpha,\alpha}$	−12.75931567	=(LN(B1/(B3^(1/B2)))+((B5-B6+(0.5*(-1+(2*B2))*B4*B4))*(B8-B7)))/(B4*SQRT(B8-B7))
13	$d_{St,K,t,T,r,q,\sigma,\alpha,0}$	−12.90073703	=(LN(B1/(B3^(1/B2)))+((B5-B6-(0.5*B4*B4))*(B8-B7)))/(B4*SQRT(B8-B7))
14	Call (NLP)	$0.00	=EXP(-B5*(B8-B7))*((EXP(B11)*NORMSDIST(B12))-(B3*NORMSDIST(B13)))
15	Put (NLP)	$29.70	=EXP(-B5*(B8-B7))*(-(EXP(B11)*NORMSDIST(-B12))+(B3*NORMSDIST(-B13)))

this section, I will extend my discussion to entertain the valuation of path-dependent exotic options. Since it is not often that one can easily arrive at accurate analytical expressions to value many of the path-dependent exotic options, I will use simplifying assumptions that are used in practice to evaluate such options whenever this is not possible. Additionally, in such instances, I will use simulations to redo the problem so as to show the reader the consequences of making such simplifying assumptions.

Averaging Options[9]

One path-dependent exotic option that gets traded in many asset classes quite extensively in the OTC market (and sometimes in the exchanges[10]) is the arithmetic-averaging option. With this type of option, the option holder gets an in-the-money payoff that is a function of the average of the underlying prices. More precisely, the owner of an averaging call option will receive the following payoff on maturity date:

$$\max\left[\frac{S_{t+\Delta t} + S_{t+2\Delta t} + \cdots + S_{t+n\Delta t}}{n} - K, 0\right]$$

where the values of stock prices are averaged every Δt years and $t + n\Delta t = T$[11].

When arithmetic-averaging options first traded in the OTC market, practitioners quickly realized that because of the lognormal distribution assumption associated with future stock/index price movements, it was not possible to obtain the pdf of the arithmetic average of stock price movements due to the fact that the sum of lognormal distributions does not

[9]These types of options are quite popular in the currency and commodity markets where hedgers are more concerned about the adverse movements in the average rates (prices) of the currency (commodity) markets during the month or quarter or year as opposed to daily movements. These are sometimes also called Asian options.

[10]Quite often, when averaging options traded on the exchange, they are written on underlyings that themselves trade as an average (e.g., average aluminum price, average gas price) thereby making such averaging options vanilla options. In such an instance, it suffices for one to use the formulae in Chapter 3 to price these options.

[11]In practice, it is not uncommon to find a payoff that is a function of the weighted average of the stock prices (where the different weights are given to different times) and the averaging is done over infrequent discrete time intervals.

result in a lognormal distribution. Given the unavailability of cheap computing power when these options first started trading, practitioners were forced to think about ways of overcoming this deficit using approximations and assumptions. In the following subsections, I will review a couple of these methods and benchmark them against the use of a Monte Carlo method.

Geometric Averaging One simplifying assumption that Kemna and Vorst made in 1990 was that an arithmetic average can be well approximated by a geometric average (although in their paper they did assume a continuous time averaging as opposed to a discrete time averaging that I discuss here).[12] Furthermore, since one can easily get the pdf for a geometric average when the underlying stock/index price movements are lognormal in nature, the authors felt that instead of valuing an arithmetic average call option, one could just as well value a geometric average call option as a good proxy. To do this, they first concluded that instead of valuing an option whose payoff is

$$\max\left[\frac{S_{t+\Delta t} + S_{t+2\Delta t} + \cdots + S_{t+n\Delta t}}{n} - K, 0\right] \tag{5.4a}$$

one should value an option whose payoff takes the form of

$$\max\left[\sqrt[n]{S_{t+\Delta t}S_{t+2\Delta t}\cdots S_{t+n\Delta t}} - K, 0\right] \tag{5.4b}$$

Using this proxy payoff, they observed that the probability density function (pdf) of the natural logarithm of the geometric average is in fact the sum of the normally distributed pdfs—which in turn produces a normal pdf. More precisely, since

$$\ln\left(\sqrt[n]{S_{t+\Delta t}S_{t+2\Delta t}\cdots S_{t+n\Delta t}}\right) = \frac{1}{n}\sum_{i=1}^{n}\ln(S_{t+i\Delta t})$$

---

[12]For a given set of four numbers $1, 2, 3, 4$, the arithmetic average is given by the value $\frac{1+2+3+4}{4} = 2.5$, while the geometric average is given by the value $\sqrt[4]{1 * 2 * 3 * 4} = 2.213$. Additionally, it can be shown that the arithmetic average would never be lesser than the geometric average.

and $\ln S_{t+i\Delta t}$ has a normal pdf with a mean of $\ln S_t + (r_{t,T} - q_{t,T} - \frac{1}{2}\sigma_{t,T}^2)i\Delta t$ and variance $\sigma_{t,T}^2 i\Delta t$, it readily follows that $\sum_{i=1}^{n} \ln(S_{t+i\Delta t})$ has a normal pdf with a mean of

$$\sum_{i=1}^{n} E\left[\ln\left(S_{t+i\Delta t}\right)\right] = \sum_{i=1}^{n}\left[\ln S_t + \left(r_{t,T} - q_{t,T} - \frac{1}{2}\sigma_{t,T}^2\right)i\Delta t\right] \quad (5.5a)$$

$$= n\ln S_t + \left(r_{t,T} - q_{t,T} - \frac{1}{2}\sigma_{t,T}^2\right)\frac{n(n+1)\Delta t}{2}$$

Similarly, it can be shown that $\sum_{i=1}^{n} \ln(S_{t+i\Delta t})$ has a variance of

$$\sum_{i=1}^{n} \mathrm{Var}[\ln(S_{t+i\Delta t})] + 2\sum_{i=1}^{n-1}\sum_{j=i+1}^{n} Covar(\ln S_{t+i\Delta t}, \ln S_{t+j\Delta t})$$

$$= \frac{\sigma_{t,T}^2 \Delta t\,(n)\,(n+1)}{2} + \frac{\sigma_{t,T}^2 \Delta t\,(n-1)\,n(n+1)}{3} \quad (5.5b)$$

$$= \frac{\sigma_{t,T}^2 \Delta t\,(n)\,(n+1)\,(2n+1)}{6}$$

With the aid of equations (5.5a) and (5.5b), one can conclude that $\frac{1}{n}\sum_{i=1}^{n} \ln(S_{t+i\Delta t})$ has a normal pdf with mean $\mu_{GA} = \ln S_t + (r_{t,T} - q_{t,T} - \frac{1}{2}\sigma_{t,T}^2)\frac{(n+1)\Delta t}{2}$ and variance $\sigma_{GA}^2 = \frac{\sigma_{t,T}^2 \Delta t(n+1)(2n+1)}{6n}$.

Using these parameters, it can be easily seen that a call option premium for a geometric averaging option is given by the expression

$$C_{S_t,K,t,T,r_{t,T},q_{t,T},\sigma_{t,T},Spot,n}\,(GA)$$

$$= e^{-r_{t,T}(T-t)} E_{S_{t+\Delta t}\cdots S_{t+n\Delta t}}\{\max[\sqrt[n]{S_{t+\Delta t}\cdots S_{t+n\Delta t}} - K, 0]\} \quad (5.6a)$$

$$= e^{-r_{t,T}(T-t)}\left[e^{\mu_{GA}+0.5\sigma_{GA}^2} N\left(d_{GA}^1\right) - KN\left(d_{GA}^2\right)\right]$$

where $d_{GA}^1 = \sigma_{GA} - \frac{\ln K - \mu_{GA}}{\sigma_{GA}}$ and $d_{GA}^2 = -\frac{\ln K - \mu_{GA}}{\sigma_{GA}}$.

It is easy to show that the formula to value the averaging put option takes the form

$$P_{S_t,K,t,T,r_{t,T},q_{t,T},\sigma_{t,T},Spot,n}(GA)$$
$$= e^{-r_{t,T}(T-t)}\left[-e^{\mu_{GA}+0.5\sigma^2_{GA}}N\left(-d^1_{GA}\right)+KN\left(d^2_{GA}\right)\right] \tag{5.6b}$$

The implementation of equations (5.6a) and (5.6b) are shown in Table 5.4.

Although the implementation in Table 5.4 shows the use of the geometric average as a proxy for the arithmetic average, by setting n (the number of averaging points) to 1, one can easily observe from equations (5.4a) and (5.4b) that the averaging option collapses to a vanilla option. As a consequence, one can expect to see the example outlined in Table 5.4 yielding the same answer as that in Table 3.4.

Moments Matching Since a geometric average can never be bigger than an arithmetic average, the consequence of using a geometric average to approximate an arithmetic average results in the geometric averaging call (put) option being lower (higher) than an arithmetic averaging call (put) option. To overcome this setback, Turnbull and Wakeman in 1991 proposed the use of moment matching to derive an approximate pdf for the arithmetic average. More precisely, they assumed that $\ln[\frac{1}{n}\sum_{i=1}^{n} S_{t+i\Delta t}]$ has a normal pdf with mean μ_{AA} and variance σ^2_{Aa} and estimated both these parameters by matching the moments of the assumed lognormal pdf of $[\frac{1}{n}\sum_{i=1}^{n} S_{t+i\Delta t}]$ with the actual values of the quantity.

To do this, they showed that

$$E\left[\frac{1}{n}\sum_{i=1}^{n} S_{t+i\Delta t}\right] = e^{\mu_{AA}+\frac{1}{2}\sigma^2_{AA}}$$
$$= \frac{1}{n}\sum_{i=1}^{n} E(S_{t+i\Delta t}) \tag{5.7a}$$
$$= \frac{S_t}{n}\sum_{i=1}^{n} e^{(r_{t,T}-q_{t,T})i\Delta t} = M_1$$

This can be summarized more succinctly as

$$e^{\mu_{AA}+\frac{1}{2}\sigma^2_{AA}} = M_1 \tag{5.7a}$$

TABLE 5.4 Using Geometric Averaging to Value Arithmetic Averaging Options

	A	B	C
1	Current Price, S_t (\$)	\$40.00	
2	Number of avg points, n	1	
3	Strike Price, K (\$)	\$40.00	
4	Volatility, σ (%)	20.00%	
5	Risk Free, r (%)	6.00%	
6	Dividend Rate, q (%)	2.00%	
7	Current Time, t (years)	0	
8	Expiry, T (years)	2	
9	Delta t, Δt	2	=(B8-B7)/B2
10	mu, μ_{GA}	3.728879454	=LN(B1)+((B5-B6-(0.5*B4*B4))*(B2+1)*B9/2)
11	sigma, σ_{GA}	0.282842712	=B4*SQRT(B9*(B2+1)*((2*B2)+1)/(6*B2))
12	$\mu_{GA} + 0.5\sigma_{GA}^2$	3.768879454	=B10+(0.5*B11*B11)
13	d_1	0.424264069	=B11-((LN(B3)-B10)/B11)
14	d_2	0.141421356	=-((LN(B3)-B10)/B11)
15	Call (GA)	\$5.80	=EXP(-B5*(B8-B7))*((EXP(B12)*NORMSDIST(B13))-(B3*NORMSDIST(B14)))
16	Put (GA)	2.842529178	=EXP(-B5*(B8-B7))*((-EXP(B12)*NORMSDIST(-B13))+(B3*NORMSDIST(-B14)))

where

$$M_1 = \frac{S_t}{n}\sum_{i=1}^{n} e^{\left(r_{t,T}-q_{t,T}\right)i\Delta t}$$

They went on to show that

$$\begin{aligned}
E\left[\frac{1}{n}\sum_{i=1}^{n} S_{t+i\Delta t}\right]^2 &= e^{2\mu_{AA}+2\sigma_{AA}^2} \\
&= \frac{1}{n^2}\sum_{i=1}^{n} E(S_{t+i\Delta t})^2 + \frac{2}{n^2}\sum_{i=1}^{n-1}\sum_{j=i+1}^{n} E(S_{t+i\Delta t}S_{t+j\Delta t}) \\
&= \frac{S_t^2}{n^2}\sum_{i=1}^{n} e^{2\left(r_{t,T}-q_{t,T}+\frac{1}{2}\sigma_{t,T}^2\right)i\Delta t} \\
&\quad + \frac{2S_t^2}{n^2}\sum_{i=1}^{n-1}\sum_{j=i+1}^{n} e^{\left(r_{t,T}-q_{t,T}\right)j\Delta t} e^{\left(r_{t,T}-q_{t,T}-\sigma_{t,T}^2\right)i\Delta t} = M_2
\end{aligned} \tag{5.7b}$$

This can be summarized more succinctly as

$$e^{2\mu_{AA}+2\sigma_{AA}^2} = M_2 \tag{5.7b}$$

where

$$\begin{aligned}
M_2 = {} & \frac{S_t^2}{n^2}\sum_{i=1}^{n} e^{2\left(r_{t,T}-q_{t,T}+\frac{1}{2}\sigma_{t,T}^2\right)i\Delta t} \\
& + \frac{2S_t^2}{n^2}\sum_{i=1}^{n-1}\sum_{j=i+1}^{n} e^{(r_{t,T}-q_{t,T})j\Delta t} e^{\left(r_{t,T}-q_{t,T}-\sigma_{t,T}^2\right)i\Delta t}
\end{aligned}$$

Solving equations (5.7a) and (5.7b) for μ_{AA} and σ_{AA}^2, they obtained

$$\mu_{AA} = \ln\left(\frac{M_1^2}{\sqrt{M_2}}\right) \tag{5.8a}$$

$$\sigma_{AA}^2 = \ln\left(\frac{M_2}{M_1^2}\right), \tag{5.8b}$$

where M_1 and M_2 are as defined in equations (5.7a) and (5.7b).

Putting all these together, they showed that the call and put option pricing formulae are given by the expressions

$$C_{S_t,K,t,T,r_{t,T},q_{t,T},\sigma_{t,T},Spot,n}(AA) = e^{-r_{t,T}(T-t)}\left[e^{\mu_{AA}+\frac{1}{2}\sigma_{AA}^2}N\left(d_{AA}^1\right) - KN\left(d_{AA}^2\right)\right] \tag{5.8c}$$

$$P_{S_t,K,t,T,r_{t,T},q_{t,T},\sigma_{t,T},Spot,n}(AA) = e^{-r_{t,T}(T-t)}\left[-e^{\mu_{AA}+\frac{1}{2}\sigma_{AA}^2}N\left(-d_{AA}^1\right) + KN\left(-d_{AA}^2\right)\right] \tag{5.8d}$$

where

$$d_{AA}^1 = \sigma_{AA} - \frac{\ln K - \mu_{AA}}{\sigma_{AA}}$$

and

$$d_{AA}^2 = -\frac{\ln K - \mu_{AA}}{\sigma_{AA}}.$$

Equations (5.8c) and (5.8d) have been implemented as shown in Table 5.5 where μ_{AA} and σ_{AA}^2 have been defined in equations (5.8a) and (5.8b) respectively.

The formulae implemented in Table 5.5 is for $n = 1$. As can be seen, the result obtained matches that in Tables 5.4 and 5.3 (where the averaging option trivially collapses to the vanilla option). Furthermore, for higher values of n, one would need to extend the terms added to in cells B10 and B11.

Monte Carlo Method The geometric averaging and moment matching approaches are just two examples of what practitioners used to do to get around the issue of finding an analytical solution to price options when the pdf of the underlying (in this case the arithmetic average) cannot be exactly derived. While this was an issue before the availability of cheap computer hardware, this is no longer a concern in the current computing environment. Practitioners nowadays resort to the use of Monte Carlo simulations (also known as the brute-force approach) to solve such problems quickly and with a greater precision.

Table 5.6 shows the implementation of Monte Carlo simulations to value both averaging call and put options.

TABLE 5.5 Using Moments Matching to Value Arithmetic Averaging Options

	A	B	C
1	Current Price, S_t (\$)	\$40.00	
2	Number of avg points, n	1	
3	Strike Price, K (\$)	\$40.00	
4	Volatility, σ (%)	20.00%	
5	Risk Free, r (%)	6.00%	
6	Dividend Rate, q (%)	2.00%	
7	Current Time, t (years)	0	
8	Expiry, T (years)	2	
9	Delta t, Δt	2	=(B8-B7)/B2
10	M_1	43.33148271	=B1*EXP((B5-B6)*B9)/B2
11	M_2	2033.998641	=(B1^2)*EXP(2*(B5-B6+(0.5*B4*B4))*B9)/(B2^2)
12	mu, μ_{AA}	3.728879454	=LN((B10^2)/SQRT(B11))
13	sigma, σ_{AA}	0.282842712	=SQRT(LN(B11/(B10^2)))
14	$\mu_{AA} + 0.5\sigma_{AA}{}^2$	3.768879454	=B12+(0.5*B13*B13)
15	d^1	0.424264069	=B13-((LN(B3)-B12)/B13)
16	d^2	0.141421356	=-((LN(B3)-B12)/B13)
17	Call (AA)	\$5.80	=EXP(-B5*(B8-B7))*((EXP(B14)*NORMSDIST(B15))-(B3*NORMSDIST(B16)))
18	Put (AA)	2.842529178	=EXP(-B5*(B8-B7))*(-(EXP(B14))*NORMSDIST(-B15))+(B3*NORMSDIST(-B16))

TABLE 5.6 Using Monte Carlo to Value Arithmetic Averaging Options

	A	B	C
1	Current Price, S_t ($)	$40.00	
2	Number of avg points, n	2	
3	Strike Price, K ($)	$40.00	
4	Volatility, σ (%)	20.00%	
5	Risk Free, r (%)	6.00%	
6	Dividend Rate, q (%)	2.00%	
7	Current Time, t (years)	0	
8	Expiry, T (years)	2	
9	Delta t, Δt	1	
10	Uniform Random Number 1	0.68393	=RAND()
11	Standard Normal Random Number 1	0.47872	=NORMSINV(B10)
12	Stock Price at Maturity, S_{1Yr} ($)	$44.908	=B1*EXP((B5-B6-(0.5*B4*B4))*B9)*EXP(B4*B11*SQRT(B9))
13	Uniform Random Number 2	0.04729	=RAND()
14	Standard Normal Random Number 2	−1.67170	=NORMSINV(B13)
15	Stock Price at Maturity, S_{2Yr} ($)	$32.795	=B12*EXP((B5-B6-(0.5*B4*B4))*B9)*EXP(B4*B14*SQRT(B9))
16	Call Option Value	$–	=MAX(AVERAGE(B12,B15)-B3,0)*EXP(-B5*(B8-B7))
17	Put Option Value	$1.018	=MAX(B3-AVERAGE(B12,B15),0)*EXP(-B5*(B8-B7))

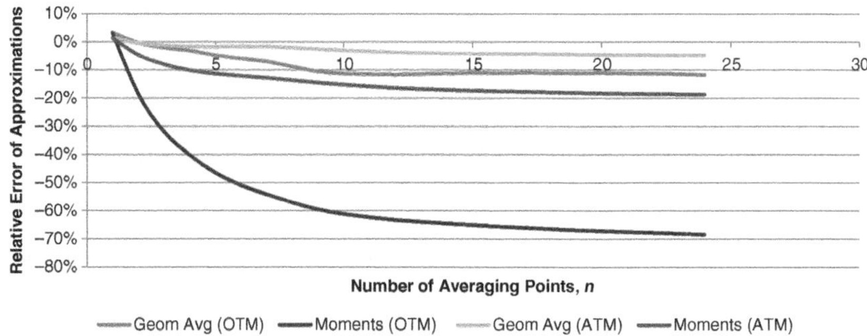

FIGURE 5.1A Relative Errors Associated with Arithmetic Averaging Call Option Approximation

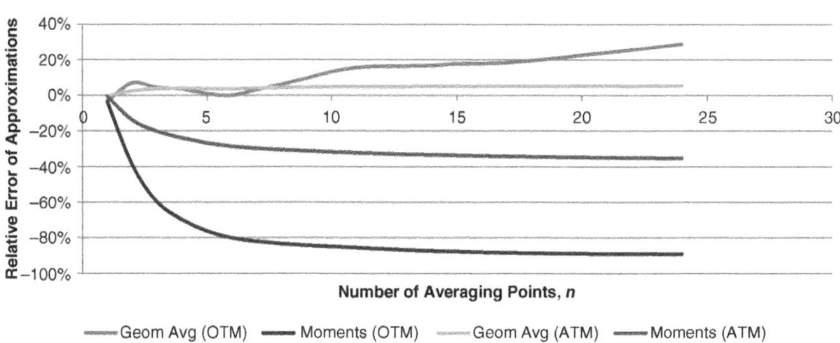

FIGURE 5.1B Relative Errors Associated with Arithmetic Averaging Put Option Approximation

Table 5.6 shows the implementation of the averaging option pricing for one simulated path when there are two averaging points.[13] In practice, one has to redo this simulation 5,000 times and average the outcomes in cell B16 (cell B17) to obtain the premiums for the averaging call (put) option of $4.41 and $2.30 respectively. In the event that there are more than two averaging points, one has to extend the rows to entertain more random numbers (and more frequent jumps).

The relative errors associated with these methods are illustrated in Figures 5.1a and 5.1b for varying numbers of averaging points and the in-the-moneyness of the option.

---

[13]Since the problem simplifies to the valuation of a vanilla call/put option when $n = 1$, the reader is referred to Table 4.9 for the valuation of vanilla options using the Monte Carlo method.

One can easily make the following observations from Figures 5.1a and 5.1b:

- The term ATM refers to an at-the-money option where the strike price is set equal to the spot price. On the other hand, the term OTM refers to an out-of-the-money option where the strike price is set to 25 percent out of the money. Thus for a call option when the spot price is \$40, the OTM strike price is \$50 (for the call option) and \$30 (for the put option).
- The relative errors that were computed to produce the graph were done so using the expression

$$\frac{Premium\,(approx) - Premium\,(Monte\ Carlo)}{Premium\,(Monte\ Carlo)}$$

- The geometric average method is a better approximation to the Monte Carlo method than the two-moments method. Furthermore, both these approximations[14] are bad when valuing out-of-the money options.

Installment Options[15]

Another path-dependent exotic option that gets used extensively by hedgers is the installment option which was discussed by Geske in 1979. In the instance of a vanilla or binary or averaging option, the option purchaser paid the premium at the inception of the option contract. In the instance of a pay-later option, the option purchaser paid the premium on the

[14]The geometric averaging and the moment-matching approaches are just two of the many approaches that are used by practitioners to value averaging options. The reader would be interested to know that some of these other approaches that have not been discussed here are surprisingly accurate even for the OTM options.

[15]These options are used when a hedger wants to lock in the potential movements in volatility and market prices today but is not sure if these options are actually required (e.g., the hedger may have submitted a bid and is waiting for the results of the tender so as to acquire the raw materials needed to fulfill the contract). Because the hedger is not sure if the option is required, the hedger is interested in paying for the option in installments. Another application of these options is discussed in Chapter 9.

maturity of the option date only *if* the option finished in-the-money. Unlike these options, an installment option purchaser pays the option premiums in two installments (a compulsory one which is paid at the inception of the contract and an optional one which is paid at some prespecified time in the future). More precisely, suppose that one is interested in purchasing a vanilla call option expiring at time T using two installments, where u is the time at which the second optional installment premium X is paid (where $t < u < T$) and t is the time at which the first (initial) compulsory installment premium CC_t is paid, the payoff to the payor of the premium at time u is given by

$$\max(C_{S_u,K,u,T,r_{t,T},q_{t,T},\sigma_{t,T},Spot}(van) - X, 0) \tag{5.9}$$

where $C_{S_u,K,u,T,r_{t,T},q_{t,T},\sigma_{t,T},Spot}(van)$ represents the market value of vanilla call option of life $T - u$ at time u when the stock price is S_u. Clearly if the value of $C_{S_u,K,u,T,r_{t,T},q_{t,T},\sigma_{t,T},Spot}(van)$ is lesser than X, the holder of this option will choose not to exercise the option (i.e., pay X).[16,17]

Taking the expectations of equation (5.9), it readily follows that

$$\begin{aligned}
CC_t &= e^{-r_{t,T}(u-t)}E_{S_u}[\max(C_{S_u,K,u,T,r_{t,T},q_{t,T},\sigma_{t,T},Spot}(van) - X, 0)] \\
&= e^{-r_{t,T}(u-t)}E_{S_u}\left[\max\left[S_u e^{-q_{t,T}(T-u)}N\left(d^1_{S_u,K,u,T,r_{t,T},q_{t,T},\sigma_{t,T}}\right)\right.\right. \\
&\quad \left.\left. - Ke^{-r_{t,T}(T-u)}N\left(d^2_{S_u,K,u,T,r_{t,T},q_{t,T},\sigma_{t,T}}\right) - X, 0\right]\right]
\end{aligned}$$

[16]This type of option is also called a call-on-call option. Other combinations include the put-on-call option, the call-on-put option, and the put-on-put option where the payoffs at time u to the payor of the option premiums are given by the expressions $\max(X - C_{S_u,K,u,T,r_{t,T},q_{t,T},\sigma_{t,T},Spot}(van), 0)$, $\max(P_{S_u,K,u,T,r_{t,T},q_{t,T},\sigma_{t,T},Spot}(van) - X, 0)$ $\max(X - P_{S_u,K,u,T,r_{t,T},q_{t,T},\sigma_{t,T},Spot}(van), 0)$ respectively. In writing these payoffs, I have assumed that X represents the second installment premium that is paid (received) at time u to receive (sell) the underlying vanilla call or put option with life $T - u$ when the stock price is S_u (where the values of the call and put option at time u are given by $C_{S_u,K,u,T,r_{t,T},q_{t,T},\sigma_{t,T},Spot}(van)$ and $P_{S_u,K,u,T,r_{t,T},q_{t,T},\sigma_{t,T},Spot}(van)$ respectively).

[17]I assumed throughout this illustration that $r_{t,T}, q_{t,T}$ and $\sigma_{t,T}$ are all constant throughout the time interval (t, T). Thus $r_{t,u} = r_{t,T}, q_{t,u} = q_{t,T}, \sigma_{t,u} = \sigma_{t,T}$ for $t \leq u \leq T$.

Taking the expectations, with respect to S_u yields

$$CC_t = e^{-r_{t,T}(u-t)}\left[e^{-q_{t,T}(T-u)} \int_{S_*}^{\infty} S_u N\left(\frac{\ln\left(\frac{S_u}{K}\right) + \left(r_{t,T} - q_{t,T} + \frac{1}{2}\sigma_{t,T}^2\right)(T-u)}{\sigma_{t,T}\sqrt{T-u}} \right) g(S_u)\, dS_u \right.$$

$$- Ke^{-r_{t,T}(T-u)} \int_{S_*}^{\infty} N\left(\frac{\ln\left(\frac{S_u}{K}\right) + \left(r_{t,T} - q_{t,T} - \frac{1}{2}\sigma_{t,T}^2\right)(T-u)}{\sigma_{t,T}\sqrt{T-u}} \right) g(S_u)\, dS_u$$

$$\left. - X \int_{S_*}^{\infty} g(S_u)\, dS_u \right] \quad (5.10)$$

where $g(S_u) = \frac{1}{\beta S_u \sqrt{2\pi}} e^{-\frac{1}{2}\left[\frac{\ln S_u - \alpha}{\beta}\right]^2}$, for $S_u > 0$

$$\alpha = \ln S_t + \left(r_{t,T} - q_{t,T} - \frac{1}{2}\sigma_{t,T}^2\right)(u-t)$$

$$\beta = \sigma_{t,T}\sqrt{u-t}$$

S_* is the solution of the equation

$$S_* e^{-q_{t,T}(T-u)} N\left(d^1_{S_*,K,u,T,r_{t,T},q_{t,T},\sigma_{t,T}}\right)$$

$$-Ke^{-r_{t,T}(T-u)} N\left(d^2_{S_*,K,u,T,r_{t,T},q_{t,T},\sigma_{t,T}}\right) - X = 0$$

To evaluate equation (5.10), first observe that the third integral and the terms accompanying it are

$$Xe^{-r_{t,T}(u-t)} \int_{S_*}^{\infty} \frac{1}{\beta S_u \sqrt{2\pi}} e^{-\frac{1}{2}\left(\frac{\ln S_u - \alpha}{\beta}\right)^2} dS_u$$

Letting $z = \frac{\ln S_u - \alpha}{\beta}$, the above simplifies to

$$Xe^{-r_{t,T}(u-t)} \int_{\frac{\ln S_* - \alpha}{\beta}}^{\infty} \frac{1}{\sqrt{2\pi}} e^{-\frac{1}{2}z^2} dz = Xe^{-r_{t,T}(u-t)} N\left(-\frac{\ln S_* - \alpha}{\beta}\right)$$

$$= Xe^{-r_{t,T}(u-t)} N\left(\frac{\ln\left(\frac{S_t}{S_*}\right) + \left(r_{t,T} - q_{t,T} + \frac{1}{2}\sigma_{t,T}^2\right)(u-t)}{\sigma_{t,T}\sqrt{u-t}} - \sigma_{t,T}\sqrt{u-t}\right)$$

$$= Xe^{-r_{t,T}(u-t)} N\left(d^2_{S_t, S_*, t, u, r_{t,T}, q_{t,T}, \sigma_{t,T}}\right) \tag{5.11a}$$

Now observe that the second integral (and the terms accompanying it) in equation (5.10) can be rewritten as

$$Ke^{-r_{t,T}(T-t)} \int_{S_*}^{\infty} \left[N\left(\frac{\ln\left(\frac{S_u}{K}\right) + \left(r_{t,T} - q_{t,T} - \frac{1}{2}\sigma_{t,T}^2\right)(T-u)}{\sigma_{t,T}\sqrt{T-u}}\right) * \frac{1}{\beta S_u \sqrt{2\pi}} e^{-\frac{1}{2}\left(\frac{\ln S_u - \alpha}{\beta}\right)^2} \right] dS_u$$

Letting $z = \frac{\ln S_u - \alpha}{\beta}$, one gets

$$Ke^{-r_{t,T}(T-t)} \int_{\frac{\ln S_* - \alpha}{\beta}}^{\infty} \left[N\left(\frac{\alpha + \beta z - \ln K + \left(r_{t,T} - q_{t,T} - \frac{1}{2}\sigma_{t,T}^2\right)(T-u)}{\sigma_{t,T}\sqrt{T-u}}\right) * \frac{1}{\sqrt{2\pi}} e^{-\frac{1}{2}z^2} \right] dz$$

$$= Ke^{-r_{t,T}(T-t)} \int_{\frac{\ln S_* - \alpha}{\beta}}^{\infty} \left[N\left(\frac{\ln\left(\frac{S_t}{K}\right) + \left(r_{t,T} - q_{t,T} - \frac{1}{2}\sigma_{t,T}^2\right)(T-t) + \sigma_{t,T}\sqrt{u-t}z}{\sigma_{t,T}\sqrt{T-u}} \right) * \frac{1}{\sqrt{2\pi}} e^{-\frac{1}{2}z^2} \right] dz$$

$$= Ke^{-r_{t,T}(T-t)} \int_{\frac{\ln S_* - \alpha}{\beta}}^{\infty} N\left(\frac{d^2_{S_t,K,t,T,r_{t,T},q_{t,T},\sigma_{t,T}} + \rho z}{\sqrt{1-\rho^2}} \right) \frac{1}{\sqrt{2\pi}} e^{-\frac{1}{2}z^2} dz,$$

where $\rho = \sqrt{\frac{u-t}{T-t}}$.

Rewriting the lower limit yields

$$Ke^{-r_{t,T}(T-t)} \int_{-d^2_{S_t,S_*,t,u,r_{t,T},q_{t,T},\sigma_{t,T}}}^{\infty} \left[N\left(\frac{d^2_{S_t,K,t,T,r_{t,T},q_{t,T},\sigma_{t,T}} + \rho z}{\sqrt{1-\rho^2}} \right) * \frac{1}{\sqrt{2\pi}} e^{-\frac{1}{2}z^2} \right] dz \tag{5.11b}$$

$$= Ke^{-r_{t,T}(T-t)} BN\left(d^2_{S_t,S_*,t,u,r_{t,T},q_{t,T},\sigma_{t,T}}, d^2_{S_t,K,t,T,r_{t,T},q_{t,T},\sigma_{t,T}}, \rho \right)$$

where $BN(\lambda, \Delta, \theta)$ represents the cumulative probability of a standard bivariate normal variate.[18]

---

[18] $BN(\lambda, \Delta, \theta)$ is the cumulative bivariate standard normal pdf that is given by the expression $\int_{-\infty}^{\lambda}\int_{-\infty}^{\Delta} \frac{1}{2\pi\sqrt{1-\theta^2}} e^{-\frac{1}{2(1-\theta^2)}(x^2-2\theta xy+y^2)} dxdy$, which can be alternatively written as $\int_{-\infty}^{\lambda} \frac{1}{\sqrt{2\pi}} N(\frac{\Delta-\theta z}{\sqrt{1-\theta^2}}) e^{-\frac{1}{2}z^2} dz$.

Finally observe that the first integral (and the terms accompanying it) in equation (5.10) can be rewritten as

$$e^{-r_{t,T}(u-t)}e^{-q_{t,T}(T-u)}\int_{S_*}^{\infty}\left[S_u N\left(\frac{\ln\left(\frac{S_u}{K}\right)+\left(r_{t,T}-q_{t,T}+\frac{1}{2}\sigma_{t,T}^2\right)(T-u)}{\sigma_{t,T}\sqrt{T-u}}\right)\right.$$

$$\left. * \frac{1}{\beta S_u\sqrt{2\pi}}e^{-\frac{1}{2}\left(\frac{\ln S_u-\alpha}{\beta}\right)^2}\right]dS_u$$

Letting $z=\frac{\ln S_u-\alpha}{\beta}$, one gets

$$e^{-r_{t,T}(u-t)}e^{-q_{t,T}(T-u)}$$

$$*\int_{\frac{\ln S_*-\alpha}{\beta}}^{\infty}\left[e^{\alpha+\beta z}N\left(\frac{\alpha+\beta z-\ln K+\left(r_{t,T}-q_{t,T}+\frac{1}{2}\sigma_{t,T}^2\right)(T-u)}{\sigma_{t,T}\sqrt{T-u}}\right)\right.$$

$$\left. * \frac{1}{\sqrt{2\pi}}e^{-\frac{1}{2}z^2}\right]dz$$

$$=S_t e^{-q_{t,T}(T-t)}\int_{\frac{\ln S_*-\alpha}{\beta}}^{\infty}\left[N\left(\frac{\ln\left(\frac{S_t}{K}\right)+\left(r_{t,T}-q_{t,T}+\frac{1}{2}\sigma_{t,T}^2\right)(T-t)+(z-\beta)\beta}{\sigma_{t,T}\sqrt{T-u}}\right)\right.$$

$$\left. * \frac{1}{\sqrt{2\pi}}e^{-\frac{1}{2}(z-\beta)^2}\right]dz$$

Making the substitution $w = z - \beta$, one gets

$$S_t e^{-q_{t,T}(T-t)} \int_{\frac{\ln S_* - \alpha}{\beta} - \beta}^{\infty} \left[N\left(\frac{\ln\left(\frac{S_t}{K}\right) + \left(r_{t,T} - q_{t,T} + \frac{1}{2}\sigma_{t,T}^2\right)(T-t) + w\beta}{\sigma_{t,T}\sqrt{T-u}} \right) * \frac{1}{\sqrt{2\pi}} e^{-\frac{1}{2}w^2} \right] dw$$

$$= S_t e^{-q_{t,T}(T-t)} \int_{-d^1_{S_t,S_*,t,u,r_{t,T},q_{t,T},\sigma_{t,T}}}^{\infty} \left[N\left(\frac{d^1_{S_t,K,t,T,r_{t,T},q_{t,T},\sigma_{t,T}} + \rho w}{\sqrt{1-\rho^2}} \right) * \frac{1}{\sqrt{2\pi}} e^{-\frac{1}{2}w^2} \right] dw \tag{5.11c}$$

$$= S_t e^{-q_{t,T}(T-t)} BN\left(d^1_{S_t,S_*,t,u,r_{t,T},q_{t,T},\sigma_{t,T}}, d^1_{S_t,K,t,T,r_{t,T},q_{t,T},\sigma_{t,T}}, \rho \right)$$

Putting equations (5.11a) to (5.11c) together, it can be seen that for the call-on-call option the initial premium can be computed using the formula,

$$\begin{aligned} CC_t = {} & S_t e^{-q_{t,T}(T-t)} BN\left(d^1_{S_t,S_*,t,u,r_{t,T},q_{t,T},\sigma_{t,T}}, d^1_{S_t,K,t,T,r_{t,T},q_{t,T},\sigma_{t,T}}, \rho \right) \\ & - K e^{-r_{t,T}(T-t)} BN\left(d^2_{S_t,S_*,t,u,r_{t,T},q_{t,T},\sigma_{t,T}}, d^2_{S_t,K,t,T,r_{t,T},q_{t,T},\sigma_{t,T}}, \rho \right) \\ & - X e^{-r_{t,T}(u-t)} N\left(d^2_{S_t,S_*,t,u,r_{t,T},q_{t,T},\sigma_{t,T}} \right) \end{aligned} \tag{5.12a}$$

where

$$\rho = \sqrt{\frac{u-t}{T-t}} \tag{5.12b}$$

and, S_* is the solution to

$$S_* e^{-q(T-u)} N\left(d^1_{S_*,K,u,T,r,q,\sigma}\right) - Ke^{-r(T-u)} N\left(d^2_{S_*,K,u,T,r,q,\sigma}\right) - X = 0 \tag{5.12c}$$

Going through similar analysis, it can be shown that the initial premiums associated with a put-on-call option, call-on-put option, and put-on-put option can be obtained using the following formulae.

$$\begin{aligned} PC_t = &-S_t e^{-q_{t,T}(T-t)} BN\left(-d^1_{S_t,S_*,t,u,r_{t,T},q_{t,T},\sigma_{t,T}}, d^1_{S_t,K,t,T,r_{t,T},q_{t,T},\sigma_{t,T}}, -\rho\right) \\ &+ Ke^{-r_{t,T}(T-t)} BN\left(-d^2_{S_t,S_*,t,u,r_{t,T},q_{t,T},\sigma_{t,T}}, d^2_{S_t,K,t,T,r_{t,T},q_{t,T},\sigma_{t,T}}, -\rho\right) \\ &+ Xe^{-r_{t,T}(u-t)} N\left(-d^2_{S_t,S_*,t,u,r_{t,T},q_{t,T},\sigma_{t,T}}\right) \end{aligned} \tag{5.13}$$

$$\begin{aligned} CP_t = &-S_t e^{-q_{t,T}(T-t)} BN\left(-d^1_{S_t,S_*,t,u,r_{t,T},q_{t,T},\sigma_{t,T}}, -d^1_{S_t,K,t,T,r_{t,T},q_{t,T},\sigma_{t,T}}, \rho\right) \\ &+ Ke^{-r_{t,T}(T-t)} BN\left(-d^2_{S_t,S_*,t,u,r_{t,T},q_{t,T},\sigma_{t,T}}, -d^2_{S_t,K,t,T,r_{t,T},q_{t,T},\sigma_{t,T}}, \rho\right) \\ &- Xe^{-r_{t,T}(u-t)} N(-d^2_{S_t,S_*,t,u,r_{t,T},q_{t,T},\sigma_{t,T}}) \end{aligned} \tag{5.14}$$

$$\begin{aligned} PP_t = &\; S_t e^{-q_{t,T}(T-t)} BN\left(d^1_{S_t,S_*,t,u,r_{t,T},q_{t,T},\sigma_{t,T}}, -d^1_{S_t,K,t,T,r_{t,T},q_{t,T},\sigma_{t,T}}, -\rho\right) \\ &- Ke^{-r_{t,T}(T-t)} BN\left(d^2_{S_t,S_*,t,u,r_{t,T},q_{t,T},\sigma_{t,T}}, -d^2_{S_t,K,t,T,r_{t,T},q_{t,T},\sigma_{t,T}}, -\rho\right) \\ &+ Xe^{-r_{t,T}(u-t)} N\left(d^2_{S_t,S_*,t,u,r_{t,T},q_{t,T},\sigma_{t,T}}\right) \end{aligned} \tag{5.15}$$

The implementation of equations (5.12a) to (5.12c) and (5.13) is shown in Table 5.7.

As can be seen from Table 5.7, implementing this algorithm involved the calculation of cumulative bivariate probabilities[19] (a function that Microsoft Excel does not come with). To do this, I used the algorithm provided in Hull (2012). Furthermore, to obtain the value of S_* (in cell B10), I manually guessed at this value (using Excel's Goal Seek feature) to

[19]The online content contains a spreadsheet that allows the reader to compute these probabilities.

TABLE 5.7 Valuation of Call-on-Call and Put-on-Call Options

	A	B	C
1	Current Price, S_t (\$)	\$40.00	
2	2nd Installment, X (\$)	\$2.00	
3	Strike Price, K (\$)	\$40.00	
4	Volatility, σ (%)	20.00%	This value was guessed so that the result in cell B13 is 0
5	Risk Free, r (%)	6.00%	
6	Dividend Rate, q (%)	2.00%	
7	Current Time, t (years)	0	
8	2nd Installment Time, u (years)	1	
9	Expiry, T (years)	2	
10	S_* (guess)	36.32320	
11	$d_1(u,T,S_*,K)$	−0.18211	=(LN(B10/B3)+((B5-B6+(0.5*B4*B4))*(B9-B8)))/(B4*SQRT(B9-B8))
12	$d_2(u,T,S_*,K)$	−0.38211	=B11-(B4*SQRT(B9-B8))
13	Check to Confirm S_* is Solution	0.00000	=(B10*EXP(-B6*(B9-B8))*NORMSDIST(B11))-(B3*EXP(-B5*(B9-B8))*NORMSDIST(B12))-B2
14	$d_1(t,u,S_t,S_*)$	0.78211	=(LN(B1/B10)+((B5-B6+(0.5*B4*B4))*(B8-B7)))/(B4*SQRT(B8-B7))
15	$d_1(t,u,S_t,S_*)$	0.58211	'=(LN(B1/B10)+((B5-B6-(0.5*B4*B4))*(B8-B7)))/(B4*SQRT(B8-B7))
16	$d_1(t,T,S_t,K)$	0.42426	=(LN(B1/B3)+((B5-B6+(0.5*B4*B4))*(B9-B7)))/(B4*SQRT(B9-B7))
17	$d_2(t,T,S_t,K)$	0.14142	'=(LN(B1/B3)+((B5-B6-(0.5*B4*B4))*(B9-B7)))/(B4*SQRT(B9-B7))
18	rho, ρ	0.707107	=SQRT((D12-D11)/(D13-D11))
19	BN($d_1(t,u,S_t,S_*),d_1(t,T,S_t,K),\rho$)	0.610088	CALCULATED USING THE ALGORITHM OUTLINED IN JOHN HULL'S BOOK
20	BN($d_2(t,u,S_t,S_*),d_2(t,T,S_t,K),\rho$)	0.504253	
21	BN($-d_1(t,u,S_t,S_*),d_1(t,T,S_t,K),\rho$)	0.054225	
22	BN($-d_2(t,u,S_t,S_*),d_2(t,T,S_t,K),\rho$)	0.051979	
23	Call-on-call premium, CC_t	4.201698	=(B1*EXP(-B6*(B9-B7))*B19)-(B3*EXP(-B5*(B9-B7))*B20)-(B2*EXP(-B5*(B8-B7))*NORMSDIST(B15))
24	Put-on-call premium, PC_t	1.115768	=-(B1*EXP(-B6*(B9-B7))*B21)+(B3*EXP(-B5*(B9-B7))*B22)+(B2*EXP(-B5*(B8-B7))*NORMSDIST(B15))

ensure the value of cell B13 is 0. In practice, this is done using Newton's method.[20]

It is not uncommon to see installment options whereby the option premium is paid in 12 installments (one of which is the compulsory premium that is paid at the inception of the contract). As the astute reader will realize, in this instance, the problem quickly gets exponentially unmanageable due to the fact that one would have to evaluate a 12-dimensional integral—further iterating the importance of use of efficient numerical methods and techniques in solving such problems.

VALUING PATH-INDEPENDENT, EUROPEAN-STYLE OPTIONS ON TWO VARIABLES

In the earlier sections, I discussed examples of exotic options where the payoffs on the option maturity were a function of the prices of a single variable. In this section, I will discuss the extension of these concepts to entertain the valuation of options on two variables to give the reader an awareness of the ad-hoc assumptions and methods practitioners use to price such options.

Exchange Options[21]

One example of a widely used exotic option on two variables is the exchange option, which was discussed by Magrabe in 1978. This option also happens to be a special case of spread option (something I will discuss in the section following this).

---

[20]By defining $f(y) = ye^{-q(T-u)}N(\frac{\ln(\frac{y}{K})+(r-q+\frac{1}{2}\sigma^2)(T-u)}{\sigma\sqrt{T-u}}) - Ke^{-r(T-u)}N(\frac{\ln(\frac{y}{K})+(r-q-\frac{1}{2}\sigma^2)(T-u)}{\sigma\sqrt{T-u}}) - X = 0$, one can use the recursive relation $y_n = y_{n-1} - \frac{f(y_{n-1})}{\frac{df(y_{n-1})}{dy}}$ for $n = 1, 2, 3, ...$ where y_0 is the initial guess at the solution. It can also be easily shown that given this form of $f(y)$, $\frac{df(y)}{dy} = e^{-q(T-u)}N(\frac{\ln(\frac{y}{K})+(r-q+\frac{1}{2}\sigma^2)(T-u)}{\sigma\sqrt{T-u}})$.

[21]This option is used when the investor is interested in taking a view on the relative movements in the two underlying assets. One application that is quite popular in the fixed income markets is to bet on the yield curve steepening or flattening. See Das (1996) and Ravindran (1997) for a more detailed discussion on this.

An exchange-option purchaser gets a maturity payoff that is of the form $\max(S_T - R_T, 0)$ where the owner of the option has the right to exchange an asset, R_T, at time T for another asset S_T—where R_T and S_T are the prices of the two underlying assets on which the exchange option is written.

To develop the pricing formulae for the exchange option, $C_{R_t,S_t,t,T,r_{t,T},qR_{t,T},qS_{t,T},\sigma R_{t,T},\sigma S_{t,T},\rho_{RS},Spot}(exc)$, I will as before assume that $\ln R_T$ and $\ln S_T$ each has normal pdf with means of

$$\mu_1 = \ln R_t + \left(r_{t,T} - qR_{t,T} - \frac{1}{2}\sigma R_{t,T}^2\right)(T-t)$$

and

$$\mu_2 = \ln S_t + \left(r_{t,T} - qS_{t,T} - \frac{1}{2}\sigma S_{t,T}^2\right)(T-t)$$

respectively and variances of $\sigma_1^2 = \sigma R_{t,T}^2 (T-t)$ and $\sigma_2^2 = \sigma s_{t,T}^2 (T-t)$ respectively. Since there are two variables at play here, it is reasonable to expect the correlation between these variables to be a contributing factor when pricing such options.

To incorporate the correlation as an assumption, I will assume that the natural logarithm of the continuously compounded stock price returns have a correlation of ρ_{RS} where (i.e., $\rho_{RS} = corr(\ln(\frac{R_T}{R_t}), \ln(\frac{S_T}{S_t})))$—an assumption that is consistent with the way the standard deviation of the natural logarithm of the continuously compounded stock price returns defined.[22]

As before, to compute the expression for $C_{R_t,S_t,t,T,r_{t,T},qR_{t,T},qS_{t,T},\sigma R_{t,T},\sigma S_{t,T},\rho_{RS},Spot}(exc)$ one has to take the present value of the expectations of the payoff with respect to R_T and S_T. Doing this yields

$$C_{R_t,S_t,t,T,r_{t,T},qR_{t,T},qS_{t,T},\sigma R_{t,T},\sigma S_{t,T},\rho_{RS},Spot}(exc)$$
$$= e^{-r_{t,T}(T-t)} E_{S_T,R_T}[\max(S_T - R_T, 0)]$$

[22]It is important for the reader to note that a correlation of ρ_{RS} between the stock returns does not imply that the stock prices have the same correlation. As pointed out by Ravindran (1997), if $\rho_{RS} = corr(\ln(\frac{R_T}{R_t}), \ln(\frac{S_T}{S_t}))$, then $corr(\ln R_T, \ln S_T) = \rho_{RS}$ and $corr(R_T, S_T) = \frac{e^{\rho_{RS}\sigma_1\sigma_2} - 1}{\sqrt{e^{\sigma_1^2} - 1}\sqrt{e^{\sigma_2^2} - 1}}$.

Letting $h(R_T, S_T)$[23] represent the joint probability density function of R_T and S_T, it readily follows that

$$C_{R_t,S_t,t,T,r_{t,T},qR_{t,T},qS_{t,T},\sigma R_{t,T},\sigma S_{t,T},\rho_{RS},Spot}(exc) = e^{-r_{t,T}(T-t)} \int_0^{\infty} \int_{R_T}^{\infty} [S_T - R_T]\, h(R_T, S_T)\, dS_T dR_T \quad (5.16)$$

Since the joint probability density function, $h(R_T, S_T)$, can be rewritten as a product of a conditional and marginal pdf, namely $h(R_T, S_T) = m(S_T|R_T)\, n(R_T)$ [24], equation (5.16) becomes

$$\begin{aligned} &C_{R_t,S_t,t,T,r_{t,T},qR_{t,T},qS_{t,T},\sigma R_{t,T},\sigma S_{t,T},\rho_{RS},Spot}(exc) \\ &= e^{-r_{t,T}(T-t)} \int_0^{\infty} n(R_T) \left\{ \int_{R_T}^{\infty} [S_T - R_T]\, m(S_T|R_T)\, dS_T \right\} dR_T \\ &= e^{-r_{t,T}(T-t)} \int_0^{\infty} e^{\alpha + \frac{1}{2}\beta^2} N\left(\beta - \frac{\ln R_T - \alpha}{\beta}\right) n(R_T)\, dR_T \\ &\quad - e^{-r_{t,T}(T-t)} \int_0^{\infty} R_T N\left(-\frac{\ln R_T - \alpha}{\beta}\right) n(R_T)\, dR_T \end{aligned} \quad (5.17)$$

To simplify the first integral (and the terms surrounding it) in equation (5.17), first observe that

$$\alpha + \frac{1}{2}\beta^2 = \left[\mu_2 - \frac{\rho_{RS}\sigma_2}{\sigma_1}\mu_1 + \frac{1}{2}\sigma_2^2\left(1 - \rho_{RS}^2\right)\right] + \frac{\rho_{RS}\sigma_2}{\sigma_1}\ln R_T$$

and

$$\beta - \frac{\ln R_T - \alpha}{\beta} = \frac{\rho_{RS}\sigma_2 - \sigma_1}{\sigma_1\sigma_2\sqrt{1 - \rho_{RS}^2}}\ln R_T + \frac{\mu_2 - \frac{\rho_{RS}\sigma_2}{\sigma_1}\mu_1 + \sigma_2^2\left(1 - \rho_{RS}^2\right)}{\sigma_2\sqrt{1 - \rho_{RS}^2}}$$

[23]Since S_T and R_T have a bivariate lognormal pdf, the joint pdf of these variables takes the form of $h(R_T, S_T) = \frac{1}{R_T S_T \sigma_1 \sigma_2 2\pi\sqrt{1-\rho_{RS}^2}} e^D$, where $D = -\frac{1}{2(1-\rho_{RS}^2)}[(\frac{\ln R_T - \mu_1}{\sigma_1})^2 - 2\rho_{RS}(\frac{\ln R_T - \mu_1}{\sigma_1})(\frac{\ln S_T - \mu_2}{\sigma_2}) + (\frac{\ln S_T - \mu_2}{\sigma_2})^2]$ for $R_T, S_T > 0$.

[24]In this representation, $n(R_T)$ represents the pdf of R_T which is given by the expression $n(R_T) = \frac{1}{R_T\sigma_1\sqrt{2\pi}} e^{-\frac{1}{2}(\frac{\ln R_T - \mu_1}{\sigma_1})^2}$ for $R_T > 0$. $m(S_T|R_T)$ represents the conditional pdf of $S_T|R_T$ which is given by the expression $m(S_T|R_T) = \frac{1}{S_T\beta\sqrt{2\pi}} e^{-\frac{1}{2}(\frac{\ln S_T - \alpha}{\beta})^2}$ for $S_T > 0$, where $\alpha = \mu_2 + \frac{\rho_{RS}\sigma_2}{\sigma_1}(\ln R_T - \mu_1)$ and $\beta = \sigma_2\sqrt{1 - \rho_{RS}^2}$.

As a consequence, it readily follows

$$e^{-r_{t,T}(T-t)}\int_0^{\infty} e^{\alpha+\frac{1}{2}\beta^2} N\left(\beta-\frac{\ln R_T-\alpha}{\beta}\right) n(R_T)\,dR_T$$

$$= e^{\mu_2-\frac{\rho_{RS}\sigma_2\mu_1}{\sigma_1}+\frac{1}{2}\sigma_2^2\left(1-\rho_{RS}^2\right)}\int_0^{\infty} R_T^{\frac{\rho_{RS}\sigma_2}{\sigma_1}} N\left(\frac{\rho_{RS}\sigma_2-\sigma_1}{\sigma_1\sigma_2\sqrt{1-\rho_{RS}^2}}\ln R_T + \frac{\mu_2-\frac{\rho_{RS}\sigma_2}{\sigma_1}\mu_1+\sigma_2^2\left(1-\rho_{RS}^2\right)}{\sigma_1\sqrt{1-\rho^2}}\right) n(R_T)\,dR_T \qquad (5.18a)$$

$$= e^{\mu_2-\frac{\rho_{RS}\sigma_2\mu_1}{\sigma_1}+\frac{1}{2}\sigma_2^2\left(1-\rho_{RS}^2\right)} e^{\mu_1\frac{\rho_{RS}\sigma_2}{\sigma_1}+\frac{1}{2}\sigma_1^2\frac{\rho_{RS}^2\sigma_2^2}{\sigma_1^2}} * \left[BN(\omega,\varphi,\theta)-BN(\varepsilon,\varphi,\theta)\right]^{25}$$

where

$$\omega=\infty$$

$$\varepsilon=-\infty$$

$$\varphi=\frac{\mu_2-\mu_1-\rho_{RS}\sigma_1\sigma_2+\sigma_2^2}{\sqrt{\sigma_1^2-2\rho_{RS}\sigma_1\sigma_2+\sigma_2^2}}$$

$$\theta=-\frac{\rho_{RS}\sigma_2-\sigma_1}{\sqrt{\sigma_1^2-2\rho_{RS}\sigma_1\sigma_2+\sigma_2^2}}$$

Equation (5.18a) can further be simplified to obtain

$$e^{\mu_2-\frac{\rho_{RS}\sigma_2\mu_1}{\sigma_1}+\frac{1}{2}\sigma_2^2\left(1-\rho_{RS}^2\right)} e^{\mu_1\frac{\rho_{RS}\sigma_2}{\sigma_1}+\frac{1}{2}\sigma_1^2\frac{\rho_{RS}^2\sigma_2^2}{\sigma_1^2}} N(\varphi)$$

$$= S_t e^{(r_{t,T}-qS_{t,T})(T-t)} N\left(\frac{\ln(S_t/R_t)+\left(qR_{t,T}-qS_{t,T}+\frac{1}{2}\sigma^2\right)(T-t)}{\sigma\sqrt{T-t}}\right)$$

where $\sigma^2=\sigma S_{t,T}^2-2\rho_{RS}\sigma S_{t,T}\sigma R_{t,T}+\sigma R_{t,T}^2$.

[25]This can be obtained by using the result in Ravindran (1997).

Hence one can conclude that the first integral (and the terms accompanying it) in equation (5.17) can be simplified to

$$S_t e^{-qS_{t,T}(T-t)} N\left(\frac{\ln\left(S_t/R_t\right) + \left(qR_{t,T} - qS_{t,T} + \frac{1}{2}\sigma^2\right)(T-t)}{\sigma\sqrt{T-t}}\right) \tag{5.18b}$$

$$= S_t e^{-qS_{t,T}(T-t)} N\left(d^1_{S_t,R_t,t,T,qR_{t,T},qS_{t,T},\sigma}\right)$$

Similarly, it can be concluded that the second integral (and the terms accompanying it) in equation (5.17) simplifies to

$$R_t e^{-qR_{t,T}(T-t)} N\left(\frac{\ln\left(S_t/R_t\right) + \left(qR_{t,T} - qS_{t,T} + \frac{1}{2}\sigma^2\right)(T-t)}{\sigma\sqrt{T-t}} - \sigma\sqrt{T-t}\right)$$

$$= R_t e^{-qR_{t,T}(T-t)} N\left(d^2_{S_t,R_t,t,T,qR_{t,T},qS_{t,T},\sigma}\right) \tag{5.18c}$$

Putting equations (5.18b) and (5.18c) together, one can arrive at the expression

$$\begin{aligned} &C_{R_t,S_t,t,T,r_{t,T},qR_{t,T},qS_{t,T},\sigma R_{t,T},\sigma S_{t,T},\rho_{RS},Spot}(exc) \\ &= S_t e^{-qS_{t,T}(T-t)} N\left(d^1_{S_t,R_t,t,T,qR_{t,T},qS_{t,T},\sigma}\right) \\ &\quad - R_t e^{-qR_{t,T}(T-t)} N\left(d^2_{S_t,R_t,t,T,qR_{t,T},qS_{t,T},\sigma}\right) \end{aligned} \tag{5.19}$$

where $\sigma = \sqrt{\sigma S^2_{T,t} + \sigma R^2_{t,T} - 2\rho_{RS}\sigma R_{t,T}\sigma S_{t,T}}$.

Equation (5.19) has been implemented in Table 5.8.

As the reader will note from the payoff of the exchange option, the notion of a call or put is immaterial since the value of this option is driven by the fact that upon exercise, one is exchanging one asset for the other (and hence the underlyings are interchangeable).

TABLE 5.8 Valuation of Exchange Options

	A	B	C
1	Current Price for Asset 1, R_t ($)	$40.00	
2	Current Price for Asset 2, S_t ($)	$40.00	
3	Volatility for Asset 1, σ_R (%)	40.00%	
4	Volatility for Asset 2, σ_S (%)	20.00%	
5	Correlation, ρ_{RS} (%)	50.00%	
6	Dividend Rate for Asset 1, q_R (%)	2.00%	
7	Dividend Rate for Asset 2, q_S (%)	1.00%	
8	Current Time, t (years)	0	
9	Expiry, T (years)	2	
10	Spread Volatility, σ	0.34641	=SQRT((B3^2)+(B4^2)-(2*B5*B3*B4))
11	d_{21}	0.28577	=(LN(B2/B1)+((B6-B7+(0.5*B10*B10))*(B9-B8)))/(B10*SQRT(B9-B8))
12	d_{22}	−0.20412	=B11-(B10*SQRT(B9-B8))
13	Call (exchange)	7.906101	=(B2*EXP(-B7*(B9-B8))*NORMSDIST(B11))-(B1*EXP(-B6*(B9-B8))*NORMSDIST(B12))

Spread Options

As mentioned, the exchange-option example discussed earlier is a special case of a more generic class of options called *spread options* that trade on the exchanges, like the CME and the OTC markets. Although spread options trade in abundance in financial markets, what makes one spread different from another is the way the underlying spread is defined. One can, for example,[26] find spreads in the CME whose differences are of the form

- Wheat and corn futures expiring on the same month (sometimes called a cross-commodity spread).
- March and May wheat futures (sometimes called a calendar spread).

For the purposes of my discussion, I will assume that a call (put) spread option purchaser gets a payoff that is of the form $\max[(S_T - R_T) - K, 0]$ $(\max[K - (S_T - R_T), 0])$ on option maturity date, where S_T and R_T are the prices of the 2 independent underlyings at time T on which the spread underlying the option is written. Making the same distributional assumption as in the exchange options, to compute the expression for

$$C_{R_t,S_t,K,t,T,r_{t,T},qR_{t,T},qS_{t,T},\sigma R_{t,T},\sigma S_{t,T},\rho_{RS},Spot}(spd)$$

observe that

$$C_{R_t,S_t,K,t,T,r_{t,T},qR_{t,T},qS_{t,T},\sigma R_{t,T},\sigma S_{t,T},\rho_{RS},Spot}(spd)$$
$$= e^{-r_{t,T}(T-t)} E_{S_T,R_T}[\max(S_T - R_T - K, 0)]$$

As before, one can rewrite the above expression as follows:

$$C_{R_t,S_t,K,t,T,r_{t,T},qR_{t,T},qS_{t,T},\sigma R_{t,T},\sigma S_{t,T},\rho_{RS},Spot}(spd)$$
$$= e^{-r_{t,T}(T-t)} \int_0^{\infty} \int_{R_T+K}^{\infty} [S_T - (R_T + K)]\, h(R_T, S_T)\, dS_T dR_T$$

[26]In theory, this spread can also be a difference of a function of one variable (e.g., average price of the first variable) and a function of the second variable (e.g., the highest price of the second variable)—where both these functions do not have to be identical.

Since the joint probability density function, $h(R_T, S_T)$, can be rewritten as a product of a conditional and marginal probability density function (i.e., $h(R_T, S_T) = m(S_T|R_T)\, n(R_T)$), the above expression becomes

$$\begin{aligned}
&C_{R_t,S_t,K,t,T,r_{t,T},q_{R_{t,T}},q_{S_{t,T}},\sigma_{R_{t,T}},\sigma_{S_{t,T}},\rho_{RS},Spot}(spd) \\
&= e^{-r_{t,T}(T-t)} \int_0^{\infty} n(R_T) \left\{ \int_{R_T+K}^{\infty} [S_T - (R_T + K)]\, m(S_T|R_T)\, dS_T \right\} dR_T \\
&= e^{-r_{t,T}(T-t)} \int_0^{\infty} e^{\alpha+\frac{1}{2}\beta^2} N\left(\beta - \frac{\ln(R_T + K) - \alpha}{\beta}\right) n(R_T)\, dR_T \qquad (5.20) \\
&\quad - e^{-r_{t,T}(T-t)} \int_0^{\infty} (R_T + K) N\left(-\frac{\ln(R_T + K) - \alpha}{\beta}\right) n(R_T)\, dR_T
\end{aligned}$$

where α, β, and $n(R_T)$ are all as defined in the section for exchange options.

Since equation (5.20) cannot be succinctly written in an analytical form similar to that of an exchange option, this equation needs to be numerically evaluated. Due to the lack of cheap, high-powered computing technology, practitioners of the past had to resort to nonsimulation-based methods, which I will now discuss.

Spread as a Normal PDF One simplifying assumption that used to be made to get around this problem was to assume that the spread $S_T - R_T$ is normally distributed with a mean of μ_{Spd} and a variance of σ^2_{Spd} (despite the fact that this distributional assumption is not true!)[27]—where μ_{Spd} and σ^2_{Spd} are then computed using the method of moment matching. To see how this is done in practice, observe that

$$\begin{aligned}
E_{R_T,S_T}(S_T - R_T) &= \mu_{Spd} \\
&= E_{S_T}(S_T) - E_{R_T}(R_T) \\
&= e^{\mu_2+\frac{1}{2}\sigma_2^2} - e^{\mu_1+\frac{1}{2}\sigma_1^2}
\end{aligned}$$

Thus, it can be easily summarized that

$$\mu_{Spd} = e^{\mu_2+\frac{1}{2}\sigma_2^2} - e^{\mu_1+\frac{1}{2}\sigma_1^2}$$

[27]If $\ln S_T$ and $\ln R_T$ each has a normal pdf, then $\ln S_T - \ln R_T = \ln(S_T/R_T)$ will also have a normal pdf, as the difference between two normal pdfs will also be a normal pdf. However, this is not the same as $S_T - R_T$ having a normal pdf.

Similarly, since

$$Var_{R_T,S_T}(S_T - R_T) = \sigma^2_{Spd}$$

$$= Var_{S_T}(S_T) + Var_{R_T}(R_T) - 2Covar_{R_T,S_T}(S_T, R_T)$$

$$= \left(e^{2\mu_2+2\sigma_2^2} - e^{2\mu_2+\sigma_2^2}\right) + \left(e^{2\mu_1+2\sigma_1^2} - e^{2\mu_1+\sigma_1^2}\right)$$

$$-2\left[e^{\mu_1+\mu_2+\frac{1}{2}\left(\sigma_1^2+\sigma_2^2+2\rho_{RS}\sigma_1\sigma_2\right)} - \left(e^{\mu_1+\frac{1}{2}\sigma_1^2}e^{\mu_2+\frac{1}{2}\sigma_2^2}\right)\right]$$

It can be easily summarized that

$$\sigma^2_{Spd} = \left(e^{2\mu_2+2\sigma_2^2} - e^{2\mu_2+\sigma_2^2}\right) + \left(e^{2\mu_1+2\sigma_1^2} - e^{2\mu_1+\sigma_1^2}\right)$$

$$-2\left[e^{\mu_1+\mu_2+\frac{1}{2}\left(\sigma_1^2+\sigma_2^2+2\rho_{RS}\sigma_1\sigma_2\right)} - \left(e^{\mu_1+\frac{1}{2}\sigma_1^2}e^{\mu_2+\frac{1}{2}\sigma_2^2}\right)\right]$$

Now that the values of μ_{Spd} and σ^2_{Spd} can be obtained from the above equations, one needs to obtain the expression used to value spread options. Given that $Spread_T = S_T - R_T$ is assumed to be normally distributed with a mean of μ_{Spd} and variance of σ^2_{Spd}, it readily follows that

$$C_{R_t,S_t,K,t,T,r_{t,T},qR_{t,T},qS_{t,T},\sigma R_{t,T},\sigma S_{t,T},\rho_{RS},Spot}(spd)$$

$$= e^{-r_{t,T}(T-t)}E_{S_T,R_T}[\max(S_T - R_T - K, 0)]$$

$$= e^{-r_{t,T}(T-t)}E_{Spread_T}[\max(Spread_T - K, 0)]$$

$$= e^{-r_{t,T}(T-t)}\int_K^{\infty}\left\{[Spread_T - K]*\frac{1}{\sigma_{Spd}\sqrt{2\pi}}e^{-\frac{1}{2}\left(\frac{Spread_T-\mu_{Spd}}{\sigma_{Spd}}\right)^2}\right\}d\ Spread_T$$

$$= e^{-r_{t,T}(T-t)}\left[\frac{\sigma_{Spd}}{\sqrt{2\pi}}e^{-\frac{1}{2}\left(\frac{K-\mu_{Spd}}{\sigma_{Spd}}\right)^2} + \left(\mu_{Spd} - K\right)N\left(\frac{\mu_{Spd} - K}{\sigma_{Spd}}\right)\right] \tag{5.21}$$

The implementation of equation (5.21) is shown in Table 5.9.

TABLE 5.9 Valuation of Spread Options Assuming Normal PDF

	A	B	C
1	Current Price for Asset 1, R_t ($)	$42.00	
2	Current Price for Asset 2, S_t ($)	$40.00	
3	Strike Price, K ($)	$2.00	
4	Volatility for Asset 1, σ_R (%)	40.00%	
5	Volatility for Asset 2, σ_S (%)	20.00%	
6	Correlation, ρ_{RS} (%)	50.00%	
7	Risk Free, r (%)	6.00%	
8	Dividend Rate for Asset 1, q_R (%)	2.00%	
9	Dividend Rate for Asset 2, q_S (%)	1.00%	
10	Current Time, t (years)	0	
11	Expiry, T (years)	2	
12	mean 1, μ_1	3.65766962	=LN(B1)+((B7-B8-(0.5*B4*B4))*(B11-B10))
13	std deviation 1, σ_1	0.56568542	=B4*SQRT(B11-B10)
14	mean 2, μ_2	3.74887945	=LN(B2)+((B7-B9-(0.5*B5*B5))*(B11-B10))
15	std deviation 2, σ_2	0.28284271	=B5*SQRT(B11-B10)
16	Mean (R_T)	45.4980568	=EXP(B12+(0.5*B13*B13))
17	Mean (S_T)	44.20684	=EXP(B14+(0.5*B15*B15))
18	Variance (R_T)	780.68207	=EXP((2*B12)+(2*B13*B13))-EXP((2*B12)+(B13*B13))
19	Variance (S_T)	162.76329	=EXP((2*B14)+(2*B15*B15))-EXP((2*B14)+(B15*B15))
20	Covariance (S_T,R_T)	167.51738	=EXP((B12+B14)+(0.5*((B13^2)+(B15^2)+(2*B6*B13*B15))))-(B16*B17)
21	mean,μ_{Spd}	−1.29122	=B17-B16
22	std deviation, σ_{Spd}	24.66598	=SQRT(B18+B19-(2*B20))
23	Call (spread)	$7.35	=EXP(-B7*(B11-B10))*((B22*EXP(-0.5*(((B3-B21)/B22)^2))/SQRT(2*PI()))+((B21-B3)*NORMSDIST((B21-B3)/B22)))

Spread as a Difference of Two Lognormal PDFs Using Gaussian Quadrature While the above approximation is reasonable for at-the-money options, because of the nature of the assumptions one should not be surprised if this does not accurately value out-of-the-money and in-the-money options. To overcome this problem, Ravindran (1993a) provided a numerical approach to the original problem (i.e., not assuming any distributional form for $Spread_T$) by first reducing this two-dimensional problem using conditioning—an idea that I had used to derive the pricing formula for exchange options.

As the reader will realize, I started the section on spread options by deploying the same conditioning idea only to arrive at a point where I had to resort to numerical methods to progress further. Given this backdrop, I will henceforth focus my discussion on the use of the Gausssian quadrature method[28] (see Abramowitz and Stegun (1965) and Burden and Faires (2010) for more details) to solve the integrals in equation (5.20).

Table 5.10 shows an example of the list of weights and roots for various values of n, where the larger the value of n the greater the accuracy of the approximation to the integral.

In order to now apply the Gaussian quadrature method to solve the one-dimensional integration problem I will, for the ease of reading, restate equation (5.20) which I am trying to numerically evaluate

$$C_{R_t,S_t,K,t,T,r_{t,T},qR_{t,T},qS_{t,T},\sigma R_{t,T},\sigma S_{t,T},\rho_{RS},Spot}(spd)$$

$$= e^{-r_{t,T}(T-t)}\int_0^\infty e^{\alpha+\frac{1}{2}\beta^2}N\left(\beta-\frac{\ln(R_T+K)-\alpha}{\beta}\right)n\left(R_T\right)dR_T \qquad (5.20)$$

$$-e^{-r_{t,T}(T-t)}\int_0^\infty (R_T+K)N\left(-\frac{\ln(R_T+K)-\alpha}{\beta}\right)n\left(R_T\right)dR_T$$

To apply the Gaussian quadrature algorithm, one has to first transform the integral limits from $(0,\infty)$ to $(-1,1)$. Furthermore, as pointed out in footnote 28, the Gaussian quadrature method can only be applied to definite integrals. As such, one has to split the domain $(0,\infty)$ into mutually

[28]The Gaussian quadrature method allows one to solve the integral $\int_{-1}^{1} f(x)\,dx$ numerically using the weights w_i, roots z_i (examples of which are given in Table 5.10 for $n = 1,2,3,4,5$) and the approximation $\sum_{i=1}^{n} w_i f(z_i)$. To perform an integral over an arbitrary interval (a,b) (i.e., $\int_a^b f(x)\,dx$), one needs to first map the integral into a $(-1,1)$ interval using the expression $\frac{b-a}{2}\int_{-1}^{1} f(\frac{b-a}{2}z+\frac{b+a}{2})dz$ which can now be evaluated using the weights w_i, roots z_i, and the approximation $\frac{b-a}{2}\sum_{i=1}^{n} w_i f(\frac{b-a}{2}z_i+\frac{b+a}{2})$. In addition to Table 5.10, weights and roots for more values of n are given in the online content.

TABLE 5.10 Weights and Coefficients for Gaussian Quadrature

n	Roots	Weights
1	2.00000000	0.00000000
2	–0.57735027	1.00000000
	0.57735027	1.00000000
3	–0.77459667	0.55555556
	0.00000000	0.88888889
	0.77459667	0.55555556
4	–0.86113631	0.34785485
	–0.33998104	0.65214515
	0.33998104	0.65214515
	0.86113631	0.34785485
5	–0.90617985	0.23692689
	–0.53846931	0.47862867
	0.00000000	0.56888889
	0.53846931	0.47862867
	0.90617985	0.23692689

exclusive subdomains $(0, M)$ and (M, ∞), where M is chosen to be the median of the pdf of R_T.[29]

Doing this allows one to rewrite the first integral (and the term accompanying it) of equation (5.20) as

$$e^{-r_{t,T}(T-t)} \int_0^\infty e^{\alpha+\frac{1}{2}\beta^2} N\left(\beta - \frac{\ln(R_T+K)-\alpha}{\beta}\right) n(R_T)dR_T$$

$$= e^{-r_{t,T}(T-t)} \int_0^M e^{\alpha+\frac{1}{2}\beta^2} N\left(\beta - \frac{\ln(R_T+K)-\alpha}{\beta}\right) n(R_T)dR_T \qquad (5.22a)$$

$$+ e^{-r_{t,T}(T-t)} \int_M^\infty e^{\alpha+\frac{1}{2}\beta^2} N\left(\beta - \frac{\ln(R_T+K)-\alpha}{\beta}\right) n(R_T)dR_T$$

While the first integral of equation (5.22a) is now a proper one (and hence can be easily mapped into the $(-1, 1)$ domain), the second integral is not. To transform the second integral into a proper one, one only needs

[29]The choice of M does influence the accuracy of the approximations. In practice I have found that a good choice for M when dealing with a lognormal pdf is the median of pdf. More precisely, if $\ln Y$ has a normal pdf with a mean of μ and a variance of σ^2, then it can be easily shown that the mean, median, and mode of Y are given by the expressions $e^{\mu+\frac{1}{2}\sigma^2}$, e^μ, and $e^{\mu-\frac{1}{2}\sigma^2}$ respectively.

to make the substitution $W_T = \frac{1}{R_T}$. Doing this transforms the second integral to

$$e^{-r_{t,T}(T-t)} \int_0^{\frac{1}{M}} e^{\alpha+\frac{1}{2}\beta^2} N\left(\beta - \frac{\ln\left(\left(\frac{1}{W_T}\right)+K\right)-\alpha}{\beta}\right) n(1/W_T)\frac{1}{W_T^2}dW_T \tag{5.22b}$$

Tables 5.11 to 5.12 show the implementation of the Gaussian quadrature algorithm to obtain the values of first integral (and the terms accompanying it) in equation (5.22a) and equation (5.18b) when $n = 5$.

The reader should note a few things from Tables 5.11 and 5.12. In order to cut down on repetition, I only identify changes in Table 5.12 vis-à-vis the formulae in Table 5.11. Furthermore, the weights and roots of the tables given in cells A21:B26 are for $n = 5$ (see also Figure 5.2).

One can apply a similar approach to solve the second integral (and the term accompanying it) of equation (5.20), namely,

$$e^{-r_{t,T}(T-t)} \int_0^{\infty} (R_T + K)N\left(-\frac{\ln(R_T+K)-\alpha}{\beta}\right) n(R_T)dR_T$$

so as to make it Gaussian-quadrature ready. Putting all the pieces together yields $C_{R_t,S_t,K,t,T,r_{t,T},qR_{t,T},qS_{t,T},\sigma R_{t,T},\sigma S_{t,T},\rho_{RS},Spot}(spd)$ value of 7.52. Clearly for more accuracy, the value of n needs to be increased.

Monte Carlo Simulation The idea of using Gausssian quadrature (or any other nonsimulation-based numerical method) to solve a one-dimensional integral worked very well when one had to solve a spread-option problem that was not analytically tractable—during the times when cheap computers were not available. Given the presence of inexpensive, powerful hardware nowadays, it is reasonable to want to take advantage of such cheapness and resort to simulations to value spread options. Other additional benefits for using simulations, despite the existence of efficient numerical methods are

- The use of a generalized methodology to value the entire book of options in the process making it easier to maintain the source-code instead of having many one-off special cases for each type of option.
- The ability to easily add new products with more complex payoffs.

Given this backdrop, I now discuss the use of Monte Carlo simulations to value the same options. As the reader will recall, all the option valuations using Monte Carlo simulations were done on a single variable. Clearly one

TABLE 5.11 Valuation of the First Integral in Equation (5.22a)

	A	B	C	D	E	F	G	H	I
1	Current Price for Asset 1, R_t ($)	$42.00							
2	Current Price for Asset 2, S_t ($)	$40.00							
3	Strike Price, K ($)	$2.00							
4	Volatility for Asset 1, σ_R (%)	40.00%							
5	Volatility for Asset 2, σ_S (%)	20.00%							
6	Correlation, ρ_{RS} (%)	50.00%							
7	Risk Free, r (%)	6.00%							
8	Dividend Rate for Asset 1, q_R (%)	2.00%							
9	Dividend Rate for Asset 2, q_S (%)	1.00%							
10	Current Time, t (years)	0							
11	Expiry, T (years)	2							
12	mean 1, μ_1	3.657669618	=LN(B1)+((B7-B8-(0.5*B4*B4))*(B11-B10))						
13	std deviation 1, σ_1	0.565685425	=B4*SQRT(B11-B10)						
14	mean 2, μ_2	3.748879454	=LN(B2)+((B7-B9-(0.5*B5*B5))*(B11-B10))						
15	std deviation 2, σ_2	0.282842712	=B5*SQRT(B11-B10)						
16	M	38.77088655	=EXP(B12)						
17	a	0	0						
18	b	38.77088655	=B16						
19	$(b-a)/2$	19.38544327	=(B18-B17)/2						
20	$(b+a)/2$	19.38544327	=(B18+B17)/2						
21	w_i	z_i	$x_i = (b-a)z_i/2 + (b+a)/2$	alpha, α	beta, β	$e^{\alpha+\frac{1}{2}\beta^2}$	$\beta - \frac{\ln(R_T + K) - \alpha}{\beta}$	$n(R_T)$	integrand
22	0.23692689	−0.90617985	1.81875	2.983998763	0.244949	20.36868684	6.956864635	1.72403E-07	0.00000
23	0.47862867	−0.53846931	8.94698	3.382290977	0.244949	30.33466073	4.283453868	0.002738856	0.08308
24	0.56888889	0.00000000	19.38544	3.575592659	0.244949	36.80348931	2.338781744	0.017172403	0.62589
25	0.47862867	0.53846931	29.82391	3.683289651	0.244949	40.98842259	1.155635667	0.021235471	0.76255
26	0.23692689	0.90617985	36.95214	3.736867949	0.244949	43.2444088	0.549233583	0.019016431	0.58270
27	Area	15.45449866							
28									

=(B19*B22)+B20

E22-[LN(C22+B3)-D22]/E22

=F26*NORMSDIST(G26)*H26

=EXP(D22+(0.5*(E22^2)))

=B14+[B6*B15*(LN(C22)-B12)/B13]

=EXP(-0.5*((LN(C26)-B12)/B13)^2)/(B13*SQRT(2*PI())*C26)

=B15*SQRT(1-(B6^2))

=SUMPRODUCT(A22:A26,I22:I26)*B19*EXP(-B7*(B11-B10))

TABLE 5.12 Valuation of Equation (5.22b)

	A	B	C	D	E	F	G	H	I
1	Current Price for Asset 1, R_t ($)	$42.00							
2	Current Price for Asset 2, S_t ($)	$40.00							
3	Strike Price, K ($)	$2.00							
4	Volatility for Asset 1, σ_R (%)	40.00%							
5	Volatility for Asset 2, σ_S (%)	20.00%							
6	Correlation, ρ_{RS} (%)	50.00%							
7	Risk Free, r (%)	6.00%							
8	Dividend Rate for Asset 1, q_R (%)	2.00%							
9	Dividend Rate for Asset 2, q_S (%)	1.00%							
10	Current Time, t (years)	0							
11	Expiry, T (years)	2							
12	mean 1, μ_1	3.657669618							
13	std deviation 1, σ_1	0.565685425							
14	mean 2, μ_2	3.748879454							
15	std deviation 2, σ_2	0.282842712							
16	M	38.77088655							
17	a	0							
18	b	0.025792549	=1/B16						
19	$(b-a)/2$	0.012896275							
20	$(b+a)/2$	0.012896275							
21	w_i	z_i	$x_i = (b-a)z_i/2 + (b+a)/2$	alpha, α	beta, β	$e^{\alpha+\frac{1}{2}\beta^2}$	$\beta - \frac{\ln\left(\frac{1}{W_T}+K\right)-\alpha}{\beta}$	$n(1/W_T)$	integrand
22	0.23692689	−0.90617985	0.00121	4.513760145	0.244949	94.0437543	−8.760392574	3.79383E-10	0.00000
23	0.47862867	−0.53846931	0.00595	4.115467931	0.244949	63.1471635	−3.920773111	0.000145851	0.01147
24	0.56888889	0.00000000	0.01290	3.922166249	0.244949	52.04799373	−1.608972168	0.004293101	72.29684
25	0.47862867	0.53846931	0.01984	3.814469257	0.244949	46.73387411	−0.344861835	0.012565494	544.64802
26	0.23692689	0.90617985	0.02458	3.76089096	0.244949	44.29584851	0.274263174	0.017274153	769.92617
27	Area	5.538662023							
28									

=F26*NORMSDIST(G26)*H26/(C22^2)

E22-[LN((1/C22)+B3)-D22]/E22

=B14+[B6*B15*(LN(1/C22)-B12)/B13]

=EXP(-0.5*((LN(1/C26)-B14)/B15)^2)/(B15*SQRT(2*PI())*(1/C26))

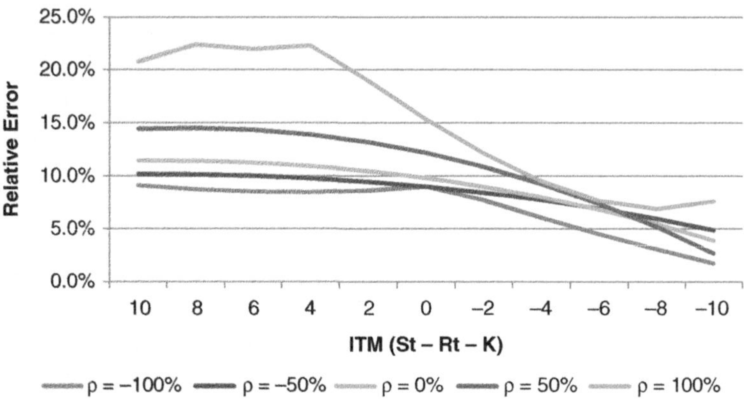

FIGURE 5.2 Relative Error from Normal Approximation

has to adapt this to entertain the fact that there are now two variables that may be correlated to each other. To do this, one has to first observe that when using Monte Carlo simulations to value options on a single variable, one had to first simulate lognormal prices (this is easily done once one is able to generate standard normal variates obtained from the generated uniform (0,1) variates). Similarly, to generate two lognormal correlated variates, one needs to be able to generate two correlated standard normal variates. To do this, one needs to first generate two independent standard normal variates, ε and ω, where in the context of the spread-option problem the first (ε) is used for generation of the price R_T. To use a correlated standard normal variate ω^* for S_T, one would have to use relation

$$\omega^* = \rho\omega + \sqrt{1-\rho^2}\varepsilon$$ [30]

Besides this minor change, the rest of the implementation is no different from what was done for pricing an option on a single variable. Table 5.13 shows the implementation of a Monte Carlo simulation for pricing a spread option.

As in the previous Monte Carlo examples, a call option value of \$1.844 is obtained using a pair of simulated paths for the two underlying stocks. If this simulation is repeated for another 5,000 times, the values can be seen to converge to 7.48 (a value that is close to 7.52). Since the Monte Carlo method is supposed to mimic the results obtained using the Gaussian

[30] ω^* is also a standard normal variate (i.e., a normal pdf with a mean of 0 and variance of 1). In addition to this, it can be easily seen that when ρ is −1, 0, and 1, ω^* is $-\omega$, ε, and ω respectively.

TABLE 5.13 Using the Monte Carlo Method for Spread Options Valuation

	A	B	C
1	Current Price for Asset 1, R_t ($)	$40.00	
2	Current Price for Asset 2, S_t ($)	$42.00	
3	Strike Price, K ($)	$2.00	
4	Volatility for Asset 1, σ_R (%)	20.00%	
5	Volatility for Asset 2, σ_S (%)	40.00%	
6	Correlation, ρ_{RS} (%)	50.00%	
7	Risk Free, r (%)	6.00%	
8	Dividend Rate for Asset 1, q_R (%)	1.00%	
9	Dividend Rate for Asset 2, q_S (%)	2.00%	
10	Current Time, t (years)	0	
11	Expiry, T (years)	2	
12	Delta t, Δt	2	
13	Uniform Random Number (for R_{2Yr})	0.04729	=RAND()
14	Standard Normal Random Number, ε	−1.67170	=NORMSINV(B13)
15	Stock Price at Maturity, R_{2Yr} ($)	$26.471	=B1*EXP((B7-B8-(0.5*B4*B4))*B12)*EXP(B4*B14*SQRT(B12))
16	Uniform Random Number (for S_{2Yr})	0.68393	=RAND()
17	Standard Normal Random Number, ω	0.47872	=NORMSINV(B13)
18	Standard Normal Random Number, ω^*	−0.42127	=(B14*B6)+(SQRT(1-(B6^2))*B17)
19	Stock Price at Maturity, S_{2Yr} ($)	$30.550	=B2*EXP((B7-B9-(0.5*B5*B5))*B12)*EXP(B5*B18*SQRT(B12))
20	Call Spread Option Value	$1.844	=MAX(B19-B15-B3,0)*EXP(-B7*(B11-B10))
21			

quadrature method (as the reasons for the introduction of the Monte Carlo method has nothing to do with increasing the efficiency over the Gaussian quadrature method), I will compare the effectiveness of the approximation associated with assuming that the spreads are normally distributed vis-à-vis not making any distributional assumption for the behavior of spreads. Figure 5.2 shows how the relative error looks for varying levels of correlation where the relative error was computed using the expression

$$\frac{Approx - Gaussian\ Quad\ (n = 5)}{Gaussian\ Quad\ (n = 5)}$$

VALUING PATH-DEPENDENT, EUROPEAN-STYLE OPTIONS ON MULTIPLE VARIABLES

In this section, I will continue my discussion on valuing path-dependent, European-style options on two variables and then extend my discussion to situations that comprise multiple variables. From the earlier sections, it is not difficult to see and understand how quickly the complications associated with the pricing of path-dependent options become. It is also easy to hypothesize how exponentially difficult the problem can get when the number of variables underlying these options starts increasing. Given this backdrop, it should not come as a surprise to the reader that it is more practical to use Monte Carlo methods to tackle such problems.

Averaging Spread Options[31]

In this example, I will discuss one variation of the spread option and averaging theme that is quite popular in the commodity markets. Called *averaging spread options*, this option gives the owner a payoff that is comprised of the difference between two correlated average prices. The payoff for such an option can be more succinctly written as follows:

$$\max\left[\sum_{i=1}^{n} S_{t+i\Delta t} - \sum_{j=1}^{m} R_{t+j\widehat{\Delta t}} - K, 0\right]$$

[31]This option is quite widely used in the commodity markets when the hedger wants protection against the relative movements in the averages of two commodity prices (e.g., crude oil versus heating oil—a variation of a crack spread).

where $\Delta t = \frac{T-t}{n}$ and $\widehat{\Delta t} = \frac{T-t}{m}$.

In particular when $n = m = 3$. Table 5.13 shows the implementation for pricing an averaging spread call option. Although the illustration in Table 5.14 shows the results associated with one path, running this over 5,000 paths yields an option premium of $4.83.

The reader may be interested in noting that it is possible for one to use the average-option-pricing algorithm and combine it with the spread-option algorithm. Clearly, doing this would only yield a proxy solution as compared to the results obtained using Monte Carlo simulation—as the effectiveness very much depends on the at-the-moneyness, correlation, and volatilities.

Lookback Basket Options

To illustrate how a pricing problem is done when there are more than two underlying variables, I will discuss a variation of the path-dependent option on four variables that is popular in the investment sector. Known as *lookback basket options*, these options pay the owner on option maturity:

$$\max[\max(W_t, W_{t+\Delta t}, \ldots, W_{t+n\Delta t}) - K, 0]$$

where $W_{t+i\Delta t} = P_{t+i\Delta t} + Q_{t+i\Delta t} + R_{t+i\Delta t} + S_{t+i\Delta t}$ for $i = 1, 2, ..., n$. $P_{t+i\Delta t}$, $Q_{t+i\Delta t}$, $R_{t+i\Delta t}$, and $S_{t+i\Delta t}$ represent the prices of four correlated stocks at time $t + i\Delta t$ with respective continuously compounded dividend rates q_P, q_Q, q_R, and q_S, respective annualized volatilities $\sigma_P, \sigma_Q, \sigma_R$, and σ_S, and the correlation matrix of returns

$$\begin{bmatrix} 1 & \rho_{PQ} & \rho_{PR} & \rho_{PS} \\ \rho_{PQ} & 1 & \rho_{QR} & \rho_{QS} \\ \rho_{PR} & \rho_{QR} & 1 & \rho_{RS} \\ \rho_{PS} & \rho_{QS} & \rho_{RS} & 1 \end{bmatrix}$$

As in the two-asset case, one needs to use the correlations to tie the generated standard normal variates. Suppose that one has already generated the four independent standard normal variates—$\varepsilon, \omega, \lambda, \theta$—for the simulation of the four respective asset prices. As pointed out by Ravindran (1997), the

TABLE 5.14 Using the Monte Carlo Method for Averaging Spread Options Valuation

	A	B	C
1	Current Price for Asset 1, R_t ($)	$40.00	
2	Current Price for Asset 2, S_t ($)	$44.00	
3	Number of avg points, n,m	3	
4	Strike Price, K ($)	$0.00	
5	Volatility for Asset 1, σ_R (%)	20.00%	
6	Volatility for Asset 2, σ_S (%)	30.00%	
7	Correlation, ρ_{RS} (%)	50.00%	
8	Risk Free, r (%)	6.00%	
9	Dividend Rate for Asset 1, q_R (%)	1.00%	
10	Dividend Rate for Asset 2, q_S (%)	2.00%	
11	Current Time, t (years)	0	
12	Expiry, T (years)	2	
13	Delta t, Δt	0.666666667	
14	Uniform Random Number (for R_{2Yr})	0.68393	
15	Standard Normal Random Number, ε_1	0.47872	
16	Stock Price at Maturity, R_{2Yr} ($)	$44.126	
17	Uniform Random Number (for S_{2Yr})	0.04729	
18	Standard Normal Random Number, ω_1	−1.67170	
19	Standard Normal Random Number, ω_1^*	−1.20838	
20	Stock Price at Maturity, $S_{2/3Yr}$ ($)	$32.618	
21	Uniform Random Number (for $R_{4/3Yr}$)	0.47398	
22	Standard Normal Random Number, ε_2	−0.06526	
23	Stock Price at Maturity, $R_{4/3Yr}$ ($)	$44.540	=B16*EXP((B8-B9-(0.5*B5*B5))*B13)*EXP(B5*B22*SQRT(B13))
24	Uniform Random Number (for $S_{4/3Yr}$)	0.99658	
25	Standard Normal Random Number, ω_2	2.70501	
26	Standard Normal Random Number, ω_2^*	2.30998	
27	Stock Price at Maturity, $S_{4/3Yr}$ ($)	$57.246	=B20*EXP((B8-B10-(0.5*B6*B6))*B13)*EXP(B6*B26*SQRT(B13))
28	Uniform Random Number (for R_{2Yr})	0.40215	
29	Standard Normal Random Number, ε_3	−0.24778	
30	Stock Price at Maturity, R_{2Yr} ($)	$43.638	
31	Uniform Random Number (for S_{2Yr})	0.95183	
32	Standard Normal Random Number, ω_3	1.66288	
33	Standard Normal Random Number, ω_3^*	1.31621	
34	Stock Price at Maturity, S_{3Yr} ($)	$78.762	
35	Call Spread Option Value	$11.799	=MAX(AVERAGE(B15,B23,B30)-AVERAGE(B19,B31,B33)-B4,0)*EXP(-B8*(B12-B11))

standard normal variates associated for the asset prices (especially second, third, and fourth asset prices) need to be modified as follows:

$$\varepsilon^* = \varepsilon$$

$$\omega^* = \rho_{\text{PQ}}\varepsilon^* + \sqrt{1-\rho_{\text{PQ}}^2}\,\omega$$

$$\lambda^* = \begin{bmatrix}\rho_{\text{PR}} & \rho_{\text{QR}}\end{bmatrix}\begin{bmatrix}\varepsilon^* \\ \omega^*\end{bmatrix} + \sqrt{1-\begin{bmatrix}\rho_{\text{PR}} & \rho_{\text{QR}}\end{bmatrix}\begin{bmatrix}1 & \rho_{\text{PQ}} \\ \rho_{\text{PQ}} & 1\end{bmatrix}^{-1}\begin{bmatrix}\rho_{\text{PR}} \\ \rho_{\text{QR}}\end{bmatrix}}\,\lambda$$

$$= \rho_{\text{PR}}\varepsilon^* + \rho_{\text{QR}}\omega^* + \sqrt{1-\begin{bmatrix}\rho_{\text{PR}} & \rho_{\text{QR}}\end{bmatrix}\begin{bmatrix}1 & \rho_{\text{PQ}} \\ \rho_{\text{PQ}} & 1\end{bmatrix}^{-1}\begin{bmatrix}\rho_{\text{PR}} \\ \rho_{\text{QR}}\end{bmatrix}}\,\lambda$$

$$\Theta^* = \begin{bmatrix}\rho_{\text{PS}} & \rho_{\text{QS}} & \rho_{\text{RS}}\end{bmatrix}\begin{bmatrix}\varepsilon^* \\ \omega^* \\ \lambda^*\end{bmatrix}$$

$$+\sqrt{1-\begin{bmatrix}\rho_{\text{PS}} & \rho_{\text{QS}} & \rho_{\text{RS}}\end{bmatrix}\begin{bmatrix}1 & \rho_{\text{PQ}} & \rho_{\text{PR}} \\ \rho_{\text{PQ}} & 1 & \rho_{\text{QR}} \\ \rho_{\text{PR}} & \rho_{\text{QR}} & 1\end{bmatrix}^{-1}\begin{bmatrix}\rho_{\text{PS}} \\ \rho_{\text{QS}} \\ \rho_{\text{RS}}\end{bmatrix}}\,\theta$$

$$= \rho_{\text{PS}}\varepsilon^* + \rho_{\text{QS}}\omega^* + \rho_{\text{RS}}\lambda^*$$

$$+\sqrt{1-\begin{bmatrix}\rho_{\text{PS}} & \rho_{\text{QS}} & \rho_{\text{RS}}\end{bmatrix}\begin{bmatrix}1 & \rho_{\text{PQ}} & \rho_{\text{PR}} \\ \rho_{\text{PQ}} & 1 & \rho_{\text{QR}} \\ \rho_{\text{PR}} & \rho_{\text{QR}} & 1\end{bmatrix}^{-1}\begin{bmatrix}\rho_{\text{PS}} \\ \rho_{\text{QS}} \\ \rho_{\text{RS}}\end{bmatrix}}\,\theta$$

In particular, when $n = 2$, Table 5.15 shows the implementation of the pricing of a lookback basket option.

The result given in cell B56 is obtained using one set of 4 correlated paths. To get a meaningful interpretation of this result, one needs to repeat this simulation for another 5,000 times and then take the average of all the results produced in cell B56 to arrive at a value of \$33.42.

One last comment I would like to make before moving on to the next chapter relates to the ability to incorporate early-exercise features into all the options we discussed in this chapter. In practice, the good news is that many of the exotic options that trade in the marketplace tend to be European style in nature. As a consequence, the Monte Carlo technique presented in this chapter is typically sufficient for the reader to use to tackle the pricing

TABLE 5.15 Using the Monte Carlo Method for Lookback Basket Options Valuation

	A	B	C	D	E
1	Current Price P_t ($)	$42.00			
2	Current Price Q_t ($)	$40.00			
3	Current Price R_t ($)	$42.00			
4	Current Price S_t ($)	$40.00			
5	Number of Lookback Points, n	2			
6	Strike Price, K ($)	$160.00			
7	Volatility for Asset 1, σ_P (%)	40.00%			
8	Volatility for Asset 2, σ_Q (%)	20.00%			
9	Volatility for Asset 3, σ_R (%)	40.00%			
10	Volatility for Asset 4, σ_S (%)	20.00%			
11	Correlation Matrix	P	Q	R	S
12	P	100%	50%	40%	60%
13	Q	50%	100%	30%	30%
14	R	40%	30%	100%	55%
15	S	60%	30%	55%	100%
16	Risk Free, r (%)	6.00%			
17	Dividend Rate for Asset 1, q_P (%)	2.00%			
18	Dividend Rate for Asset 2, q_Q (%)	1.00%			
19	Dividend Rate for Asset 2, q_R (%)	1.50%			
20	Dividend Rate for Asset 2, q_S (%)	2.00%			
21	Current Time, t (years)	0			
22	Expiry, T (years)	2			
23	Delta t, Δt	1			
24	Uniform Random Number (for P_{1Yr})	0.68393			
25	Standard Normal Random Number, ε_1	0.478716958			
26	Standard Normal Random Number, ε_1*	0.478716958	=B25		
27	Stock Price at Maturity, P_{1Yr} ($)	48.86964277			
28	Uniform Random Number (for Q_{1Yr})	0.04729			
29	Standard Normal Random Number, ω_1	−1.67170			
30	Standard Normal Random Number, ω_1*	−1.20838			
31	Stock Price at Maturity, Q_{1Yr} ($)	$32.369			
32	Uniform Random Number (for R_{1Yr})	0.06727			
33	Standard Normal Random Number, λ_1	−1.49640			
34	Standard Normal Random Number, λ_1*	−1.53157			
35	Stock Price at Maturity, R_{1Yr} ($)	$21.978			
36	Uniform Random Number (for S_{1Yr})	0.54826			
37	Standard Normal Random Number, θ_1	0.12126			
38	Standard Normal Random Number, θ_1*	−2.00060			
39	Stock Price at Maturity, R_{1Yr} ($)	$27.351			
40	Uniform Random Number (for P_{2Yr})	0.75912			
41	Standard Normal Random Number, ε_2	0.703486216			
42	Standard Normal Random Number, ε_2*	0.703486216			
43	Stock Price at Maturity, P_{2Yr} ($)	62.21218544			
44	Uniform Random Number (for Q_{2Yr})	0.69106			
45	Standard Normal Random Number, ω_2	0.49885			
46	Standard Normal Random Number, ω_2*	0.78376			
47	Stock Price at Maturity, Q_{2Yr} ($)	$ 39.015			
48	Uniform Random Number (for R_{2Yr})	0.14909			
49	Standard Normal Random Number, λ_2	−1.04034			
50	Standard Normal Random Number, λ_2*	−0.42937			
51	Stock Price at Maturity, R_{2Yr} ($)	$17.873			
52	Uniform Random Number (for S_{2Yr})	0.57211			
53	Standard Normal Random Number, θ_2	0.18174			
54	Standard Normal Random Number, θ_2*	0.55259			
55	Stock Price at Maturity, R_{2Yr} ($)	$31.164			
56	Call Lookback Basket Option Value	$3.548			

```
'=(C12*B26)+(SQRT(1-(C12^2))*B29)
```

```
'=(B14*B26)+(C14*B30)
+(SQRT(1-MMULT(B14:C14,MMULT(MINVERSE(B12:C13),D12:D13)))*B33)
```

```
'=(D19*D30)+(E19*D34)+(F19*D38)
+(SQRT(1-MMULT(D19:F19,MMULT(MINVERSE(D16:F18),G16:G18)))*D37)
```

```
'=MAX(MAX(SUM(B1:B4),SUM(B27,B31,B35,B39),SUM(B43,B47,B51,B55))-D10,0)
*EXP(-B16*(B22-B21))
```

of exotic options. Having said that, it is tempting for the reader to question the necessity and value of discussing approximation methods. The reasons for this stem from the following:

- One motivation for this book is to show the reader how quantitative methods are applied in practice and in this instance how such techniques are applied to the pricing of exotic options (regardless of the fact that the Monte Carlo method can easily do all of these things with very little effort).
- Regardless of the fact that the use of the Monte Carlo method is the most common today, knowing such approximating methods (and improving on them) allows one to use them as great control variates to improve on the efficiency of the Monte Carlo runs—which as a consequence reduces run time.
- In the event that one is able to find great approximation methods that produce very few relative errors compared to a Monte Carlo method, it is often much easier to use them (this a big reason why the Black-Scholes model is still coded as is in a program even though one can use Monte Carlo methods)—as it is much more efficient to use such methods vis-à-vis Monte Carlo methods, especially when running various stress tests.

Having said the above, if needed, one can still incorporate early-exercise features into the problems discussed here by using the methodologies identified in Chapter 3. Given that this not a frequently encountered problem, I will not discuss this here and refer the interested reader to Hull (2012) and Ravindran (1997).

REFERENCES

Abramowitz, M., and I. A. Stegun, eds. 1965. *Handbook of Mathematical Functions with Formulas, Graphs, and Mathematical Tables*. New York: Dover Publications.

Boyle, P. P. 1977. "Options: A Monte Carlo Approach." *Journal of Financial Economics* 4:323–338.

Burden, R. and D. Faires. 2010. *Numerical Analysis*. 7th ed. Belmont, CA: Thomson Brooks/Cole.

Das, S. 1996. *Exotic Options*. London: IFR Publishing.

Geske, R. 1979. "The Valuation of Compound Options." *Journal of Financial Economics* 7:63–81.

Haug, E. G. 2006. *The Complete Guide to Option Pricing Formulas*. 2nd ed. New York: McGraw-Hill.

Hull, J. C. 2012. *Options, Futures and Other Derivatives*. 8th ed. Upper Saddle River, NJ: Prentice Hall.

Kemna, A. G. Z., and A. C. F. Vorst. 1990. "A Pricing Method for Options Based on Average Asset Values. *Journal of Banking and Finance* 14:113–129.

Margrabe, W. 1978. "The Value of an Option to Exchange One Asset for Another." *Journal of Finance* 33:177–186.

Nelken, I., ed. 1995. *The Handbook of Exotic Options: Instruments, Analysis and Applications*. New York: McGraw-Hill.

Ravindran, K.,1993a. "Low Fat Spreads." *RISK* 6:56–57.

Ravindran, K. 1993b. "LIBOR Binary Notes." *Derivatives Week* (December 6):5.

Ravindran, K. 1997. *Customized Derivatives: A Step-by-Step Guide to Using Exotic Options, Swaps and Other Customized Derivatives*. New York: McGraw-Hill.

Turnbull, S. M., and L. M. Wakeman. 1991. "A Quick Algorithm for Pricing European Average Options." *Journal of Financial and Quantitative Analysis* 26:77–389.

CHAPTER 6

Estimating Model Parameters

In Chapters 3, 4, and 5, I discussed the valuation of options when the variability entered only through future price (value or rate) movements. As a consequence, the bulk of my discussion in this chapter will focus on the estimation of model parameters when there is only price stochasticity. As in Chapter 5, I will continue to assume that the underlying is an index that pays continuous dividends.

I showed in Chapter 3 how equations (3.7a) and (3.7b)—were used to value European-style options on a stock that pays a continuously compounded dividend. For the ease of reading, I have re-stated these equations again:

$$C_{S_t,K,t,T,r_{t,T},q_{t,T},\sigma_{t,T},Spot}(van) = S_t e^{-q_{t,T}(T-t)} N\left(d^1_{S_t,K,t,T,r_{t,T},q_{t,T},\sigma_{t,T}}\right) - Ke^{-r_{t,T}(T-t)} N\left(d^2_{S_t,K,t,T,r_{t,T},q_{t,T},\sigma_{t,T}}\right) \tag{3.7a}$$

$$P_{S_t,K,t,T,r_{t,T},q_{t,T},\sigma_{t,T},Spot}(van) = -S_t e^{-q_{t,T}(T-t)} N\left(-d^1_{S_t,K,t,T,r_{t,T},q_{t,T},\sigma_{t,T}}\right) + Ke^{-r_{t,T}(T-t)} N\left(-d^2_{S_t,K,t,T,r_{t,T},q_{t,T},\sigma_{t,T}}\right) \tag{3.7b}$$

where

$$d^1_{S_t,K,t,T,r_{t,T},q_{t,T},\sigma_{t,T}} = \frac{\ln\left(S_t/K\right) + \left(r_{t,T} - q_{t,T} + \frac{1}{2}\sigma^2_{t.T}\right)(T-t)}{\sigma_{t,T}\sqrt{T-t}}$$

$$d^2_{S_t,K,t,T,r_{t,T},q_{t,T},\sigma_{t,T}} = \frac{\ln\left(S_t/K\right) + \left(r_{t,T} - q_{t,T} - \frac{1}{2}\sigma^2_{t.T}\right)(T-t)}{\sigma_{t,T}\sqrt{T-t}}$$

When illustrating the implementation of equations (3.7a) and (3.7b) in Table 3.4, I assumed that all the inputs going into the model (e.g.,

$S_t, K, t, T, r_{t,T}, q_{t,T}, \sigma_{t,T})$ are known—which is far from the truth in practice. In reality, the only inputs that are known with 100 percent objectivity are S_t, K, t, T. In fact, while S_t represents the value of the observable index at the time of valuation, the other three inputs (i.e., K, t, T) are terms associated with the European-style vanilla option contract. Furthermore, the input $r_{t,T}$, which used to be thought of as known, transparent, and objective in the past has been shown to be none of those for the following reasons:

- As seen in Figure 2.5, there can be a big discrepancy in the zero rates arising from how the zero-rate curve is constructed (i.e., linear function versus cubic polynomial). In the event that the option maturity lies in the region where this discrepancy is great, the value of $r_{t,T}$ that is used for both growing the stock and present valuing the option payoff can be drastically different—leading to differing option values.
- Since the decision to implement Dodd-Frank, the market has started to move away from the use of the uncollateralized LIBOR as a floating rate to the use of a collateralized overnight indexed swap (OIS) rate as a floating rate—in the process redefining the term *risk-free rate*. See also footnote 20 of Chapter 2.

Despite this, relative to both $q_{t,T}$ and $\sigma_{t,T}$, there is a lesser degree of uncertainty associated with the estimation of $r_{t,T}$.

Given the above backdrop, I will now discuss methods used by practitioners to estimate the unknown parameters $r_{t,T}, q_{t,T}$, and $\sigma_{t,T}$. Before doing this, it would be useful for the reader to recognize that since an option premium is supposed to reflect the risks embedded in the option, it is imperative for the parameters $r_{t,T}, q_{t,T}$, and $\sigma_{t,T}$ to accurately represent the average value of the parameters during the life of the option, as it would be these factors (among other things) that determine the value of S_T. Clearly the longer the option maturity, the greater the difficulty to accurately guesstimate these values.

To help with the estimation of the parameters $r_{t,T}, q_{t,T}$, and $\sigma_{t,T}$, one typically resorts to using at least one of the two following methods in practice:

1. Implied:[1] Refers to the use of currently available liquid market information (e.g., option price, zero risk-free rate curve, and so on) to determine

[1]This is sometimes referred to as calibrating the model to market information (as the inputs in the model are adjusted so that the resulting output matches the market value of the option)—although there are some exceptions to this when the model is an all-encompassing model with a lesser number of estimable parameters relative to the amount of available liquid market data. See also the section in this chapter on Calibration of Interest Rate Option Model Parameters.

the implied values of the parameters, as this would be the market's perception of the realized values.

2. Historical: Refers to the use of historical data to statistically estimate the values of the parameters, as this would be the practitioner's view on the realized values.

Starting with a discussion on how parameter values can be implied from market data, I conclude this chapter with a discussion on various statistical methods that can be deployed to estimate the parameter values using historical data.

CALIBRATION OF PARAMETERS IN THE BLACK-SCHOLES MODEL

As mentioned earlier, there are three input parameters (namely $r_{t,T}$, $q_{t,T}$, and $\sigma_{t,T}$) that need to be estimated for use in equations (3.7a) and (3.7b). However, before one can decide how to best estimate these parameters, it is important to first understand the function of these parameters. To do this, I will provide a quick description for each of these parameters—the reader is referred to Hull (2012) for more details:

$r_{t,T}$: The annualized continuously compounded risk-free rate that represents the fully collateralized risk-free rate (that is obtained for the time period (t, T) using the zero risk-free rate curve at time t) is the rate at which money can be borrowed or lent for the life of the option (i.e., $T - t$).

$q_{t,T}$: The annualized continuously compounded dividend rate that represents the rate (that is obtained for the time period (t, T) using the zero dividend rate curve at time t), is the rate at which dividends are paid out to shareholders of the underlying shares for the life of the option (i.e., $T - t$) (where it is assumed that the dividends are not reinvested).

$\sigma_{t,T}$: The annualized rate that represents the spot volatility rate (that is obtained for the time period (t, T) using the spot volatility rate curve at time t) is the volatility experienced by the underlying stock for the life of the option (i.e., $T - t$).

When I discussed the construction of a zero risk-free rate curve in Chapter 2, the reader will recall that for the constructed curve to be deemed effective, the curve should be able to

- Serve as a platform that can be used to compare the relative value of one interest-bearing instrument over the other.

- Reproduce the market prices of actively trading financial instruments.
- Infer (deduce) prices of nonliquid and/or complex financial instruments (so as to assess how much premium is attached to such instruments—relative to where liquid instruments trade).

The reason for my drawing reference to the zero risk-free rate curve construction is to show the striking similarity between what was discussed in Chapter 2 and what will be discussed in this chapter.

To infer $r_{t,T}$, $q_{t,T}$, and $\sigma_{t,T}$, from market information, it is important for the reader to first understand that for a given maturity T, these parameters can be estimated by going through the following steps:

Step 1: Estimate $r_{t,T}$ using the zero risk-free rate curve.

Step 2: Estimate $q_{t,T}$ using the value of $r_{t,T}$ (in step 1) and the value of forward/futures contract with the same maturity.

Step 3: Estimate $\sigma_{t,T}$ using the values of $r_{t,T}$ and $q_{t,T}$ (in steps 1 and 2) and the value of an options contract with the same maturity.

Since the implementation of step 1 is straightforward (given the backdrop of Chapter 2), I will henceforth only focus on the inference of $q_{t,T}$ and $\sigma_{t,T}$.

Inferring $q_{t,T}$

For a given maturity T and implied $r_{t,T}$, to infer $q_{t,T}$ one needs the price of the forward/futures contract expiring at same time T. In footnote 29 of Chapter 3, I pointed out that the value of a forward/futures contract is given by the expression

$$F_{S_t,t,T,r_{t,T},q_{t,T}} = S_t * e^{(r_{t,T}-q_{t,T})(T-t)}$$

This can be solved for $q_{t,T}$ (since S_t and $r_{t,T}$ are observables) and shown to be:

$$q_{t,T} = r_{t,T} - \frac{\ln(F_{S_t,t,T,r_{t,T},q_{t,T}}/S_t)}{T-t} \tag{6.1}$$

Table 6.1 shows the implementation of equation (6.1) when all the other relevant information is given.[2]

[2]An alternative method to imply $q_{t,T}$ involves the use of both call and put options that are struck at the same level and mature at the same time. In this case, using the put-call parity of the option, it can be shown that $q_{t,T}$ is the solution to the equation $-\frac{1}{T-t}\ln(\frac{put\ premium-call\ premium+Ke^{-r_{t,T}(T-t)}}{S_t})$.

TABLE 6.1 Implying Dividend Rate, $q_{t,T}$

	A	B	C
1	Current Price, S_t ($)	$40.00	
2	Futures Price, F_t ($)	$42.00	
3	Risk Free, r (%)	6.00%	
4	Current Time, t (years)	0	
5	Expiry, T (years)	2	
6	Implied Dividend, q	3.560%	=B3-(LN(B2/B1)/(B5-B4))

Inferring $\sigma_{t,T}$

For a given maturity T, to infer $\sigma_{t,T}$, one would need the inferred values of $r_{t,T}$, $q_{t,T}$, and the options contract value expiring at time T. Knowing all the relevant information allows one to solve equations (3.7a) and (3.7b) for $\sigma_{t,T}$. Putting all these together, it is easy to see that solving for $\sigma_{t,T}$ is equivalent to finding the solution of the equation

$$f(\sigma_{t,T}) = C_{Market\ Price} - C_{S_t,K,t,T,r_{t,T},q_{t,T},\sigma_{t,T},Spot}(van) = 0 \qquad (6.2)$$

where $C_{Market\ Price}$ refers to the observed market price of the call option.

Thus the implied volatility, σ_*, is the value of $\sigma_{t,T}$ that is the root of equation (6.2).

Although the root of equation (6.2) is easily solved using Excel's Goal Seek function, this unfortunately is not a practical method for arriving at the solution. The reason for this is that in practice one is faced with the problem of finding implied volatilities for hundreds of option contracts instantaneously so as to allow the trader to make real-time trading decisions. As a consequence, one has to resort to more robust and powerful numerical methods.[3]

For the purposes of illustration, I will again use Newton's method to show how to compute the implied volatility associated with a market-based, vanilla call option premium. Newton's method suggests that the root of equation (6.2) can be obtained by recursively using equation (6.3) to solve for σ_{n+1}.

$$\sigma_{n+1} = \sigma_n - \frac{f(\sigma_n)}{\frac{df(\sigma_n)}{d\sigma_n}} \text{ for } n = 0, 1, 2, 3, \ldots \qquad (6.3)$$

where σ_0 is the initial guessed value of the iteration.

[3]Examples of these methods include the Bisection algorithm, Newton method, Secant method, and a hybrid of these methods. See Burden and Fraires (2010).

Combining equations (6.2) and (6.3), one can arrive at

$$\sigma_{n+1} = \sigma_n + \frac{C_{MarketPrice} - C_{S_t,K,t,T,r_{t,T},q_{t,T},\sigma_n,Spot}(van)}{\dfrac{dC_{S_t,K,t,T,r_{t,T},q_{t,T},\sigma_n,Spot}(van)}{d\sigma_n}} \qquad (6.4a)$$

where $C_{S_t,K,t,T,r_{t,T},q_{t,T},\sigma_n,Spot}(van)$ is defined by equation (3.7a) and

$$\frac{dC_{S_t,K,t,T,r_{t,T},q_{t,T},\sigma_n,Spot}(van)}{d\sigma} = \frac{S_t}{\sqrt{2\pi}} e^{-q_{t,T}(T-t)-\frac{1}{2}(d^1_{S_t,K,t,T,r_{t,T},q_{t,T},\sigma_n})^2} \qquad (6.4b)$$

One can similarly write analogs to equations (6.4a) and (6.4b) that can be used to obtain implied volatilities from put option premiums and arrive at

$$\sigma_{n+1} = \sigma_n + \frac{P_{MarketPrice} - P_{S_t,K,t,T,r_{t,T},q_{t,T},\sigma_n,Spot}(van)}{\dfrac{dP_{S_t,K,t,T,r_{t,T},q_{t,T},\sigma_n,Spot}(van)}{d\sigma_n}} \qquad (6.5a)$$

where $P_{S_t,K,t,T,r_{t,T},q_{t,T},\sigma_n,Spot}(van)$ is defined by equations (3.7b),

$$\frac{dP_{S_t,t,T,r_{t,T},q_{t,T},\sigma_n,Spot}(van)}{d\sigma} = \frac{S_t}{\sqrt{2\pi}} e^{-q_{t,T}(T-t)-\frac{1}{2}(d^1_{S_t,K,t,T,r_{t,T},q_{t,T},\sigma_n})^2} \qquad (6.5b)$$

and $P_{MarketPrice}$ represents the market price of the put option from which one is trying to the implied value of σ_n.

Table 6.2 shows the implementation of equations (6.4a), (6.4b), (6.5a), and (6.5b) assuming that all the other relevant inputs to the Black-Scholes model and the option prices are given.

As the reader will note[4] in Table 6.2:

- The formulae used in cells B10 through B13 have not been displayed simply because these formulae are no different from those presented in Table 3.4.

---

[4]In addition, a few more technical observations need to be made as follows:

- One needs to start with the right σ_0 so as to converge faster. In practice, one uses the implied volatility that was last used to obtain a new implied volatility for an updated option price. In the absence of this, one typically starts off with the historical volatility as a good proxy.

TABLE 6.2 Implying Volatility Rate, $\sigma_{t,T}$

	A	B	C
1	Current Price, S_t ($)	$40.00	
2	Strike Price, K ($)	$40.00	
3	Volatility, σ_0 (%)	20.00%	
4	Risk Free, r (%)	6.00%	
5	Dividend Rate, q (%)	2.00%	
6	Current Time, t (years)	0	
7	Expiry, T (years)	2	
8	c(market price) ($)	$5.00	
9	p(market price) ($)	$3.00	
10	$d^1(\sigma_0)$	0.424264069	
11	$d^2(\sigma_0)$	0.141421356	
12	Call(σ_0)	5.797289275	
13	Put(σ_0)	2.842529178	
14	dCall(σ_0)/$d\sigma_0$	14.01237574	=B1*EXP(-B5*(B7-B6))*EXP(-0.5*B10*B10)/SQRT(2*PI())
15	dPut(σ_0)/$d\sigma_0$	14.01237574	=B1*EXP(-B5*(B7-B6))*EXP(-0.5*B10*B10)/SQRT(2*PI())
16	σ_1 (call)	0.143101064	=B3+((B8-B12)/B14)
17	σ_1 (put)	0.21123798 2	=B3+((B9-B13)/B15)

- Unlike Table 3.4, I have put in the argument σ_0 in cells B10 and B11—just to emphasize that all these values are for the initial guess of sigma (σ_0) that is given in cell B3.

- Existence of the functional form of the differentials. In implementing equations (6.4b) and (6.5b), $\frac{dC_{S_t,K,t,T,r_{t,T},q_{t,T},\sigma_n,Spot}(van)}{d\sigma_n}$ and $\frac{dP_{S_t,K,t,T,r_{t,T},q_{t,T},\sigma_n,Spot}(van)}{d\sigma_n}$ existed as functional forms. In practice, when dealing with path-dependent and early-exercise options, this is seldom the case. In such an event, it is customary to compute these differentials numerically—no different how the premiums are computed. Thus one would, for example, compute $\frac{dC_{S_t,K,t,T,r_{t,T},q_{t,T},\sigma_n,Spot}(van)}{d\sigma_n}$ (assuming this does not have a functional form) using the numerical approximation $\frac{C_{S_t,K,t,T,r_{t,T},q_{t,T},\sigma_n+0.01,Spot}(van)-C_{S_t,K,t,T,r_{t,T},q_{t,T},\sigma_n,Spot}(van)}{0.01}$ for each value of n.
- When using Monte Carlo simulations to value these options, due to the randomness associated with the simulation, there is noise associated with the computed premium. This noise can potentially lead to a large error when computing the differentials numerically. Fortunately, this problem can be easily overcome by ensuring that the same set of random numbers are used when computing the option premiums (for both the base volatility and shifted volatility cases).

- Table 6.2 only contains the result for one iteration (whose results are given in cells B16 and B17). In practice this iteration has to be continued until the desired error bound is satisfied.

Table 6.3 shows the convergence of the implied volatility for both the call and put option.

As in the zero risk-free rate term structure where each liquid interest rate instrument is used to construct a zero risk-free rate that uniquely corresponded to the maturity of the instrument, one also constructs a zero-dividend rate term structure and spot volatility term structure based on the forward/futures and vanilla European-style option contracts. This should not come as any surprise since practitioners use prices of liquid instruments of varying maturities to infer a series of q and σs, each of which uniquely corresponds to a given maturity. However, unlike the zero risk-free rate curve construction (where one had to sometimes bootstrap using zero risk-free rates of shorter maturities to obtain those for the longer maturities), the zero-dividend rate and spot volatility rate curve construction are more straightforward. The reason for this stems from the fact that while the longer-dated instruments that were used to calibrate the zero risk-free rates were coupon bearing instruments, those used for calibrating the dividend and volatility rates seem to naturally embed the zero-rate or spot-rate structure-like features. Figure 6.1 shows an example of how an implied spot volatility term structure may look in practice.

As can be seen in Figure 6.1, to connect the data points I assumed the fitting of a linear function, hence the presence of kinks at the data points. Like the zero risk-free rate curve construction, one can use a cubic polynomial to smooth out the kinks at the data points. Whatever the methodology, the constructed term structure of zero risk-free rates, zero-dividend rates, and spot-volatility rates can be used to reproduce the price of liquid instruments (consistent with the second objective) and price complex options (e.g., early exercise and path dependent) on the same underlying in the process fulfilling the third objective.

Unlike the term structures associated with the zero risk-free rates and zero-dividend rates, the term structure of the spot-volatility rates unfortunately does not tell the whole story about the exact market sentiments in regard to how likely the price movements will be. In fact, since future movements in price/rate distribution in practice are not exactly lognormal, practitioners make adjustments[5] to the volatilities of lognormal pdf (depending

[5]These are sometimes called the volatility smiles or frowns.

TABLE 6.3 Convergence of σ_n

	A	B	C	D	E	F	G	H	I	J	K	L	M
1													
2													
3		n	0	1	2	3	4	5	6	7	8	9	
4		σ_{call}	20.00%	14.31%	16.64%	15.66%	16.06%	15.89%	15.96%	15.93%	15.95%	15.94%	
5		σ_{put}	20.00%	21.12%	20.66%	20.85%	20.77%	20.80%	20.79%	20.80%	20.79%	20.79%	
6													

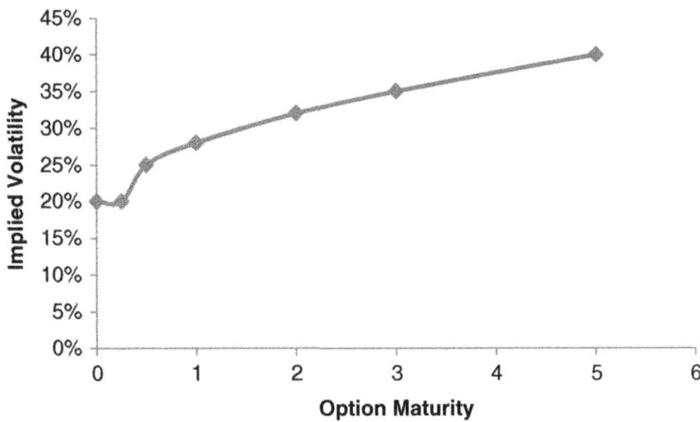

FIGURE 6.1 Implied Volatility Term Structure

on the in-the-moneyness of the option) so as to better capture the nonlogarithmic behavior of the pdf—all in the spirit of dressing the volatility inputs going into a lognormal pdf so as to ensure that market prices can be reproduced. As a consequence, it is not uncommon to see an implied volatility surface associated with options on an underlying, as shown in Figure 6.2, rather than that presented in Figure 6.1—although in the absence of any in-the-moneyness effects, the volatility surface trivially collapses to a volatility term structure.

From Figure 6.2, it is important for the reader to make the following two observations:

- One needs[6] to use a cubic polynomial to smooth the kinks at the data points so the implied volatility surface can be more readily used with complex stochastic processes for the price or price volatility models.
- A less obvious but a very important issue is one relating to the use of the implied volatility surface to price options. While valuing vanilla European-style options is quite easy (since one only needs to read off the implied surface for the appropriate implied volatility for a given maturity and the in-the-moneyness of the option), the same cannot be said when valuing early-exercise and/or path-dependent options. The reason for this stems from the fact in valuing early-exercise or path-dependent options, one would need to use the applicable forward risk-free rate,

[6]Clearly the need to use a cubic polynomial for smoothing the interpolation around the data points is a mute point if the data grid is fine enough to mimic a continuous surface.

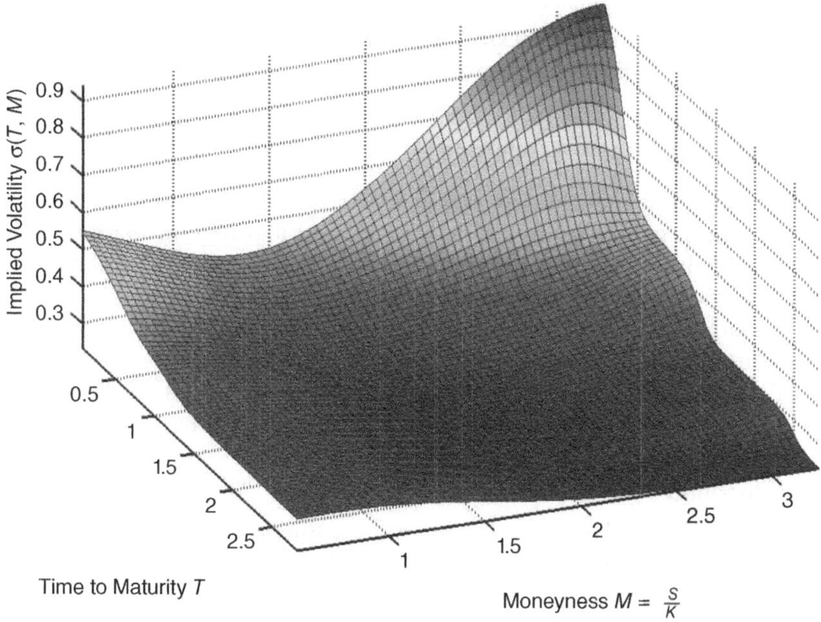

FIGURE 6.2 Implied Volatility Surface
Source: www.mathworks.com.

forward dividend rate, and forward volatility rates—all of which are easy to do when time to maturity is the only dimension for the implied volatility (i.e., there is no in-the-money effect). The moment an in-the-money effect enters the picture, one needs to capture both the forward volatility rates and the in-the-moneyness effect created by the asset-price movements during the life of the option.

USING IMPLIED BLACK-SCHOLES VOLATILITY SURFACE AND ZERO RATE TERM STRUCTURE TO VALUE OPTIONS

In this section, I discuss how an implied Black-Scholes volatility surface together with the term structure of zero risk-free and dividend rates can be used to value path dependent options. To do this, I start with the special case when the volatility surface is assumed to be parallel to the in-the-money axis (i.e., no in-the-moneyness effects)—a consequence of which is that the implied volatility surface collapses to an implied volatility term structure. Following this, I revisit the problem of pricing path-dependent options in the presence of in-the-moneyness effects, so as to help the reader better appreciate the nuances and complexity associated with extraction of information that is inherent in the volatility surface.

Using Volatility Term Structure

I will first assume that the zero risk-free rate, zero-dividend rate, and spot-volatility term structures are the only sources of market information available. In this instance, the valuation of vanilla European-style options is an easy exercise simply because to infer the inputs $r_{t,T}, q_{t,T}$, and $\sigma_{t,T}$ one just has to read them off the appropriate term structures. Given this backdrop, I will focus my discussion on path-dependent option valuation.

To understand how term structures can be used to price path-dependent options, one needs to first observe that when valuing these options, one major underlying assumption (given by equation (3.5)) is that $\ln S_T$ is normally distributed with a mean of $\ln S_t + (r_{t,T} - q_{t,T} + \frac{1}{2}\sigma^2_{t.T})(T-t)$ and a variance of $\sigma^2_{t.T}(T-t)$. The consequence of this assumption is that S_T does not depend on any information prior to time t. Thus, if S_u represents some time in the future (where $t < u < T$), then the pdf of $\ln S_T$ given $\ln S_t$ can be easily decomposed as a sum of the following two pdfs:

1. $\ln S_u$ is normally distributed with a mean $\ln S_t + (r_{t,u} - q_{t,u} + \frac{1}{2}\sigma^2_{t.u})(u-t)$ and a variance of $\sigma^2_{t.u}(u-t)$.
2. $\ln S_T$ is normally distributed with a mean $\ln S_u + (r_{u,T} - q_{u,T} + \frac{1}{2}\sigma^2_{u.T})$ $(T-u)$ and a variance $\sigma^2_{u.T}(T-u)$.

Thus, a conditional pdf of $\ln S_T$ on $\ln S_u$ is dependent on the forward rates $r_{u,T}$, $q_{u,T}$, and $\sigma_{u,T}$—among other things. Hence it is important for one to be able extract these forward rates from the given sources of market term structures.

As stated in equation (2.7), for any two given zero risk-free rates $r_{t,u}$ and $r_{t,T}$ (where $T > u > t$), the forward risk-free rate $r_{t,u,T}$ (a rate that is applicable from time u to T using the zero rates at time t) is given by the expression

$$r_{t,u,T} = \frac{r_{t,T}(T-t) - r_{t,u}(u-t)}{T-u} \tag{2.7}$$

Since the zero-dividend rates work the same way as the zero risk-free rates, one can go through similar arithmetic to show that for any two given zero-dividend rates $q_{t,u}$and $q_{t,T}$ (where $T > u > t$), the forward dividend rate

$q_{t,u,T}$ (a rate that is applicable from time u to T using the zero rates at time t) is given by the expression

$$q_{t,u.T} = \frac{q_{t,T}(T-t) - q_{t,u}(u-t)}{T-u} \tag{6.6}$$

Unlike forward risk-free and dividend rates, forward volatility rates cannot be obtained using a formula that is similar to equations (2.7) and (6.6). The reason for this stems from my earlier comment on the ability to decompose the conditional pdf of $\ln S_T$ (given $\ln S_t$) as a sum of the conditional pdfs of $\ln S_u$ (given $\ln S_t$) and $\ln S_T$ (given $\ln S_u$). Given this decomposition, it is easy to see that

$$\mathrm{Var}\left[\ln\left(\frac{S_T}{S_t}\right)\right] = \mathrm{Var}\left[\ln\left(\frac{S_u}{S_t}\right)\right] + \mathrm{Var}\left[\ln\left(\frac{S_T}{S_u}\right)\right]$$

As a consequence, it readily follows that if $\sigma_{t,u}$ and $\sigma_{t,T}$ are any two spot-volatility rates (where $T > u > t$), the forward volatility rate $\sigma_{t,u,T}$ (a rate that is applicable from time u to T using the spot volatility rates at time t) is given by the expression

$$\sigma_{t,u,T} = \sqrt{\frac{\sigma^2_{t.T}(T-t) - \sigma^2_{t.u}(u-t)}{T-u}} \tag{6.7}$$

Table 6.4 shows the implementation of equations (2.7), (6.6), and (6.7).

TABLE 6.4 Calculation of Forward Rates $r_{u,T}, q_{u,T}, \sigma_{u,T}$

	A	B	C
1	Current Time (t)	0.000	
2	Future Time (u)	0.500	
3	Future Time (T)	1.500	
4	Zero Risk Free rate ($r_{t,u}$)	6.00%	
5	Zero Risk Free rate ($r_{t,T}$)	10.00%	
6	Zero Dividend rate ($q_{t,u}$)	1.00%	
7	Zero Dividend rate ($q_{t,T}$)	2.00%	
8	Spot Volatility rate ($\sigma_{t,u}$)	20.00%	
9	Spot Volatility rate ($\sigma_{t,T}$)	35.00%	
10	Forward Risk Free rate ($r_{u,t}$)	12.0%	=((B5*(B3-B1))-(B4*(B2-B1)))/(B3-B2)
11	Forward Dividend rate ($q_{u,t}$)	2.50%	=((B7*(B3-B1))-(B6*(B2-B1)))/(B3-B2)
12	Forward Volatility rate ($\sigma_{u,t}$)	40.47%	=SQRT(((B9*B9*(B3-B1))-(B8*B8*(B2-B1)))/(B3-B2))
13			
14			

Now that I have illustrated how to imply forward rates from the appropriate zero (risk-free and dividend) and spot-volatility rate term structures, I will show how forward rates can be used to value path-dependent options. To do this, I discuss one example involving the derivation of an accurate analytical solution and another involving the use of the Monte Carlo method.

Installment Options In Chapter 5, I discussed the valuation of a call-on-call option and showed for a flat term structure of a zero risk-free rate, zero-dividend rate, and spot-volatility rate (i.e., $r_{t,T} = r_{t,u}, q_{t,T} = q_{t,u}, \sigma_{t,T} = \sigma_{t,u}$ for all $T > u > t$), the formula for the first installment premium is given by equations (5.12a), (5.12b), and (5.12c) which can be rewritten for ease of reading as follows:

$$
\begin{aligned}
CC_t = S_t e^{-q_{t,T}(T-t)} BN\left(d^1_{S_t,S_*,t,u,r_{t,T},q_{t,T},\sigma_{t,T}}, d^1_{S_t,K,t,T,r_{t,T},q_{t,T},\sigma_{t,T}}, \rho\right) \\
-Ke^{-r_{t,T}(T-t)} BN\left(d^2_{S_t,S_*,t,u,r_{t,T},q_{t,T},\sigma_{t,T}}, d^2_{S_t,K,t,T,r_{t,T},q_{t,T},\sigma_{t,T}}, \rho\right) \\
-Xe^{-r_{t,T}(u-t)} N\left(d^2_{S_t,S_*,t,u,r_{t,T},q_{t,T},\sigma_{t,T}}\right)
\end{aligned}
\tag{5.12a}
$$

where

$$
\rho = \sqrt{\frac{u-t}{T-t}} \tag{5.12b}
$$

and, S_* is the solution to

$$
\begin{aligned}
S_* e^{-q_{t,T}(T-u)} N\left(d^1_{S_*,K,u,T,r_{t,T},q_{t,T},\sigma_{t,T}}\right) \\
-Ke^{-r_{t,T}(T-u)} N\left(d^2_{S_*,K,u,T,r_{t,T},q_{t,T},\sigma_{t,T}}\right) - X = 0
\end{aligned}
\tag{5.12c}
$$

To consider the presence of the term structure of rates and obtain an analogous expression to value an installment option, I will as before assume that the:

- Current time is t.
- Second optional premium of X is paid at time u.
- Underlying option expiry upon payment of the second optional premium is time T (i.e., option life of $T - u$).

Given the above assumptions, it is straightforward to see that the first installment premium (associated with the installment option), in the presence of term structures, is given by

$$\begin{aligned} CC_{t.TS} = e^{-r_{t,u}(u-t)} E_{S_u} \{ \max [S_u e^{-q_{u,T}(T-u)} N \left(d^1_{S_u,K,u,T,r_{u,T},q_{u,T},\sigma_{u,T}} \right) \\ - K e^{-r_{u,T}(T-u)} N \left(d^2_{S_u,K,u,T,r_{u,T},q_{u,T},\sigma_{u,T}} \right) - X, 0] \} \end{aligned} \tag{6.8}$$

Since the values of $r_{u,T}$, $q_{u,T}$, and $\sigma_{u,T}$ are unknown and assumed to be deterministic at time t, one needs to find an estimate for these variables using the forward zero rate ($r_{t,u,T}$), forward dividend rate ($q_{t,u,T}$), and forward volatility rate ($\sigma_{t,u,T}$)—all of which have been defined in equations (2.7), (6.6), and (6.7).

Putting all these together with (6.8), one gets

$$\begin{aligned} & CC_{t,TS} \\ &= e^{-r_{t,u}(u-t)} \Bigg[\int_{S_*}^{\infty} e^{-q_{t,u,T}(T-u)} S_u N \left(\frac{\ln(S_u/K) + \left(r_{t,u,T} - q_{t,u,T} + \frac{1}{2}\sigma^2_{t,u,T} \right)(T-u)}{\sigma_{t,u,T}\sqrt{T-u}} \right) g(S_u)\, dS_u \\ & - K e^{-r_{t,u,T}(T-u)} \int_{S_*}^{\infty} N \left(\frac{\ln(S_u/K) + \left(r_{t,u,T} - q_{t,u,T} - \frac{1}{2}\sigma^2_{t,u,T} \right)(T-u)}{\sigma_{t,u,T}\sqrt{T-u}} \right) g(S_u)\, dS_u \\ & - X \int_{S_*}^{\infty} g(S_u)\, dS_u \Bigg] \end{aligned} \tag{6.9a}$$

where

$$g(S_u) = \frac{1}{\beta S_u \sqrt{2\pi}} e^{-\frac{1}{2}\left[\frac{\ln S_u - \alpha}{\beta}\right]^2}, \text{ for } S_u > 0 \tag{6.9b}$$

$$\alpha = \ln S_t + \left(r_{t,u} - q_{t,u} - \frac{1}{2}\sigma^2_{t,u} \right)(u-t) \tag{6.9c}$$

$$\beta = \sigma_{t,u}\sqrt{u-t} \tag{6.9d}$$

and S_* is the solution of the equation

$$\begin{aligned} S_* e^{-q_{t,u,T}(T-u)} N \left(d^1_{S_*,K,u,T,r_{t,u,T},q_{t,u,T},\sigma_{t,u,T}} \right) \\ - K e^{-r_{t,u,T}(T-u)} N \left(d^2_{S_*,K,u,T,r_{t,u,T},q_{t,u,T},\sigma_{t,u,T}} \right) - X = 0 \end{aligned} \tag{6.9e}$$

To evaluate equation (6.9a), first observe that the third integral and the terms accompanying it (after expansion and substitution of equation (6.9b)) becomes

$$Xe^{-r_{t,u}(u-t)}\int_{S_*}^{\infty}\frac{1}{\beta S_u\sqrt{2\pi}}e^{-\frac{1}{2}(\frac{\ln S_u-\alpha}{\beta})^2}dS_u$$

Letting

$$z=\frac{\ln S_u-\alpha}{\beta}\text{ yields } Xe^{-r_{t,u}(u-t)}\int_{\frac{\ln S_*-\alpha}{\beta}}^{\infty}\frac{1}{\sqrt{2\pi}}e^{-\frac{1}{2}z^2}dz$$
$$=Xe^{-r_{t,u}(u-t)}N\left(-\frac{\ln S_*-\alpha}{\beta}\right)$$

Substituting equations (6.9c) and (6.9d), one gets

$$Xe^{-r_{t,u}(u-t)}N\left(\frac{\ln\left(S_t/S_*\right)+\left(r_{t,u}-q_{t,u}-\frac{1}{2}\sigma_{t,u}^2\right)(u-t)}{\sigma_{t,u}\sqrt{u-t}}\right) \tag{6.10a}$$
$$=Xe^{-r_{t,u}(u-t)}N\left(d^2_{S_t,S_*,t,u,r_{t,u},q_{t,u},\sigma_{t,u}}\right)$$

Now observe that the second integral and the terms accompanying it in equation (6.9a) (after expansion and substitution of equation (6.9b)) becomes

$$Ke^{-r_{t,T}(T-t)}\int_{S_*}^{\infty}N\left(\frac{\ln(S_u/K)+\left(r_{t,u,T}-q_{t,u,T}-\frac{1}{2}\sigma_{t,u,T}^2\right)(T-u)}{\sigma_{t,u,T}\sqrt{T-u}}\right)\frac{1}{\beta S_u\sqrt{2\pi}}e^{-\frac{1}{2}(\frac{\ln S_u-\alpha}{\beta})^2}dS_u$$

Letting $z=\frac{\ln S_u-\alpha}{\beta}$ the above simplifies to

$$Ke^{-r_{t,T}(T-t)}\int_{\frac{\ln S_*-\alpha}{\beta}}^{\infty}N\left(\frac{\alpha+\beta z-\ln K+(r_{t,u,T}-q_{t,u,T}-\frac{1}{2}\sigma_{t,u,T}^2)(T-u)}{\sigma_{t,u,T}\sqrt{T-u}}\right)\frac{1}{\sqrt{2\pi}}e^{-\frac{1}{2}z^2}dz$$

Making the substitution with equations (6.9c) and (6.9d) and letting

$$\tilde{\rho} = \frac{\sigma_{\mathrm{t,u}}}{\sigma_{\mathrm{t,T}}}\sqrt{\frac{u-t}{T-t}}$$

one gets

$$Ke^{-r_{t,T}(T-t)}\int_{-d^2_{S_t,S_*,t,u,\mathrm{r_{t,u}},\mathrm{q_{t,u}},\sigma_{\mathrm{t,u}}}}^{\infty} N\left(\frac{d^2_{S_t,K,t,T,\mathrm{r_{t,T}},\mathrm{q_{t,T}},\sigma_{\mathrm{t,T}}} + \tilde{\rho}z}{\sqrt{1-\tilde{\rho}^2}}\right)\frac{1}{\sqrt{2\pi}}e^{-\frac{1}{2}z^2}dz$$

$$= Ke^{-r_{t,T}(T-t)}BN\left(d^2_{S_t,S_*,t,u,\mathrm{r_{t,u}},\mathrm{q_{t,u}},\sigma_{\mathrm{t,u}}}, d^2_{S_t,K,t,T,\mathrm{r_{t,T}},\mathrm{q_{t,T}},\sigma_{\mathrm{t,T}}}, \tilde{\rho}\right) \tag{6.10b}$$

Finally observe that the first integral and the terms accompanying it in equation (6.9a) (after expansion and substitution of equation (6.9b)) becomes

$$e^{-r_{t,u}(u-t)}e^{-q_{t,u,T}(T-u)}$$

$$*\int_{S_*}^{\infty} S_u N\left(\frac{\ln\left(\mathrm{S_u/K}\right) + \left(\mathrm{r_{t,u,T}} - \mathrm{q_{t,u,T}} + \frac{1}{2}\sigma^2_{\mathrm{t,u,T}}\right)(\mathrm{T-u})}{\sigma_{\mathrm{t,u,T}}\sqrt{\mathrm{T-u}}}\right)\frac{1}{\beta S_u\sqrt{2\pi}}e^{-\frac{1}{2}\left(\frac{\ln S_u-\alpha}{\beta}\right)^2}dS_u$$

Letting $z = \frac{\ln S_u - \alpha}{\beta}$, it is easy to see that

$$e^{-r_{t,u}(u-t)}e^{-q_{t,u,T}(T-u)}$$

$$*\int_{\frac{\ln S_*-\alpha}{\beta}}^{\infty} e^{\alpha+\beta z}N\left(\frac{\alpha+\beta z - \ln\mathrm{K} + \left(\mathrm{r_{t,u,T}} - \mathrm{q_{t,u,T}} + \frac{1}{2}\sigma^2_{\mathrm{t,u,T}}\right)(T-u)}{\sigma_{\mathrm{t,u,T}}\sqrt{\mathrm{T-u}}}\right)\frac{1}{\sqrt{2\pi}}e^{-\frac{1}{2}z^2}dz$$

$$= S_t e^{-q_{t,T}(T-t)}$$

$$*\int_{\frac{\ln S_*-\alpha}{\beta}}^{\infty} N\left(\frac{\ln\left(\frac{\mathrm{S_t}}{\mathrm{K}}\right) + \left(\mathrm{r_{t,T}} - \mathrm{q_{t,T}} + \frac{1}{2}\sigma^2_{\mathrm{t,T}}\right)(T-t) + (z-\beta)\beta}{\sigma_{\mathrm{u,T}}\sqrt{\mathrm{T-u}}}\right)\frac{1}{\sqrt{2\pi}}e^{-\frac{1}{2}(z-\beta)^2}dz$$

Letting $w = z - \beta$ and then substituting with equations (6.9c) and (6.9d),

$$S_t e^{-q_{t,T}(T-t)} \int_{\frac{lnS_*-\alpha}{\beta}-\beta}^{\infty} N\left(\frac{\ln\left(\frac{S_t}{K}\right) + \left(\mathrm{r_{t,T}} - \mathrm{q_{t,T}} + \frac{1}{2}\sigma_{\mathrm{t,T}}^2\right)(T-t) + w\beta}{\sigma_{\mathrm{u,T}}\sqrt{\mathrm{T-u}}}\right) \frac{1}{\sqrt{2\pi}} e^{-\frac{1}{2}w^2} dw$$

$$= S_t e^{-q_{t,T}(T-t)} \int_{-d^1_{S_t,S_*,t,u,\mathrm{r_{t,u}},\mathrm{q_{t,u}},\sigma_{\mathrm{t,u}}}}^{\infty} N\left(\frac{d^1_{S_t,K,t,u,\mathrm{r_{t,T}},\mathrm{q_{t,T}},\sigma_{\mathrm{t,T}}} + \tilde{\rho} w}{\sqrt{1-\tilde{\rho}^2}}\right) \frac{1}{\sqrt{2\pi}} e^{-\frac{1}{2}w^2} dw$$

$$= S_t e^{-q_{t,T}(T-t)} BN\left(d^1_{S_t,S_*,t,u,\mathrm{r_{t,u}},\mathrm{q_{t,u}},\sigma_{\mathrm{t,u}}}, d^1_{S_t,K,t,u,\mathrm{r_{t,T}},\mathrm{q_{t,T}},\sigma_{\mathrm{t,T}}}, \tilde{\rho}\right) \tag{6.10c}$$

Putting all the pieces together, equation (6.9a) can be simplified with the aid of equations (6.10a), (6.10b), and (6.10c) to arrive at the formula,

$$\begin{aligned} CC_{t,TS} = {} & S_t e^{-q_{t,T}(T-t)} BN\left(d^1_{S_t,S_*,t,u,\mathrm{r_{t,u}},\mathrm{q_{t,u}},\sigma_{\mathrm{t,u}}}, d^1_{S_t,K,t,u,\mathrm{r_{t,T}},\mathrm{q_{t,T}},\sigma_{\mathrm{t,T}}}, \tilde{\rho}\right) \\ & -K e^{-r_{t,T}(T-t)} BN\left(d^2_{S_t,S_*,t,u,\mathrm{r_{t,u}},\mathrm{q_{t,u}},\sigma_{\mathrm{t,u}}}, d^2_{S_t,K,t,T,\mathrm{r_{t,T}},\mathrm{q_{t,T}},\sigma_{\mathrm{t,T}}}, \tilde{\rho}\right) \\ & -X e^{-r_{t,u}(u-t)} N\left(d^2_{S_t,S_*,t,u,\mathrm{r_{t,u}},\mathrm{q_{t,u}},\sigma_{\mathrm{t,u}}}\right) \end{aligned} \tag{6.11a}$$

where

$$\tilde{\rho} = \frac{\sigma_{\mathrm{t,u}}}{\sigma_{\mathrm{t,T}}}\sqrt{\frac{u-t}{T-t}} \tag{6.11b}$$

and, S_* is the solution to

$$\begin{aligned} & S_* e^{-q_{t,u,T}(T-u)} N\left(d^1_{S_*,K,u,T,r_{t,u,T},q_{t,u,T},\sigma_{t,u,T}}\right) \\ & -K e^{-r_{t,u,T}(T-u)} N\left(d^2_{S_*,K,u,T,r_{t,u,T},q_{t,u,T},\sigma_{t,u,T}}\right) - X = 0 \end{aligned} \tag{6.11c}$$

Table 6.5 shows the implementation of a call-on-call installment option (equations (6.11a), (6.11b), and (6.11c)) in the presence of term structures.

TABLE 6.5 Calculation of Installment Option Premium in the Presence of Term Structures

	A	B	C
1	Current Price, S_t ($)	$40.00	
2	2nd Installment, X ($)	$ 2	
3	Strike Price, K ($)	$40.00	
4	Volatility, $\sigma_{t,u}$(%)	20.00%	
5	Volatility, $\sigma_{t,T}$(%)	30.00%	
6	Risk Free, $r_{t,u}$(%)	4.00%	
7	Risk Free, $r_{t,T}$(%)	5.00%	
8	Dividend Rate, $q_{t,u}$(%)	1.00%	
9	Dividend Rate, $q_{t,T}$(%)	2.00%	
10	Current Time, t (years)	0	
11	Second Installment Time, u (years)	1	
12	Expiry, T (years)	2	
13	Forward Volatility, $\sigma_{u,t}$(%)	37.42%	=SQRT(((B5*B5*(B12-B10))-(B4*B4*(B11-B10)))/(B12-B11))
14	Forward Risk Free, $r_{u,t}$(%)	6.00%	=((B7*(B12-B10))-(B6*(B11-B10)))/(B12-B11)
15	Forward Dividend Rate, $q_{u,t}$(%)	3.00%	=((B9*(B12-B10))-(B8*(B11-B10)))/(B12-B11)
16	S_* (guess)	30.68863	
17	$d_1(u,T,S_*,K)$	−0.44095	=(LN(B16/B3)+((B14-B15+(0.5*B13*B13))*(B12-B11)))/(B13*SQRT(B12-B11))
18	$d_2(u,T,S_*,K)$	−0.81511	=(LN(B16/B3)+((B14-B15-(0.5*B13*B13))*(B12-B11)))/(B13*SQRT(B12-B11))
19	Check To Confirm S_* Is Solution	0.00000	=(B16*EXP(-B15*(B12-B11))*NORMSDIST(B17))-(B3*EXP(-B14*(B12-B11))*NORMSDIST(B18))-B2
20	$d_1(t,u,S_t,S_*)$	1.57494	=(LN(B1/B16)+((B6-B8+(0.5*B4*B4))*(B11-B10)))/(B4*SQRT(B11-B10))
21	$d_2(t,u,S_t,S_*)$	1.37494	=(LN(B1/B16)+((B6-B8-(0.5*B4*B4))*(B11-B10)))/(B4*SQRT(B11-B10))
22	$d_1(t,T,S_t,K)$	0.35355	=(LN(B1/B3)+((B7-B9+(0.5*B5*B5))*(B12-B10)))/(B5*SQRT(B12-B10))
23	$d_2(t,T,S_t,K)$	−0.07071	=(LN(B1/B3)+((B7-B9+(0.5*B5*B5))*(B12-B10)))/(B5*SQRT(B12-B10))
24	rho, ρ	0.471405	=(B4/B5)*SQRT((B11-B10)/(B12-B10))
25	$BN(d_1(t,u,S_t,S_*),d_1(t,T,S_t,K)\rho)$	0.623405	CALCULATED USING THE ALGORITHM OUTLINED IN JOHN HULL'S BOOK
26	$BN(d_2(t,u,S_t,S_*),d_2(t,T,S_t,K)\rho)$	0.459142	
27	Call-on-call premium, CC_t	5.581426	=(B1*EXP(-B9*(B12-B10))*B25)-(B3*EXP(-B7*(B12-B10))*B26)-(B2*EXP(-B6*(B11-B10))*NORMSDIST(B21))
28			

This value was guessed so that the result in cell B19 is 0.

As can be seen from Table 6.5, the calculations are quite similar to Table 5.4 except that one has to factor in the concepts of forward risk-free rate, dividend rate, and volatility rate.

Averaging Options In the implementation of the Monte Carlo method to value path-dependent options described in Chapter 5, one had to recursively generate a stock price using the immediately generated stock price. More precisely, I used the recursive relationship derived using the idea in footnote 21 of Chapter 4:

$$S_{t+\Delta t} = S_t e^{\left(r_{t,T} - q_{t,T} - 0.5\sigma_{t,T}^2\right)(\Delta t)} * e^{\sigma_{t,T}\sqrt{\Delta t}z} \tag{6.12a}$$

where z represents the random standard normal variate and Δt represents time over which the simulation is done.

Equation (6.12a) can be more generally written as

$$S_{t_i} = S_{t_{i-1}} e^{(r_{t,t_{i-1},t_i} - q_{t,t_{i-1},t_i} - 0.5\sigma_{t,t_{i-1},t_i}^2)(t_i - t_{i-1})} * e^{\sigma_{t,t_{i-1},t_i}\sqrt{t_i - t_{i-1}}z_i} \tag{6.12b}$$

where

$i = 1, \ldots, n$.
$t_0 = t$.
$t_n = T$, z_i the ith random standard normal variate.
r_{t,t_{i-1},t_i}, q_{t,t_{i-1},t_i}, and σ_{t,t_{i-1},t_i} represent the forward risk-free rate, dividend rate, and volatility rate respectively.

Table 6.6 shows the revaluation of the averaging option illustrated in Table 5.6.

As can be seen from Table 6.6, I have only demonstrated the formulae involving the computation of the forward rates and the generation of the stock price since the rest of the formulae is no different from those produced in Table 5.6.

USING VOLATILITY SURFACE

In the previous section, I discussed the use of zero-rate risk-free, zero-rate dividend, and volatility term structures to infer the appropriate forward (risk-free, dividend, and volatility) rates to value path-dependent options.

TABLE 6.6 Calculation of Averaging Option Premium in the Presence of Term Structures

	A	B	C
1	Current Price, S_t ($)	$40.00	
2	Number of avg points, n	2	
3	Strike Price, K ($)	$40.00	
4	Volatility, $\sigma_{t,t+\Delta t}$ (%)	20.00%	
5	Volatility, $\sigma_{t,T}$ (%)	30.00%	
7	Risk Free, $r_{t,t+\Delta t}$ (%)	4.00%	
8	Risk Free, $r_{t,T}$ (%)	5.00%	
9	Dividend Rate, $q_{t,u}$ (%)	1.00%	
10	Dividend Rate, $q_{t,T}$ (%)	2.00%	
11	Current Time, t (years)	0	
12	First Averaging Time, t+Δt (years)	1	
13	Second Averaging Time/Expiry, T (years)	2	
14	Forward Volatility, $\sigma_{t,t+\Delta t,T}$ (%)	37.42%	=SQRT(((B5*B5*(B13-B11))-(B4*B4*(B12-B11)))/(B13-B12))
15	Forward Risk Free, $r_{t,t+\Delta t,T}$ (%)	6.00%	=((B8*(B13-B11))-(B7*(B12-B11)))/(B13-B12)
16	Forward Dividend Rate, $q_{t,t+\Delta t,T}$ (%)	3.00%	=((B10*(B13-B11))-(B9*(B12-B11)))/(B13-B12)
17	Uniform Random Number 1	0.68393	
18	Standard Normal Random Number 1	0.47872	
19	Stock Price at Maturity, S_{1Yr} ($)	$44.461	=B1*EXP((B7-B9-(0.5*B4*B4))*(B12-B11))*EXP(B4*B18*SQRT(B12-B11))
20	Uniform Random Number 2	0.04729	
21	Standard Normal Random Number 2	−1.67170	
22	Stock Price at Maturity, S_{2Yr} ($)	$22.854	=B19*EXP((B15-B16-(0.5*B14*B14))*(B13-B12))*EXP(B14*B21*SQRT(B13-B12))
23	Call Option Value	$ –	=MAX(AVERAGE(B19,B22)-B3,0)*EXP(-B8*(B13-B11))
24	Put Option Value	$5.739	=MAX(B3-AVERAGE(B19,B22),0)*EXP(-B8*(B13-B11))

As was seen, the adjustments made were done to capture the presence of additional market information that took the form of forward rates. While this was not a huge step up in terms of complexity, as compared to a flat-term structure of rates (i.e., constant risk-free, dividend, and volatility rates), trying to do this for a collection of spot-volatility rate term structures across varying in-the-moneyness of the option (i.e., the spot-volatility rate surface) becomes much trickier. This is simply due to the fact that in addition to the term of the option maturity, the in-the-moneyness of the option needs to be captured (which intuitively is equivalent to saying that the implied volatility is a function of both the time and prevailing stock price). The problem of trying to use the implied volatility surface to value path-dependent options was tackled in 1994, when Dupire published his paper on volatility smiles set in continuous time. Derman and Kani in the same year independently published their paper on the same topic but set in discrete time.

In this section, I discuss the implementation of the methodology proposed by Derman and Kani (1994)—which was basically motivated by the desire to construct a stock-price tree that is consistent with the term structure of zero rates and implied volatility surface in discrete time. More precisely they assumed a generalized version of equation (3.5)

$$\frac{dS}{S} = (r(t) - q(t))\,dt + \sigma(t, S)\,dz \tag{6.13}$$

where

S is the price of the stock.
$r(t)$ is the annualized continuously compounded risk-free rate that is a function of time.
$q(t)$ is the annualized continuously compounded dividend rate that is a function of time.
$\sigma(t, S)$ is the annualized volatility of the stock price return that is a function of both time and stock price level.
dz is the random variable drawn from a standard normal probability density function.
dS is the small change in the stock price over a small time interval dt.

They constructed a binomial tree of stock prices and probabilities that was consistent with above diffusion equations—a more complex version of the binomial tree that was discussed in Chapter 3. Derman and Kani showed that equations (3.14a) to (3.14c) can be generalized to accommodate the presence of more market information and written out to be

$$S_{t+(i+1)\Delta t,j+1} = \begin{cases} \dfrac{S_{t+(i+1)\Delta t,j}\left[e^{\Gamma_i \Delta t} Ca^{S_{t+i\Delta t,j},(i+1)\Delta t} - \sum^{U}\right] - \lambda_{i,j} S_{t+i\Delta t,j}(F^{i,j} - S_{t+(i+1)\Delta t,j})}{e^{\Gamma_i \Delta t} Ca^{S_{t+i\Delta t,j},(i+1)\Delta t} - \sum^{U} - \lambda_{i,j}(F^{i,j} - S_{t+(i+1)\Delta t,j})} & j = \frac{i+2}{2} + 1, \ldots, i+1 \\ \dfrac{S_t\left[e^{\Gamma_i \Delta t} Ca^{S_t,(i+1)\Delta t} + \lambda_{i,j} S_t - \sum^{U}\right]}{-e^{\Gamma_i \Delta t} Ca^{S_t,(i+1)\Delta t} + \sum^{U} + \lambda_{i,j} F^{i,j}} & j = \frac{i+2}{2} = \frac{i+2}{2} \\ \dfrac{S_{t+(i+1)\Delta t,j+2}\left[e^{\Gamma_i \Delta t} Pu^{S_{t+i\Delta t,j+1},(i+1)\Delta t} - \sum^{D}\right] + \lambda_{i,j+1} S_{t+i\Delta t,j+1}(F^{i,j+1} - S_{t+(i+1)\Delta t,j+2})}{e^{\Gamma_i \Delta t} Pu^{S_{t+i\Delta t,j+1},(i+1)\Delta t} - \sum^{D} + \lambda_{i,j+1}(F^{i,j+1} - S_{t+(i+1)\Delta t,j+2})} & j = 0, \ldots, \frac{i+2}{2} - 1 \end{cases}$$

(6.14a)

$$p_{t+i\Delta t,j} = \frac{F^{i,j} - S_{t+(i+1)\Delta t,j}}{S_{t+(i+1)\Delta t,j+1} - S_{t+(i+1)\Delta t,j}} \tag{6.14b}$$

where

$i = 0, 1, 2, \ldots$

$\lfloor a \rfloor$ is the floor function of a.[7]

$$\sum^{U} = \sum_{k=j+1}^{i+1} \lambda_{i,k}(F^{i,k} - S_{t+i\Delta t,k})$$

$$\sum^{D} = \sum_{k=1}^{j-1} \lambda_{i,k+1}(S_{t+i\Delta t,k+1} - F^{i,k+1})$$

$$\Gamma_i = r_{t,t+i\Delta t,t+(i+1)\Delta t}$$

$\lambda_{i,j}$ is the Arrow-Debreu price associated with the stock price $S_{t+i\Delta t,j}$ (where $\lambda_{0,1}$ is defined to be 1).

$Ca^{S_{t+i\Delta t,j},t+(i+1)\Delta t} = C_{S_t,S_{t+i\Delta t,j},t,t+(i+1)\Delta t,r_{t,t+(i+1)\Delta t},q_{t,t+(i+1)\Delta t},\sigma_{S_t,S_{t+i\Delta t,j}},Spot}(van)$.

$Pu^{S_{t+i\Delta t,j},t+(i+1)\Delta t} = P_{S_t,S_{t+i\Delta t,j},t,t+(i+1)\Delta t,r_{t,t+(i+1)\Delta t},q_{t,t+(i+1)\Delta t},\sigma_{S_t,S_{t+i\Delta t,j}},Spot}(van)$.

$S_{t+i\Delta t,j}$ is the jth node of the stock-price tree at time $t + i\Delta t$ (where $S_{t,1}$ is defined to be S_t).

---

[7]The floor function is defined such that $\lfloor a \rfloor$ is the largest integer that is no greater than a. For example, $\lfloor 1.2 \rfloor = 1$, $\lfloor 2 \rfloor = 2$.

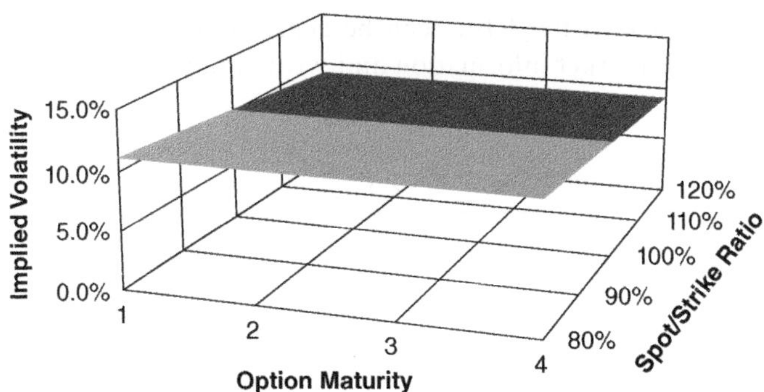

FIGURE 6.3 Implied Volatility Surface Used for Table 6.7, A to C

$F^{i,j}$ is the forward price associated with the stock price $S_{t+i\Delta t,j}$ and applied to time $t + (i + 1)\Delta t$.

$\sigma_{S_t,S_{t+i\Delta t,j}}$ is the implied volatility of the option when the stock price is S_t and the strike price is $S_{t+i\Delta t,j}$.

$p_{t+i\Delta t,j}$ is the probabilty of moving from stock price $S_{t+i\Delta t,j}$ to $S_{t+(i+1)\Delta t,j+1}$ (where $p_{t,1}$ is defined to be probability of upward movement at time t).

To illustrate the use of the above algorithm to calibrate a tree that is consistent with the term structures of zero rates and volatility rates, I will reproduce the example contained in their paper, using their assumptions that the current stock price is \$100, the term structure of zero dividend rates is 0 percent, the term structure of zero risk-free rates is 3 percent, and the implied volatility surface is 10 percent for at-the-money options increasing (decreasing) linearly by 0.5 percent per every \$10 drop (increase) in the strike rate of the option.[8] The assumed implied volatility surface is shown in Figure 6.3.

Using the above information (and assuming that one is interested in generating a binomial tree with annual time steps), it is of interest to find the values of the following implied stock-price tree (shown in Figure 6.4a) and the implied probability tree (shown in Figure 6.4b).

[8]When the stock price is \$100, the implied volatility is 10 percent. When the stock price goes to \$110, \$120, and \$130, the implied volatility decreases to 9.5, 9, and 8.5 percent respectively. When the stock prices go to \$90, \$80, and \$70 the implied volatility increases to 10.5, 11, 11.5 percent respectively.

					$S_{t+4\Delta t,5}$
				$S_{t+3\Delta t,4}$	
			$S_{t+2\Delta t,3}$		$S_{t+4\Delta t,4}$
		$S_{t+\Delta t,2}$		$S_{t+3\Delta t,3}$	
	S_t		$S_{t+2\Delta t,2}$		$S_{t+4\Delta t,3}$
		$S_{t+\Delta t,1}$		$S_{t+3\Delta t,2}$	
			$S_{t+2\Delta t,1}$		$S_{t+4\Delta t,2}$
				$S_{t+3\Delta t,1}$	
					$S_{t+4\Delta t,1}$
i	0	1	2	3	4
Time (years)	t	$t+\Delta t$	$t+2\Delta t$	$t+3\Delta t$	$t+4\Delta t$

FIGURE 6.4A Implied Stock-Price Tree

Given the assumptions (including one in which the authors assume that the price tree is centered around the initial stock price S_t), it readily follows that $S_{t,1} = S_{t+2\Delta t,2} = S_{t+4\Delta t,3} = 100$.

Getting the Implied Stock Prices When $i = 0$

When $i = 0$, first note that $j = 0, 1$. To get $S_{t+\Delta t,2}$ (see Figure 6.4a), one would need to use the equation (6.14a) by noting that $\frac{i+2}{2} = \frac{i+2}{2} = 1$ when

				$P_{t+3\Delta t,4}$
			$P_{t+2\Delta t,3}$	
		$p_{t+\Delta t,2}$		$P_{t+3\Delta t,3}$
	p_t		$P_{t+2\Delta t,2}$	
		$P_{t+\Delta t,1}$		$P_{t+3\Delta t,2}$
			$P_{t+2\Delta t,1}$	
				$P_{t+3\Delta t,1}$
i	0	1	2	3
Time (years)	t	$t+\Delta t$	$t+2\Delta t$	$t+3\Delta t$

FIGURE 6.4B Implied Probability Tree

$i = 0$. Given this observation, it is straightforward to see that $S_{t+\Delta t,2}$ can be obtained by using the middle of equation 6.14a (which is given by case 1A when $j = 1$). Similarly, it can be seen that $S_{t+\Delta t,1}$ can be obtained by using the last of equation 6.14a (which is given by case 1B when $j = 0$).

Case 1A: When $j = 1$

$$S_{t+\Delta t,2} = \frac{S_t\left[e^{\Gamma_0 \Delta t} Ca^{S_t,\Delta t} + \lambda_{0,1} S_t - \sum^U\right]}{-e^{\Gamma_0 \Delta t} Ca^{S_t,\Delta t} + \sum^U + \lambda_{0,1} F^{0,1}} \tag{6.15}$$

where

$$\begin{aligned} S_t &= 100, \Gamma_0 = 0.03, \Delta t = 1, \\ \sum^U &= \sum_{k=2}^{1} \lambda_{0,k}\left(F^{0,k} - S_{t,k}\right) = 0, \\ F^{0,1} &= S_t e^{0.03(1)} = 103.046, \lambda_{0,1} = 1 \text{ and} \\ Ca^{S_t,\Delta t} &= C_{S_t,S_t,t,t+\Delta t,0.03,0,\sigma_{S_t,S_t},Spot}(van) \end{aligned}$$

Since $\sigma_{S_t,S_t} = 0.1$, one can value $C_{100,100,0,1,0.03,0,0.1,Spot}(van)$ using the 1-step binomial tree to obtain a value of 6.40.[9]

Making the appropriate substitutions in equation (6.15) yield $S_{t+\Delta t,2} =$ 110.52.

Case 1B: When $j = 0$

$$S_{t+\Delta t,1} = \frac{S_{t+\Delta t,2}\left[e^{\Gamma_0 \Delta t} Pu^{S_{t,1},\Delta t} - \sum^D\right] + \lambda_{0,1} S_{t,1}(F^{0,1} - S_{t+\Delta t,2})}{e^{\Gamma_0 \Delta t} Pu^{S_{t,1},\Delta t} - \sum^D + \lambda_{0,1}(F^{0,1} - S_{t+\Delta t,2})} \tag{6.16}$$

where

$$\begin{aligned} S_{t+\Delta t,2} &= 110.52, \Gamma_0 = 0.03, \Delta t = 1. \\ \sum^D &= \sum_{k=1}^{-1} \lambda_{0,k+1}(S_{t,k+1} - F^{0,k+1}) = 0 \\ F^{0,1} &= 103.046, \lambda_{0,1} = 1. \\ Pu^{S_{t,1},\Delta t} &= P_{S_t,S_t,t,t+\Delta t,0.03,0,\sigma_{S_t,S_t},Spot}(van). \end{aligned}$$

---

[9]Using equations (3.14a) to (3.14c) for the inputs given, it can be shown that $u = e^{0.1\sqrt{1}} = 1.1052$, $d = \frac{1}{u} = 0.9048$, $p = \frac{e^{0.03(1)} - d}{u-d} = 0.6270$, and $C_{100,100,0,1,0.03,0,0.1,Spot}(van) = e^{-0.03(1)}\{[p * max(100u - 100, 0)] + [(1 - p) * \max(100d - 100, 0)]\}$ which simplifies to 6.40.

					$S_{t+4\Delta t,5}$
				$S_{t+3\Delta t,4}$	
			$S_{t+2\Delta t,3}$		$S_{t+4\Delta t,4}$
		110.52		$S_{t+3\Delta t,3}$	
	100		100		100
		90.48		$S_{t+3\Delta t,2}$	
			$S_{t+2\Delta t,1}$		$S_{t+4\Delta t,2}$
				$S_{t+3\Delta t,1}$	
					$S_{t+4\Delta t,1}$
i	0	1	2	3	4
Time (years)	*t*	*t*+Δ*t*	*t*+2Δ*t*	*t*+3Δ*t*	*t*+4Δ*t*

FIGURE 6.5A Implied Stock Price Tree with One Year of Information

As before, since $\sigma_{S_t,S_t} = 0.1$, one can value $P_{100,100,0,1,0.03,0,0.1,Spot}(van)$ using the one-step binomial tree to obtain a value of 3.44.[10]

Making the appropriate substitutions into equation (6.16) yields $S_{t+\Delta t,1} = 90.48$.

Getting the Implied Probabilities When $i = 0$

To get the value of $p_t = p_{t,1}$ (see Figure 6.4b), one can use equation (6.14b) and obtain the expression

$$p_{t,1} = \frac{F^{0,1} - S_{t+\Delta t,1}}{S_{t+\Delta t,2} - S_{t+\Delta t,1}}$$

Since $F^{0,1} = S_t e^{0.03(1)} = 103.046$, $S_{t+\Delta t,1} = 90.48$ (from case 1B) and $S_{t+\Delta t,2} = 110.52$ (from case 1A), it readily follows that $p_{t,1} = 0.6270$.

Putting all these values together, one can arrive at Figures (6.5a) and (6.5b)—which are updates of Figures (6.4a) and (6.4b).

Getting the Implied Stock Prices When $i = 1$

When $i = 1$, first note that $j = 0, 1, 2$ from equation (6.14a). From Figure 6.5a, it can be seen that since $S_{t+2\Delta t,2}$ is known, one only needs to find $S_{t+2\Delta t,1}$ and $S_{t+2\Delta t,3}$. To get $S_{t+2\Delta t,3}$, one would need to use the equation

---

[10]Using equations (3.14a) to (3.14c), for the inputs given, it can be shown that $u = e^{0.1\sqrt{1}} = 1.1052$, $d = \frac{1}{u} = 0.9048$, $p = \frac{e^{0.03(1)} - d}{u-d} = 0.6270$, and $P_{100,100,0,1,0.03,0,0.1,Spot}(van) = e^{-0.03(1)}\{[p*max(-100u + 100, 0)] + [(1-p)*\max(-100d + 100, 0)]\}$ which simplifies to 3.44.

				$P_{t+3\Delta t,4}$
			$P_{t+2\Delta t,3}$	
		$p_{t+\Delta t,2}$		$P_{t+3\Delta t,3}$
	0.6270		$P_{t+2\Delta t,2}$	
		$P_{t+\Delta t,1}$		$P_{t+3\Delta t,2}$
			$P_{t+2\Delta t,1}$	
				$P_{t+3\Delta t,1}$
i	0	1	2	3
Time (years)	*t*	$t+\Delta t$	$t+2\Delta t$	$t+3\Delta t$

FIGURE 6.5B Implied Probability Tree with One Year of Information

(6.14a) by noting that $\frac{i+2}{2} = 1.5$ (and hence $\left\lfloor \frac{i+2}{2} \right\rfloor = 1$). Given this observation, it is straightforward to see that $S_{t+2\Delta t,3}$ can be obtained by using the top of equation 6.14a (which is given by case 2A when $j = 2$). Similarly, it can be seen that $S_{t+2\Delta t,1}$ can be obtained by using the last of equation 6.14a (which is given by case 2B when $j = 0$).

Case 2A: When $j = 2$

$$S_{t+2\Delta t,3} = \frac{S_{t+2\Delta t,2}\left[e^{\Gamma_1 \Delta t} Ca^{S_{t+\Delta t,2},2\Delta t} - \sum^U\right] - \lambda_{1,2} S_{t+\Delta t,2}(F^{1,2} - S_{t+2\Delta t,2})}{e^{\Gamma_1 \Delta t} Ca^{S_{t+\Delta t,2},2\Delta t} - \sum^U - \lambda_{1,2}(F^{1,2} - S_{t+2\Delta t,2})} \tag{6.17}$$

where

$$\begin{aligned}
S_{t+2\Delta t,2} &= 100, \Gamma_1 = 0.03, \Delta t = 1. \\
F^{1,2} &= S_{t+\Delta t,2} e^{0.03(1)} = 113.883, \ \lambda_{1,2} = 0.6085.^{11} \\
\sum^U &= \sum_{k=3}^{2} \lambda_{1,k}(F^{1,k} - S_{t+\Delta t,k}) = 0. \\
Ca^{S_{t+\Delta t,2},2\Delta t} &= C_{S_t, S_{t+\Delta t,2}, t, t+2\Delta t, 0.03, 0, \sigma_{S_t, S_{t+2\Delta t,2}}, Spot}(van).
\end{aligned}$$

[11]This is the Arrow-Debreu value, $\lambda_{1,2}$, corresponding to the stock price node $S_{t+\Delta t,2}$. This value can be obtained by calculating the probability of present value of \$1 obtained in this node which is $p * e^{-0.03*1} * \$1$, where p the probability of an upward move from a stock price level of S_t to a level of $S_{t+\Delta t,2}$ that is consistent to the implied volatility and is given by the expression in equation (6.14b) where $p_{t,1} = 0.6270$. As a consequence $\lambda_{1,2} = p_{t,1} e^{-0.03(1)} = 0.6085$.

Since $\sigma_{S_t,S_{t+2\Delta t,2}} = 0.0947$[12], one can value $C_{100,110.52,0,2,0.03,0,0.0947,Spot}(van)$ using the 2-step binomial tree to obtain a value of 3.951.[13]

Making the appropriate substitution in equation (6.17) yields $S_{t+2\Delta t,3} = 120.30$.

Case 2B: When $j = 0$

$$S_{t+2\Delta t,1} = \frac{S_{t+2\Delta t,2}\left[e^{\Gamma_1 \Delta t} Pu^{S_{t+\Delta t,1},2\Delta t} - \sum^D\right] + \lambda_{1,1} S_{t+\Delta t,1}(F^{1,1} - S_{t+2\Delta t,2})}{e^{\Gamma_1 \Delta t} Pu^{S_{t+\Delta t,1},2\Delta t} - \sum^D + \lambda_{1,1}(F^{1,1} - S_{t+2\Delta t,2})} \tag{6.18}$$

where

$$\begin{aligned} S_{t+2\Delta t,2} &= 100, \Gamma_1 = 0.03, \Delta t = 1. \\ \sum^D &= \sum_{k=1}^{-1} \lambda_{1,k+1}(S_{t+\Delta t,k+1} - F^{1,k+1}) = 0,\ F^{1,1} = 103.046. \\ \lambda_{1,1} &= 1. \\ Pu^{S_{t+\Delta t,1},\Delta t} &= P_{S_t,S_{t+\Delta t,1},t,t+2\Delta t,0.03,0,\sigma_{S_t,S_{t+\Delta t,1}},Spot}(van). \end{aligned}$$

As before, since $\sigma_{S_t,S_{t+\Delta t,1}} = 0.1047$[14], one can value $P_{100,90.48,0,1,0.03,0,0.1047,Spot}(van)$ using the 2-step binomial tree to obtain a value of 1.283.[15]

Making the appropriate substitutions in equation (6.18) yield $S_{t+2\Delta t,1} = 79.28$.

---

[12]Since the implied volatility when the stock prices are at \$110 and \$115 are 9.5 percent and 9 percent respectively, using linear interpolation, it can be shown the implied volatility would be 9.47 percent when the stock price is \$ 110.52.

[13]Using equations (3.14a) to (3.14c), for the inputs given, it can be shown that $u = e^{0.0947\sqrt{1}} = 1.0993$, $d = \frac{1}{u} = 0.9096$, $p = \frac{e^{0.03(1)} - d}{u-d} = 0.6368$, and $C_{100,110.52,0,2,0.03,0,0.0947,Spot}(van) = e^{-0.03(2)}[p^2 * max(100u^2 - 110.52, 0)]$, which simplifies to 3.95.

[14]Since the implied volatility when the stock prices are at \$110 and \$90 are 10 percent and 10.5 percent respectively, using linear interpolation, it can be shown the implied volatility would be 10.47 percent when the stock price is \$90.48.

[15]Using equations (3.14a) to (3.14c), for the inputs given, it can be shown that $u = e^{0.0947\sqrt{1}} = 1.0993$, $d = \frac{1}{u} = 0.9096$, $p = \frac{e^{0.03(1)} - d}{u-d} = 0.6368$, and $P_{100,110.52,0,2,0.03,0,0.0947,Spot}(van) = e^{-0.03(2)}[(1-p)^2 * max(-100d^2 + 110.52, 0)]$, which simplifies to 1.283.

Getting the Implied Probabilities When $i = 1$

To get the values of $p_{t+\Delta t,1}$ and $p_{t+\Delta t,2}$ (see Figure 6.5b), one can use equation (6.5b) and obtain the expressions

$$p_{t+\Delta t,1} = \frac{F^{1,1} - S_{t+2\Delta t,1}}{S_{t+2\Delta t,2} - S_{t+2\Delta t,1}}$$

$$p_{t+\Delta t,2} = \frac{F^{1,2} - S_{t+2\Delta t,2}}{S_{t+2\Delta t,3} - S_{t+2\Delta t,2}}$$

Since $F^{1,1} = S_{t+\Delta t,1}e^{0.03(1)} = 93.24$, $F^{1,2} = S_{t+\Delta t,2}e^{0.03(1)} = 113.89$, $S_{t+2\Delta t,1} = 79.28$ (from case 2B), $S_{t+2\Delta t,2} = 100$ and $S_{t+2\Delta t,3} = 120.30$ (from case 2A), it readily follows that $p_{t+\Delta t,1} = 0.6736$ and $p_{t+\Delta t,2} = 0.6838$.

Putting all these values together, one arrives at Figure 6.6a and Figure 6.6b—an update of Figure 6.5a and Figure 6.5b.

One can go through similar steps and arrive at the implied price tree and an implied probability tree given in the Derman and Kani paper (reproduced in Figures 6.7a and 6.7b).

With the implied stock-price trees and the corresponding probabilities, it is straightforward for one to use the methodology outlined in Chapters 3 and 5 to value path-dependent options. Furthermore, although the

					$S_{t+4\Delta t,5}$
				$S_{t+3\Delta t,4}$	
			120.30		$S_{t+4\Delta t,4}$
		110.52		$S_{t+3\Delta t,3}$	
	100		100		100
		90.48		$S_{t+3\Delta t,2}$	
			79.29		$S_{t+4\Delta t,2}$
				$S_{t+3\Delta t,1}$	
					$S_{t+4\Delta t,1}$
i	0	1	2	3	4
Time (years)	t	$t+\Delta t$	$t+2\Delta t$	$t+3\Delta t$	$t+4\Delta t$

FIGURE 6.6A Implied Stock-Price Tree with Two Years of Information

				$P_{t+3\Delta t,4}$
			$P_{t+2\Delta t,3}$	
		0.6840		$P_{t+3\Delta t,3}$
	0.6270		$P_{t+2\Delta t,2}$	
		0.6735		$P_{t+3\Delta t,2}$
			$P_{t+2\Delta t,1}$	
				$P_{t+3\Delta t,1}$
i	0	1	2	3
Time (years)	*t*	$t+\Delta t$	$t+2\Delta t$	$t+3\Delta t$

FIGURE 6.6B Implied Probability Tree with Two Years of Information

					139.78
				130.08	
			120.30		120.51
		110.52		110.57	
	100		100		100
		90.48		90.44	
			79.29		79.43
				73.91	
					59.02
i	0	1	2	3	4
Time (years)	*t*	$t+\Delta t$	$t+2\Delta t$	$t+3\Delta t$	$t+4\Delta t$

FIGURE 6.7A Implied Stock-Price Tree with Four Years of Information

				0.7000
			0.6820	
		0.6840		0.6780
	0.6270		0.6240	
		0.6735		0.6660
			0.5410	
				0.0.711
i	0	1	2	3
Time (years)	*t*	$t+\Delta t$	$t+2\Delta t$	$t+3\Delta t$

FIGURE 6.7B Implied Probability Tree with Four Years of Information

example discussed the use of a flat term structure of zero risk-free and dividend rates, the above methodology can be easily extended to incorporate a nonflat, deterministic zero risk-free and dividend rate term structure.

As an alternative to the above approach, one can also use stochastic volatility models (in which the volatility itself is a random variable). Two widely used stochastic volatility models are Heston (1993) and Hagan et al. (2002) (which is sometimes better known as the SABR model—Stochastic Alpha Beta Rho model). The reader is referred to the excellent treatment of implied volatility surface and stochastic volatility models by Gatheral (2006) for more details.

CALIBRATION OF INTEREST RATE OPTION MODEL PARAMETERS

In the previous section, I discussed how and why practitioners use market prices to imply the volatility, risk-free, and dividend inputs for the Black-Scholes model. Although it was easy to incorporate information from a term structure of implied spot-volatility rates to value early exercise and path dependent options, to do so using a surface of implied spot-volatility rates, trying to value path-dependent options was a challenge. Regardless, one was still able to find a way to solve the problem using the concept of local volatilities—while trying to keep the stochastic component contained to stock-price movements. Although I concluded the previous section by commenting on the use of stochastic volatility models, throughout my discussion I have primarily kept to the use of a lognormal pdf for price-rate movements. While this is, in general, true for the valuation of options on equities and currencies, practitioners use a plethora of models when valuing interest rate options, ranging from equilibrium models to market-based models (models that describe the movements of the entire term structure of interest rates). The reader is referred to Hull (2012) for an overview of some of the models.

In using models that are all encompassing (that describe all term structure movements), the practitioner needs to balance between the ability to reproduce liquid market prices and the need to value path-dependent options. The reason for this stems from the fact that many of these models have only a finite number of parameters that need to be inferred vis-à-vis the abundance of available market information. As a consequence, the practitioner is faced with the problem of a possible overfill, simply because after fitting, the user is not able to reproduce *all* the market prices that were used to estimate or infer the parameters of this model. In this section, I will present one example in the context of the widely used Hull-White one-factor model that is used to model short interest rates (e.g., overnight rate).

Unlike equation (3.5) where the underlying index was assumed to follow the diffusion process, the Hull-White one-factor model for the short rates is assumed to follow the diffusion process

$$dr = (\theta(t) - ar)dt + \sigma dz \tag{6.19}$$

where

r is the annualized continuously compounded short rate.
$\theta(t)$ is a time-related function that is chosen so as to ensure that the model fits the term structure.
a is the mean reversion rate associated with the short rates.
σ is the annualized standard deviation of the short rate.
dz is the random variable drawn from a standard normal probability density function.
dr is the small change in the short rate over a small time interval dt.

See Hull (2012) for further details of this model and the use of this model to value options.

Using the short-rate process assumption in equation (6.19), it can be shown that the formulae to price European-style call and put options on zero coupon bonds are given by the equations (6.20a) and (6.20b) respectively.

$$LP(t,s)\,N(h) - KP(t,T)\,N(h - \sigma_p) \tag{6.20a}$$

$$-LP(t,s)\,N(-h) + KP(t,T)\,N(-h + \sigma_p) \tag{6.20b}$$

where

K is the strike price of the option.
L is the face value of the zero coupon bond.
$T - t$ is the option life.
$s - t$ is the zero coupon bond life (where $s > T$).
$P(t,s)$ is the s-t-year discount factor using the yield curve at time t.
$P(0,T)$ is the T-year discount factor using the yield curve at time

$$\sigma_p = \frac{\sigma}{a}\left[1 - e^{-a(s-T)}\right]\sqrt{\frac{1 - e^{-2a(T-t)}}{2a}}$$

$$h = \frac{1}{\sigma_p}\ln\left[\frac{LP(t,s)}{KP(t,T)}\right] + \frac{\sigma_p}{2}.$$

Table 6.7 shows the implementation of equations (6.20a) and (6.20b) on a spreadsheet.

TABLE 6.7 Valuing Options on Zero Coupon Bonds

	A	B	C
1	Mean Reversion Rate (*a*)	5.000%	
2	Short Rate Volatility (sigma)	1.000%	
3	Bond Strike Price	$55.00	
4	Bond Face Value	$100.00	
5	Current Time (*t*)	0	
6	Bond Maturity Time (*T*)	3	
7	Bond Maturity (*s*)	9	
8	*T*-Year Discount Factor (*P*(*0*,*T*))	0.8554373	
9	*s*-year Discount Factor (*P*(*0*,*s*))	0.4693248	
10	sigma(*p*)	0.08345199	=(B2*(1-EXP(-B1*(B7-B6)))*SQRT((1-EXP(-2*B1*(B6-B5)))/(2*B1)))/B1
11	h	0.01199952	=((LN((B4*B9)/(B3*B8)))/B10)+(0.5*B10)
12	Call Prem	1.50639231	=(B4*B9*NORMSDIST(B11))-(B3*B8*NORMSDIST(B11-B10))
13	Put Prem	1.62296381	=(-B4*B9*NORMSDIST(-B11))+(B3*B8*NORMSDIST(-B11+B10))

Now that I have illustrated how the Hull-White one-factor model can be applied to value options on zero coupon bonds, I will show how a practitioner can imply the parameters of the model using market information.

In the Black-Scholes framework, I discussed a practitioner's dilemma in trying to estimate values of $r_{t,T}$, $q_{t,T}$, and $\sigma_{t,T}$. Similarly, as can be seen from the description of the Hull-White one-factor model in equation (6.8), there are essentially three unknowns associated with the model. These are

a: The mean reversion rate which the short rate reverts back to its long-term mean $\theta(t)$ (identifying one of the characteristics in the interest rate market in that interest rates cannot keep increasing or decreasing indefinitely).

σ: The standard deviation associated with the short rates (which is different from the definition of the volatility in the Black-Scholes framework).

$\theta(t)$: The long-term, time-dependent mean rate.

While $\theta(t)$ is calibrated to be consistent with the zero curve (i.e., the term structure of zero rates),[16] the other two parameters of the Hull-White model are calibrated using option prices on the underlying bonds/rates. Furthermore, as can be seen by the option-pricing formulae on zero coupon bonds given in this section, unlike the explicit presence of a and σ, the only way values of $\theta(t)$ enter the formulae is through the presence of discount factors $P(0,T)$ and $P(0,s)$. As a consequence, to illustrate the computation of the implied values of a and σ from a list of option premiums, I will assume the discount factors take the form in Table 6.8 and the option prices for various maturities in Table 6.9.

Given the market information in Tables 6.8 and 6.9, to find the best estimates for both a and σ using the seven option premiums, I have used equation (6.20b) to compute the premiums for each of the seven options (where $P_{i,calc}$ represents the calculated premium for put option i for $i = 1,2,3,\ldots,7$). Letting $P_{i,obs}$ represent the observed market premium for put option i and defining the error function

$$f(a,\sigma) = \sum_{i=1}^{7} \left(\frac{P_{i,calc} - P_{i,obs}}{P_{i,obs}} \right)^2$$

[16]Like the bootstrapping of the yield curve discussed in Chapter 2 or the calculation of implied volatility that was discussed earlier in this chapter, $\theta(t)$ can be uniquely implied from the zero risk-free rate curve.

TABLE 6.8 Curve of Discount Factors

Time	Discount Factors
0	1.00000
1	0.97045
1.5	0.95238
2	0.92302
2.5	0.89131
3	0.85544
3.5	0.81621
4	0.78650
4.5	0.64317
5	0.59139
5.5	0.54859
6	0.50645
6.5	0.46932
7	0.42908
7.5	0.38644

one would be interested in finding the values of a and σ that minimize the value of the function $f(a, \sigma)$.

From Table 6.10, it can be seen that $f(a, \sigma)$ is minimized when $a =$ 10 percent and $\sigma = 1.6$ percent. It should be pointed out that sometimes these values can be quite unstable (i.e., there could be several local minimums) and the global minimum would be achieved at values of a and σ that may be unrealistic or impractical. As a consequence, it is imperative for the user to ensure common sense checks are applied to whatever combinations of a and σ are produced as optimal values. Furthermore, when the number of market-data points increases, it is important for the reader to note

TABLE 6.9 Option Premiums by Term

	Option Life (Yrs)	Bond Life (Yrs)	Put Option Premium
1	1	6	0.578
2	1.5	6.5	2.423
3	2	7	4.150
4	2.5	7.5	5.958
5	3	8	7.165
6	3.5	8.5	8.609
7	4	9	10.929

TABLE 6.10 Relative Errors from Fitting

		a								
		8.0%	8.5%	9.0%	9.5%	10.0%	10.5%	11.0%	11.5%	12.0%
sigma	1.00%	52.88%	55.78%	58.65%	61.48%	64.27%	67.00%	69.68%	72.31%	74.88%
	1.10%	35.96%	38.87%	41.78%	44.68%	47.58%	50.45%	53.30%	56.13%	58.91%
	1.20%	21.31%	23.95%	26.66%	29.41%	32.19%	35.00%	37.83%	40.67%	43.50%
	1.30%	9.90%	12.01%	14.24%	16.58%	19.02%	21.54%	24.13%	26.77%	29.46%
	1.40%	2.57%	3.85%	5.33%	7.01%	8.84%	10.83%	12.94%	15.17%	17.50%
	1.50%	0.01%	0.17%	0.62%	1.34%	2.32%	3.52%	4.93%	6.51%	8.27%
	1.60%	2.80%	1.53%	0.66%	0.16%	0.01%	0.17%	0.62%	1.34%	2.29%
	1.70%	11.43%	8.42%	5.94%	3.95%	2.40%	1.26%	0.51%	0.10%	0.03%
	1.80%	26.29%	21.25%	16.87%	13.09%	9.87%	7.18%	4.97%	3.21%	1.87%
	1.90%	47.73%	40.36%	33.78%	27.93%	22.78%	18.26%	14.35%	10.99%	8.16%
	2.00%	76.04%	66.03%	56.96%	48.77%	41.40%	34.81%	28.94%	23.74%	19.18%

that despite finding the optimal values of a and σ (which minimize the sum of squareds of the relative error), it would not be possible for the user to reproduce the market prices—thereby not achieving one of the objectives of this exercise. Hence, unlike the Black-Scholes model where the parameters in the model can be uniquely inferred from market information, practitioners using more powerful models are faced with the problem of not being able to uniquely infer model parameters (hence the inability to reproduce market prices accurately). As a consequence, it should not be a surprise to see traders keep a variety of models in their arsenal and use what, in their judgment, seems to be best suited for their objectives.

STATISTICAL ESTIMATION

In earlier sections, I discussed the use of calibration to estimate model parameters from market information. As mentioned, it is not uncommon for practitioners to resort to the use of statistical methods to estimate these model parameters. Reasons why a practitioner would want to go through this process include:

- Estimating the parameters using historical information to understand the estimated parameter values better and then make a decision if the currently traded prices (implied model parameters) are cheaper than what they have been historically.
- Calibration of model parameters makes good sense only if the prices that are used for calibration are from a liquidly traded market. If these prices change only sporadically (or if the trading volume is very thin) then calibrating to such prices would be pointless, as it would not give a true representation of the market sentiments on true value of the derivative. In such an instance, supplementing the calibration method with the estimation of these parameters using historical information would provide more insights to what is going on in the marketplace.
- Derivative prices are not going to always be readily available. In such an event, trying to estimate what the value of an embedded option is or what value one would assign to a customized derivative (which has no active market) can only be made feasible if one is able to estimate these parameters historically.

Given the above backdrop, it would be of interest to look at two methods one can use to calculate historical parameter values.

Using Historical Implied Volatilities

In the earlier sections of this chapter I discussed the extraction of zero risk-free/dividend rates and spot-volatility rates from liquidly traded financial instruments. In practice, for liquidly traded options (e.g., options on the S&P index) it is quite common to find historical implied values that can be analyzed to better understand the behavior of current implied values during a defined period (e.g., trading hours in a day). As a consequence, one can better estimate the relative cheapness associated with the implied value of a currently traded option vis-à-vis the realized values or even where the implied values of similar instruments have been trading during the last six months and so on.

To understand this better, I will use historical implied volatility values to illustrate how such an analysis can be done.

Figure 6.8 shows the historical daily closing implied volatility values of a one-year at-the-money (ATM) option and how it fluctuates over time. To better understand the behavior of this implied volatility and make practical trading decisions, one can statistically analyze the data supporting Figure 6.9. One simple analysis is to compute the cumulative probabilities associated with the observations.

From Figure 6.9, it can be seen that:

- 100 percent of the observations lie in the interval [10.18%, 23.21%].
- 95 percent of the observations lie in the interval [10.95%, 20.34%].
- 90 percent of the observations lie in the interval [11.33%, 19.95%].
- The average value of the 273 observations is 14.98 percent.

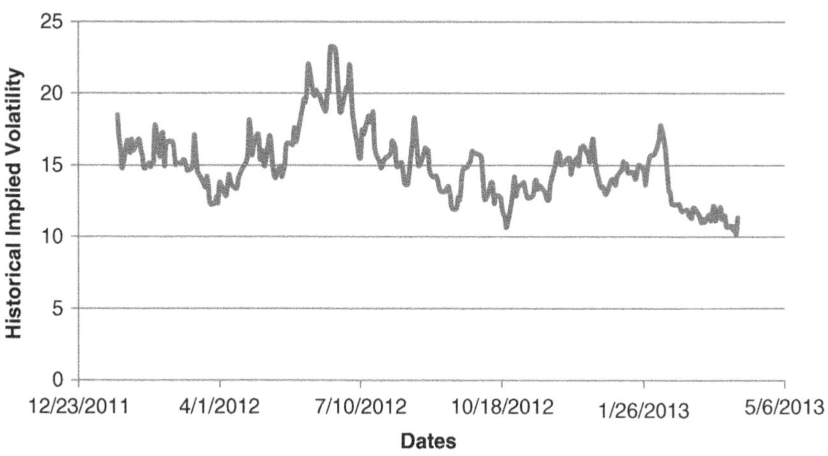

FIGURE 6.8 Historical One-Year ATM Option Volatilities

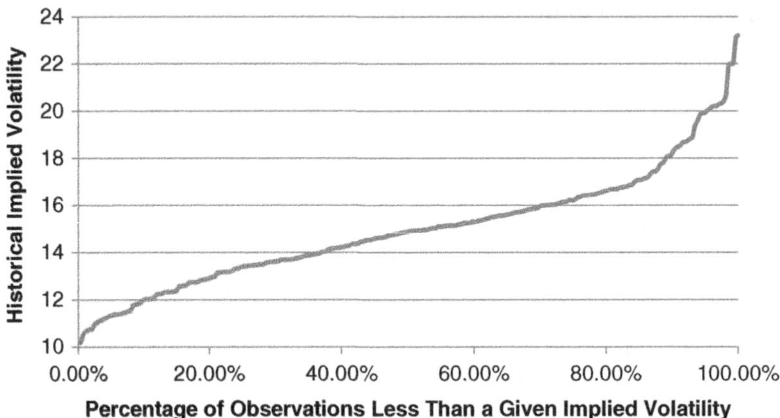

FIGURE 6.9 Cumulative Probabilities of One-Year ATM Implied Volatilities

Depending on what the current implied volatility level is, a trader can ask the question: How relatively cheap or expensive is the current implied volatility vis-à-vis where it used to trade historically? Using this type of analysis, the trader can monitor charts of a similar constant maturity option (taking into consideration the time decay) daily to decide if that trade should be unwound.

While the above illustrates a simple example of the kind of analysis that is used to help with decision making associated with the assessment of the relative cheapness of an actively trading 1-year ATM implied volatility, one can deploy rigorous statistical approaches (e.g., generalized autoregressive conditional heteroskedasticity (GARCH), exponential generalized autoregressive conditional heteroskedasticity (EGARCH) models) to understand the impact of seasons, trading volumes, earnings, and more on the implied volatility of the option to fine-tune the decisions.

Using Historical Underlying Values

In the previous section I discussed how, due to the high liquidity of actively traded options, historical implied volatilities are readily available for analysis. In such an instance, one could perform the analysis on historical implied volatility values to help decide the relative cheapness of current implied volatility vis-à-vis implied volatilities experienced during history. While it is important for one to understand this type of relative value analysis, the data (even if readily available) does not readily lend itself to the estimation of the volatility that the option owner is going to be realizing during the life of the option.

The question of estimating the realized volatility (that the option holder is going to experience during the life of the option) can be actually done using historical data of the underlying asset. More precisely, to do this, one has to first recall that the underlying assumption regarding the movements in stock price is that future prices are lognormally distributed; that is $\ln S_T$ is normally distributed with a mean of $\ln S_t + \left(r_{t,T} - q_{t,T} - \frac{1}{2}\sigma^2_{t,T}\right)(T - t)$, and, variance of $\sigma^2_{t,T}(T-t)$ or, equivalently, $\frac{1}{\sqrt{T-t}}\ln(\frac{S_T}{S_t})$ is normally distributed with a mean of $\left(r_{t,T} - q_{t,T} - \frac{1}{2}\sigma^2_{t,T}\right)\sqrt{T-t}$, and, variance of $\sigma^2_{t,T}$.

Since equation (3.5) is equivalent to saying that continuously compounded daily returns are normally distributed with a mean of zero[17] (i.e., $(r_{t,T} - q_{t,T} - \frac{1}{2}\sigma^2_{t,T})\sqrt{T-t} \sim 0$) and variance of $\sigma^2_{t,T}$, it readily follows that the volatility of the underlying stock, $\sigma_{t,T}$, can be obtained by computing the standard deviation of the annualized continuously compounded (i.e., natural logarithm) of the returns. Succinctly put, this standard deviation can be computed using the expression $\sqrt{\frac{1}{n}\sum_{i=1}^{n} u_i^2}$, where u_i represents the ith annualized continuously compounded daily return.[18] This result is obtained using a statistical method called method of moments. Another method of parameter estimation, called maximum likelihood estimate, also produces a similar result for the average volatility—except that the denominator used in the computation of the standard deviation is $n - 1$.[19]

Figure 6.10 shows the historical path of the index.

Table 6.11 shows the sample calculations related to the historical volatility.

---

[17]This assumption has very little impact on the volatility estimation since over a small time interval the quantity $(r_{t,T} - q_{t,T} - \frac{1}{2}\sigma^2_{t,T})\sqrt{T-t}$ would be very small.

[18]The formula to calculate standard deviation (as typically seen in standard statistics textbooks) is of the form $\sqrt{\frac{1}{n}\sum_{i=1}^{n} u_i^2 - (\frac{1}{n}\sum_{i=1}^{n} u_i)^2}$. Since mean of this population is assumed to be 0, $\frac{1}{n}\sum_{i=1}^{n} u_i = 0$. From this, the result for the standard deviation readily follows.

[19]The formula for σ_n obtained using a maximum likelihood estimating method takes the form $\sqrt{\frac{1}{n-1}\sum_{i=1}^{n} u_i^2 - (\frac{1}{n}\sum_{i=1}^{n} u_i)^2}$.

FIGURE 6.10 Historical S&P 500 Index Values

As can be seen in Table 6.11, to arrive at the annualized volatility of 8.4 percent, I had to make a few assumptions, such as:

Number of Days Used to Convert Days into Years In arriving at the 8.4 percent annualized volatility number, I used 365 days (as a day-count convention) to calculate the time (in years) between each data point. Practitioners sometimes also use 250 or 360 days. While using 360 days as a day-count convention only slightly changes the result, using 250 days would yield a volatility change of about 2 percent.

Choice of Return Period In the example discussed, I used daily returns to arrive at the volatility. I could have just as well used a weekly return to arrive

TABLE 6.11 Computation of Daily Historical Volatility

	A	B	C	D
1	Dates	Index Values	Daily Returns	
2	1/17/2012	1289.09		
3	1/18/2012	1293.67	0.067757646	=LN(B3/B2)/(1/SQRT(365))
4	1/19/2012	1308.04	0.211046778	=LN(B4/B3)/(1/SQRT(365))
5	1/20/2012	1314.50	0.094121254	=LN(B5/B4)/(1/SQRT(365))
6	1/21/2012	1315.38	0.012785661	=LN(B6/B5)/(1/SQRT(365))
7	1/22/2012	1316.00	0.009002944	=LN(B7/B6)/(1/SQRT(365))
8	Annualized Volatility		0.084055408	=STDEV(C3:C7)

at a volatility of 10.9 percent or a monthly return to arrive at a volatility of 10.7 percent. The question of what return period one should use in practice is a tricky one, as it is usually a function of how frequently the hedger wants to rebalance the portfolio or positions.

Amount of Data Used In the computation carried out, I used the entire data set to compute the returns. In practice, despite the fact that one may have access to a large historical database, it may not be prudent to use the entire dataset simply because going back too much into history may not be reflective of the current financial markets/economic environment, and using too little may not be enough to give a good estimate for what the reality could be. Hence, herein lie the balance and the art of deciding how much data to use and which part of an historical period should be considered. Another related question is how (if at all) should the life of the option matter to how much data is used?

Weighting the Observations Throughout the example, by using the formula $\sqrt{\frac{1}{n}\sum_{i=1}^{n} u_i^2}$, I implicitly assumed that the observations used to compute the standard deviation were equally weighted (i.e., weights of $\frac{1}{n}$). In practice, it is common to assume that the more recent historical observations should weigh more than the less recent historical observations. To do this, practitioners assume that the standard deviation is given by the formula $\sqrt{\sum_{i=1}^{n} w_i u_i^2}$ where w_i is the weight attached to u_i (the return i days ago), $\sum_{i=1}^{n} w_i = 1$, and $w_i > w_j \geq 0$ (for $1 \leq i < j \leq n$).[20] A further extension to this weighting scheme is to assume that there is a long-run, average variance with its appropriate weight. As a consequence, the expression for the volatility would take the form

$$\sqrt{w_0 V + \sum_{i=1}^{n} w_i u_i^2}$$

where V and w_0 represent the long-run variance and its respective weight.[21]

It is this thinking that led to the development of different weighting schemes associated with weighting of the historical returns.

[20]In particular, by setting $w_i = (1-\beta)\beta^{i-1}$ and assuming n is large enough, one can arrive at the exponentially weighted moving average (EWMA) model. See Hull (2012).

[21]Known as the ARCH (n) model, this was first introduced by Engle in 1982.

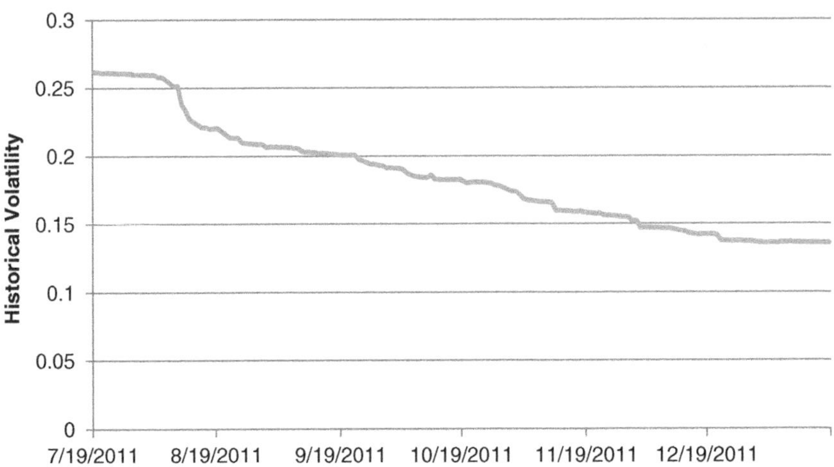

FIGURE 6.11 Rolling Historical Volatilities

Rolling History One criterion in choosing an appropriate estimate for realized volatility is to ensure that the estimate has some noise. While too little noise typically implies too much data, too much noise implies too little data. To understand what the right amount of noise should be, one needs to study how the volatility rolls through time and how much noise should one accept. To do this, one needs to calculate the volatility for a given data set (as discussed earlier) and then recalculate the volatility for a new data set (which comprises a new data point and loses the oldest data point). This is then repeated over the entire data set. In the context of our example, by adding more old data to the original data set, the following illustrates an example of a rolling volatility.

As can be seen from Figure 6.11, the rolling volatility (or volatility of the rolling data) is slowly trending downwards. The consequence of the resulting exhibit is the need to look at a longer historical period to better understand how much of an up-and-down fluctuation this volatility measure was subjected to. Should this be all the historical information that is available (or should further historical information support the same trend as above) then it clearly means that the number of data points for computing volatility needs to be reduced to introduce more noise to the rolling volatility. In running the above analysis, it is imperative to do a reality check to see if the results make intuitive sense—as it is very easy to get caught up in theoretical results that may not make any sense in practice.

REFERENCES

Burden, R., and D. Faires. 2010. *Numerical Analysis*. 7th ed. Belmont, CA: Thomson Brooks/Cole.

Derman, E., and I. Kani. 1994. "Pricing with a Smile." *RISK* 7:18–20.

Dupire, B. 1994. "Riding on a Smile." *RISK* 7:32–39.

Engle, R. 1982. "Autoregressive Conditional Heteroscedasticity with Estimates of the Variance of UK Inflation." *Econometrica* 50:987–1008.

Gatheral, J. 2006. *The Volatility Surface: A Practitioner's Guide*. Hoboken, NJ: Wiley Finance.

Hagan, P., D. Kumar, A. Lesniewski, and D. Woodward. 2002. "Managing Smile Risk." *Wilmott Magazine* (September):84–108.

Heston, S. L. 1993. "A Closed-Form Solution for Options with Stochastic Volatility with Applications to Bond and Currency Options." *The Review of Financial Studies* 6:327–343.

Hull, J. C. 2012. *Options, Futures and Other Derivatives*. 8th ed. Upper Saddle River, NJ: Prentice Hall.

REFERENCES

CHAPTER 7

The Effectiveness of Hedging Strategies

In Chapters 3, 4, and 5, I presented examples of option pricing and showed how one can use models to analyze and value various customized options. In this chapter, I discuss how sellers of these options (or any guarantees for that matter) can analyze the effectiveness and efficiency of a hedging strategy to understand and mitigate the risks arising from the initiation of these option transactions.

Black-Scholes developed the famous option-pricing model in 1973 to value European-style vanilla options on non-dividend paying stocks. One assumption used by the authors to arrive at their final result was that the hedger had the ability to construct a riskless portfolio at the time the option is sold and maintain this riskless portfolio continuously and dynamically throughout the life of the option as market conditions changed and the option life diminishes. Applying Ito's lemma to the resulting diffusion equations in continuous time, the authors were able to arrive at equations (3.4a) and (3.4b). As mentioned in Chapter 3, each of the assumptions used by Black-Scholes has since been violated by many subsequent publications in the spirit of building more realistic models. The assumption tampering, fuelled by the cheapness of fast computing power, has resulted in the use of simulations as a tool to value options and analyze risk-management strategies associated with the sale of these options in discrete time.

Starting with an example of delta hedging the sale of a vanilla call option on nondividend-paying stocks, I go on to discuss delta hedging other vanilla options and the impact of changing the assumptions underlying a delta-hedging program. I conclude the chapter with a discussion on the hedging of a 10-year put option and an analysis of two strategies used to hedge the put option.

DELTA HEDGING

One key assumption used to derive equations (3.4a) and (3.4b) was that the hedger can construct an instantaneously riskless portfolio by buying $\Delta_{S_t,K,t,T,r_{t,T},q_{t,T},\sigma_{t,T},Spot,van\,call}$[1] number of shares for every unit of call option sold at the time of option transaction. By continuously adjusting $\Delta_{S_t,K,t,T,r_{t,T},q_{t,T},\sigma_{t,T},Spot,van\,call}$ as the stock price path changes throughout the life of the option so as to maintain the risklessness of the portfolio under a slew of assumptions, Black-Scholes showed that the hedger would end up with a hedge profit and loss (P&L) of zero regardless of the stock price path realized during this rebalancing process. Known as delta hedging, the consequence of this process is the result that theoretically, a fair premium was charged by the hedger for this option.

As in Chapter 5, I will assume that the stock price process follows equation (3.5). In such an instance, as was already discussed, the vanilla European-style options can be priced using equations (3.7a) and (3.7b).

$$C_{S_t,K,t,T,r_{t,T},q_{t,T},\sigma_{t,T},Spot}(van) = S_t e^{-q_{t,T}(T-t)} N\left(d^1_{S_t,K,t,T,r_{t,T},q_{t,T},\sigma_{t,T}}\right) - K e^{-r_{t,T}(T-t)} N\left(d^2_{S_t,K,t,T,r_{t,T},q_{t,T},\sigma_{t,T}}\right) \quad (3.7a)$$

$$P_{S_t,K,t,T,r_{t,T},q_{t,T},\sigma_{t,T},Spot}(van) = -S_t e^{-q_{t,T}(T-t)} N\left(-d^1_{S_t,K,t,T,r_{t,T},q_{t,T},\sigma_{t,T}}\right) + K e^{-r_{t,T}(T-t)} N\left(-d^2_{S_t,K,t,T,r_{t,T},q_{t,T},\sigma_{t,T}}\right) \quad (3.7b)$$

where

$$d^1_{S_t,K,t,T,r_{t,T},q_{t,T},\sigma_{t,T}} = \frac{\ln(S_t/K) + \left(r_{t,T} - q_{t,T} + \frac{1}{2}\sigma^2_{t,T}\right)(T-t)}{\sigma_{t,T}\sqrt{T-t}}$$

$$d^2_{S_t,K,t,T,r_{t,T},q_{t,T},\sigma_{t,T}} = \frac{\ln(S_t/K) + \left(r_{t,T} - q_{t,T} - \frac{1}{2}\sigma^2_{t,T}\right)(T-t)}{\sigma_{t,T}\sqrt{T-t}}$$

[1] Known as the call option delta, this can be obtained by calculating the sensitivity of the call option premium to a change in the underlying stock price (i.e., $\frac{\partial C_{S_t,K,t,T,r_{t,T},q_{t,T},\sigma_{t,T},Spot,van\,call}}{\partial S_t}$).

In the context of my discussion, since the hedger of a call (put) would need to hold $\Delta_{S_t,K,t,T,r_{t,T},q_{t,T},\sigma_{t,T},Spot,van\,call}$ ($\Delta_{S_t,K,t,T,r_{t,T},q_{t,T},\sigma_{t,T},Spot,van\,put}$) shares for every unit of option sold, and since $\Delta_{S_t,K,t,T,r_{t,T},q_{t,T},\sigma_{t,T},Spot,van\,call}$ ($\Delta_{S_t,K,t,T,r_{t,T},q_{t,T},\sigma_{t,T},Spot,van\,put}$) represents the sensitivity of the call (put) option price to a change in the underlying stock price, it readily follows from equations (3.7a) and (3.7b) that

$$\Delta_{S_t,K,t,T,r_{t,T},q_{t,T},\sigma_{t,T},Spot,van\,call} = e^{-q_{t,T}(T-t)} N\left(d^1_{S_t,K,t,T,r_{t,T},q_{t,T},\sigma_{t,T}}\right) \tag{7.1}$$

$$\Delta_{S_t,K,t,T,r_{t,T},q_{t,T},\sigma_{t,T},Spot,van\,put} = -e^{-q_{t,T}(T-t)} N\left(-d^1_{S_t,K,t,T,r_{t,T},q_{t,T},\sigma_{t,T}}\right) \tag{7.2}$$

Table 7.1 shows the implementation of Equations (7.1) and (7.2).

From Table 7.1, it can be seen from cells B9 (B10) that if the underlying stock price increases by a dollar, the value of the call (put) option increases (decreases) by \$0.63 (\$0.32).[2] Furthermore, as was seen in Table 3.4, for selling this call (put) option, the seller of the option would have received an approximate premium of \$5.80 (\$2.84).

To understand how delta hedging works, I will first start my discussion on the hedging of the sale of a European-style call option on a nondividend-paying stock. Following this, I will revisit the example in the presence of dividends and then discuss the hedging of the sale of European-style vanilla put options.

---

[2]The reader should observe that by the virtue of equations (7.1) and (7.2), the delta of a vanilla European style call (put) option is bounded in the interval [0,1] ([−1,0])—where 1 (−1) indicates that the call (put) option is finishing in-the-money if the option is expiring or highly likely to finish in-the-money if the option has not already expired.

Additionally, just because $0 \leq |\Delta_{S_t,K,t,T,r_{t,T},q_{t,T},\sigma_{t,T},Spot,van\,call}| \leq 1$ and $0 \leq |\Delta_{S_t,K,t,T,r_{t,T},q_{t,T},\sigma_{t,T},Spot,van\,put}| \leq 1$, not all option deltas have this property. To see this, consider the binary call option premium in equation (5.1a) where I showed that $C_{S_t,K,t,T,r_{t,T},q_{t,T},\sigma_{t,T},Spot}(bin) = e^{-r_{t,T}(T-t)} N(d^2_{S_t,K,t,T,r_{t,T},q_{t,T},\sigma_{t,T}})$. The delta for a binary call, $\Delta_{S_t,K,t,T,r_{t,T},q_{t,T},\sigma_{t,T},Spot,bincall} = \frac{\partial C_{S_t,K,t,T,r_{t,T},q_{t,T},\sigma_{t,T},Spot}(bin)}{\partial S_t}$, can be shown to be $\frac{1}{\sigma_{t,T} S_t \sqrt{2\pi(T-t)}} e^{-r_{t,T}(T-t)} e^{-0.5(d^2_{S_t,K,t,T,r_{t,T},q_{t,T},\sigma_{t,T}})^2}$. As can be seen, this is clearly not restricted to the [0,1] interval.

TABLE 7.1 Deltas for Vanilla European-Style Options

	A	B	C
1	Current Price, S_t ($)	$40.00	
2	Strike Price, K ($)	$40.00	
3	Volatility, σ (%)	20.00%	
4	Risk Free, r (%)	6.00%	
5	Dividend Rate, q (%)	2.00%	
6	Current Time, t (years)	0	
7	Expiry, T (years)	2	
8	d^1	0.424264069	=(LN(B1/B2)+((B4-B5+(0.5*B3*B3))*(B7-B6)))/(B3*SQRT(B7-B6))
9	Delta Call	0.63826528	=EXP(-B5*(B7-B6))*NORMSDIST(B8)
10	Delta Put	–0.32252416	=-EXP(-B5*(B7-B6))*NORMSDIST(-B8)

TABLE 7.2 Premium and Deltas for Vanilla European-Style Call Option on a Nondividend Paying Stock at Contract Inception

	A	B
1	Current Price, S_t ($)	$40.00
2	Strike Price, K ($)	$40.00
3	Volatility, σ (%)	20.00%
4	Risk Free, r (%)	6.00%
5	Dividend Rate, q (%)	0.00%
6	Current Time, t (years)	0
7	Expiry, T (years)	2
8	d^1	0.565685425
9	d^2	0.282842712
10	Delta Call	0.714196178
11	Call Premium	6.879048813

Hedging the Sale of a Vanilla European-Style Call Option on a Nondividend-Paying Stock

Keeping the stock price, risk-free rate, volatility rate, and expiry the same as in Table 6.1 and setting the dividend rate to 0, one can easily arrive at the results shown in Table 7.2.

As can be seen from Table 7.2, if a unit of the option contract stipulates the delivery of 100 shares at an exercise price of $40/share, then for a unit of call option contract sold, the option seller would receive an up front premium of $687 (=$6.87*100). To be instantaneously riskless at the time of the sale, the option holder has to buy[3] 71.4 (=0.714*100) shares. To acquire these shares, the option seller would need $2856 (=$40*71.4). Since the option writer would receive an amount of $687 for selling this option, only an amount of $2169 needs to be borrowed. Assuming that this can be done at a risk-free rate of 6 percent (which is one of the inputs used to obtain the option premium of $687), one can surmise that the option seller would, in addition to selling a unit of option contract, buy 71.4 shares of stock to have a riskless portfolio.

[3]The reason for buying shares as opposed to selling shares comes from the fact that the moment a call is sold, the exposure to the seller of the option is actually $-\Delta_{S_t,K,t,T,r_{t,T},q_{t,T},\sigma_{t,T},Spot,van\,call}$ shares. Since $0 \leq \Delta_{S_t,K,t,T,r_{t,T},q_{t,T},\sigma_{t,T},Spot,van\,call} \leq 1$, to neutralize this (i.e., be riskless), the hedger has to acquire $\Delta_{S_t,K,t,T,r_{t,T},q_{t,T},\sigma_{t,T},Spot,van\,call}$ shares resulting in a net portfolio delta of 0.

TABLE 7.3 Premium and Deltas for Vanilla European-Style Call Option on a Nondividend-Paying Stock Six Months into the Contract

	A	B
1	Current Price, S_t ($)	$45.00
2	Strike Price, K ($)	$40.00
3	Volatility, σ (%)	20.00%
4	Risk Free, r (%)	6.00%
5	Dividend Rate, q (%)	0.00%
6	Current Time, t (years)	0.5
7	Expiry, T (years)	2
8	d^1	0.970745178
9	d^2	0.725796204
10	Delta Call	0.834162406
11	Call Premium	9.533793495

Suppose for the moment that the next rebalancing is done 6 months later when the share price is $45 and both the risk-free and the volatility rates remain unchanged. Table 7.3 shows the impact of these changes in the option premium and delta.

As can be seen from Table 7.3, the delta has now changed from 71.4 to 83.4. The consequence of this is that the option writer now has to buy an additional (83.4 – 71.4) = 12 shares. To do this, the option writer has to borrow another 12*$45 = $540 at the continuously compounded risk-free rate of 6 percent.

Table 7.4 captures the impact of rebalancing once every six months (continuing with the scenario in Table 7.3), until the option expires (assuming both the risk-free and volatility rates are kept constant).

The reader should note that to obtain the value of cell E11 in Table 7.4 (i.e., delta value on option maturity), I had to hard-code a delta value of 1 simply because substituting a value of 0 for $T - t$ would yield a #Div/0 comment as an output for cell C11.[4]

[4]This should not be surprising to the reader, as given the definition for $d^1_{S_t,K,t,T,r_{t,T},q_{t,T},\sigma_{t,T}}$, the denominator would be 0 when $T - t = 0$. Applying L'Hopital's rule, it can be easily shown that as $T - t \to 0$, $d^1_{S_t,K,t,T,r_{t,T},q_{t,T},\sigma_{t,T}} \to \infty$. This readily implies that $N(d^1_{S_t,K,t,T,r_{t,T},q_{t,T},\sigma_{t,T}}) \to 1$ (consistent with what has been hard-coded for delta). Further, should the option finish out-of-the-money, the corresponding delta value would be 0.

TABLE 7.4 Delta Hedging for Vanilla European-Style Call Option on a Nondividend-Paying Stock

	A	B	C	D	E	F	G	H	I	J	K
1	Strike Price, K ($)	$40.00									
2	Volatility, σ (%)	20.00%									
3	Risk Free, r (%)	6.00%									
4	Dividend Rate, q (%)	0.00%									
5	Expiry, T (years)	2									
6	Time	Current Stock Price	d^1	d^2	Delta	Incoming Premium	Cost of Shares	Amt Borrowed	Interest On Amt Borrowed	Cumulative Amt Owing	
7	0	40	0.57	0.28	0.71	687.90	2856.78	2168.88		2168.88	
8	0.5	45	0.97		0.83		539.85	2708.73	66.05	2774.78	
9	1	39	0.27		0.61		−883.08	1891.70	84.50	1976.20	
10	1.5	44	0.96		0.83		980.90	2957.10	60.18	3017.29	
11	2	42			1.00		711.22	3728.50	91.89	3820.39	
12											
13											
14											
15											

=B15*E15*100

=B16*(E16-E15)*100

=L15*(EXP(0.06*0.5)-1)

=I15-H15

=L15+I16-H16

=H16+I16

Table 7.5 illustrates the settlement value associated with the delta-hedging program on option maturity for an option finishing in-the-money.

As can be seen from Table 7.5, the entry in cell J12 refers to the fact that the option has been exercised (as it finished in-the-money). The seller of the option receives a strike price of $40 for each underlying share and would in turn deliver 100 shares to the buyer of the option. The entry in cell J13 refers to the fact that the option seller would have made a profit of about $179 on option maturity should this scenario materialize (funds received from the option exercise less the cumulative amount owing on option maturity just prior to settlement of option).

Table 7.6 shows the illustration associated when the option finishes out-of-the money.

As can be seen in cell J12 of Table 7.6, the option finishing out-of-the-money implies no incoming cash from option exercise. What the hedger is left with is the hedging P&L of $86 (before present valuing).

Since Black-Scholes assumed in their paper that one should arrive at a total hedge profit of 0 whatever the stock-price path realized during the life of the option, it should be rather surprising for the reader to see that the final answers in cell J13 of both Tables 7.5 and 7.6 are not 0. The simple reason for this is that the hedging was not done in continuous time. By doing the hedging over an infinitesimal time interval, one would be able to see a value of 0 in cell J13—regardless the nature of the path. From a practical implementation standpoint, it is difficult to do this in continuous time. As a consequence, one would need to run a daily simulation 5,000 times to arrive at an average value of 0—implying that the theoretical option premium charged for the sale of this option is a fair-value premium if interest rates and volatility rates remain constant.

Hedging the Sale of a Vanilla European-Style Call Option on a Dividend-Paying Stock

To discuss this, I will revisit the example illustrated in Table 7.1 and show how the delta-hedging mechanics carried out in Table 7.7 is affected by a dividend paying stock.

As can be seen in Table 7.7, column J illustrates how dividends play the role of reducing the borrowing costs. Running a daily simulation over 5,000 paths, it can be seen that the final result in cell K13 averages to 0—confirming the theoretical fair value charged for the sale of this option (i.e., premium of $580).

TABLE 7.5 Settlement Associated with a Delta-Hedging Program for Vanilla European-Style Call Option on a Nondividend-Paying Stock (In-The-Money Expiry)

	A	B	C	D	E	F	G	H	I	J	K
1	Strike Price, K ($)	$40.00									
2	Volatility, σ (%)	20.00%									
3	Risk Free, r (%)	6.00%									
4	Dividend Rate, q (%)	0.00%									
5	Expiry, T (years)	2									
6	Time	Current Stock Price	d^1	d^2	Delta	Incoming Premium	Cost of Shares	Amt Borrowed	Interest On Amt Borrowed	Cumulative Amt Owing	
7	0	40	0.57	0.28	0.71	687.90	2856.78	2168.88		2168.88	
8	0.5	45	0.97		0.83		539.85	2708.73	66.05	2774.78	
9	1	39	0.27		0.61		–883.08	1891.70	84.50	1976.20	
10	1.5	44	0.96		0.83		980.90	2957.10	60.18	3017.29	
11	2	42			1.00		711.22	3728.50	91.89	3820.39	
12							Cash from Option Exercise			4000.00	=(40*100)
13							Total Hedge Profit			179.61	=L20-L19
14							PV (Hedging Program)			159.30	=L21*EXP(-0.06*2)
15											

TABLE 7.6 Settlement Associated with a Delta-Hedging Program for Vanilla European-Style Call Option on a Nondividend-Paying Stock (Out-Of-The-Money Expiry)

	A	B	C	D	E	F	G	H	I	J	K
1	Strike Price, K ($)	$40.00									
2	Volatility, σ (%)	20.00%									
3	Risk Free, r (%)	6.00%									
4	Dividend Rate, q (%)	0.00%									
5	Expiry, T (years)	2									
6	Time	Current Stock Price	d^1	d^2	Delta	Incoming Premium	Cost of Shares	Amt Borrowed	Interest On Amt Borrowed	Cumulative Amt Owing	
7	0	40	0.57	0.28	0.71	687.90	2856.78	2168.88		2168.88	
8	0.5	45	0.97		0.83		539.85	2708.73	66.05	2774.78	
9	1	39	0.27		0.61		–883.08	1891.70	84.50	1976.20	
10	1.5	38	–0.08		0.47		–530.31	1445.89	60.18	1506.08	
11	2	35			0.00		–1638.62	–132.54	45.87	–86.67	
12							Cash from Option Exercise			0.00	
13							Total Hedge Profit			86.67	
14							PV (Hedging Program)			76.87	
15											

TABLE 7.7 Settlement Associated with a Delta-Hedging Program for a Vanilla European-Style Call Option on a Dividend-Paying Stock (In-The-Money Expiry)

	A	B	C	D	E	F	G	H	I	J	K	L
1	Strike Price, K ($)	$40.00										
2	Volatility, σ (%)	20.00%									=I8+H8-J8	
3	Risk Free, r (%)	6.00%										
4	Dividend Rate, q (%)	2.00%						=B8*(EXP(B4*0.5)-1)*100*E7				
5	Expiry, T (years)	2										
6	Time	Current Stock Price	d^1	d^2	Delta	Incoming Premium	Cost of Shares	Amt Borrowed	Interest On Amt Borrowed	Dividend	Cumulative Amt Owing	
7	0	40	0.42	0.14	0.64	579.73	2553.06	1973.33			1973.33	
8	0.5	45	0.85		0.78		629.52	2602.85	60.10	28.87	2634.08	
9	1	39	0.17		0.56		–860.28	1773.80	80.22	30.50	1823.51	
10	1.5	44	0.89		0.80		1084.86	2908.37	55.53	24.66	2939.25	
11	2	42			1.00		822.65	3761.90	89.51	33.94	3817.47	
12							Cash from Option Exercise				4000.00	
13							Total Hedge Profit				182.53	
14							PV (Hedging Program)				161.89	
15												

Hedging the Sale of a Vanilla European-Style Put Option on a Dividend-Paying Stock

Hedging the sale of a put option is philosophically similar to that of the call option that was discussed earlier. The only exception is that to have a riskless portfolio, the hedger would now need to short the shares as opposed to buying the shares.[5] Table 7.8 shows an illustration associated with hedging the sale of the put option when the option finishes in-the-money.

As can be seen in Table 7.8, one big difference between Tables 7.7 and 7.8 is the way the terms in columns E and F are computed. Additionally, in cell E11, I hard-coded a value of −1 to reflect the fact that the put option finished in-the-money. In the event that the put option finishes out-of-the-money, this would have a value of 0.

ASSUMPTIONS UNDERLYING DELTA HEDGING

In this section, I review the assumptions used by Black-Scholes to obtain their famous option pricing formulae and explain the implications of violating them. These assumptions can be more succinctly summarized as follow:

Stock Price Process

In modeling stock price movements, Black-Scholes assumed that

$$\frac{dS}{S} = \mu dt + \sigma dz \tag{7.1}$$

where

S is the price of the stock.
μ is the annualized, continuously compounded growth rate.
σ is the annualized volatility of the stock price return.
dz is the random variable drawn from a standard normal probability density function.
dS is the small change in the stock price over a small time interval.
μ and σ are both assumed to be constants.

[5]The implication of this is that in a market where shorting of shares is not allowed, it becomes impossible for one to risk-manage the sale of the put option using delta hedging. In such an instance, the only risk-management strategies available to the hedger are that of taking the risk naked or buying a structurally similar put from another counterparty. As the astute reader will realize, the problem of shorting also exists if the hedger decides to delta-hedge the purchase of a call option.

TABLE 7.8 Settlement Associated with a Delta-Hedging Program for Vanilla European-Style Put Option on a Dividend-Paying Stock (In-The-Money Expiry)

	A	B	C	D	E	F	G	H	I	J	K	L
1	Strike Price, K ($)	$40.00										
2	Volatility, σ (%)	20.00%										
3	Risk Free, r (%)	6.00%										
4	Dividend Rate, q (%)	2.00%										
5	Expiry, T (years)	2										
6	Time	Current Stock Price	d^1	d^2	Delta	Incoming Premium	Cost of Shares	Amt Borrowed	Interest On Amt Borrowed	Dividend	Cumulative Amt Owing	
7	0	40	0.42	0.14	−0.32	284.25	−1,290.10	−1,574.35			−1,574.35	
8	0.5	45	0.85		−0.19		586.06	−988.28	−47.95	−14.59	−1,021.64	
9	1	39	0.17		−0.42		−898.32	−1,919.97	−31.11	−7.54	−1,943.54	
10	1.5	38	−0.15		−0.55		−500.25	−2,443.79	−59.19	−16.14	−2,486.84	
11	2	35			−1.00		−1,560.05	−4,046.89	−75.74	−19.50	−4,103.13	
12							Cash from Option Exercise				−4,000.00	
13							Total Hedge Profit				103.13	
14							PV (Hedging Program)				91.47	
15												

As mentioned previously, the implication of this assumption is that $\ln S_T$ is normally distributed with a mean of $lnS_t + (\mu_{t,T} - \frac{1}{2}\sigma^2_{t,T})(T - t)$, and a variance of $\sigma^2_{t,T}(T - t)$ where

S_t is the price of the stock at time t.
t is the current time.
T is the future time.

The lognormal distributional assumption used to describe future stock price movements is only an assumption because:

- Stock prices do not exactly follow this distribution in practice.
- $\mu_{t,T}$ and $\sigma_{t,T}$ are never constants.

Given this backdrop, it is not unreasonable for a practitioner to use:

- Implied market information so as to ensure that the simulated stock price is consistent with the market view (i.e., future stock prices are not lognormally distributed).
- Historical information to estimate parameters of a guessed probability density function (pdf) for price returns or trying to fit distributions on price-return data so as to derive an empirical pdf that would serve as a great proxy for future price returns.
- A mixture of pdfs (e.g., a mixture of lognormals or mean-reverting double lognormals, and so on) or the standard diffusion equation for movements in stock price but with expressions for μ and σ that are functions of the underlying stock price and time.

Whatever the methodology, the reader should note that the consequences of using a different return distribution to simulate future stock price movements are completely different simulated stock price paths and hence different option values.

Short Selling

As was pointed out in footnote 2, the delta of a vanilla European-style call option lies in the interval $[0, 1]$. Furthermore, as discussed in footnote 3, to manage a riskless portfolio associated with the sale of the call option, the hedger needs to acquire Δ_{Call} shares, in the process making the net portfolio delta neutral 0—all of which is illustrated in Tables 7.5 to 7.7.

By the same token, if the hedger has instead bought a call option or sold a put option, the sensitivity of this position to movements in the underlying stock price results in a positive delta. As a consequence, for the hedger to have a riskless portfolio, the hedger has to short delta shares, which would not be possible if short selling was not allowed—something that was touched on in footnote 5.

Given the above backdrop, it is easy to conclude that if short selling is not allowed (which has happened in certain markets and during financial crisis), some of the positions like going short a call or long a put cannot be initiated and delta hedged—forcing risk-managers to take unhedged positions. As a consequence, market makers during such times will either not transact in any positions resulting in them needing to short the markets or simply price in a hefty premium to take into account the inability to short the market while trying to capitalize on the fact that other market makers are no longer making markets on such products or do a mirror trade with another counterparty.

Transactions Costs, Continuous Trading, and Divisibility

In illustrating the implementation of a delta-hedging program outlined in Tables 7.5 to 7.8, I assumed that there are no transaction costs associated with rebalancing the portfolio. As a consequence, it is easy to rebalance the portfolio delta as frequently as one desires. All the delta-hedging dynamics fall apart in the presence of transaction costs simply because the hedging P&L associated with a continuously rebalanced delta-hedging program far outweigh the theoretical premium charged for the option in the absence of transactions costs—pointing to the fact that the generated premium is inadequate.

Before discussing the impact of transactions cost on a delta-hedging program, it is important for the reader to first understand that in practice there are two types of transaction costs that a trader has to deal with. These are:

1. Bid-offer spread.[6]
2. Commissions associated with each transaction.[7]

[6]The price paid to buy a stock is different from the price obtained by selling the same stock. The more illiquid the stock, the wider the bid-offer spread.

[7]An example of this would be paying $7 for each transaction (regardless of the number of shares bought or sold in that transaction) or $7 plus $1.25/option contract (regardless of the number of option contracts bought or sold).

Table 7.9 illustrates the impact of transaction costs on the hedging P&L along a sample path associated with the sale of a European-style call option. In fact, Table 7.9 represents the rerun of Table 7.7 in the presence of transaction costs.

As can be seen from Table 7.9, running the delta-hedging program in the presence of transaction costs results in a lower hedge P&L compared to Table 7.7. Thus, the more frequent the rebalancing of the deltas, the lower the hedge P&L of this scheme—which, as a consequence, implies that the option premium generated from the sale of this option has to be higher than the theoretical one without any transaction costs.[8]

The disadvantage of hedging less frequently is that there will be a deviation from the theoretically expected result of 0 (due to continuous rebalancing). In fact, there have been several publications discussing the impact of hedging frequency on the standard deviation of the hedge P&L. See, for example, Leland (1985).[9]

In addition to the above, there are two more issues I would like to touch on before moving to the assumption relating to dividends. The first relates to the fact that it is not possible to transact in a fractional number of shares (e.g., 10.25 shares, 13.57 shares). This problem can easily be rectified in the simulations by ensuring that one is only transacting in an integer number of shares (or number of lots—where each lot would contain 100 shares). The second issue relates to the fact that financial markets are only open during certain times of the day. While this may be a small concern for most options, trying to model a delta-hedging program on an hourly basis involving a very short-term option means stopping all hedging at market close and starting again at market open—something that can be easily incorporated in a simulation-based methodology.

---

[8]In practice, this is done through implied volatilities. In fact when trading, practitioners use implied volatility as a currency to compensate them for the cost associated with manufacturing the option they are selling (by taking into consideration the transactions cost, risks exposed, and the cost of capital needed to execute the transaction).

[9]Most of these papers were published before the availability of cheap, high-powered computer hardware and hence were focused on finding the bounds of errors associated with running a delta-hedging program in the presence of transaction costs. Given the current environment of cheap, high-powered computers, this problem has morphed into a simulation-based one in which hedging strategies are simulated in practice so as to be able to numerically identify bounds for various error or loss functions.

TABLE 7.9 Settlement Associated with a Delta-Hedging Program for Vanilla European-Style Call Option on a Dividend-Paying Stock (In-The-Money Expiry) With Transaction Costs

	A	B	C	D	E	F	G	H	I	J	K	L	M	N	O
1	Strike Price, K ($)	$40.00													
2	Volatility, σ (%)	20.00%													
3	Risk Free, r (%)	6.00%													
4	Dividend Rate, q (%)	2.00%													
5	Expiry, T (years)	2													
6	Flat Commision/Trade	$10													
7	Bid-Offer Spread	1.00%													
8	Time	Current Mid-Market Stock Price	Current Bid Stock Price	Current Offer Stock Price	d^1	d^2	Delta	Incoming Premium	Cost of Shares	Flat Commission	Amt Borrowed	Interest On Amt Borrowed	Dividend	Cumulative Amt Owing	
9	0	40	39.60	40.40	0.42	0.14	0.64	579.73	2578.59	10.00	2008.86			2008.86	
10	0.5	45	44.55	45.45	0.85		0.78		635.81	10.00	2654.67	61.18	28.87	2686.99	
11	1	39	38.61	39.39	0.17		0.56		−851.68	10.00	1845.31	81.83	30.50	1896.64	
12	1.5	44	43.56	44.44	0.89		0.80		1095.70	10.00	3002.34	57.76	24.66	3035.45	
13	2	42	41.58	42.42			1.00		830.88	10.00	3876.33	92.44	33.94	3934.83	
14									Cash from Option Exercise					4000.00	
15									Total Hedge Profit					65.17	
16									PV (Hedging Program)					57.80	
17															

Dividends

Although this assumption was not considered in the original Black-Scholes paper, I did discuss the incorporation of dividends in the previous section (see Tables 7.7 and 7.8). To summarize, the impact of a continuous dividend rate can be implemented by reducing the interest on the amount borrowed by the dividend amount received (as dividends are paid on the stocks held). As the astute reader will realize, equations (3.7a) and (3.7b) are the consequence of running a delta-hedging program in the presence of continuously compounded dividends and absence of transaction cost.

Arbitrage Opportunities and Constant Risk-Free Rate

The assumption relating to the lack of arbitrage opportunities is a crucial one as only with it were the authors able to remove the notion of risk-preference in the valuation of the options. More precisely, using equation (7.1) the authors assumed that it was possible for the hedger to hold a riskless portfolio comprising the sale of the option and the purchase of the appropriate number of shares which was continuously rebalanced so as not to allow any arbitrage opportunities.

The consequence of applying these assumptions and Ito's lemma to the equation (7.1) is

$$\frac{\partial f}{\partial t} + rS\frac{\partial f}{\partial S} + \frac{1}{2}\sigma^2\frac{\partial^2 f}{\partial S^2} = rf \tag{7.2}$$

which shows the absence of $\mu_{t,T}$ (the hedger's view on the growth rate of the stock price). Solving equation (7.2) using the boundary conditions $\max(S_T - K, 0)$ and $\max(K - S_T, 0)$ resulted in the Black-Scholes formulae given by equations (3.4a) and (3.4b).

The implication of this result is that one can conveniently replace $\mu_{t,T}$ for $r_{t,T}$ (assuming that $r_{t,T}$ is also constant) to arrive at the same set of equations. Succinctly put, as stated in the previous chapters, to value these options (or even run the delta-hedging program discussed in this chapter) one can assume that for a nondividend-paying stock, $\ln S_T$ is normally distributed with a mean of $\ln S_t + (r_{t,T} - \frac{1}{2}\sigma^2_{t,T})(T-t)$, and a variance of $\sigma^2_{t,T}(T-t)$. With this distributional assumption, one can now take the expected value of the payoff associated with the option and discount the result using the continuously compounded risk-free rate so as to obtain equations (3.4a) and (3.4b).

The concept of no-arbitrage and continuous rebalancing of a riskless portfolio that has been discussed in this section only matters if the hedger is interested in dynamically replicating the exposure using delta-hedging or other hedging methodologies. In the event that the hedger wants to take on risks without doing any kind of hedging, the hedger is free to use any value for $\mu_{t,T}$ (the growth rate of the stock price) or even any price distribution that is reflective of its view on the market.[10]

BEYOND DELTA HEDGING

Despite the fact that the Black-Scholes model was built on a platform that one is able to continuously manage a delta-neutral portfolio, there are practical shortcomings associated with this strategy. Examples of these are discussed in the following subsections.

Buy High and Sell Low

In the examples discussed earlier, the hedger shorted an option and then went on to delta-hedge the risk by buying (selling) shares when the share price went up (down). This is also referred to as the buy-high-and-sell-low strategy. The consequence of this is that the risk-manager would be exposed to a lower hedge P&L if the stock price path turns out to be more volatile than what was anticipated when selling the option.[11] To reduce this, one in practice would need to create a strategy that would be robust to changes in delta as the underlying stock price changes. More precisely, by immunizing against the changes in sensitivity of option delta to the underlying stock price movements, one can avoid the need to constantly

[10]An example of this can be found in the insurance industry. More precisely, it is not uncommon to find an insurance company selling a policy containing an embedded market guarantee which is priced using the insurance company's view on the market growth rate and volatility. In this instance, instead of running a hedging program, the insurance company would set aside the required capital and reserves for the risks it is exposed to.

[11]The intuition underlying this stems from the fact that the higher the volatility, the greater the premium. Hence, by selling an option for an implied volatility that turns out to be lower than that realized during the life of the option, the hedger incurs a lower hedge P&L. The converse of this happens when the hedger goes long an option. More precisely, the hedger would want the realized volatility to be higher than the implied volatility paid. In this instance, ignoring transaction costs, to generate as much profit as possible, the hedger would buy-low-and-sell-high on every trade in the hope of generating as much revenue as possible during the life of the option.

delta hedge. Called *gamma hedging*,[12] practitioners use this approach to reduce the frequency of trading associated with rebalancing of the deltas. Denoting $\Gamma_{S_t,K,t,T,r_{t,T},q_{t,T},\sigma_{t,T},Spot,van\,call}$ for a vanilla European-style call and $\Gamma_{S_t,K,t,T,r_{t,T},q_{t,T},\sigma_{t,T},Spot,van\,put}$ for a vanilla European-style put, it can be easily shown that for dividend paying stocks,

$$\begin{aligned}\Gamma_{S_t,K,t,T,r_{t,T},q_{t,T},\sigma_{t,T},Spot,van\,call} &= \frac{\partial\Delta_{S_t,K,t,T,r_{t,T},q_{t,T},\sigma_{t,T},Spot,van\,call}}{\partial S_t}\\ &= \frac{1}{S_t\sigma_{t,T}\sqrt{2\pi(T-t)}} * e^{-q_{t,T}(T-t)-0.5(d^1_{S_t,K,t,T,r_{t,T},q_{t,T},\sigma_{t,T}})^2}\end{aligned} \tag{7.2a}$$

$$\begin{aligned}\Gamma_{S_t,K,t,T,r_{t,T},q_{t,T},\sigma_{t,T},Spot,van\,put} &= \frac{\partial\Delta_{S_t,K,t,T,r_{t,T},q_{t,T},\sigma_{t,T},Spot,van\,put}}{\partial S_t}\\ &= \frac{1}{S_t\sigma_{t,T}\sqrt{2\pi(T-t)}} * e^{-q_{t,T}(T-t)-0.5(d^1_{S_t,K,t,T,r_{t,T},q_{t,T},\sigma_{t,T}})^2}\end{aligned} \tag{7.2b}$$

Changes in Volatility and Risk-Free Rates

One of the assumptions made by Black-Scholes is that $\sigma_{t,T}$ and $r_{t,T}$ must remain constant during the life of the hedging program. In practice, this is far from true as stock price volatility and interest rates change just as frequently as stock prices. As a consequence, for the hedger to be immunized against these movements, the hedger needs to ensure that sensitivities of the option premium to changes in volatility (called *vega*) and risk-free rate (called *rho*) need to be also rebalanced. The expressions for vega and rho in the instance of calls and puts on dividend-paying stocks are given as follow:

$$\begin{aligned}Vega_{S_t,K,t,T,r_{t,T},q_{t,T},\sigma_{t,T},Spot,van\,call} &= \frac{\partial C_{S_t,K,t,T,r_{t,T},q_{t,T},\sigma_{t,T},Spot}}{\partial\sigma_{t,T}}\\ &= \frac{1}{\sqrt{2\pi}}S_t\sqrt{T-t} * e^{-q_{t,T}(T-t)-0.5(d^1_{S_t,K,t,T,r_{t,T},q_{t,T},\sigma_{t,T}})^2}\end{aligned} \tag{7.3a}$$

[12]While delta hedging involves the use of stocks, gamma hedging involves the use of stock options (simply because stocks only have delta and stock options have both delta and gamma). Having said that, it is imperative for the reader to note that while it is theoretically possible to neutralize deltas using stock options as opposed to using stocks, this is not done in practice simply due to the transaction costs and the fact that the consequence of such a hedge might increase the total gamma/vega/rho of the portfolio.

$$Vega_{S_t,K,t,T,r_{t,T},q_{t,T},\sigma_{t,T},Spot,van\,put} = \frac{\partial P_{S_t,K,t,T,r_{t,T},q_{t,T},\sigma_{t,T},Spot}}{\partial \sigma_{t,T}}$$
$$= \frac{1}{\sqrt{2\pi}} S_t \sqrt{T-t} * e^{-q_{t,T}(T-t)-0.5(d^1_{S_t,K,t,T,r_{t,T},q_{t,T},\sigma_{t,T}})^2} \tag{7.3b}$$

$$Rho_{S_t,K,t,T,r_{t,T},q_{t,T},\sigma_{t,T},Spot,van\,call} = \frac{\partial C_{S_t,K,t,T,r_{t,T},q_{t,T},\sigma_{t,T},Spot}}{\partial r_{t,T}}$$
$$= K(T-t) * N\left(d^2_{S_t,K,t,T,r_{t,T},q_{t,T},\sigma_{t,T}}\right) e^{-r_{t,T}(T-t)} \tag{7.4a}$$

$$Rho_{S_t,K,t,T,r_{t,T},q_{t,T},\sigma_{t,T},Spot,van\,put} = \frac{\partial P_{S_t,K,t,T,r_{t,T},q_{t,T},\sigma_{t,T},Spot}}{\partial r_{t,T}}$$
$$= -K(T-t) * N\left(-d^2_{S_t,K,t,T,r_{t,T},q_{t,T},\sigma_{t,T}}\right) e^{-r_{t,T}(T-t)} \tag{7.4b}$$

At first glance, it may seem counterintuitive to the reader as to how it is possible to assume that $\sigma_{t,T}$ and $r_{t,T}$ are constants on one hand and then calculate both vega and rho as though these variables are in fact random on the other hand. On a closer examination, this is not counterintuitive if one recognizes the fact that the option premiums are correct for a given $\sigma_{t,T}$ and $r_{t,T}$ and that the values of $\sigma_{t,T}$ and $r_{t,T}$ are subject to change. In practice, it is more appropriate to use the relevant distributions for both volatilities and risk-free rates so as to allow for extra variability inherent in these options, which tend to be more pronounced as the maturities get longer. The consequence of doing this is higher option premiums as compared to those obtained using constant $\sigma_{t,T}$ and $r_{t,T}$—an issue that is discussed further in Chapter 8.

As in the gamma risks, hedging vega risks also involves the use of stock options. Despite this, one cannot use the same set of options to simultaneously mitigate both gamma and vega risks—unless the hedge option is identical to the initial option sold. In this case, all sensitivities, like delta/gamma/vega/rho and so on, of the entire portfolio after hedging would be identically zero and continue to be such as the option life decays and market conditions change. Like delta risks, hedging rho risks can easily be done using interest rate swaps as well as stock options although the use of interest rate swaps tends to be cleaner and cheaper. Thus, to implement delta, gamma, vega, and rho hedging in practice, every time a rebalancing needs to done (i.e., neutralize the net portfolio delta/vega/rho values to zero), the hedger has to transact in a combination of stocks, stock options, and interest rate swaps.

Redoing the example discussed in Table 7.7 (and not taking into consideration any transaction costs), one can see in Table 7.10 how the gamma, vega, and rho change over the option life.

From Table 7.10, the reader can easily observe that I only computed the deltas, gammas, vegas, rhos of an option. In practice, one can mathematically compute higher order derivatives[13]—although only some of them are hedged, while the others are monitored. Furthermore, it is important for the reader to note that one is able to compute any of these derivatives with ease as long as the analytical expressions for the option-pricing formulae are readily available. As was seen in Chapter 5, this can be quite a challenge for many of the path-dependent options. In such an instance, a practitioner's only recourse is to do this numerically.[14]

As mentioned earlier, to hedge the delta, gamma, vega, and rho risks simultaneously, one needs to transact in stocks, two non-identical stock options, and interest rate swaps. While finding the number of shares required to neutralize only the deltas was easy to do, finding the number of shares/options/swaps required to neutralize the deltas/gammas/vegas/rhos simultaneously is more challenging for the following four reasons:

1. One now has to contend with solving for the 4 variables (i.e., the number of stocks, two non-identical stock options, and interest rate swaps).

[13]Examples of such derivatives are $Vanna = \frac{\partial Vega}{\partial S_t}$, $Speed = \frac{\partial \Gamma}{\partial S_t}$, $Vomma = \frac{\partial Vega}{\partial \sigma}$, $Zomma = \frac{\partial \Gamma}{\partial \sigma}$, $Ultima = \frac{\partial Vomma}{\partial \sigma}$, $Theta = \frac{\partial C}{\partial (T-t)}$, $Charm = \frac{\partial \Delta}{\partial (T-t)}$, $Veta = \frac{\partial Vega}{\partial (T-t)}$, $Color = \frac{\partial \Gamma}{\partial (T-t)}$, $Totto = \frac{\partial Vanna}{\partial (T-t)}$—where I have suppressed the subscripts for the purposes of brevity. As the reader will note, being able to capture all these derivatives (and more) means having the ability to recreate the option. To see this, consider the call option premium $C_{S_t,K,t,T,r_{t,T},q_{t,T},\sigma_{t,T},Spot}$. Since this is a function of the variables $S_t, T-t, r_{t,T}, q_{t,T}$, and $\sigma_{t,T}$ one can use Taylor's expansion to expand the call option premium in terms of the variables $S_t, T-t, r_{t,T}, q_{t,T}$, and $\sigma_{t,T}$. Doing this yields $C_{S_t+\Delta S,K,t+\Delta t,T,r_{t,T}+\Delta r,q_{t,T}+\Delta q,\sigma_{t,T}+\Delta\sigma,Spot} = C_{S_t,K,t,T,r_{t,T},q_{t,T},\sigma_{t,T},Spot} + (\Delta S^{*} \, Call\ Delta) + (\Delta t^{*} \, Call\ Theta) + (\Delta\sigma^{*} \, Call\ Vega) + \ldots$.

[14]$\Delta_{S_t,K,t,T,r_{t,T},q_{t,T},\sigma_{t,T},Spot,van\ call}$ for example can be computed using the numerical difference $\frac{C_{S_t+\Delta S_t,K,t,T,r_{t,T},q_{t,T},\sigma_{t,T},Spot} - C_{S_t,K,t,T,r_{t,T},q_{t,T},\sigma_{t,T},Spot}}{\Delta S_t}$. The other derivatives can similarly be calculated numerically. It is important for the reader to note that to use simulations to compute these derivatives, one has to ensure that the same set of random numbers are reused to compute option premiums associated with the shifted parameters (be they S_t or $r_{t,T}$, $q_{t,T}$ or $\sigma_{t,T}$, etc.). In doing so, any noise arising from the use of the random numbers is systematically removed.

TABLE 7.10 Illustration of Gamma, Vega, and Rho for a Vanilla European-Style Call Option on a Dividend-Paying Stock (In-The-Money Expiry)

	A	B	C	D	E	F	G	H	I	J	K	L
1	Strike Price, K ($)	$40.00										
2	Volatility, σ (%)	20.00%										
3	Risk Free, r (%)	6.00%										
4	Dividend Rate, q (%)	2.00%										
5	Expiry, T (years)	2										
6	Time	Current Stock Price	d^1	d^2	Delta	Gamma	Vega	Rho				
7	0	40	0.42	0.14	0.64	0.03	19.82	27.91				
8	0.5	45	0.85	0.60	0.78	0.02	14.89	32.54				
9	1	39	0.17	−0.03	0.56	0.05	15.02	18.44				
10	1.5	44	0.89	0.74	0.80	0.04	8.30	21.18				
11	2	42			1.00							
12												
13												
14												
15												

```
=EXP(-B4*(B5-A7))*
  EXP(-0.5*C7*C7)/
  (B7*B2*SQRT(2*PI()*(B5-A7)))
```

```
=B7*SQRT(B5-A7)*
  EXP(-B4*(B5-A7))*
  EXP(-0.5*C7*C7)/SQRT(2*PI())
```

```
=B1*SQRT(B5-A7)*
  EXP(-B3*(B5-A7))*
  NORMSDIST(D7)
```

2. The presence of a multitude of options across varying maturities and strikes available.[15]
3. The presence of a multitude of interest rate swaps across varying maturities.[16]
4. The term structure of implied volatilities does not trade as a single entity.[17] More precisely, the implied volatility associated with a 1-year European-style vanilla option, for example, does not trade in step with the implied volatility of a 10-year European-style vanilla option. As a consequence, trying to hedge the sale of a 10-year European-style vanilla option with a 1-year European-style vanilla option by simply matching vegas can lead to potentially disastrous consequences. In such an instance, it is customary to "bucket" similar risks together (e.g., short-term volatilities that are made up of volatilities from options with maturities less than three years, mid-term volatilities that are made up of volatilities from options with maturities larger than three years and less

---

[15]If the available hedge options are identical to the originating option, then the hedge options trivially reduce to one option that has the same maturity and strike as the originating option—see footnote 13. In the event no hedge options with the originating option strike are available, then the hedge options would comprise two non-dentical options each of which has the same maturity and a different strike when compared to the originating option. Furthermore, even if the hedge options have the same maturity as the originating option, in practice it is often the case that due to cost of the hedge options, it is often more cost effective for the hedger to transact in shorter dated options and keep rolling them over.

In the event that available hedge options have maturities shorter than the originating option, the hedger is faced with the choice of selecting the right combination of maturity/strike for each of the two required options so as to minimize the transaction costs both at the time of the hedge execution as well as ensure that the cumulative hedging costs incurred in risk-managing the originating option does not exceed the cost of the originating option. As a consequence, to optimally select the appropriate options requires the use of complex multi-stage optimization methods.

[16]The ideal rho hedge is a zero risk-free rate with maturity matching the originating option. Given that this is difficult to trade in practice, one often resorts to the use of a spot start semiannually reset swap with maturity set equal to that of the originating option. In the event that this is difficult to transact (i.e., not readily available), it is not unreasonable for the hedger to use liquid interest rate swaps with the maturities that are as close as possible to the maturity of the originating option as great proxy hedges.

[17]The same holds true when dealing with the term structure of zero risk-free rates.

than seven years, and long-term volatilities which are made up of volatilities from options with maturities longer than seven years) and try to find options in the buckets that are closest to what has been sold to hedge the risks. The result of this is the existence of a short-term vega, mid-term vega, and a long-term vega, all of which need to be managed, in the process making the risk-management of long-term options very tricky.

For the purposes of discussion, I will only focus on the first issue, which fortunately is nothing more than finding solutions to four simultaneous equations.

To see this, assume that to hedge these risks one needs to use stocks (S), two nonidentical options (O_1 and O_2), and an at-the-market interest rate swap (SR). Denoting the delta, gamma, vega, and rho associated with the

- Stock (S) by $\Delta_S, \Gamma_S, Vega_S, Rho_S$ respectively.[18]
- Option (O_1) by $\Delta_{O_1}, \Gamma_{O_1}, Vega_{O_1}, Rho_{O_1}$ respectively.
- Option (O_2) by $\Delta_{O_2}, \Gamma_{O_2}, Vega_{O_2}, Rho_{O_2}$ respectively.
- Swap rate (SR) by $\Delta_{SR}, \Gamma_{SR}, Vega_{SR}, Rho_{SR}$ respectively.[19]
- Option that is being hedged by Δ, Γ, *Vega*, and *Rho* respectively.[20]
- Notionals associated with S, O_1, O_2, and SR by N_S, N_{O_1}, N_{O_2}, and N_{SR} respectively.

It can be shown that the simultaneous equations one needs to solve take the form of

$$N_S\Delta_S + N_{O_1}\Delta_{O_1} + N_{O_2}\Delta_{O_2} + N_{SR}\Delta_{SR} + \Delta = 0 \qquad (7.5a)$$

$$N_S\Gamma_S + N_{O_1}\Gamma_{O_1} + N_{O_2}\Gamma_{O_2} + N_{SR}\Gamma_{SR} + \Gamma = 0 \qquad (7.5b)$$

$$N_S\mathrm{Vega}_S + N_{O_1}\mathrm{Vega}_{O_1} + N_{O_2}\mathrm{Vega}_{O_2} + Vega = 0 \qquad (7.5c)$$

$$N_S\mathrm{Rho}_S + N_{O_1}\mathrm{Rho}_{O_1} + N_{O_2}\mathrm{Rho}_{O_2} + Rho = 0 \qquad (7.5d)$$

[18]The gamma, vega, and rho for a stock is trivially zero while the delta of a stock is 1. Hence $\Delta_S = 1, \Gamma_S = Vega_S = Rho_S = 0$.

[19]Since the interest rate swaps are not sensitive to stock price movements, the delta, gamma, and vega for an interest rate swap is trivially zero. Hence $\Delta_{SR} = \Gamma_{SR} = Vega_{SR} = 0$.

[20]Where these Greeks take into consideration the position of the option (i.e., long or short) that one is trying to hedge. Additionally, I have conveniently assumed that the entire volatility term structure and zero risk-free rate term structure moves as a single entity in the process resulting in the use of a single vega and rho.

Equations (7.5a) to (7.5d) can be easily solved to obtain values for N_S, N_{O_1}, N_{O_2}, and N_{SR}.[21] Just like what was done in the delta-hedging example, in Tables 7.5 to 7.9 one has to rebalance these notionals every 6 months and then unwind these hedges.

Scenario-Based Hedging

In practice, hedgers want to hedge their risks in a prudent fashion so as to minimize transaction costs while ensuring that they do not take on risks they are not comfortable with while running a hedging program. As a consequence, it is not uncommon for one to hedge catastrophic scenarios (i.e., scenarios that expose them to risks they cannot stomach) as opposed to hedging their exposure to every possible scenario outcome. To do this, one has to first construct a portfolio comprising the option that needs to be hedged and the assets (i.e.,stock, stock options,[22] and swaps) needed to hedge the risks, and stress test the portfolio against the scenarios of concern so as to see how much of each asset one has to acquire so that the hedger is comfortable with the resulting exposure.

TESTING HEDGING STRATEGIES

My discussion thus far focused on replicating risks arising from the options sold. In doing this, I briefly touched on the tradeoff between transaction costs

[21]Using Cramer's rule (see for example Anton (2010) or the online content on matrices) one can show that $N_S = \frac{A}{Z}, N_{O_1} = \frac{B}{Z}, N_{O_2} = \frac{C}{Z}$, and $N_{SR} = \frac{D}{Z}$ where A, B, C, D, Z are the determinants of the 4×4 matrices $\begin{bmatrix} -\Delta & \Delta_{O_1} & \Delta_{O_2} & \Delta_{SR} \\ -\Gamma & \Gamma_{O_1} & \Gamma_{O_2} & \Gamma_{SR} \\ -Vega & Vega_{O_1} & Vega_{O_2} & Vega_{SR} \\ -Rho & Rho_{O_1} & Rho_{O_2} & Rho_{SR} \end{bmatrix}$, $\begin{bmatrix} \Delta_S & -\Delta & \Delta_{O_2} & \Delta_{SR} \\ \Gamma_S & -\Gamma & \Gamma_{O_2} & \Gamma_{SR} \\ Vega_S & -Vega & Vega_{O_2} & Vega_{SR} \\ Rho_S & -Rho & Rho_{O_2} & Rho_{SR} \end{bmatrix}$, $\begin{bmatrix} \Delta_S & \Delta_{O_1} & -\Delta & \Delta_{SR} \\ \Gamma_S & \Gamma_{O_1} & -\Gamma & \Gamma_{SR} \\ Vega_S & Vega_{O_1} & -Vega & Vega_{SR} \\ Rho_S & Rho_{O_1} & -Rho & Rho_{SR} \end{bmatrix}$, $\begin{bmatrix} \Delta_S & \Delta_{O_1} & \Delta_{O_2} & -\Delta \\ \Gamma_S & \Gamma_{O_1} & \Gamma_{O_2} & -\Gamma \\ Vega_S & Vega_{O_1} & Vega_{O_2} & -Vega \\ Rho_S & Rho_{O_1} & Rho_{O_2} & -Rho \end{bmatrix}$ and $\begin{bmatrix} \Delta_S & \Delta_{O_1} & \Delta_{O_2} & \Delta_{SR} \\ \Gamma_S & \Gamma_{O_1} & \Gamma_{O_2} & \Gamma_{SR} \\ Vega_S & Vega_{O_1} & Vega_{O_2} & Vega_{SR} \\ Rho_S & Rho_{O_1} & Rho_{O_2} & Rho_{SR} \end{bmatrix}$ respectively.

[22]It is not uncommon for these options to also include exotic or more customized options.

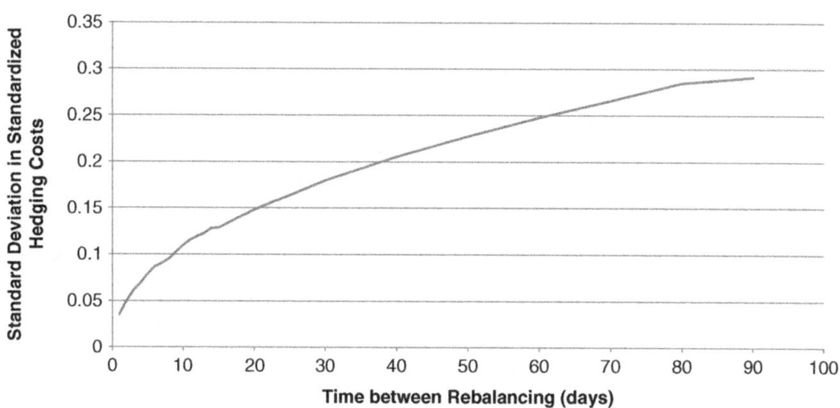

FIGURE 7.1 Impact of Trading Frequency on Standardized Hedge P&L Standard Deviation

and hedging errors. Succinctly stated, the more frequent the hedging, the less volatile—albeit higher—the hedging costs. On the contrary, the less frequent the hedging, the more volatile—albeit lower—the hedging costs. In this section, I will discuss a couple of practical ways to evaluate the effectiveness of hedging strategies.

Assuming that there are no transaction costs, one can rerun the delta-hedging analysis presented in Tables 7.7 and 7.8 to arrive at Figure 7.1.[23]

As can be seen from Figure 7.1, the bigger the time between rebalancing, the greater the standard deviation in the simulated standardized hedge P&L. As a consequence, one would like to rebalance as frequently as possible so as to reduce the noise in the simulated standardized hedge P&L. Doing this will be ineffective if there were transaction costs associated with the hedging program. Rerunning the analysis that resulted in Figure 7.1 across varying transaction costs yields the results in Table 7.11.[24]

---

[23]To arrive at data supporting the chart, I computed the hedge P&L using the delta-hedging example in Tables 7.7 and 7.8, standardized it (by dividing with option premium), and then calculated the standard deviation of the standardized-hedge P&L obtained by using 2,500 runs. To avoid any error introduced by the generation of random numbers, I used the same set of random numbers so as to ensure the same stock price path scenarios.

[24]To put this table together, I assumed that transaction costs of 0, 2, and 4 percent of the stock price were incurred when buying and selling the shares during the delta-hedging activity. For example, when the transaction cost of 2 percent was used, I simulated a mid-market stock price S and then assumed a stock price of $1.02S$ when purchasing shares and a stock price of $0.98S$ when selling the shares—all consistent with the mechanics presented in Table 7.9.

TABLE 7.11 Effect of Transaction Costs on Rebalancing Intervals

	Transaction Costs					
	0%		2%		4%	
Rebalancing Interval (days)	Average	Std Deviation	Average	Std Deviation	Average	Std Deviation
1	0.00	0.04	1.30	0.45	2.59	0.89
2	0.00	0.05	0.95	0.32	1.91	0.64
3	0.00	0.06	0.80	0.27	1.61	0.53
4	0.00	0.07	0.72	0.25	1.43	0.47
5	0.00	0.08	0.66	0.23	1.31	0.43
6	0.00	0.09	0.61	0.22	1.22	0.39
7	0.00	0.09	0.58	0.20	1.15	0.37
8	0.00	0.10	0.55	0.20	1.10	0.36
9	0.00	0.10	0.53	0.20	1.05	0.34
10	0.00	0.11	0.51	0.20	1.01	0.34
11	0.00	0.12	0.49	0.20	0.97	0.32
12	0.00	0.12	0.48	0.20	0.95	0.32
13	0.00	0.12	0.46	0.20	0.92	0.31
14	0.00	0.13	0.45	0.20	0.90	0.31
15	0.00	0.13	0.44	0.19	0.88	0.30
20	0.00	0.15	0.40	0.20	0.80	0.29
30	0.01	0.18	0.36	0.22	0.72	0.28
40	0.01	0.21	0.33	0.24	0.66	0.29
50	0.00	0.23	0.31	0.25	0.62	0.30
60	0.01	0.25	0.30	0.27	0.60	0.31
70	0.00	0.27	0.29	0.29	0.57	0.32
80	0.00	0.29	0.28	0.30	0.55	0.34

As can be seen from Table 7.11, when there are no transaction costs, the average hedge P&L associated with the delta-hedging program using 2,500 paths is 0 (as expected). Consistent with Figure 7.1, the standard deviation of the standardized hedge P&L increased from 0.04 to 0.29 in the absence of transaction costs. As the transaction costs increased, the average standardized hedge P&L also increased by roughly the same amount (i.e., a two-fold increase in transaction costs resulted in approximately a two-fold increase in the average standardized hedge P&L). Not surprisingly the standard deviation of these standardized hedge P&L also increased as transaction costs increased—illustrating the fact that the more frequent the rebalancing, the bigger the increase in standard deviation. Based on the analysis done, for a given transaction-cost level, the hedger can now decide (using the table) on how much fluctuation the hedger can stomach in the realized hedge

P&L—in the process making a decision on how frequently the hedger has to rebalance. It is important for the reader to understand that for a given transaction cost, it is not unusual to have two hedgers selling identical options and choosing different rebalancing frequencies simply due to the fact that each of them would have different appetites for risks given their level of capital, risk limits, etc.

In practice, instead of waiting once every day, or 10 days, or 50 days, and so on to rebalance their positions, practitioners tend to work with the notion of a *delta-trading limit*. More precisely, with this approach, hedgers only neutralize their deltas if the absolute value of the total net portfolio delta exceeds a certain pre-defined level. In this way, one can avoid hedging costs due to rollercoaster market movements (i.e., an upward movement followed by a downward movement or a downward movement followed by an upward movement) as long as the trading limits are not breached during such rollercoaster rides. Thus, a delta-trading limit of 0 would be akin to rebalancing continuously (as this would mean that any slippages in the portfolio delta need to be rebalanced immediately). Similarly, a very large delta-trading limit would imply an infrequent rebalancing of deltas. In taking this approach, one can replace all references to rebalancing frequency with portfolio-delta limits. One can also extend this philosophy to implement portfolio gamma, vega, and rho trading limits when hedging gamma, vega, and rho risks respectively.

In discussing the implementation of delta hedging and the impact of transaction costs on standard deviation associated with standardized hedge P&L, I pointed out that for the hedger to decide how best to run a delta hedging program, the hedger must decide how much standard deviation in standardized hedge P&L he/she is prepared to stomach for a given level of transaction costs—which is done in the guise of a delta-trading limit (or time interval between rebalancing periods or both). Once the delta-trading limit and the frequency of delta monitoring has been established, the hedger can now more readily compare different strategies by looking at both the average standardized hedge costs and the standard deviation of the simulated standardized hedge P&L. To understand this better, suppose for a given transaction-cost level and a specified delta-trading limit frequency of delta monitoring, the distribution of the hedge P&L associated with the use of stocks produced an average and standard deviation of 1.00 and 0.40 respectively. If the distribution of hedge P&L using another hedging strategy (e.g., using at-the-money options[25]) with the same trading limits and frequency of

[25]When the delta trading limit is breached, in order to neutralize the deltas, I have assumed that the hedger unwinds the existing option positions and then puts on new at-the-money option positions.

TABLE 7.12 Comparison of Hedging Strategies for a Given Trading Limit Constraint

Statistics from Delta Hedging Profit Distribution At-the-Money Options			
Standard Deviation	Average		
	0.5	1	1.5
0.2	Better than using stocks.	Better than using stocks.	
0.4	Better than using stocks.	No advantage over using stocks.	Worse than using stocks.
0.6		Worse than using stocks.	Worse than using stocks.

monitoring constraints produced an average and standard deviation of 1.00 and 0.2 respectively, then it is obvious that the strategy based on using at-the-money options is more effective than the one based on stocks. Table 7.12 better summarizes all possible scenarios and instances when one strategy dominates the other.

From Table 7.12, one can make the following four observations:

1. While the comments given for seven of the nine scenarios are intuitively reasonable, nothing can be concluded in the two instances (that are shaded in grey). In such an instance, one would need to look at other metrics[26] to arrive at a decision.
2. Since I only ran 2,500 paths to produce the distribution of simulated hedge P&L for both the strategies, some allowance has to be made to allow for simulation errors that possibly arise from not running sufficient paths or biasedness in the sampling of the random numbers—as discussed in Chapter 4. This is despite the fact that the same stock price paths are used to compare the stock-based strategy against an at-the-money-option strategy. As a consequence, the effectiveness of one strategy over the other cannot be established with certainty if the average and the standard deviation associated with the hedge-P&L distributions are close to each other. To overcome this impasse, one can either run more simulations, or use different decision metrics, or do a combination of both.

[26]Examples of these metrics are the coefficient of variations (which is computed by dividing the standard deviation by the mean) or conditional tail expectations (which is computed by calculating the worst-case scenarios and taking the average of the selected worse-case scenarios).

3. I have kept the stock price volatility and risk-free rate constant thus far. In practice, these variables have their own distribution (and sometimes can even be correlated to stock price movements). To do a more rigorous analysis of the hedge–P&L distribution, one must test these strategies against movements in volatilities and risk-free rates so as to ensure that the results obtained are a more realistic indication of what can be achieved in practice—especially when vega and rho risks turn out to be the biggest risk drivers in the option sold.
4. In addition to simulating stock prices into the future, another sensibility check that is usually carried out in practice is the *experience check*. With this type of check, instead of solely relying on simulated stock prices, one would additionally use real-world scenarios (which may contain historical stock prices, risk-free rates, volatilities) to test the effectiveness of the hedging strategies. In doing so, one can get a better sense of how well or badly the strategies perform under market scenarios that are deemed catastrophic.

ANALYSIS ASSOCIATED WITH THE HEDGING OF A EUROPEAN-STYLE VANILLA PUT OPTION

In this section, I will assemble many of the ideas discussed earlier in this chapter to illustrate how one goes about evaluating hedging strategies. To help with the crystallization of the ideas discussed, I will discuss the hedging of the sale of a 10-year, European-style vanilla put option on a nondividend-paying stock. Table 7.13 illustrates the premium and all the risk parameters (delta, gamma, vega, rho, and theta) associated with the sale of this option.

As can be seen from Table 7.13, the put delta is quite small relative to the put vega and/or put rho—all of it pointing to the fact that the biggest risks for this type of option are the volatility and interest-rate risks (but not delta risks). Despite this, I start with the hedging of the delta risks, and then introduce the hedging of the volatility and rho risks.

Delta Hedging

To do this, one needs to redo what has been done in Tables 7.8 and 7.9 in the presence of transaction costs to arrive at Table 7.14.

As can be seen from Table 7.14, regardless of the nature of commission, a daily hedging program results in a lower average hedge P&L relative to the annual hedging program—something that is intuitively

TABLE 7.13 Put Option Premium and Greeks

	A	B
1	Current Price, S_t ($)	$40.00
2	Strike Price, K ($)	$40.00
3	Volatility, σ (%)	20.00%
4	Risk Free, r (%)	6.00%
5	Dividend Rate, q (%)	0.00%
6	Current Time, t (years)	0
7	Expiry, T (years)	10
8	d^1	1.264911064
9	d^2	0.632455532
10	Delta Put	–0.102951605
11	Gamma Put	0.007085728
12	Vega Put	22.67433045
13	Rho Put	–18.29521304
14	Put Premium	1.667390134

TABLE 7.14 Hedge P&L in the Presence of Transaction Costs

Flat Commission	Bid-Offer Spread	Hedge Frequency	Average	Std Deviation
$–	2.00%	Daily	$695.16	$349.13
		Weekly	$287.98	$143.72
		Monthly	$135.53	$79.10
		Quarterly	$81.78	$78.68
		Semiannually	$59.29	$96.27
		Annually	$43.51	$130.41
$10	2.00%	Daily	$27,708.53	$403.08
		Weekly	$4,799.78	$149.27
		Monthly	$1,045.89	$80.19
		Quarterly	$391.56	$79.31
		Semiannually	$218.87	$96.75
		Annually	$127.93	$130.86
$10	0.00%	Daily	$27,013.10	$167.21
		Weekly	$4,510.92	$30.75
		Monthly	$910.94	$38.86
		Quarterly	$309.34	$64.35
		Semiannually	$157.59	$89.25
		Annually	$81.30	$125.79

TABLE 7.15 Hedge – P&L Statistic Summary in the Presence of Transaction Costs

Hedge Frequency	0 FC/2% BO	10 FC/2% BO	10 FC/0% BO
Daily	0.50	0.01	0.01
Weekly	0.50	0.03	0.01
Monthly	0.58	0.08	0.04
Quarterly	0.96	0.20	0.21
Semi annually	1.62	0.44	0.57
Annually	3.00	1.02	1.55

consistent.[27] Since the magnitude of the standard deviation of any data tends to be highly correlated to the magnitude of the average of the data, unlike the average hedge P&L that can be easily compared (and ranked) across varying hedging frequencies, it is difficult to compare standard-deviation of hedge P&L across varying hedging frequencies. As a consequence, I will use the coefficient of variation metric[28] to compare the effectiveness of these strategies. Doing this yields Table 7.15.

Table 7.15 shows how the coefficient of variation associated with the hedge P&L increases as the hedging frequency drops for varying trading commission structures. As seen in the table, the less frequent the hedging program the lesser the average hedge P&L and the bigger the standard deviation associated with the hedge–P&L distribution.

The results in Tables 7.14 and 7.15 were obtained using a delta-hedging strategy in which the rebalancing is done at every predefined time interval (e.g., daily, weekly, monthly). In practice, such hedging is done only if the absolute value of the net portfolio delta breaches a predefined delta-trading limit. Figure 7.2 illustrates the impact of various delta-trading limits on hedge – P&L distribution when the only transaction cost is the 2 percent bid-offer spread.

[27]To arrive at these numbers, I used 2,500 independent paths where the same price paths were used to compute deltas/hedge P&L so that the stock prices used in an annual rebalancing scheme are a subset of those used in a semi-annual rebalancing scheme, which in turn are a subset of those used in a quarterly rebalancing scheme, and so on.

[28]The coefficient of variation for a given data set can be computed using the formula $\frac{\textit{Standard deviation}}{\textit{mean}}$ where the *mean* is assumed to be greater than 0. A higher coefficient of variation indicates a bigger dispersion of the data.

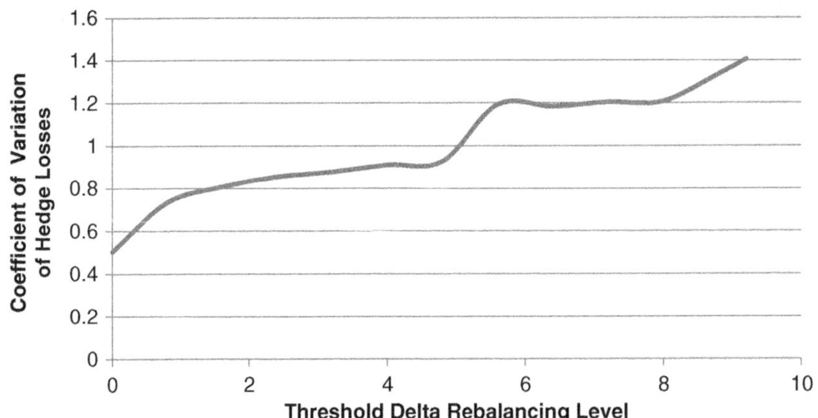

FIGURE 7.2 Coefficient of Variation of Hedge–P&L Statistics for Varying Delta-Trading Limits When the Transaction Cost Is a 2 Percent Bid-Offer Spread

As can be seen in Figure 7.2, when the delta-trading limit is zero, the hedge P&L trivially collapses to those outlined in Tables 7.13 and 7.14 for a daily delta-hedging program where there is only a 2 percent, bid-offer transaction cost. In practice, one would have to run the analysis underlying Figure 7.2 taking into consideration all the transaction costs as opposed to only using a bid-offer spread.

In addition to looking at Figure 7.2 for an indication of the kind of net-portfolio delta-threshold trading limit that should be deployed when implementing a delta-hedging program, practitioners also analyze the impact of implementing such a strategy when daily realized values of stock prices, risk-free rates, and volatility rates during the life of the option keep changing. Although these scenarios (also sometimes called real-world scenarios) are a digression from what was proposed under the risk-neutral world of Black-Scholes, they are chosen in practice to highlight how bad the hedging program can get in the event the worst-case scenario happens. Table 7.16 illustrates an example of a real-world scenario path for the first 10 days of the simulation.

In practice, the scenarios produced in Table 7.16 are done so for the entirety of the option life (10 years in this case) so as to evaluate the efficiency of the hedging strategy under various real-world scenarios (examples of real-world scenarios include the historical values of risk-free rates, volatility rates, and stock prices). By using real-world scenarios, the hedger's objective is to identify catastrophic scenarios which, when realized, would lead to a drastic negative impact on the hedge P&L, and, in the process, motivate the hedger to contemplate deploying other types of hedging strategies (including a different net-portfolio delta-threshold-trading limits) so that the

TABLE 7.16 Real-World Sample Stock-Price Path and Put Option Delta for the First 10 Days

Index	Time (years)	Risk-Free Rate	Volatility Rate	Current Mid-Market Stock Price	Current Bid Stock Price	Current Offer Stock Price	d^1	Put Delta
0	0	6.00%	20.00%	40.00	39.20	40.80	1.26	−0.10
1	0.002778	6.05%	21.00%	43.50	42.63	44.37	1.37	−0.09
2	0.005556	5.90%	19.00%	45.00	44.10	45.90	1.48	−0.07
3	0.008333	5.80%	19.00%	47.00	46.06	47.94	1.53	−0.06
4	0.011111	6.10%	18.80%	45.50	44.59	46.41	1.54	−0.06
5	0.013889	6.30%	19.30%	42.60	41.75	43.45	1.44	−0.07
6	0.016667	6.20%	18.70%	47.60	46.65	48.55	1.64	−0.05
7	0.019444	6.00%	19.10%	50.70	49.69	51.71	1.69	−0.05
8	0.022222	5.90%	17.00%	53.20	52.14	54.26	1.90	−0.03
9	0.025	5.80%	16.00%	49.50	48.51	50.49	1.82	−0.03
10	0.027778	5.94%	16.50%	46.00	45.08	46.92	1.67	−0.05

decrease in hedge P&L is more effectively stymied under these catastrophic scenarios.

Delta/Vega Hedging

Although I have only discussed the hedging of delta risks thus far, as can be seen in Table 7.13, the vega risks inherent in the put option are, in fact, the largest risks vis-à-vis the delta, gamma, and rho risks. Despite this, there is no necessity for the hedger to hedge the vega risks. In fact, it is not uncommon for some practitioners to take on these risks unhedged and only run a delta-hedging program.[29]

[29]One rationale for this behavior is due to the mindset that the 10-year historical volatility is a better measure for the 10-year realized volatility. Since the 10-year implied volatility tends to exceed the 10-year historical volatility by a big margin (which sometimes can be as much as 15 percent—when the 10-year historical volatility is as low as 17 percent) and the historical volatility is quite stable (in that the distribution of 10-year historical volatility tends to have a small standard deviation), practitioners think of this risk as negligible. As a consequence of this, deltas are computed using these historical volatilities. It is important for the reader to understand that with this thinking, the hedger cannot expect the mark-to-market value of his/her 10-year put option to be consistent with what the capital markets would indicate, because the capital markets' pricing of these options is driven off implied volatilities. (See Chapter 6 and footnote 30).

Given the above backdrop, should the hedger decide to hedge the vega risks, he or she is now faced with the task of trying the extend the delta-hedging analysis to incorporate delta-vega hedging attributes. To do this, one has to incorporate the following mechanics:

- Introduce option assets that can be used to manage the vega risks.[30]
- Be able to simulate implied volatilities (and/or produce a real-world scenario of implied volatilities).
- Introduce bid-offer spreads on implied volatilities.

Given the above caveats, to illustrate the implementation of the vega-hedging program and keep the illustration manageable, I will assume that:

- The hedge asset is a nine-year, at-the-money put option.
- Every time the net portfolio vega risks are neutralized, the hedger sells all the existing assets at market price and transacts into the then-prevailing 9-year at-the-money put option.[31]

---

[30]Since there is a large variety of options that can be used (e.g., at the-money, in-the-money, and out-of-the-money options with maturities of one, two, or six months, and so on), the hedger is faced with the daunting task of deciding how best to select the right option to manage this risk and to neutralize the vega risks, the hedger first needs to identify the option's maturity and strike before deciding on the quantity of such options needed. See also footnote 15.

Furthermore, the consequence of using options as hedge assets and managing the vega risks to historical volatility (though this can be done) would be a nightmare of trying to keep track of the cash flow going in and out of the hedging program. To understand this better, consider the instance when the 10-year option (in Table 7.13) is underwritten when the implied and historical volatilities are 35 and 20 percent, respectively. A 35 percent (20 percent) implied (historical) volatility gives a premium of about \$560 (\$166) and a vega of about 2770 (2267) for this 10-year option and charges \$560 for the sale of the option. Suppose now that 1 year has passed and the 9-year hedge option has the same implied (historical) volatilities, giving it a respective premium of \$578 (\$179) and a vega of about 2790 (2330). If the hedger uses the historical volatility to manage the hedging program, then he/she would be needing 0.97, 9-year, at-the-money put options leading to a cost of \$174—which unfortunately would not be the actual amount paid out as the market would demand a premium of \$562, making it difficult (but not impossible) to keep track of the cash flow going in and out of the hedging program. This problem does not occur if the hedger runs the entire hedging program using implied volatilities.

[31]This is a departure from what I did for the delta-hedging program where it was sufficient for me to top up or scale down the deltas by buying (selling) additional (redundant) shares.

- Liquidating options are done at mid-market volatility levels, while the purchase (sales) of new at-the-money options are done at higher (lower) implied-volatility levels.
- The monitoring and neutralizing of the net portfolio vega/delta risks would last until the first year of hedging is completed. Once this one-year mark is reached, the hedger will enter into a 9-year put option that perfectly replicates the option sold (hence this asset may not be an at-the-money option).
- Spot-implied volatilities across all maturities and strikes are assumed to be constant (i.e., the implied volatility surface is trivially parallel to the strike and term axis).[32]
- Term structure of spot-implied volatilities is assumed to move as an entity[33] and is simulated using the simple lognormal pdf.[34] More precisely, I will assume that $\ln\sigma_{t+u}$ is normally distributed with mean $\ln\sigma_t - 0.02u$ and variance $0.04u$—where σ_{t+u} represents the term structure of spot volatilities at time $t + u$.

One can now use the above assumptions and implement a vega-hedging program (similar to what was done to a delta-hedging program) and obtain the results in Table 7.17.[35]

Table 7.17 shows the impact of the correlation between the volatility and stock-price jumps and net portfolio volatility-trading limits. From the table, two important observations can be made:

---

[32]As a consequence of this, forward volatilities would trivially also be the same as the spot volatilities.

[33]See comment following Table 7.10 on the bucketing of vegas.

[34]This is an example of a simple volatility generator. One can easily use something that is more complex like the Heston's model or any other volatility generator to customize the generation of implied volatilities.

[35]To do this, I had to first simulate the volatility of the stock using the lognormal assumption for future spot-volatility movements, use that volatility to simulate stock prices, which are used to compute the vega of the 10-year put as it decays through time. At each time of rebalancing, I had to compute the amount of 9-year at-the-money options that I had to buy so that the vegas are neutralized. Once this amount is determined, I had to compute the net deltas of the portfolio (comprising the sold put and the newly acquired 9-year put) and then check to see what the portfolio delta is and if I should neutralize it (in which case I would need to transact in stocks). I continued this process until the end of the first year when I unwound all my positions to transact in a 9-year option with a strike price of \$40 (the same level as the original 10-year put option that was originally sold). In this way, all the Greeks will be completely neutralized until the maturity of the sold option.

TABLE 7.17 Hedge P&L in a 2 Percent Bid-Offer Spread in Both Volatility and Stock Price Movements and $0

Volatility Trading Limit	Perfect Positive Correlation		No Correlation		Perfect Negative Correlation	
	Average	Stdev	Average	Stdev	Average	Stdev
$–	$4,477.20	$508.90	$4,397.81	$1,113.30	$4,367.66	$1,364.96
$5.00	$328.83	$158.41	$1,891.63	$900.02	$1,945.53	$1,234.27
$10.00	$127.32	$66.94	$1,076.97	$742.27	$1,208.11	$1,040.31
$15.00	$76.68	$41.35	$669.61	$588.34	$703.59	$926.68
$20.00	$56.45	$25.92	$451.75	$455.59	$499.35	$751.46
$25.00	$48.13	$19.43	$317.78	$362.52	$389.95	$604.90
$30.00	$43.04	$17.99	$231.49	$297.91	$310.49	$495.19
$35.00	$38.67	$17.76	$171.77	$239.34	$252.40	$407.82
$40.00	$34.19	$16.97	$132.74	$197.57	$205.75	$338.47
$45.00	$29.43	$12.42	$105.07	$164.08	$171.08	$289.13
$50.00	$28.27	$11.75	$84.01	$135.93	$139.90	$240.09
$55.00	$27.37	$11.03	$68.27	$111.97	$116.33	$204.33
$60.00	$26.48	$10.41	$55.88	$93.07	$96.59	$171.13
$65.00	$25.71	$9.81	$46.64	$77.21	$80.69	$147.30
$70.00	$25.10	$8.97	$39.39	$62.11	$67.40	$123.29

1. Correlations between stock-price and volatility-rate jumps do matter, in that the more negative the correlation, the higher the hedge costs. While all the information is computed when the net portfolio delta-trading limit is 0, having a nonzero limit would definitely have an impact on the results
2. In the hedging strategy discussed, I used a 9-year option that I rolled over each vega rebalancing moment. In practice nothing stops me from using options of other maturities (e.g., a 3-year put or 1-year call option—assuming that such options are available in abundance). In such an instance, the reader should realize that while it is theoretically possible to neutralize the vega of a 10-put option using short-dated options, volatilities trade like yield curves.[36] As a consequence, in practice, as

[36]Like the yield curves where different maturities have different characteristics (i.e., the short end of the yield curve does not trade like the long end of the yield curve), the volatility term structures are similar. As a consequence, as in the yield curve, the trader needs to understand the dynamics between short-, medium-, and long-term volatility movements and how one may (or may not) affect the other.

discussed earlier, it is customary to have three net portfolio vega-trading limits (short term, medium term, and long term)—where the short term would possibly contain option maturities that are three years and lesser, the long term would possibly contain option maturities that are seven years and longer. Doing this allows the hedger to more prudently quantify and manage vega risks.

Additional Considerations

In addition to what has been discussed, there are a few other pertinent observations a hedger should be concerned about when running this kind of analysis. For instance:

One can extend the discussion of the delta/vega-hedging strategy to include the hedging of rho risks. To do this, the hedger needs to use at-market interest rate swaps to manage the rho risks. More precisely, like the vega risks, it is customary to monitor the short-, mid-, and long-term risks and then hedge these risks respectively, using swaps of the appropriate maturity.

I discussed two strategies to help hedge the risks underlying the sale of a 10-year put option. One was a delta-hedging strategy (in which the delta risks are managed for the entire 10-year period). The second was a delta/vega strategy (in which the delta/vega risks are managed for one year after which the strategy rolls into a 9-year option that perfectly mimicked the option sold). These strategies are by no means exhaustive; other strategies a hedger might want to test are a delta/rho-based strategy (which, with an at-market swap rate matching the maturity of the sold option, is rolled over every time the net portfolio rho risk is neutralized), a delta/vega strategy (in which short-dated options are used), and so on.

To test a collection of strategies, it is imperative for the hedger to ensure that a unique set of trading limits and the frequency of trading limit monitoring (whenever applicable) is used. Once these are identified, the strategies can be put through a series of real-world scenarios and simulated scenarios (as was done in Tables 7.13, 7.14, and 7.16) to obtain the mean and standard and whatever statistics (or metrics) the hedger wants to use to rank the strategies from the best to the worst.

When the 10-year option was sold, the predominant risks happened to be the volatility and interest-rate risks. When options are short-dated or path-dependent in nature, other types of risks tend to be more predominant (e.g., gamma risks). As such, it is imperative for the hedger to not try to naively apply what was an effective hedge strategy for one type of option to another option.

REFERENCES

Anton, H. 2010. *Elementary Linear Algebra.* 10th ed. Hoboken, NJ: John Wiley & Sons.

Black, F., and M. Scholes. 1973. "The Pricing of Options and Corporate Liabilities." *Journal of Political Economy* 81:673–659.

Garman, M. B., and S. W. Kohlhagen. 1983. "Foreign Currency Option Values." *Journal of International Money and Finance* 2:231–237.

Hull, J. C. 2012. *Options, Futures and Other Derivatives.* 8th ed. Upper Saddle River, NJ: Prentice Hall.

Ito, K. 1951. "On Stochastic Differential Equations." *Memoirs of the American Mathematical Society* 4:1–51.

Leland, H. E. 1985. "Option Pricing and Replication with Transaction Costs." *The Journal of Finance* 40:1283–1301.

CHAPTER 8

Valuing Variable Annuity Guarantees

In Chapter 5, I presented examples of exotic–option pricing that traded in the capital-markets arena. In this chapter, I will discuss an example of an exotic option that is couched as a retail investment product that is prevalent in the insurance industry. Known as *variable annuities* (*VAs*), these products are essentially mutual fund investments with performance guarantees that are linked to the time of death—hence making it possible to be manufactured only by life insurance companies.[1]

VAs have been sold in the United States by life insurance companies since the late 1960s.[2,3] Although variable annuities were originally sold

---

[1]Other examples of exotic options that are sold by insurance companies as investment products include the indexed (or fixed-indexed) annuities. Unlike variable annuities, in which investments are made directly by policyholders into units of mutual funds, deposits in indexed annuities are credited using market returns (which sometimes may be path dependent). Because of the nature of the deposits, the Securities Exchange Commission (SEC) does not regulate indexed annuities.

[2]It is more correct to say that the first forms of VA contracts were not really VA contracts. Issued by Teachers Insurance and Annuities Association College Retirement Equities Fund (TIAA-CREF) in 1952, a special fund was used to provide VA-like coverage within the retirement-income program of TIAA. Thus, although it was not an individual annuity contract, the development of this first VA concept by TIAA helped with the development of the VA market during the 1960s when the regulatory environment for VAs became better defined. See Kalberer and Ravindran (2009).

[3]To sell such a product, an insurance company has to file a prospectus with the SEC and the state it wants to sell the product in (as these products are regulated by the state regulators, federal regulator, and the SEC). Such a filed prospectus typically tends to be 200 to 300 pages in length and contains detailed information associated with the VA product—examples of which include the nature/names of funds, types of fees/penalties charged for funds/guarantees/policy surrenders, and so on.

as mutual funds containing embedded death benefits (sometimes known as guaranteed minimum death benefits or GMDBs), in recent decades variable annuities have morphed to include living benefits (sometimes known as guaranteed minimum accumulation benefits or GMABs, guaranteed minimum income benefits or GMIBs, and guaranteed minimum withdrawal benefits or GMWBs). VAs have gained tremendous popularity with consumers so much so that in the U.S. market new annual sales volume easily exceeds USD$110 billion and the current total volume of the U.S. marketplace for such products far exceeds 1 trillion U.S. dollars—making it an important investment tool in any retiree's investment-product arsenal. The interested reader is referred to the classic 2009 reference on this topic by Kalberer and Ravindran for further details.

This chapter starts with a discussion on how a GMDB product works in practice. I then discuss how a GMDB can be priced, using the previously used assumptions in conjunction with mortality probabilities, so as to more accurately quantify the risks. In doing so, I will discuss a caveat relating to valuing long-dated options and suggest a solution to get around this problem. Using the suggested solution, I value the long-dated options embedded in a GMDB product followed by a discussion of other nuances/features associated with GMDB. The chapter concludes with a brief discussion of the living benefits that are often attached as riders to the basic GMDB product as well as death-benefit riders.

BASIC GMDB

The GMDB, in its basic form, is constructed to protect the beneficiary against the drop in value of the initial investment (in mutual funds) at the time of the annuitant's death.[4] Succinctly put, a GMDB in its basic form has the following characteristics:

[4]The three words that get used very frequently when dealing with insurance contracts are *annuitant*, *policyholder*, and *beneficiary*. The word annuitant refers to the person whose life is used to determine the time at which the policy is paid off and, as a consequence, the actuarial risks associated with the insurance product. While this typically refers to a single life, in practice it is not uncommon to also see joint lives used to determine if the death has happened. More precisely, in the instance of a couple, the measuring life would be the life of the first member to die while the beneficiary would be the surviving member of the couple. The word policyholder refers to the person who is the legal owner of the policy. While it is usual for a policyholder to be a single individual, it is not uncommon to have multiple people or even a corporation (entity) owning a policy. The word beneficiary refers to the person who is deriving the "benefit" from the annuitant's death. Similar to the

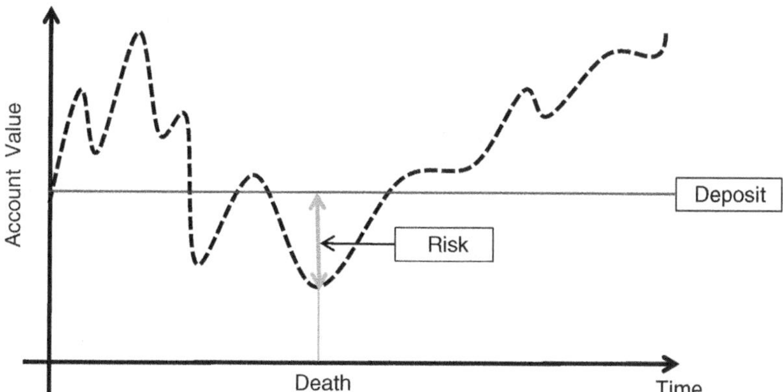

FIGURE 8.1 Risks to the Insurance Company Underwriting a Basic GMDB

- A single upfront premium that is deposited at the inception of contract by purchasing units of a fund.[5]
- The premium is returned to the beneficiary at the time of the annuitant's death and is guaranteed to be no less than the deposited amount.
- Fees for fund management and the guarantee of principal are deducted daily from the fund price returns.

Figure 8.1 aptly describes most of the characteristics described above and the risk to the insurance company for offering such a product (where the Account Value associated with the investment is trivially the same as the number of fund units multiplied by the fund unit value).

As can be seen from Figure 8.1, the insurance company's risk in selling this product only happens when the value of the investment drops to a level lower than the deposit at the time of the annuitant's death. To quantify these risks, the insurance company needs to think through the issues like how to

policyholder, while it is usual for a policy to have one beneficiary, it is not uncommon to have multiple beneficiaries or even a corporation as beneficiaries of a policy. Given the backdrop, while in theory it is possible for the annuitant, policyholder, and beneficiary to be three different people, in practice it is often the case that the policyholder is also either the annuitant or the beneficiary—but NOT both—for a single life. On the other hand, when considering joint lives, it is quite common for these three parties (policyholders/annuitants/beneficiaries) to be the one and same.

[5]This is only a simplifying assumption in that the policyholders are allowed to deposit additional premiums during the life of the contract—subject to certain restrictions imposed by the contracts.

model future fund value movements, what does the payoff associated with the guarantee look like, and how to go about valuing these guarantees.

Modeling Future Fund Value Movements

As in the earlier chapters, I assume that index-value movements best mimic fund movements. As a consequence, I will use a diffusion equation that is a slight modification of equation (3.5) that is given by the expression

$$\frac{dS}{S} = (g - q)dt + \sigma dz \tag{8.1}$$

where

S is the value of the fund.
g is the annualized continuously compounded growth rate.
q is the annualized continuously compounded fees.[6]
σ is the annualized volatility of the fund return.
dz is the random variable drawn from a standard normal probability density function.
dS is the small change in the fund value over a small time interval dt.

As the reader will recall, the characterization in equation (8.1) is equivalent to assuming that $\ln S_T$ is normally distributed with a mean of $\ln S_t + (g_{t,T} - q_{t,T} - \frac{1}{2}\sigma^2_{t,T})(T - t)$, and, variance of $\sigma^2_{t,T}(T - t)$, where $g_{t,T}$ represents the continuously compounded growth rate that is applied from time t to T, and the rest of the notations are consistent with those used before.

Payoff Associated with the Guarantees

First observe that the beneficiary stands to receive from the annuitant's death a benefit of $N * \max(S_t, S_T)$, where N represents the number of fund units, S_t represents the fund unit value at time t (inception of the contract), and S_T represents the fund unit value net of fees at time T (where T represents the time of the annuitant's death).

[6]This is used to represent the sum of the fund management fees as well as the fees associated with the basic death benefit. The fact that this is continuously compounded is only a simplifying assumption. See the section on Other Details Associated with GMDB Products later in this chapter.

$N * \max(S_t, S_T)$ can be rewritten as $N * [S_T + \max(S_t - S_T, 0)]$, from which it can be easily seen that an investment in a GMDB can be alternatively viewed as the sum of investment value[7] at the time of death, and N units of put option (which has a strike of S_t and a life of $(T - t)$).

Thus, purchasing a basic GMDB is equivalent to purchasing N fund units and N put options (where each at-the-money spot option has a life of $T - t$ years)—assuming that the annuitant dies at time T and the fund units are redeemed only at time T.

Valuing the Guarantees Using Annualized Options

Given the comment in the earlier section, one can assume without a loss of generality that the policyholder purchases one unit of a fund instead of the N units (and hence deposits an amount of $\$S_t$). From this, it readily follows that the value of the return of premium option (expiring at time T) can be obtained using the expression

$$-S_t e^{(g_{t,T} - q_{t,T} - r_{t,T})(T-t)} N\left(-d^1_{S_t,S_t,t,T,g_{t,T},q_{t,T},\sigma_{t,T}}\right) + S_t e^{-r_{t,T}(T-t)} N\left(-d^2_{S_t,S_t,t,T,g_{t,T},q_{t,T},\sigma_{t,T}}\right) \quad (8.2)$$

where $d^1_{S_t,K,t,T,g_{t,T},q_{t,T},\sigma_{t,T}}$ and $d^2_{S_t,K,t,T,g_{t,T},q_{t,T},\sigma_{t,T}}$ are as defined earlier.

As the reader will realize, equation (8.2) holds true only if the annuitant dies at time T. Equation (8.2) can alternatively be viewed as a put option that was described in equation (3.7b) with the dividend rate, $q_{t,T}$ in that equation, set to $r_{t,T} - g_{t,T} + q_{t,T}$.

Since the probability of the annuitant dying precisely at one moment (i.e., exactly at time T) is 0, it is more realistic to consider the probability of the annuitant dying in a time interval. More precisely, by assuming that the annuitant can die within the ith year of policy purchase (where $i = 1, 2, 3, \ldots$), I will, for the purposes of option valuation, assume that the market risks associated with the death of the annuitant during the ith policy year can be hedged by an option that has a life of i years (where $i = 1, 2, 3, \ldots$). It is intuitively reasonable to expect the probability of the annuitant dying during the ith policy year to change as the value i increases and for these probabilities to be a function of the annuitant's age.[8]

---

[7]This is actually N times the fund unit value at the time of death (i.e., T).

[8]In practice, life insurance companies do this using mortality tables. Mortality tables are created by the life insurance sector, using historical death patterns, to quantify

TABLE 8.1 Sample Annual Mortality Rates for Annuitants Aged from 50 to 60

	A	B
1	50	0.451800%
2	51	0.493800%
3	52	0.537000%
4	53	0.581100%
5	54	0.626000%
6	55	0.671800%
7	56	0.718400%
8	57	0.765800%
9	58	0.814600%
10	59	0.867100%
11	60	0.926600%

Given the above backdrop, if the age of the policyholder is x when the current time is t (i.e., at the policy inception), it readily follows from equation (8.2) that the value of the $116 - x$ options is given by the expression

$$S_t \sum_{i=1}^{116-x} q_{x,x+i} * \left\{ -e^{(g_{t,t+i}-q_{t,t+i}-r_{t,t+i})i} N\left(-d^1_{S_t,S_t,t,t+i,g_{t,t+i},q_{t,t+i},\sigma_{t,t+i}}\right) \right.$$
$$\left. + e^{-(r_{t,t+i})i} N\left(-d^2_{S_t,S_t,t,t+i,g_{t,t+i},q_{t,t+i},\sigma_{t,t+i}}\right) \right\} \tag{8.3a}$$

where $q_{x,x+y}$ denotes the probability of an x-year-old annuitant dying during the age $x + y - 1$ and $x + y$ for $y = 1, 2, 3, \ldots$.

Table 8.1 gives a snapshot of a typical mortality table capturing the probability of an individual dying within a year for a given age.

The 0.4518 percent entry in cell B1 of Table 8.1 refers to the probability that a 50-year-old would die in the coming year (i.e., before reaching age 51). Similarly, the 0.4938 percent entry in cell B2 refers to the probability that a 51-year-old will die before reaching 52, and so on. Since Table 8.1 is

---

the probability of dying in any given year for any given age (where this age can go as long as 115). These country-specific industry-based tables are typically revised when the industry, as a whole, feels that that has been a marked deviation from what has been produced. Although the life insurance industry as a whole produces different mortality tables for male smokers, male nonsmokers, female smokers, female nonsmokers, and so on, insurance companies in practice revise these industry-based mortality tables to reflect their company specific experience.

an example of what a typical mortality table looks like, one would need to arithmetically manipulate these rates to obtain the values of $q_{x,x+i}$ that are needed to solve equation (8.3a). Table 8.2 shows how all these components are put together to obtain the value of the options when the annuitant is 100 years old.[9]

There are a few observations the reader should make (some obvious and some not so obvious) from Table 8.2.

Since the current age of the annuitant is 100, the mortality table goes until age 115 and assumes that any death happening in any one year can be hedged by a put option expiring at the end of the death year. It is easy to see that only 116 – 100 = 16 put options contributed to the total cost of the put options embedded in this GMDB. The costs associated with each of these options are given from cells G9:G24, and the total of these costs is given in cell G25. In the event that the age of the annuitant is now 50 (instead of 100), this would imply one would have a total of 116 – 50 = 66 put options (ranging in maturities from 1 to 66 years) that would be contributing toward the cost of these options.

The mortality rates (extracted directly from the mortality table) are given in cells B9:B24, where cell B9 refers to the probability of a 100-year-old dying before age 101 (i.e., $q_{100,101}$), cell B10 refers to the probability of a 101-year-old dying before age 102 (i.e., $q_{101,102}$), and so on. To compute the $q_{x,x+i}$ factor that is present in equation (8.3a), namely $q_{100,101}, q_{100,102}, q_{100,103}, \ldots, q_{100,151}$, one has to derive them with the aid of the mortality rates given in cells B9:B24 using the following approach:

$q_{100,101}$, the value in cell C9, refers to the probability that a 100-year-old would die before 101 and this is trivially the mortality probability given in cell B9.

$q_{100,102}$, the value in cell C10, refers to the probability that a 100-year-old would die after 101 but before 102. This is trivially the probability of surviving until age 101 and then dying in the year of age 101. As a consequence,

$$q_{100,102} = (1 - q_{100,101}) * q_{101,102}$$

$q_{100,103}$, the value in cell C11, can similarly be obtained using the expression

$$(1 - q_{100,101}) * (1 - q_{101,102}) * q_{102,103}$$

[9]I used 100 here for the purposes of illustration so that the exhibit associated with the illustration of the number of put options valued is manageable.

TABLE 8.2 Valuation of Embedded Put Options When Annuitant Is 100 Years Old

	A	B	C	D	E	F	G	H
1	Current Fund Value (*St*)	10						
2	Risk Free Rate (*r*)	5.00%						
3	Growth Rate (*g*)	10.00%						
4	Management/Basic Death Benefit Fees (*q*)	2.00%						
5	Volatility (σ)	20.00%						
6	Current Age (*x*)	100						
7	Current Time	0						
8	Age	$q_{x+i,x+i+1}$	$q_{x+i,x+i+1}$	Expiry (*T*)	d^1	d^2	Put Premium	
9	100	0.3007160	0.3007160	1	1	0	0.1368859	
10	101	0.3235920	0.226283	2	1	0	0.1112551	
11	102	0.3487800	0.164973	3	1	1	0.0795338	
12	103	0.3765290	0.115981	4	1	1	0.0529527	
13	104	0.4070880	0.07818	5	1	1	0.0332321	
14	105	0.4407070	0.050182	6	1	1	0.0196680	
15	106	0.4776340	0.030418	7	1	1	0.0109262	
16	107	0.5181200	0.017236	8	1	1	0.0056515	
17	108	0.5624120	0.009016	9	2	1	0.0026909	
18	109	0.6107600	0.004284	10	2	1	0.0011617	
19	110	0.6634170	0.001811	11	2	1	0.0004456	
20	111	0.7206260	0.000662	12	2	1	0.0001476	
21	112	0.7826400	0.000201	13	2	1	0.0000406	
22	113	0.8497080	4.74E-05	14	2	1	0.0000087	
23	114	0.9220770	7.73E-06	15	2	1	0.0000013	
24	115	1.0000000	6.54E-07	16	2	1	0.0000001	
25				Total			0.4546017	

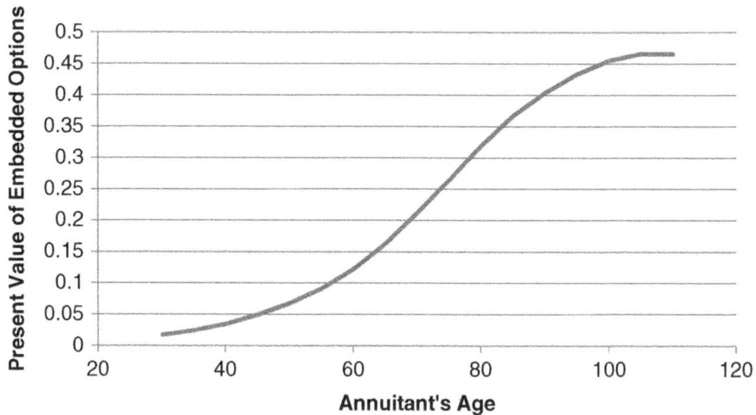

FIGURE 8.2 Impact of Issue Age on Guaranteed Value

In general, $q_{100,i}$ (for $i = 102, \ldots, 116$) can be obtained using the expression

$$\left\{ \prod_{j=100}^{i-2} (1 - q_{j,j+1}) \right\} * q_{i-1,i}$$

In practice, although most of the annuitants purchasing such investment products tend to be in their fifties, the exact age breakdown is not known to the insurance company a priori to launching the product. As a consequence, when developing these products, it is difficult for the insurance company to accurately forecast the actual breakdown of the age of potential purchasers of the product. Given this backdrop, an insurance company typically runs the type of analysis outlined in Table 8.2 across differing ages and then probability weighs[10] the results across the ages to estimate how much these guarantees are in fact worth. Doing this across differing ages when the investment policy is issued, one can arrive at Figure 8.2.

[10]Since the development of any product is done with the input of the sales force (or insurance agents), the estimation of the age distribution of potential clients is done using inputs from its agents, distribution of competitors' sales (if available), positioning of the product (e.g., if the product can be purchased in a retirement account using pretax funds or using after-tax dollars), and its own desire to target a certain age segment of the market—just to name a few.

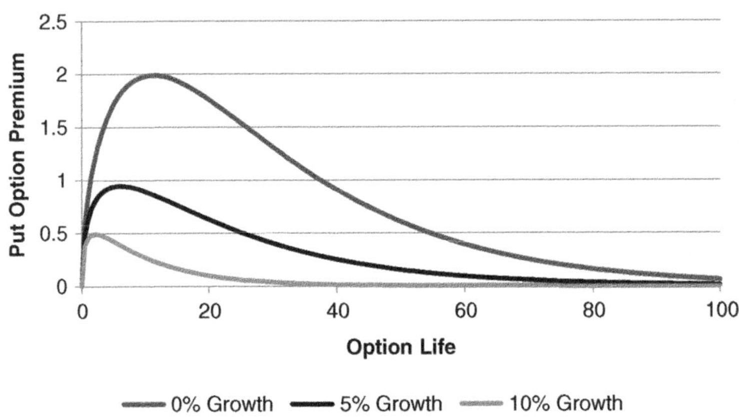

FIGURE 8.3 Impact of Maturity on Option Premium

The younger the annuitant's age on the date of issue, the greater the number of options needed to quantify the risks accurately—which intuitively translates to the younger the annuitant, the larger the cumulative value of the options used to hedge the risks. Figure 8.2 seems to contradict this intuition and the reason for this lies in the way put-option values behave as the maturity of the option increases (a consequence of the Black-Scholes equation). To understand this better, I will digress for a bit to discuss the valuation of long-dated vanilla put options.

Ignoring the mortality component in Table 8.2, Figure 8.3 shows the impact of the option life on the option value for varying growth rates when all other inputs (fund value, risk-free rate, volatility, management fees) are kept the same.

As can be seen from Figure 8.3, regardless of the fund growth rate, the option value increases as option maturity increases until a certain point in time and then starts decreasing to 0.[11] In reality, even if one could possibly buy a 100-year-option, the value of the 100-year option will definitely not be anywhere close to zero—underlining the importance of using the Black-Scholes model prudently. As in Ravindran and Edelist (1977), I will assume that the option premiums are bounded from below (i.e., floored). Figure 8.4 illustrates the consequence of flooring these premiums.

[11]This is contrary to what is usually presented in many finance textbooks. More precisely, one of the properties of the Black-Scholes model, as described in this literature, is that option premiums are nondecreasing functions of option lives—which although true in practice is not the consequence of the Black-Scholes model.

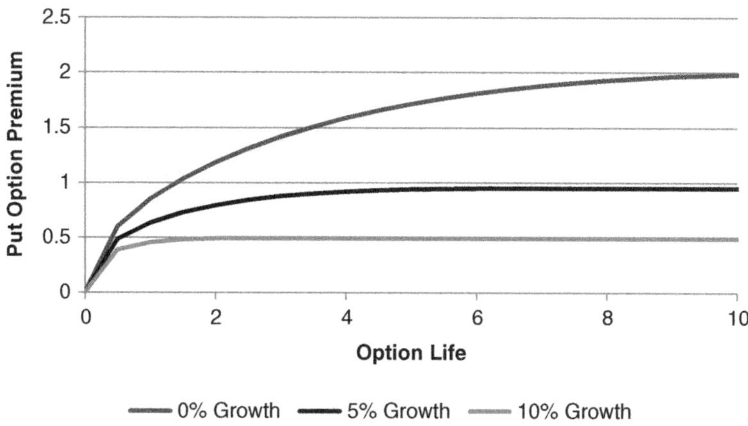

FIGURE 8.4 Impact of Maturity on a Floored Option Premium

Before applying the concept of flooring to redo the analysis required to reproduce Figure 8.2, one first needs to apply some of the ideas discussed in Chapter 6. More precisely, one has to imply inputs from the floored option premiums used to produce Figure 8.4. To do this, I will first imply the volatility of the options from the floored premiums and then use this implied volatility to price the embedded at-the-money options. Figure 8.5a shows the implied volatilities extracted from the at-the-money option premiums shown in Figure 8.4 over varying maturities.

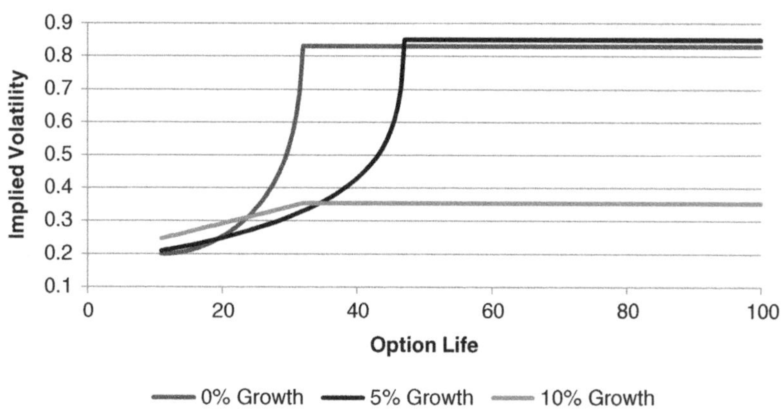

FIGURE 8.5A Term Structure of Implied Volatilities for At-The-Money Options

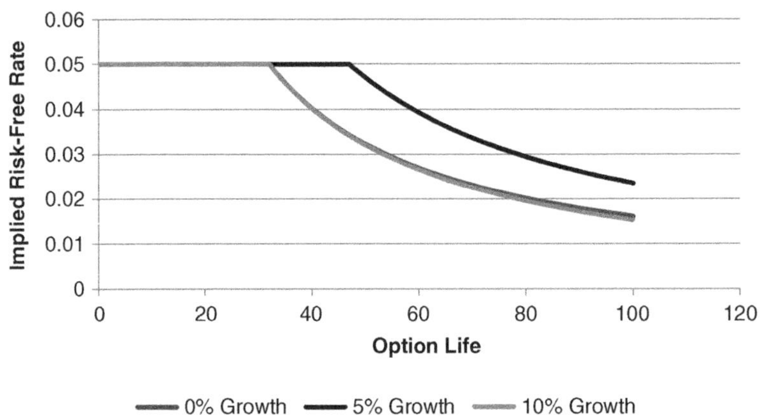

FIGURE 8.5B Term Structure of Implied Risk-Free Rates for At-The-Money Options

As can be seen from Figure 8.5a, the implied volatility keeps increasing as the option maturity increases (an intuitively reasonable result) and then flattens out after a period of 30 years or more. The reason for this is simply due to the fact that since the start time of the flattening is also the start time for which no implied volatility exists (i.e., no volatility can be high enough to match the option premium), I had for convenience kept the implied volatility flat for this time period. As a consequence, I needed to calibrate another input of the option pricing model (e.g., the continuously compounded risk-free rate) so as to ensure that the option premiums in Figure 8.4 can be reproduced. To do this, I started with the term structure of zero rates and then calibrated it in conjunction with the volatility term structure given in Figure 8.5a, so that the option premiums in Figure 8.4 can be reproduced. Doing this yields the implied term structure of zero rates as given in Figure 8.5b.

Using the implied parameters in Figures 8.5a and 8.5b, one can now revalue the embedded options in the GMDB. Figure 8.6 illustrates the difference in premiums obtained by using the implied information (i.e., volatilities and risk-free rates) and the non-implied information (i.e., same as what was used to generate the premiums in Figure 8.2).

As can be seen from Figure 8.6, consistent with intuition, the difference in the total value of the embedded option premiums decrease as the annuitant's age gets higher—illustrating the fact that implied information affects longer dated options. Furthermore, in approximating a death incurring in a year by an option expiring at the end of the year, I have made a

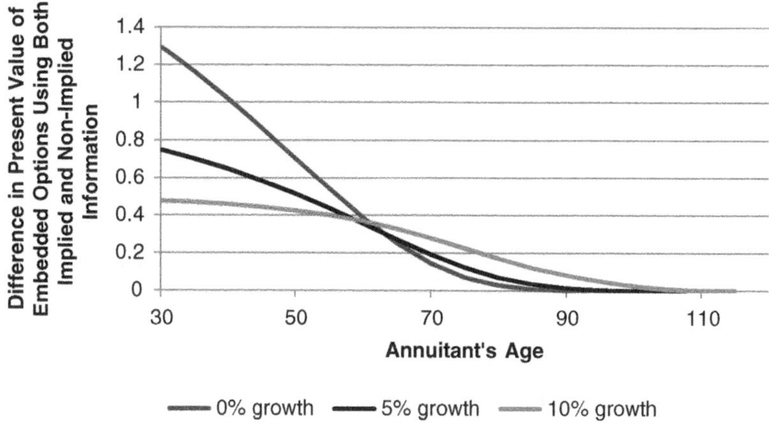

FIGURE 8.6 Impact of Using Implied Information to Value GMDB Guarantees Across Varying Growth Rates

departure from the way these policies are settled in practice (as seen in Figure 8.1). More precisely, the insurance company is contractually on the hook for any downturn in investment performance at market closing on the day of death.[12] Ravindran and Edelist (1997) discuss the use of continuous pdfs and their impact on the total-option premium when compared to the annual approximation. In practice, instead of using an annual time-step approximation, insurance companies use a monthly time-step approximation that I discuss next.

Valuing the Guarantees Using More Frequent Options

Equation (8.3a) contains the expression when annual mortality rates are used to value annualized options (i.e., options with maturities $1, 2, 3, \ldots$

[12]It is not uncommon for there to be a time lag between the actual time of the annuitant's death and the time when the insurance company is notified of the death. While in some insurance contracts this can be as long as a year, there are also instances when the insurance companies are never notified. As a practical matter, it is important for the reader to note that even if the beneficiary informs the insurance company of the passing of the annuitant months after the death, it is often the case that the insurance company is contractually required to pay the beneficiary using the closing market values at the time of the annuitant's death and not at the time the death notification is received by the insurance company.

years). In the event that this is done once every six months (as opposed to once a year), equation (8.3a) becomes equation (8.3b).

$$\begin{aligned} S_t \sum_{i=1}^{232-2x} q_{x,x+0.5i} \Big\{ & -e^{(g_{t,t+0.5i}-q_{t,t+0.5i}-r_{t,t+0.5i})0.5i} \\ & N\left(-d^1_{S_t,S_t,t,t+0.5i,g_{t,t+0.5i},q_{t,t+0.5i},\sigma_{t,t+0.5i}}\right) \\ & + e^{-(r_{t,t+i})0.5i} N\left(-d^2_{S_t,S_t,t,t+0.5i,g_{t,t+0.5i},q_{t,t+0.5i},\sigma_{t,t+0.5i}}\right)\Big\} \end{aligned} \tag{8.3b}$$

Since $q_{x,x+0.5i}$ refers to the probability that the x-year-old annuitant dies during age $x + 0.5(i-1)$ and $x + 0.5i$, one needs to extract this probability from the table of annual mortality rates $q_{x,x+1}$ for $x = 0, 1, \ldots, 115$.

To do this, one has to observe that given $q_{x,x+1}$ a population of 100 when the annuitant is x years old reduces to a size of $100(1 - q_{x,x+1})$ at the end of one year (when the annuitant reaches $x + 1$ years). To obtain the semiannual equivalent mortality rates $q_{x,x+0.5}$ and $q_{x+0.5,x+1}$ from $q_{x,x+1}$, one has to first assume that $q_{x,x+0.5} = q_{x+0.5,x+1}$. Then it readily follows that

$$100 * (1 - q_{x,x+1}) = 100 * (1 - q_{x,x+0.5}) * (1 - q_{x,x+0.5})$$

from which one can obtain the expression

$$q_{x,x+0.5} = q_{x+0.5,x+1} = 1 - (1 - q_{x,x+1})^{\frac{1}{2}}$$

Similarly it can be shown that

$$\begin{aligned} q_{x+1,x+1.5} &= q_{x+1.5,x+2} = 1 - (1 - q_{x+1,x+2})^{\frac{1}{2}} \\ q_{x+2,x+2.5} &= q_{x+2.5,x+3} = 1 - (1 - q_{x+2,x+3})^{\frac{1}{2}} \\ q_{x+(115-x),x+(115-x)+0.5} &= q_{x+(115-x)+0.5,x+(116-x)} \\ &= 1 - (1 - q_{x+(115-x),x+(116-x)})^{\frac{1}{2}} \end{aligned}$$

Table 8.3 shows an example of an implementation of the extraction of semiannual mortality probabilities from the standard mortality tables.

TABLE 8.3 Extracting Semiannual Mortality Rates from Annual Mortality Rates

	A	B	C	D
1	Age	Annual Mortality Prob	Semiannual Mortality Prob	
2	50	0.451800%	0.226156%	=1-(1-B2)^(1/2)
3	50.5		0.226156%	=1-(1-B2)^(1/2)
4	51	0.493800%	0.247206%	=1-(1-C2)^(1/2)
5	51.5		0.247206%	=1-(1-C2)^(1/2)
6	52	0.537000%	0.268861%	=1-(1-D2)^(1/2)
7	52.5		0.268861%	=1-(1-D2)^(1/2)
8	53	0.581100%	0.290973%	=1-(1-E2)^(1/2)
9	53.5		0.290973%	=1-(1-E2)^(1/2)
10	54	0.626000%	0.313491%	=1-(1-F2)^(1/2)
11	54.5		0.313491%	=1-(1-F2)^(1/2)
12	55	0.671800%	0.336466%	=1-(1-G2)^(1/2)
13	55.5		0.336466%	=1-(1-G2)^(1/2)

The results of Table 8.3 have been extended further using similar ideas to obtain quarterly,[13] monthly,[14] and so on mortality rates as shown in Table 8.4.

Given the backdrop of Table 8.4, it is useful to see how much of an approximation error is being made by keeping to the original paradigm of annualized options (in the context of the 100-year-old annuitant, this would be moving from 16 options with maturities ranging from $1, 2, \ldots, 16$ years to as many as 192 options with maturities ranging from $\frac{1}{12}, \frac{2}{12}, \ldots, \frac{192}{12}$ years. Figure 8.7 captures these differences based on the information outlined in Table 8.2. As the reader can expect, these differences would be a function of volatility rates, risk-free rates, growth rates, and mortality rates.

[13]This can be obtained using a similar expression that is adjusted for the compounding frequency. For example, $q_{x,x+0.25} = q_{x+0.25,x+0.5} = q_{x+0.5,x+0.75} = q_{x+0.75,x+1} = 1 - (1 - q_{x,x+1})^{\frac{1}{4}}$.

[14]The expression for the monthly mortality rates can also be obtained using similar expressions for the quarterly and semiannual rates—but adjusted for the frequency of compounded.

TABLE 8.4 Extracting Quarterly and Monthly Mortality Rates from Annual Mortality Rates

	A	B	C	D	E
1	Age	Annual Mortality Prob	Semiannual Mortality Prob	Quarterly Mortality Prob	Monthly Mortality Prob
2	50	0.451800%	0.226156%	0.113142%	0.037728%
3	50.0833333				0.037728%
4	50.1666667				0.037728%
5	50.25			0.113142%	0.037728%
6	50.3333333				0.037728%
7	50.4166667				0.037728%
8	50.5		0.226156%	0.113142%	0.037728%
9	50.5833333				0.037728%
10	50.6666667				0.037728%
11	50.75			0.113142%	0.037728%
12	50.8333333				0.037728%
13	50.9166667				0.037728%
14	51	0.493800%	0.247206%	0.123679%	0.041243%
15	51.0833333				0.041243%
16	51.1666667				0.041243%
17	51.25			0.123679%	0.041243%
18	51.3333333				0.041243%
19	51.4166667				0.041243%
20	51.5		0.247206%	0.123679%	0.041243%
21	51.5833333				0.041243%
22	51.6666667				0.041243%
23	51.75			0.123679%	0.041243%
24	51.8333333				0.041243%
25	51.9166667				0.041243%

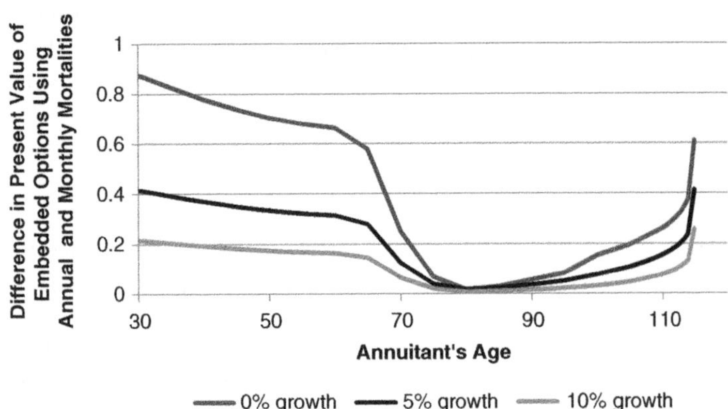

FIGURE 8.7 Impact of Issue Age and Settlement Frequency on Guaranteed Values Across Varying Growth Rates

DEATH BENEFIT RIDERS

In many of the GMDB products sold in the marketplace, the return of the premium feature discussed earlier is provided as a standard death benefit feature in the product for no additional premium (although in reality the fees associated with the basic death benefit are covered by the mortality and expense fees, which are also known as the M&E fees).[15] It is quite often the case that policyholders can add on additional death guarantees (called *death benefit riders*) for an additional premium. Depending on the insurance company, some of these riders are sold on a stand-alone basis while others are sold as packaged riders or standard benefits. Regardless of the way these riders are packaged and offered, all these death benefit riders can be broken down to their three basic building blocks: roll-up riders, ratchet riders, and earnings benefit riders.

Roll-Up Rider

This rider essentially provides the beneficiary the added comfort that regardless of how the market performs, the initial deposit is guaranteed to grow every year at a certain rate. More precisely, unlike the basic death benefit product in the earlier section whereby the beneficiary got a payoff of $\max(S_t, S_T)$ where S_t represents the fund unit value at time t (inception of the policy) and S_T represents the fund unit value net of fees at time T (time of annuitant's death), the beneficiary of a roll-up rider would get a payoff of $\max[S_t(1+R)^M, S_T]$ where R represents the annual roll-up rate and M represents the number of completed policy anniversary years before the annuitant's death.[16] Figure 8.8 illustrates the types of risks the insurance company is on the hook for when offering a roll-up rider.

---

[15]In practice, although the fund manager of the investments may be external to the insurance company, part of the M&E fees collected from the policyholder are given to the insurance company for bringing in the asset to manage. Insurance companies use a portion of these fees as a charge for the principal guarantee provided at the time of the annuitant's death.

[16]This is just one representation of how an insurance company may offer a roll-up rider to the beneficiary. In practice there are many variations on this rolling-up theme. One example of such a variation is to allow the deposit to be rolled up using a continuously compounding rate. Thus, the beneficiary would receive a payoff of $\max[S_t e^{RM}, S_T]$ instead of $\max[S_t(1+R)^M, S_T]$. Other variations include rolling up until the moment of death as opposed to rolling up *only* on policy anniversary dates, qualifying age for such a rider (i.e., the minimum and maximum age of the annuitant at the time of policy issue), age at which the roll-up stops, and so on.

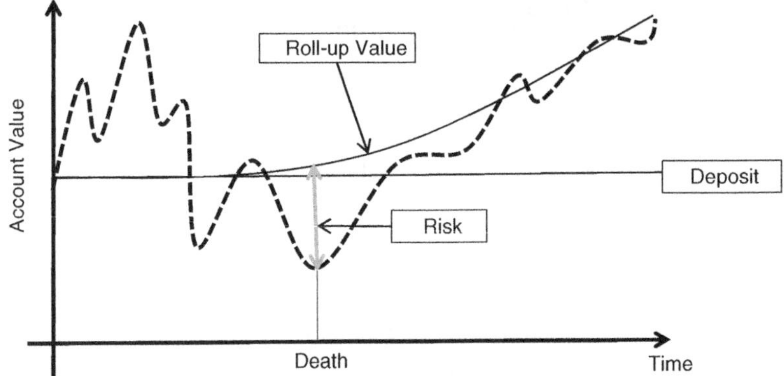

FIGURE 8.8 Risks to the Insurance Company Underwriting a Basic GMDB with a Continuously Compounded Roll-Up Rider

This roll-up rider payoff can, of course, be rewritten as $S_T + \max[S_t(1+R)^M - S_T, 0]$. Taking the relevant expectations of the optionality component, it can be seen that equation (8.3b) morphs into equation (8.4) when the mortality settlement is done semiannually

$$\begin{aligned} S_t \sum_{i=1}^{232-2x} q_{x,x+0.5i} \Bigg\{ \Bigg[-e^{(g_{t,t+0.5i}-q_{t,t+0.5i}-r_{t,t+0.5i})0.5i} \\ * N\left(-d^1_{S_t,S_t(1+R)^i,t,t+0.5i,g_{t,t+0.5i},q_{t,t+0.5i},\sigma_{t,t+0.5i}}\right)\Bigg] \\ + \Bigg[(1+R)^i e^{-(r_{t,t+i})0.5i} N\left(-d^2_{S_t,S_t(1+R)^i,t,t+0.5i,g_{t,t+0.5i},q_{t,t+0.5i},\sigma_{t,t+0.5i}}\right)\Bigg]\Bigg\} \end{aligned} \tag{8.4}$$

For offering this benefit, the insurance company typically charges a rider fee (in annual basis points) that is a function of R,[17] among other factors. Like the M&E fees, although this additional charge could be calculated and subtracted from the daily fund returns, it is a common

[17]In addition to R, it is intuitively reasonable to expect this additional charge to be a function of the annuitant's age and the nature of the investment. Despite this, in practice, an insurance company presents this rider charge as something that is independent of the nature of investment, age, and sex of the annuitant. Because of this, an insurance company offering such a rider has to make assumptions relating to investment styles, sex, and the ages of annuitants.

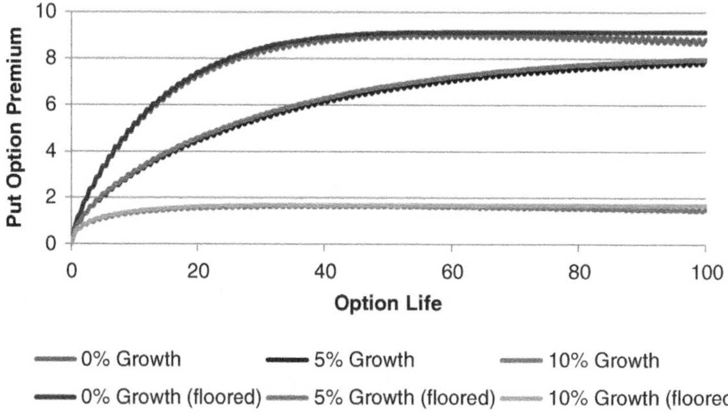

FIGURE 8.9 Impact of Maturity on Roll-Up Option Premiums

practice for this deduction to be made annually from the account at the end of each calendar year.

Before illustrating the implementation of equation (8.4), it is useful to see how such a roll-up feature affects a simple long-dated put option with no mortality effects. Figure 8.9 shows the impact of time on the premium of a put option that has a strike price that rolls up annually at a 5 percent rate (in a manner that is consistent with the roll-up death benefit rider) when there is no flooring of the option premium. It also shows the incremental amount of increase in the option premiums if the concept of the bounding of the premiums was to be introduced to the option premiums.

Figure 8.9 may seem to appear different to the reader when compared to Figure 8.3 even though both graphs are supposed to depict the sensitivity of option premiums when there is no notion of using implied information to value the embedded options. While the need to apply such a correction is obvious from Figure 8.3, the same cannot be said about Figure 8.9. In fact, by looking at Figure 8.9, one would have never guessed that such a correction is needed—simply because the premiums seem to be nondecreasing as the option maturity increases. On a closer look, the reader will realize that this nondecrease of premiums is actually due to the increase in the strike price (or the option becoming more in-the-money) as the option maturity increases.[18] As a consequence, one needs to introduce the flooring concept

[18]In the context of the example discussed, the strike price for the one-year option is $S_t(1.05)$, the two-year option is $S_t\left(1.05^2\right)$, and the three-year option is $S_t\left(1.05^3\right)$, and so on, showing that the longer the option maturity, the higher the strike price and hence the more in-the-money the option gets.

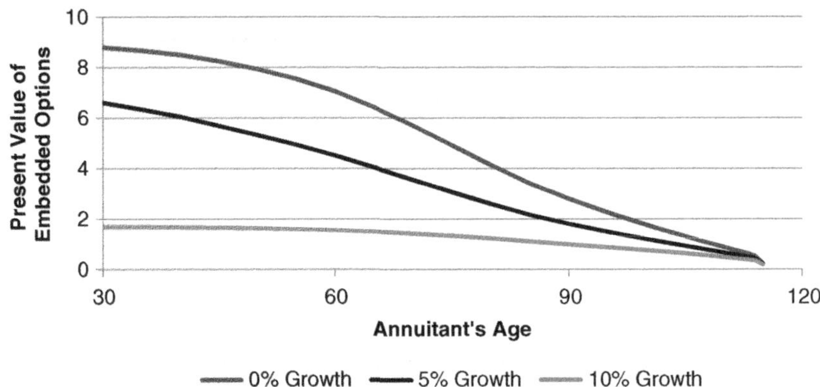

FIGURE 8.10 Sensitivity of Fund Growth on the Present Value of Roll-Up Death Benefit Riders Using a Calibrated Volatility and Risk-Free Rate Term Structure

to the in-the-money options so that results obtained can be consistent with those illustrated in Figure 8.4.

To apply the flooring idea to value these riders, one can basically use either of the following approaches:

- Use the results of Figures 8.5a and 8.5b to revalue these in-the-money options. The only setback of this strategy is that one would end up using the parameters for at-the-money options to value in-the-money options—potentially making the in-the-money options more expensive.
- Use the results of Figure 8.9 to extract the implied volatility term structure and zero rates. This would be a much more accurate approach to valuing the roll-up riders simply because the implied parameters from the in-the-money options are used to value the same in-the-options.

Given the above backdrop, I will use the implied information extracted from Figure 8.9 to value the roll-up riders.

Figure 8.10 illustrates the sensitivity of the growth rate of the funds on the present value of the embedded options (where I assumed that the deposit is annually rolled up at 5 percent and no extra premiums are charged for this rider).

Rachet Rider

Unlike the roll-up rider, this rider provides for the growth of the initial deposit that takes advantage of the investment volatility. More precisely,

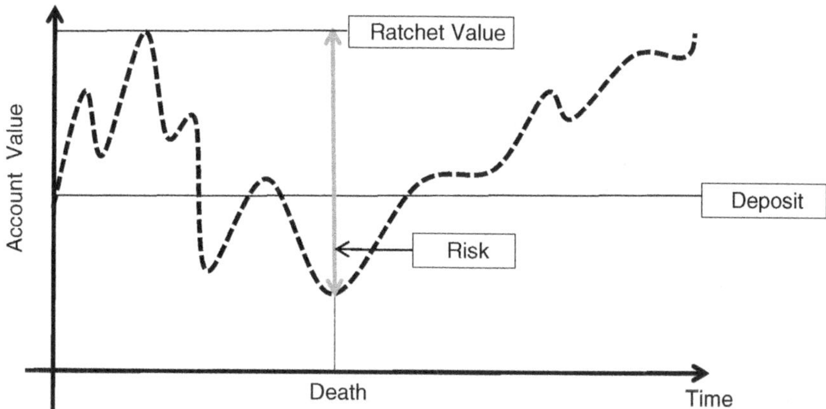

FIGURE 8.11 Risks to the Insurance Company Underwriting a Basic GMDB with a Ratchet Rider

unlike the roll-up rider, the beneficiary of this rider would get a payoff of $\max[S_t, S_{t+1}, S_{t+2}, \cdots, S_{t+M}, S_T]$ where M represents the number of elapsed policy anniversary years before the annuitant's death.[19] Figure 8.11 illustrates the types of risks the insurance company is on the hook for when offering a ratchet rider.

This payoff can of course be similarly rewritten as $S_T + \max[\max(S_t, S_{t+1}, \cdots, S_{t+M}) - S_T, 0]$.[20] For offering this benefit, the insurance company charges an additional rider fee, which is a function of the frequency of ratcheting.[21] As in the roll-up rider, fees for this rider are

[19]This is just one example of a representation on how an insurance company may offer a ratchet rider to a policyholder. In practice, the ratcheting can be done as frequently as daily to as infrequently as once every 10 years.

[20]As the reader will recognize, the payoff $[\max(S_t,S_{t+1}, \cdots, S_{t+M}) - S_T, 0]$ is an example of an exotic option that trades in the capital markets under the name of a lookback option. While it is possible to find a closed-form solution for a lookback option when there is continuous sampling of stock prices (see Hull (2012)), trying to obtain one when only discrete sampling is performed is much more mathematically challenging (see Kou (2008)). As a consequence of this, I use simulations to solve this problem.

[21]As in the roll-up rider, despite the fact that the cost of this rider is also a function of the nature of the investment and the annuitant's age, when sold by the insurance companies they are typically presented as independent of the investment choices and the annuitant's age/sex.

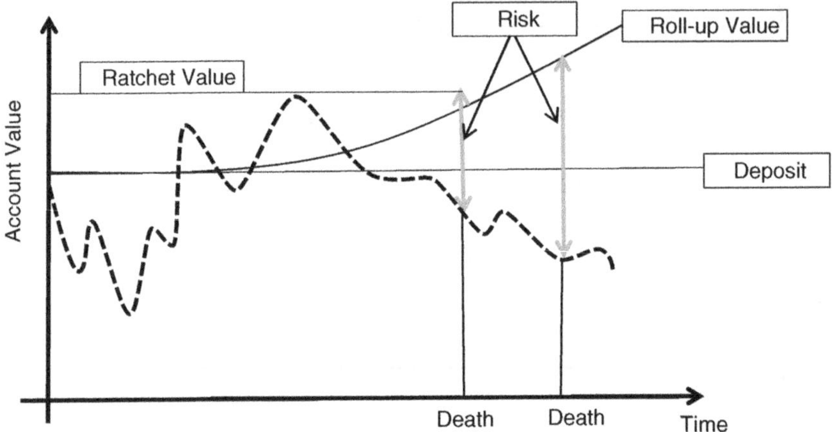

FIGURE 8.12 Risks to the Insurance Company Underwriting a Basic GMDB with a Roll-Up and Ratchet Rider

typically calculated using the account value and then deducted annually from the account value.

As mentioned earlier in this section, insurance companies sometimes offer a roll-up/ratchet rider combo. An example of such a combo payoff is $\max[S_t, S_{t+1}, S_{t+1}, \ldots, S_{t+M}, S_T, S_t(1+R)^M]$ which can be simplified to be $S_T + \max[\max(S_t, S_{t+1}, \ldots, S_{t+M}, S_t(1+R)^M) - S_T, 0]$. Figure 8.12 illustrates the risks the insurance company is exposed to when selling this combo.

As the reader will recall, to value the roll-up riders, one needs to capture the flooring of the option premiums through the calibration of the volatility and interest rate term structures, which are then used as inputs to value the embedded options. Thus, to value these roll-up/ratchet combo riders, one has to continue using these calibrated volatility and interest rate structures as inputs. Figures 8.13a and 8.13b show the respective impacts of introducing annual and monthly ratchet features to the 5 percent rollup rider that was considered in the earlier section when no fees are charged for the rider.

Earnings Rider

Unlike the previous death benefit riders in which the beneficiary is protected against a downturn in the annuitant's investment portfolio at the

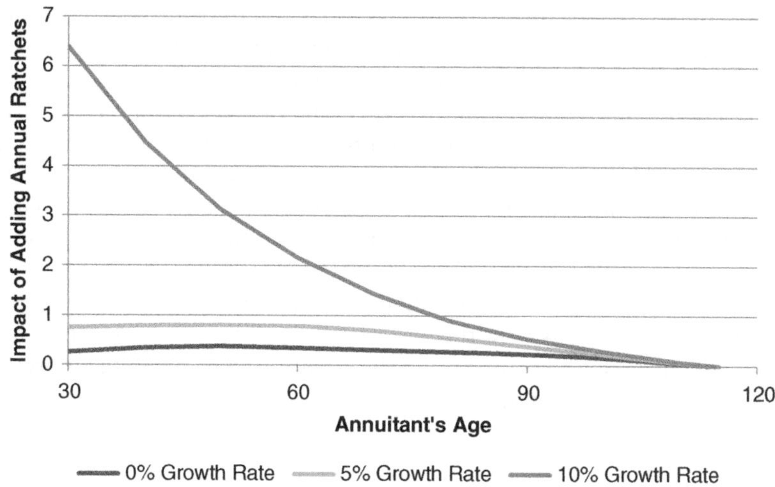

FIGURE 8.13A Impact of Adding an Annual Ratchet Rider to the 5 Percent Roll-Up Death Rider Benefit Using a Calibrated Volatility and Risk-Free Rate Term Structure

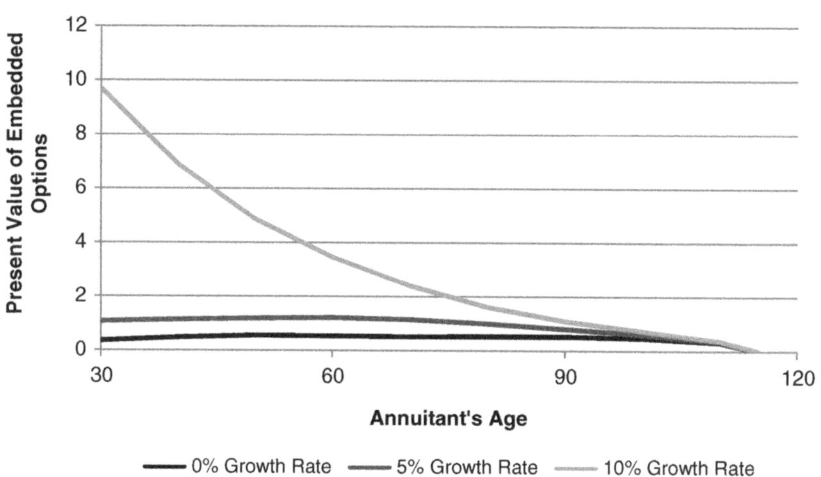

FIGURE 8.13B Impact of Adding a Monthly Ratchet Rider to the 5 Percent Roll-Up Death Rider Benefit Using a Calibrated Volatility and Risk-Free Rate Term Structure

time of annuitant's death, the earnings rider is motivated by the beneficiary's need to pay the taxes due to the annuitant's death. More precisely, since taxes are typically paid on an increase in investment value (i.e., capital gains), it is not surprising to see that this type of rider has a payoff of the form $Y\% * \max[S_T - S_t, 0]$, where Y represents the prespecified percentage of the upside that is paid out at the time of annuitant's death. For offering this benefit, like the other riders, the insurance company typically charges a rider fee that is calculated and subtracted from the account value on an annual basis.

The earnings rider payoff is similar to a vanilla call option that expires at the time of death T. Given this backdrop, it is easy to see that the earnings rider benefit can be valued using the equation (8.5) when the mortality settlement is done semiannually.

$$
\begin{aligned}
Y\% * S_t \sum_{i=1}^{232-2x} q_{x,x+0.5i} & \left[e^{(g_{t,t+0.5i} - q_{t,t+0.5i} - r_{t,t+0.5i})0.5i} \right. \\
& \left. * N\left(d^1_{S_t,S_t,t,t+0.5i,g_{t,t+0.5i},q_{t,t+0.5i},\sigma_{t,t+0.5i}}\right)\right] \\
- & \left[e^{-(r_{t,t+i})0.5i} N\left(d^2_{S_t,S_t,t,t+0.5i,g_{t,t+0.5i},q_{t,t+0.5i},\sigma_{t,t+0.5i}}\right)\right]
\end{aligned} \tag{8.5}
$$

Figure 8.14 shows the implementation of equation (8.5) assuming no rider fees for a variety of growth rates.

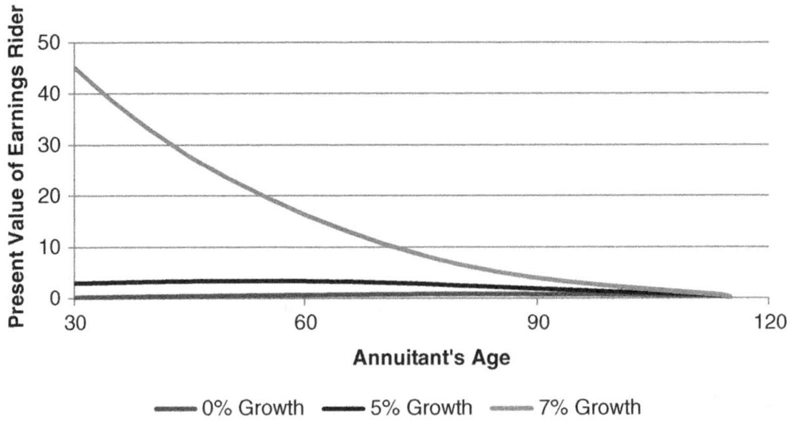

FIGURE 8.14 Sensitivity of Growth Rates to Present Value of a 100 Percent Earnings Benefit Rider

OTHER DETAILS ASSOCIATED WITH GMDB PRODUCTS

In the previous section, I discussed three death rider enhancements to the basic death benefit product. All these riders had tangible economic enhancements to the basic death benefit theme—in the process creating additional risks to the insurance company. In addition to these tangible economic benefits, the basic GMDB product also has other embedded features which, on the first glance, may seem intangible but can easily turn out to pose an immense amount of financial risk to the insurance company should it not be careful. In this section, I discuss many of these features and assumptions so one can better understand the risks that are undertaken by insurance companies when selling such products.

Fees

In running the illustrations to show the present value of the options, I assumed that the M&E fees are continuously compounded and that no rider fees are charged. In practice, the rider fees are quite often calculated on a less frequent basis (e.g., monthly, quarterly, semiannually, annually) and units of funds are redeemed to pay for the rider fees. Furthermore, some insurance companies link their death rider fees to current guarantee levels instead of account values.[22]

[22]Suppose that the policyholder initiated a GMDB policy (which includes the 5 percent roll-up rider) on February 15, 2010, by investing $1,000 to acquire 100 units of a fund whose unit fund value is $10. Assume further that the rider fee charged for the roll-up feature is 50 basis points (an amount computed annually using the account value at market closing on every policy-anniversary day) and that the unit fund values on February 15, 2011, and February 15, 2012, are $9 and $11 respectively (after the deduction of the M&E). The rider fee collected on February 15, 2011 is $\$9 * 100 * 0.0050 = \$4.50$. To pay the $4.50, the insurance company will liquidate 0.5 units of the fund to end up with 99.5 units of the fund. The rider fee collected on February 15, 2012, is $\$11 * 99.5 * 0.0050 = \$5.4725$, which is obtained by liquidating another 0.4975 units, leaving a total of 99.0025 units. In the event the fees are linked to the running guarantee, the fee collected on February 15, 2011, is $\$10 * 1.05 * 100 * 0.0050 = \$5.25$. To pay the $5.25, the insurance company will liquidate 0.5833 units of the fund to end up with 99.4167 units of the fund. The rider fee collected on February 15, 2012, is $\$10 * 1.05 * 1.05 * 99.4167 * 0.0050 = \$5.4803$, which is obtained by liquidating another 0.4982 units, leaving a total of 98.9185 units.

Commissions

The insurance company has to pay commissions[23] to the agent for closing the deal. There are usually two components to this aspect: one an up-front amount that is applied to a new deposit and paid out at the inception of the contract, while the other is a continuing amount that is typically paid out on policy anniversaries and is linked to the size of the account value; it is also paid out annually to the agent as long as the policy is in force or still active. Depending on the fee structure selected, the initial commission amount is typically prefunded by the insurance company from reserves it has to set aside for writing such business in the hope of recovering it from the policyholder over time through the M&E and rider fees paid by the policyholder during the life of the policy. To recoup these up-front costs, insurance companies try to discourage their policyholders from surrendering early by imposing high surrender fees.[24]

On-Risk and Off-Risk Age

In many of the GMDB products offered, insurance companies typically have age restrictions associated with them. On the deposit side, the insurance companies typically require that the annuitant cannot exceed a certain age before the basic product (and its rider) can be issued. Furthermore, even after issuance, an insurance company may have restrictions on cutoff age after which no additional deposits can be made into the policy. These are sometimes called on-risk age. In addition, riders quite often come equipped with the notion of off-risk age. As described by the name, off-risk age refers to the age beyond which the rider no longer rolls up or ratchets.

---

[23]In practice, there are few types of fee options that are offered to the policyholder. One simple example is the front-end load fee structure, which refers to the fees that are taken off from the deposit—in the process affecting the actual amount invested. Front-end fees typically do not carry any surrender charges. Another example is the back-end load fee structure, in which surrender charges are typically included.

[24]Starting anywhere from 7 to 10 percent in the first policy year, these surrender charges reduce over a period of 7 to 10 years after which no charges are imposed on any surrender. An example of this would be the following surrender charge schedule: 1st policy year—7 percent, 2nd policy year—6 percent, 3rd policy year—5 percent, 4th policy year—4 percent, 5th policy year—3 percent, 6th policy year—2 percent, 7th policy year—1 percent, 8th policy year and later—0 percent. The reader should note that all these charges only apply to surrender amounts in excess of the free allowable surrender amount in a policy year.

From a pricing standpoint, it is important to be able to embed these features into calculations so that the frequency and cut-off time associated with the roll-ups and ratchets are more accurately captured.

Investment Allocation

In my discussion thus far, I have conveniently assumed that the policyholder makes an investment in one fund. In practice, insurance companies offer a multitude of funds (sometimes hundreds of them) in which the policyholder can allocate investments. The inputs required to value the optionality embedded in the basic product and its riders when there is only one fund are the fund fee, fund growth rate, and fund volatility rate. In the event the policyholder invests in a multitude of funds, the fund values, growth rates, and volatilities associated with each of these funds (in addition to the correlation between the fund returns) become instrumental in helping to determine the value of the optionalities.

Since how well the total investment in a GMDB product performs is really a function of how the investment is distributed among all the available funds, the insurance company is left with the task of guessing at this distribution. Clearly, the more accurate the predicted breakdown of investments among the policyholders, the lesser the risks exposed to when making these assumptions. The biggest risk the insurance company is exposed to when doing this is to assume that all the investments are deposited into a money market fund, only to experience that all policyholders have actually made their investments into a fund that has the highest volatility. Over the last decade, in order to reduce the risks embedded in these products, insurance companies have introduced restrictions into the types of funds a policyholder can allocate the investments into if certain types of riders (including living benefits) are chosen.

Continued Investments Reallocation

In addition to the initial fund allocation discussed earlier, many products also allow a policyholder to reallocate their fund holdings a few times in each policy year for free (subject to certain constraints) to ensure that the investment objectives are continually met. As such, the insurance company has to make an additional assumption relating to how it expects the investment behavior of the policyholder to evolve over time (namely, what criteria needs to be triggered before the policyholder re-allocates the investment portfolio—if at all) and if the switches are made with full economic rationality.

Surrenders and Withdrawals

Although in my simplifying assumption I assumed that the policyholder holds on to the policy until the death of the annuitant, in practice the policyholder has the ability to surrender the policy in its entirety or even partially withdraw[25] from the policy. To discourage a policyholder from withdrawing or surrendering, insurance companies typically allow for 10 percent of the account value to be withdrawn annually penalty free, and then institute heavier penalties for additional amounts to serve as a deterrent to the policyholder from quickly terminating the policy.[26]

As in the fund allocation, the insurance company has to make assumptions regarding a policyholder's behavior as it relates to the timing of the surrenders and withdrawals (subject to the maximum number of allowable withdrawals per year) and the size of the withdrawals each time a withdrawal is made. This is usually the most difficult one to estimate, as it is very much a function of the distribution channel (e.g., types of agents used), the rationality of policyholders (to understand the impact of rationality on surrendering and withdrawals), and the age of the annuitant, among other things. Among all the risks discussed in this section, this tends to be the most predominant risk underlying this product.

Minimums and Maximums

To ensure that policy-processing costs and other administrative-related expenses are met, insurance companies often institute minimums on deposits, withdrawal amount sizes, switch amount sizes, administration fees, total account value after withdrawals, and so on. While this is not something one typically models due to the lack of severity of this risk, it is good for the modeler to ensure that these charges do not surprise them. In practice, it is

---

[25]Throughout this chapter, the word *surrender* is used to refer to the action of completely surrendering or lapsing the policy after which the policy is terminated. The word *withdraw* is used to refer to the action of withdrawing a proportion of the account value (or investment) from the policy, after which the policy continues to be in force. Furthermore, in practice the number of allowable withdrawals in any one given year is usually capped and subject to penalties.

[26]The reason for wanting a policyholder not to surrender early is to avoid losses paid to the insurance broker/advisor for putting the deal together. In practice, it is customary for the advisors to be paid 4 percent of the initial deposit and 50 basis points of the account value annually thereafter as long as the account is active. Thus, when the policyholder withdraws or surrenders during the early years, the insurance company is out of pocket from the heavy commissions paid to the brokers at the inception of the contract. See also the comment on commissions.

good to embed the constraints that need to be quantified in order to better ascertain the risks the insurance company is exposed to.

Joint Mortality

In the examples discussed thus far, the beneficiary got paid as soon as the annuitant died. Although my discussion was centered around the life of a single annuitant, it is not uncommon to purchase GMDBs and GMDB riders on joint (or two) lives. As mentioned before, in this instance, the death benefit would pay off as soon as one member of the couple dies (regardless of which person that is). Thus, one has to use both the male and female mortality tables and compute the first-die probabilities as the mortality rates.

Regulatory Requirements and Return

To sell a GMDB product, an insurance company has to ensure it sets aside adequate reserves and capital so it stays solvent to pay off the claims when they are due (something that regulators look at before allowing an insurance company to offer such products). For an insurance company to model the profitability associated with offering this product, in addition to modeling all the above features, the insurance company also must:

- Factor in the amount of reserve and capital it has to set aside.
- Use the appropriate accounting metrics to ensure fees/expenses (including commissions) are accounted for in a manner that meets the accounting guidelines set out by the tax authorities.
- Ensure that the fees collected should exceed the required expected return associated with investing in this business.

Unfortunately, these requirements cannot be modeled by simply reading a product prospectus.

IMPROVING MODELING ASSUMPTIONS

In modeling the basic GMDB and its riders, I assumed that movements in the underlying fund prices (which are similar to index values, stock prices, etc.) and can be modeled using a lognormal pdf where the growth rates, risk-free rates, and volatility rates are all assumed to be deterministic throughout the life over which this modeling is done. The consequence of these assumptions when valuing long-dated options was illustrated in Figures 8.3 and 8.9 and discussed earlier. To artificially get around the problem, I had suggested the flooring of the premiums as a makeshift solution. A cleaner way to get around this problem is to simply incorporate stochastic risk-free rates and volatility rates in the entire analysis, as doing anything else is potentially prone to modeling inconsistency. In this section, I provide a brief overview on how such modeling can be done in practice.

Stochastic Growth and Risk-Free Rates

Since the models used to mimic growth-rate movements and risk-free rate movements are pretty much identical (albeit with different parameters), I will focus my discussion on the modeling of risk-free rate movements throughout this section.

One of the assumptions I have used thus far is that $r_{t,T}$, the continuously compounded risk-free rate, is deterministic. To understand how best to model stochastic zero rates, recall that in Chapter 3, I discussed the valuation of swaptions, caps, and floors, and the assets underlying the options were the corresponding forward rates. In theory, one can use this idea to model future interest rates (and hence more complex interest rate derivatives), but to do this one has to also capture the correlation between these forward rates to be able to model the entire yield curve. Called the LIBOR Market Model (LMM), this approach was pioneered by Brace, Gatarek, and Musiela in 1997. Since the implementation of an LMM can be quite painstakingly complex I will discuss a simpler alternative to the LMM. Although there are a few easily implementable alternative models (each with its pros and cons),[27] I will only discuss the no-arbitrage, one-factor model that was proposed by Hull and White in 1990 (something I briefly discussed in Chapter 6).

The diffusion equation given by equation (6.8) has the form

$$dr = (\theta(t) - ar)dt + \sigma dz \tag{6.8}$$

Equation (6.8) can be equivalently rewritten as $r_{T,T+dt}$ and has a normal pdf with a mean of $r_{t,t+dt}e^{-a(T-t)} + \frac{\theta(t)}{a}(1 - e^{-a(T-t)})$ and variance

$$\frac{\sigma_r^2}{2a}(1 - e^{-2a(T-t)})$$

[27]The reader is referred to Hull (2012) for more details.

where

$r_{t,t+dt}$ is the short (or overnight rate) at time t.
σ_T is the volatility of the short rate $r_{T,T+dt}$.
a is the reversion rate (or speed of reversion) of the short rate to its mean value of $\theta(t)$.

Using the above distributional properties of $r_{T,T+dt}$, one can recursively obtain the short rate for any time in the future. Once this short rate is obtained, it is easy (using the properties of the model) to deduce the zero-rate curve at that time. The reader is again referred to Hull (2012) for details.

One can now combine this short interest rate model with the lognormal price behavior of the fund to better capture the effect of the long-term interaction between short rates and fund prices. As the astute reader will observe, the correlation between short rates and fund prices (or equity markets) are also fundamental in deciding how short-rate movements affect the actual fund-value movements—if at all.

Stochastic Volatility Rates

One common stochastic volatility model that is used in practice often is due to Heston (1993). Like the Hull-White one-factor model, the Heston model also allows for volatility to be pulled back toward some predefined, long-term mean. More precisely, the proposed stochastic volatility of the fund has a diffusion equation which can be represented as follows:

$$d\sigma = b\,(\sigma_L - \sigma)\,dt + \omega\sqrt{\sigma}dz_3 \tag{8.6}$$

where

σ is the annualized volatility of the fund's value.
b is the mean reversion rate.
σ_L is the mean reversion level.
ω is the annualized volatility of the fund volatility.
dz_3 is the random variable drawn from a standard normal probability density function.[28]
$d\sigma$ is the small change in the fund volatility over a small time interval dt.

---

[28]In addition to this, it is assumed that this random variable is correlated to the random variable used to generate the fund returns.

While equation (8.6) is something that can be easily used to model the stochastic volatility associated with a single fund, modeling the stochastic volatilities of multiple funds gets more complex because one must contend with the correlation between all the stochastic volatilities of these funds. In addition to the introduction of stochastic growth rates, risk-free rates, and volatilities, there is one more inconsistency in the model that one needs to fix in the event stochastic-free rates are introduced. This relates to the fact that in modeling fund returns I have assumed all these funds are equity funds (or have very high equity components in the funds). If such funds were actually bond funds or money market funds, then assuming that such fund-unit returns are lognormally distributed contradicts the fact that risk-free rates are normally distributed as given by equation (6.8). The reason is that when risk-free rate movements are normally distributed, the price movement of a bond in a bond fund unit value would *not* be lognormally distributed. As a consequence, it is important to model movements in these fund units in a manner that is consistent with all the other assumptions used for modeling.

LIVING BENEFIT RIDERS

In the beginning of this chapter, I mentioned three living benefit riders (e.g., GMAB, GMIB, and GMWB) briefly. In this section, I will briefly discuss the features associated with each of these riders to give the reader an appreciation of how such riders work in practice—without getting into the details of modeling (although the methodology discussed in this chapter can be easily extended to value living benefit riders). The reader should consult the reference by Kalberer and Ravindran (2009) for more details on these benefits.

GMABs

The GMAB is a living benefit rider that has been in the marketplace since the 1990s. In its basic form, a GMAB rider is structured to protect the policyholder against a drop in value of the initial investment on the maturity of the GMAB rider provided the annuitant has not died by then. Thus, on expiry of the GMAB rider, assuming that the policyholder purchases 1 unit of the fund for $\$S_t$ at the inception of the contract, the policyholder would receive a payoff of

$$\max[S_t, S_{Mat}] = S_{Mat} + \max[S_t - S_{Mat}, 0]$$

where S_{Mat} represents the fund value net of fees on the maturity of the GMAB rider.

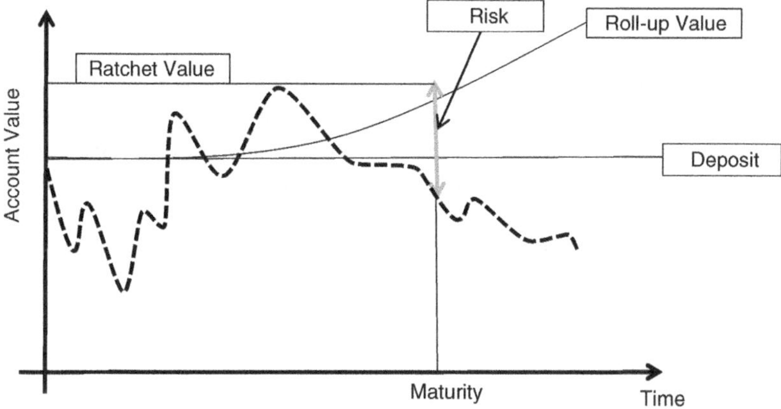

FIGURE 8.15 Risks to the Insurance Company Underwriting a Basic GMAB with a Roll-Up and Ratchet Rider

As long as the GMAB rider matures when the annuitant is alive, the policyholder can choose to:

- Continue with the standard GMDB product (which may also possibly include the roll-up/ratchet death benefit riders).[29]
- Continue with the standard GMDB product (and its riders) and renew the GMAB rider.
- Surrender the policy to receive a total investment value of max $[S_t, S_{Mat}]$.

In the event the annuitant dies before the rider matures, the beneficiary will get the traditional death benefits (courtesy of the GMDB product and its riders).

To get the principal protection feature on the maturity of the GMAB rider (which typically ranges anywhere from 7 to 10 years), the policyholder would have to pay an extra charge annually that would typically be deducted from the account value by redeeming units of the fund. It may be of interest for the reader to note that insurance companies sometimes also offer roll-up and ratchet feature enhancements to the standard principal guarantee on rider maturity for additional charges (in excess of those required for the standard GMAB rider). Figure 8.15 more aptly describes the risk to the insurance company for offering such a product.

[29]In the event that the fund value on the GMAB rider maturity (i.e., S_{Mat}) is less than the initial investment (i.e., S_t), the insurance company would pay the policyholder an amount of $S_t - S_{Mat}$—which goes into the policy as an additional deposit.

GMIBs

The GMIB is another living benefit rider that has been in the marketplace since the late 1990s. In its basic form, a GMIB rider is structured to allow the policyholder, for an extra annual rider fee, the ability to annuitize (i.e., convert the account value to a stream of fixed cash flows that are paid out by the insurance company until the time of the annuitant's death at some prespecified annuity rate).[30] While the beneficiary gets paid by the GMDB (and its death benefit riders) if the annuitant dies before the annuitization is carried out, once the annuitization is done, the entire VA contract is replaced by a standard annuity contract. Thus at the time of the annuitization[31], the policyholder gets a payoff of

$$S_{Ann} * \max\left[Mkt\,Ann_{Ann}, Gtee\,Ann_{Ann}\right]$$

where

- S_{Ann} refers to the VA account value at the time of annuitization.
- $Gtee\,Ann_{Ann}$ refers to the life annuity that the policyholder can buy using \$1 and the prescribed annuitization rates in the GMIB rider contract.[32]

---

[30]The GMIB rider policyholder typically has this option on every policy-anniversary date starting from the tenth policy-anniversary year. Once annuitized, the policyholder would receive a steady monthly (or annual) income until the death of the annuitant. To illustrate, suppose the account value at the time of annuitization is \$50,000 and this translates to a \$297/month annuity based on the prescribed annuitization rates, in the event the annuitant dies after collecting an amount of \$29,700, the beneficiary would still receive the unused amount of \$21,300. On the other hand, if the insurance company has already paid out a cumulative amount exceeding \$50,000, upon the death of the annuitant, the beneficiary would not receive anything.

[31]Another option that is available to the policyholder at the time of annuitization is to simply surrender the policy and collect the underlying account value. This can be a logical decision in the event the accumulated account value is very high relative to economic value associated with the annuitization.

[32]Suppose the age of the annuitant is 100 and the policyholder wants to receive an annual cash flow starting 1 year from now. Using a prescribed annuitization rate of x percent, then the present value of this annuity can be computed using the equation $\{[(1-q_{100,101}) * q_{100,102} * e^{-r_{0,1}}] + [(1-q_{100,101}) * (1-q_{100,102}) * q_{100,103} * e^{-2r_{0,2}})] + \cdots + [\prod_{i=101}^{115}(1-q_{100,i}) * q_{100,116} * e^{-15r_{0,15}}]\}$. Hence, in buying an annuity for \$1, the policyholder would get an annual payment of \$$x$, where $x = \frac{1}{y}$ and $y = [(1-q_{100,101}) * q_{100,102} * e^{-r_{0,1}}] + [(1-q_{100,101}) * (1-q_{100,102}) * q_{100,103} * e^{-2r_{0,2}})] + \cdots + [\prod_{i=101}^{115}(1-q_{100,i}) * q_{100,116} * e^{-15r_{0,15}}]$.

- $Mkt\,Ann_{Ann}$ refers to the life annuity that can be purchased using $1 and the prevailing market annuity rates at the time of annuitization.

From the payoff, it can be easily seen that the policyholder would only annuitize the VA contract if the size of the coupon obtained using the prescribed annuitization rate is higher than that obtained using the market-based annuity rate. In the event that this is not the case, the rational policyholder would wait for a later time to annuitize.

GMWBs

The GMWB is the final example of a living benefit rider that has been in the marketplace since the early 2000s and is still a popular version of the living benefit sold in the market. Although it may seem to have some resemblance to the GMIB at the first glance, it is quite different from the GMIB.

In its simplest form, a GMWB rider allows the annuitant (once he/she reaches the age of 65) to withdraw penalty-free annually no more than 5% of the $\max[S_t, S_{time\ at\ which\ policyholder\ turns\ 65}]$. To discourage the policyholder from withdrawing before age 65 or withdrawing more than the annual capped amount after age 65, penalties are associated with such withdrawals. As the astute reader will see given the nature of the guarantee and the conditions attached to the withdrawals, as long as these conditions are not violated, the insurance company's risks rise when the market drops and the annuitant lives for a long time. The reason for this stems from the fact that when this happens, the account value gets quickly depleted every time the policyholder withdraws the capped annual penalty-free amount. The consequence of this is that the insurance company is contractually on the hook for fulfilling its commitment to ensure that the annuitant gets paid the capped annual lifetime withdrawal amount as long as the annuitant is alive.

Compared to the GMAB and GMIB living benefit riders, the GMWB rider in reality is more complex than the simplest form of GMWB that was described earlier. An example of this complexity is the fact that, although eligible, the policyholder is not obligated to withdraw his annual penalty free capped amount and instead can choose to leave it in the account and let it grow—making it very important for the insurance company to be able to accurately model the policyholder behavior.

REFERENCES

Brace, A., D. Gatarek, and M. Musiela. 1997. "The Market Model of Interest Rate Dynamics." *Mathematical Finance* 7:127–155.

Heston, S. L. 1993. "A Closed Form Solution for Options with Stochastic Volatility with Applications to Bonds and Currency Options." *Review of Financial Studies* 6:327–343.

Hull, J. C. 2012. *Options, Futures and Other Derivatives*. 8th ed. Upper Saddle River, NJ: Prentice Hall.

Hull, J. C., and A. White. 1990. "Pricing Interest Rate Derivative Securities." *Review of Financial Studies* 3:573–592.

Kalberer, T., and K. Ravindran. 2009. *Variable Annuities: A Global Perspective*. London: Incisive Financial Publication Limited.

Kou, S. G. 2008. "Discrete Barrier and Lookback Options. "In *Handbooks in OR and MS*, Vol. 15, edited by J. Birge and V. Linetsky. Amsterdam: Elsevier B.V.

Ravindran, K., and A. W. Edelist. 1977. "Deriving Benefits from Death." In *Frontiers in Derivatives*, edited by A. Konishi and R. E. Dattatreya. Chicago: Irwin Professional Publishing.

CHAPTER 9

Real Options

In previous chapters, I restricted my discussion to the explicit valuation of financial options. In practice, the concept of optionality is something one faces daily in both a personal and business capacity. As such, it is important and interesting to see if one can use ideas discussed in the earlier chapters to value such options or decisions. Before discussing how to do this, I will first illustrate some practical examples of real options.

Real options[1] are options couched as decisions that one can optimize on. Examples of this include decisions to abandon a project, expand on an investment, scale down an operation, defer an investment, or cancel a project.[2] Although this has been the traditional definition of a real option, for the purpose of this book I will use the term *real options* in a broader context so as to also include the ability to quantify the value of a choice. More precisely, in addition to the above, I will use the term real options to also include the quantification of choices associated with operations management, optimal allocation, decision making under uncertainty, amongst others. As such, additional examples of real options include:

- Deciding when to turn on and off power generating units (e.g., hydroelectric stations, fossil units, coal plants, nuclear stations) so to optimize profits.
- Operating a gas storage facility in a manner to optimize storage facilities and manage the supply and demand for storage space as gas prices fluctuate and gas producers move between pumping out their stored gas and storing more gas.

---

[1]After the publication of the seminal paper by Black and Scholes in 1973, the term *real options* was coined by Myers in 1977 to discuss the use of quantitative methods to value corporate liabilities.

[2]See Hull (2012).

- Pricing airline seats to maximize the profitability associated with a flight route while taking into consideration the costs associated with the operation of that flight.
- Valuing a company by taking into consideration its revenue, operating costs, debts, employee options, pension plans.
- Shutting down a mine production facility due to a drop in commodity prices, taking into consideration the cost of layoffs and restarting the mine.
- Determining the number of phone operators to be hired to ensure that incoming calls are not lost due to long waiting times.
- Quantifying consumer behavior as it relates to the timing of optimally lapsing (or surrendering) an insurance policy or any other investment products.

Given the above backdrop, it is easy to realize how prevalent real options are in one's daily life. To add more color to the subject of real options, I next discuss two nontraditional applications of real options. While the first concerns the quantification of rational policyholder behavior when deciding when to optimally surrender a GMAB rider, the second relates to the quantification of the value associated with the hiring of servers so as to simultaneously minimize the waiting time in a queue and the cost of operating the queue.

SURRENDERING A GMAB RIDER

The purpose of this section is to illustrate via an example how the embedded optionality associated with consumer behavior can be quantified. One living benefit rider that was briefly mentioned in Chapter 8 was the GMAB rider. As the reader will recall, this rider can be added on by the policyholder to the basic GMDB product should the policyholder be interested in protecting the investment on the maturity date of the GMAB rider.

Although Figure 8.15 shows a GMAB rider with a roll-up and ratchet guarantee, for the ease of explanation, I will henceforth keep my discussion focused on the return-of-principal guarantee at maturity (i.e., no roll-ups or ratchets) GMAB rider. In this instance, as can be seen from Figure 8.15, the insurance company is exposed to the risk that the value of the investment drops below the initial deposit on GMAB maturity and the annuitant is alive to receive this benefit. To value this benefit, as in Chapter 8, I will assume that $\ln S_T$ is normally distributed with a mean of $\ln S_t + \left(g_{t,T} - q_{t,T} - \frac{1}{2}\sigma^2_{t,T}\right)(T-t)$ and variance of $\sigma^2_{t,T}(T-t)$.

As outlined in Chapter 8, an investment into a unit of fund value with a GMAB rider without any roll-up or ratchet features that is attached to a standard GMDB policy can be reinterpreted as the sum of

- Investment into a fund unit.
- At-the-money put option maturing at the time of the GMAB rider, provided the annuitant is still alive.
- At-the-money put option expiring at the time of death (where the rider falls away at the time of death provided this death happens before GMAB rider maturity).

Since I have already discussed the valuation of the death benefit option embedded in a standard GMDB product in Chapter 8, I will focus my attention on the valuation of a GMAB rider and the impact of policyholder optionality on this valuation.

Using the notations of Chapter 8, assuming that the annuitant is x years old and the GMAB has a y-year maturity, the value of the embedded maturity option is given by the expression

$$S_t * \prod_{i=1}^{y}(1 - q_{x,x+i}) *$$
$$\{ - e^{y*(g_{t,t+y}-q_{t,t+y}-r_{t,t+y})} N(-d^1_{S_t,S_t,t,t+y,g_{t,t+y},q_{t,t+y},\ \sigma_{t,t+y}})$$
$$+ e^{-y*(r_{t,t+y})} N(-d^2_{S_t,S_t,t,t+y,g_{t,t+y},q_{t,t+y},\ \sigma_{t,t+y}})\} \qquad (9.1)$$

Figure 9.1 shows how the present value of the 7-year option embedded in the GMAB rider changes across varying annuitant ages when the fund is assumed to grow at varying growth rates and no rider fee is charged. To produce Figure 9.1, for the sake of consistency, I used the implied information in Figures 8.5a and 8.5b for the term structure of volatilities and zero rates respectively.

Although Figure 9.1 is the consequence of implementing equation (9.1), the reader should be mindful that this is only an approximation. The reason for this stems from the fact that in putting this illustration together, I assumed no GMAB rider fees and 2 percent continuously compounded M & E charges. In practice, as mentioned in Chapter 8, the rider fees are taken off annually while the M & E charges are taken off daily from the fund returns before the fund values are reported. Rerunning the analysis that was used to produce Figure 9.1 for the seven-year GMAB rider when the rider fees are 50 basis points and the M & E charges are 1.5 percent,

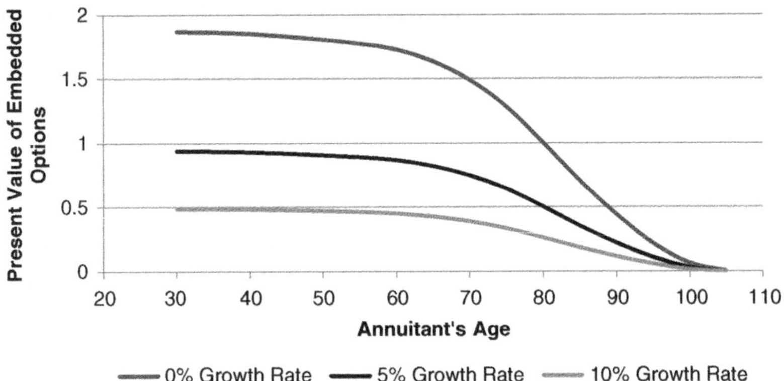

FIGURE 9.1 Present Value of an Option Embedded in a GMAB Rider

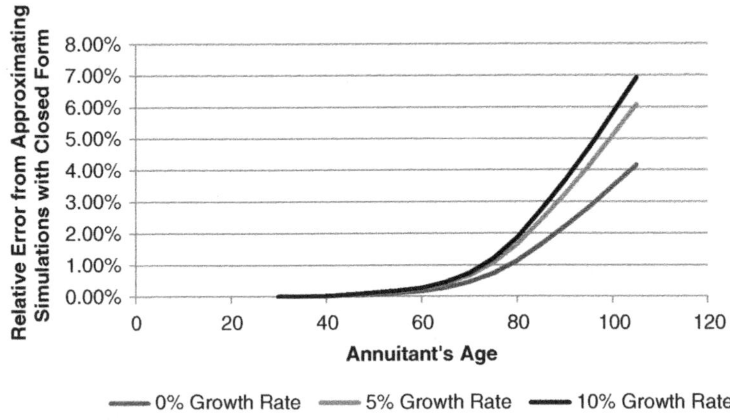

FIGURE 9.2 Relative Errors from Approximating Annual Rider Fees

one obtains the results in Figure 9.2,[3] which demonstrates the relative error arising from approximating the annual GMAB rider fee with 0.5 percent of M & E charges so as to result in a total of 2 percent of M & E charges.

As can be seen from Figure 9.2, the relative error associated with the approximation increases as the annuitant's age increases—reiterating the need to accurately capture the nuances associated with the cash flows especially when the annuitant gets older.

[3]The relative errors were computed using the expression $100\% * \frac{approx-exact}{approx}$ where *exact* refers to the number obtained using simulations to precisely capture the annual rider-fee deduction at the beginning of each year and *approx* refers to the number obtained using equation (9.1).

TABLE 9.1A Inputs Used to Value GMAB Rider Optionality

Current Fund Value (St)	10
Continuously Compounded Growth Rate (g)	5.00%
Management Fees (q)	1.50%
Accumulation Benefit Fees	0.50%
Current Age	80
Term	7
# of units	1

Tables 9.1a and 9.2a show the inputs and simulations that have been put together to obtain the results in Figure 9.2.

As can be seen from Table 9.1b, a positive value in cell H13 implies that the premiums charged for the maturity benefit rider are insufficient to cover the benefit (when only mortalities and account-value returns are in play) for that particular path. To find the fair value of the rider, one has to do these runs over multiple simulated paths to ensure that on average the value of cell H13 turns out to be 0.

One critical element that has still not been factored in the pricing of the GMAB rider benefit is that associated with lapses or surrenders (something I had briefly discussed in Chapter 8). More precisely, to do the above calculations, I implicitly assumed that the policyholder will not surrender the policy or withdraw any amount from the policy before the GMAB rider maturity date. In practice, to keep the cost of the guarantees down, insurance companies make assumptions about how their policyholders behave to ensure that their pricing reflects the fact that a fraction of them would not be around by the time the GMAB maturity date comes around. Depending on the product design, there are products in the marketplace which allow a policyholder to either surrender the GMAB rider without having to surrender the GMDB contract or surrender the entire contract (i.e., the underlying GMDB and the GMAB rider). Given this backdrop, for the purposes of my discussion, I will henceforth assume that the policyholder is able to surrender only the GMAB rider without impacting the underlying GMDB contract. For the ease of explanation, I will also make the simplifying assumption that the policyholder is only allowed to make a full surrender.[4]

[4]The consequence of this assumption is that a policyholder is not allowed to partially withdraw from the contract—an assumption that is NOT made by an insurance company in practice. More precisely, in addition to making an assumption on the percentage of full surrenders in each policy year, assumptions on the frequency, amount and timing of partial withdrawals are also made.

TABLE 9.1B Simulation Layout to Value GMAB Rider Optionality

	A	B	C	D	E	F	G	H	I	J	K	L
1	Time (yrs)	Implied Volatility	Implied Risk-Free Rate	Forward Volatility	Account Value (beginning of year)	Number of Policyholders alive	Number of policyholders dead	Maturity Benefit (fees)	Account Value (after fees)	Normal Random #s	PV (GMAB Fees)	
2	0				10	1		0.05	9.95	−1.866446	0.05	
3	1	0.2	0.05	0.2	6.953765778	0.936868	0.063132	0.0325738	6.921191975	−0.346234	0.029029	
4	2	0.2	0.05	0.2	6.555741774	0.871734126	0.065133874	0.02857432	6.527167455	0.245468	0.022539	
5	3	0.201837	0.05	0.205461	6.960838869	0.805005494	0.066728632	0.02801757	6.932821301	0.196211	0.019413	
6	4	0.206374	0.05	0.219424	7.317339792	0.737200686	0.067804808	0.02697174	7.290368052	−1.637934	0.016279	
7	5	0.211757	0.05	0.232043	5.025682964	0.669011097	0.068189589	0.01681119	5.008871776	1.018199	0.008759	
8	6	0.217409	0.05	0.243712	6.453740746	0.601266364	0.067744733	0.01940209	6.43433866	−0.528668	0.008642	
9	7	0.223115	0.05	0.254678	5.638278501	0.534872127	0.066394237					
10												
11	Total Present Value (GMAB Fees)/simulaton							0.155	=SUM(K3:K13)			
12	Present Value (Maturity Benefit)/simulation							1.64401142	=MAX(E9-Deposit,0)*F9*EXP(-A9*C9)			
13	Net Present Value/simulation							1.48935034	=H12-H11			
14												

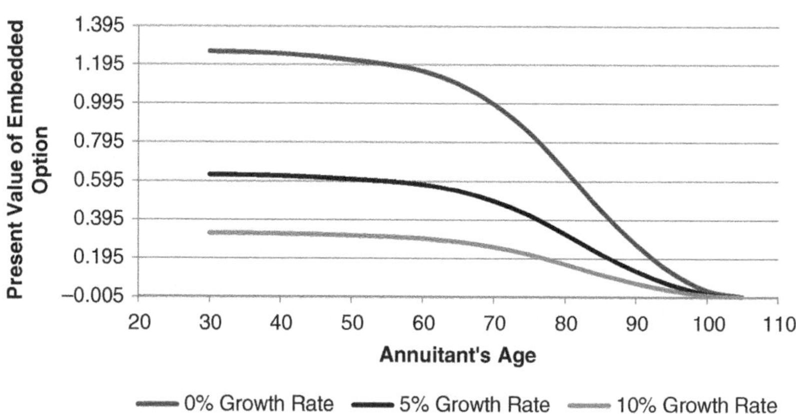

FIGURE 9.3A Impact of Surrenders on the Present Value of GMAB Riders for Varying Growth Rates

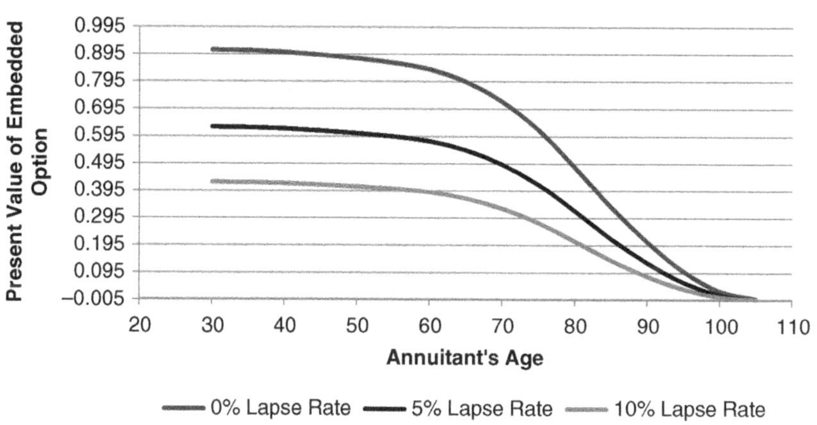

FIGURE 9.3B Impact of Surrenders on the Present Value of GMAB Riders for Varying Lapse Rates

Figure 9.3a shows the impact of the surrenders on the present value of the GMAB rider for varying fund growth rates when the lapse rate is 5 percent.

Consistent with intuition, Figure 9.3a shows that the higher the growth rate of the underlying fund, the lower the value of the embedded option in the GMAB (as the option becomes highly out-of-the-money). Figure 9.3b shows the impact of surrenders on the present value of the GMAB rider for varying

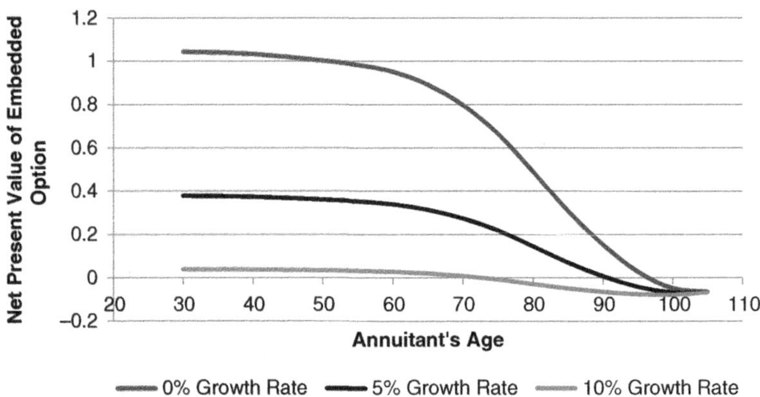

FIGURE 9.3C Impact of Surrenders on Net Present Value of GMAB Riders for Varying Growth Rates When Lapse Rate Is 5 Percent

lapse rates[5] (i.e., 0 percent per year, 5 percent per year, and 10 percent per year) when the growth rate is 5 percent.

As can be seen from Figure 9.3b, the higher the surrender rate, the lower the present value of the GMAB rider—confirming the intuition that the higher the lapse rate, the lower the risks. Redoing the analysis that was done to produce Figures 9.3a and 9.3b so as to understand the impact on the net present value of the GMAB rider (where the net present value is defined to be the difference of the present value of embedded options obtained in Figures 9.3a and 9.3b and the present value of rider fees collected during the life of the GMAB rider), one can arrive at Figures 9.3c, 9.3d, and 9.3e.

As can be observed from Figures 9.3a to 9.3e the insurance company is exposed to risks when the annuitant is alive on GMAB maturity date and when either realized lapse rates turn out to be much lower than what was used to price the guarantee decrease or the underlying fund value turns out to be lower than that initial deposit at the end of seven years. Furthermore, the greater the expected growth rate, expected lapse rates, or rider premium charged, the lower the expected breakeven issue age. As a consequence, one can conclude that if the target market for this product is much younger (e.g., 50), based on the economics associated with the GMAB rider, the insurance company should be charging more than 50 basis points or use a fund with

[5]These types of lapse rates are called static lapse rates. In practice, practitioners also use dynamic lapse rates (where the word dynamic is used to refer to factors like remaining life, value of the underlying funds and the in-the-moneyness of the rider—among other things).

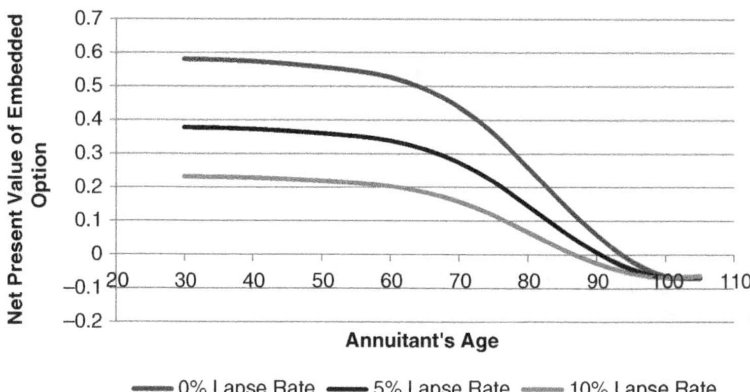

FIGURE 9.3D Impact of Surrenders on Net Present Value of GMAB Riders for Varying Lapse Rates When Growth Rate Is 5 percent

a higher growth rate or encourage surrendering as much as possible so the breakeven age shifts more to the left (i.e., gets lower).

Although I used a constant lapse rate to illustrate the impact of deterministic lapse rates (as seen in Figures 9.3a to 9.3e), one can also use dynamic lapse rates where the surrenders are driven by factors linked to market behavior. In fact, dynamic lapse rates can be neatly broken down into two categories: economic rationality (i.e., the policyholder is better off surrendering if surrendering offers the policyholder a higher payoff than continuing—a decision that is strictly based on financial market dynamics) and economic irrationality (i.e., the policyholder surrenders based on some

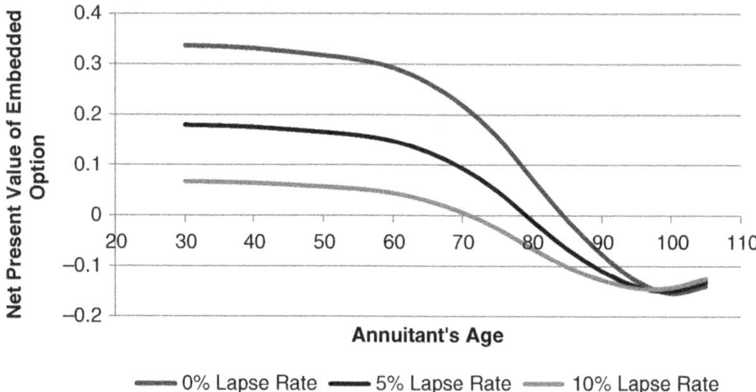

FIGURE 9.3E Impact of Surrenders on Net Present Value of GMAB Riders for Varying Lapse Rates When Rider Fee Is Increased by 50 Bps and Growth Rate Is 5 percent

predefined criteria that are not economically rational—e.g., if the fund value exceeds 120 percent of the deposit). Given the above backdrop, for ease of understanding, I will decompose the entire spectrum of lapse-rates into the following three groups:

1. Economic rational behavior.
2. Noneconomic rational behavior (which also includes static lapse rates).
3. A hybrid of economic and noneconomic rationality.

Modeling Economic Rational Behavior in a GMAB Rider

It is first important for the reader to understand that the modeling of rational behavior is done from the viewpoint of a policyholder and not an insurance company as it is the policyholder that has the ability to optimize the value of the option. Since it is easier to model optionality with early exercise features using a binomial method, I will use the same techniques described in Chapter 3 to value the early-exercise features.

As in Chapter 3, I use the binomial method to generate the account values and then use backward induction to roll back down the option tree. Letting S_t be the account value at time t, and assuming that this would move up to $S_t u$ with a probability p or move down to $S_t d$ with probability $1 - p$ over the time interval Δt, the values of u, d, and p are given by equations (3.14a), (3.14b), and (3.14c), which are restated here for convenience.[6]

$$u = e^{\sigma\sqrt{\Delta t}} \tag{3.14a}$$

$$d = \frac{1}{u} \tag{3.14b}$$

$$p = \frac{e^{r\Delta t} - d}{u - d} \tag{3.14c}$$

[6]The reader should note that equations (3.14a) – (3.14c) are only valid when both the implied term structure of volatility rates and zero rates are both flat (i.e., constants). In the event that only the term structure of volatility rates is constant, one can easily use the discount factors to capture the forward rates associated with non-constant zero rate term structure when discounting on the option tree (as shown in Table 3.12) over varying maturities. More precisely, if the zero rates corresponding to times w and $w + \Delta t$ (where $t < w < w + \Delta t$) are given by $r_{t,w}$ and $r_{t,w+\Delta t}$ respectively, as shown by equation (2.7), the continuously compounded forward rate applicable for the time interval $(w, w + \Delta t)$ is given by the equation $r_{t,w,w+\Delta t} = \dfrac{[r_{t,w+\Delta t}*(w + \Delta t - t)] - [r_{t,w}*(w - t)]}{\Delta t}$. Thus, to discount the cash flows in the option tree from time $w + \Delta t$ to time w, one would use the discount factor $e^{-r_{t,w,w+\Delta t}\Delta t}$. Doing

While equations (3.14a) to (3.14c) are valid as long as the fund grows at the risk-free rate r, when the fund grows at a rate g and has a continuously compounded MER rate of q, equation (3.14c) needs to be replaced by equation (9.2).

$$p = \frac{e^{(g-q)\Delta t} - d}{u - d} \tag{9.2}$$

In addition to the adaptation of equation (9.2) needed to value the optionality embedded in a GMAB rider, as was seen in Figure 9.2, one needs to also capture the annual GMAB rider fees discretely instead of

---

this over each time w, one can easily embed the term structure of zero rates into the binomial tree.

In the event that the term structure of volatility is not a constant, because of potentially different forward volatilities for varying maturities, one is left with varying values of u (given by equation (3.14a)). The consequence of this is that the recombining nature of the tree as shown in Table 3.11 would no longer be present. To see this, assume that the spot 1-year and 2-year volatilities are 20 percent and 25 percent respectively. Then using a binomial time step of 1 year, it readily follows that the volatility applicable for the time interval (0,1) is 20 percent and the forward volatility applicable for the time interval (1,2) can be computed using equation (6.7) and shown to be 29.16 percent. As a consequence, $u = 1.2214$ (for the time interval $(0, 1)$) and $u = 1.3385$ (for time interval $(1, 2)$). Thus if the stock price at time 0 is \$100, then the stock prices at time 1 year are $\$100 * 1.2214 = \$122.14$ and $\$100/1.2214 = \$81.87$. Furthermore, while the stock price of \$122.14 (at time 1 year) generates stock prices of $\$122.14 * 1.3385 = \$163.48$ and $\$122.14/1.3385 = \$91.25$ (at time 2 years), the stock price of \$81.87 (at time 1 year) generates stock prices of $\$81.87 * 1.3385 = \$109.58$ and $\$81.87/1.3385 = \$61.16$ (at time 2 years). Since the stock prices at time 2 years take values of \$163.48, \$91.25, \$109.58, and \$61.16, it can be easily seen that the tree does not recombine like what was seen in Table 3.11. To force the tree to recombine, the second time step in the binomial tree needs to be 0.547 years as opposed to the original value of 1 year since using this value of Δt, the stock prices at time 1.547 years become \$149.18, \$100, \$67.03—a recombining tree. In order to arrive at a second time step value of 0.547 years, one has to first guess at this second time step (e.g., x). One then interpolates the spot volatility for $1 + x$ years using the 1-year spot volatility and 2-year spot volatility. Using this spot volatility, one then infers the forward volatility for the time interval $(1, 1 + x)$. Using the second time step value of x, one needs to find the stock prices using the stock prices at time 1 year and the value u that is used to generate the stock prices at time $1 + x$ years. This step is repeated until the value of x is found such that the two middle price nodes match. One can then use this idea to bootstrap out a price tree for any required maturity and any given volatility term structure. As the astute reader will realize, in lieu of doing this, one can alternatively apply the methodology outlined in Chapter 6 to calibrate the stock price from the option prices.

TABLE 9.2A Assumptions and Tree Metrics

Current Fund Value (St)	10
Risk Free Rate (r)	5.00%
Growth Rate (g)	5.00%
Management Fees (q)	1.50%
Accumulation Benefit Fees	0.50%
Volatility (σ)	20.00%
Current Age	50
Term	7
Δt	1.00000
u	1.22140
d	0.81873
p	0.53862

approximating it with a continuously compounded rate. As discussed in Hull (2012), while valuing an option on discrete dividends is tantamount to creating stock price trees with non-recombining nodes at times when dividends are paid, such problems do not exist when the dividends are expressed as rates that are a function of the stock price.

Given the above backdrop, since the rider fees are a function of the account values, one can apply both the upward jump (u) and downward jump (d) to an account value that is net of fees. In the context of modeling the fund movements, consistent with the Tables 9.1a and 9.1b, I will use equation (9.2) in conjunction with equations (3.14a) and (3.14b) to value the GMAB riders.

For the seven-year GMAB rider example considered in Table 9.1a, assuming an annual time step, a constant volatility of 20 percent and a constant risk-free rate of 5 percent,[7] one can easily arrive at Tables 9.2a through 9.2d.[8]

Using the generated net account value tree in Table 9.2d, one can now compute the option payoff on GMAB maturity and then roll back down the option tree using backward induction. At any node on the 7-year time, the policyholder receives a payoff of max $\left[S_0 - S_{7years}, 0\right]$. Since this payoff in actuality can only be received if the annuitant is alive, it would be instructive

[7]I made the constant assumptions for both the risk-free and volatility rates so as to ensure that the illustration is more easily understood by the reader. To consider the case when the risk-free rate and volatility rates are non-constant, one has to use the suggestions provided in footnote 6.

[8]Since the rider fee is a function of the account value, one can generate the account-value (stock-price) tree assuming dividends (i.e., M & E fees), and then discretely adjust the account values for the GMAB rider fees.

TABLE 9.2B Account Value Projection[9]

Account Values with No Fees							
Time (Years)							
0	1	2	3	4	5	6	7
							39.15
						32.22	
					26.51		26.25
				21.81		21.6	
			17.95		17.77		17.59
		14.77		14.62		14.48	
	12.15		12.03		11.91		11.79
10		9.9		9.8		9.7	
	8.15		8.07		7.98		7.91
		6.64		6.57		6.5	
			5.41		5.35		5.3
				4.4		4.36	
					3.59		3.55
						2.92	
							2.38

to look at the mortality and survival probabilities of the annuitant. Table 9.3 shows the mortality and survival probabilities associated with a 50-year-old annuitant.

With the probabilities mapped out in Table 9.3, it is easy to see that the option payoff of max $\left[S_0 - S_{7years}, 0\right]$ needs to be weighted by the probability that the policyholder would still be alive at year 7 (which is given by cell I4 in Table 9.3). Doing this, one can easily fill up all the nodes for year 7 in Table 9.4 (cells I6:I20).

To fill up the 6-year nodes on the option tree, it is imperative to understand—from the policyholder's standpoint—that the GMAB rider can be viewed as an option that allows a policyholder to pay the annual rider fee so as to be able to continue with the rider for one last year.[10] Hence by not

[9]Where the values are projected using Table 9.2d. For example, the fund values at the 1-year time, 12.1530 and 8.1463 (in Table 9.2b), are obtained using the adjusted fund value 9.95 (in Table 9.2d) and multiplying it by the value of u and d respectively.
[10]In practice, depending on the contract, the policyholder may make this decision every business day the underlying fund trades. Furthermore, as the astute reader may realize, this option is an extension of the installment options discussed in Chapter 5 (where I discussed the finding of the first compulsory premium when the second optional installment option was known). Unlike Chapter 5, which discussed an

TABLE 9.2C GMAB Rider Fees

GMAB Rider Fees							
Time (Years)							
0	1	2	3	4	5	6	7
						0.16	
					0.13		
				0.11		0.11	
			0.09		0.09		
		0.07		0.07		0.07	
	0.06		0.06		0.06		
0.05		0.05		0.05		0.05	
	0.04		0.04		0.04		
		0.03		0.03		0.03	
			0.03		0.03		
				0.02		0.02	
					0.02		
						0.01	

TABLE 9.2D Account Value Net of Fees

Account Value Net of Fees							
Time (Years)							
0	1	2	3	4	5	6	7
							39.15
						32.06	
					26.38		26.25
				21.7		21.49	
			17.86		17.68		17.59
		14.7		14.55		14.4	
	12.09		11.97		11.85		11.79
9.95		9.85		9.75		9.66	
	8.11		8.02		7.94		7.91
		6.6		6.54		6.47	
			5.38		5.33		5.3
				4.38		4.34	
					3.57		3.55
						2.91	
							2.38

TABLE 9.3 Mortality and Survival Probabilities Associated with a 50-Year-Old Annuitant

	A	B	C	D	E	F	G	H	I
1	Time (years)	0	1	2	3	4	5	6	7
2	Age	50	51	52	53	54	55	56	57
3	Mortality Table Probability		0.4518%	0.4938%	0.5370%	0.5811%	0.6260%	0.6718%	0.7184%
4	Number Living	1	0.995482	0.99056631	0.985246969	0.9795217	0.97338989	0.96685066	0.9599048
5	Number Dying		0.004518	0.00491569	0.005319341	0.00572527	0.00613181	0.00653923	0.00694586
6									

TABLE 9.4 Option Values Due to Policyholder Behavior Relating to the Surrender of a GMAB Rider

	A	B	C	D	E	F	G	H	I
1	Time (years)	0	1	2	3	4	5	6	7
2	Age	50	51	52	53	54	55	56	57
3	Mortality Table Probability		0.4518%	0.4938%	0.5370%	0.5811%	0.6260%	0.6718%	0.7184%
4	Number Living	1	0.995482	0.99056631	0.985246969	0.9795217	0.97338989	0.96685066	0.9599048
5	Number Dying		0.004518	0.00491569	0.005319341	0.00572527	0.00613181	0.00653923	0.00694586
6									0
7								0	
8							0		0
9						0		0	
10					0		0		0
11				0.07986949		0.06390024		0	
12			0.32199116		0.348664993		0.30877564		0
13		0.672479		0.7782639		0.85490696		0.83565965	
14			1.27030881		1.478004359		1.69686029		2.01098668
15				2.07829311		2.46020192		2.97936612	
16					3.084935768		3.69806404		4.5126184
17						4.21777111		5.00740252	
18							5.34234736		6.18951229
19								6.36683597	
20									7.31356788

paying the annual fee, the policyholder is effectively choosing to surrender the rider and forego the maturity benefit. As a consequence, the following two things can happen at any option node on the sixth year time:

1. The policyholder surrenders the rider on year 6 by not paying any more rider fees.
2. The policyholder pays the rider fees on year 6 so as to continue holding on to the policy for another year (i.e., maturity).

Since the optionality (and decision-making component) only exists when the policyholder is alive at year 6, to quantify this optionality one needs to incorporate the probability of living at this time.

Cells I6 and I8 of Table 9.4 correspond to the net account values 39.15 and 26.25 (in Table 9.2d) respectively. To calculate the optional value at cell H7 of Table 9.4 (which corresponds to an account value of 32.05 in Table 9.2d), one needs to calculate the following two values and then pick the higher of these values.

Value from Surrendering The policyholder would only get a value of 0 by surrendering since by surrendering, the GMAB rider just drops away.

Value from Continuing If the policyholder chooses to continue with the policy, the policyholder would get an option value of 0 (cell I6 of Table 9.4) with a probability 0.5386, and an option value of 0 (cell I8 of Table 9.4) with probability (1–0.5386) one year later—provided the policyholder does not die during this year.[11] Hence the present value of this expectation to the policyholder is given by the expression

$$[(0*0.5386) + (0*(1 - 0.5386))]\, e^{-0.05(1)}$$

where the term $e^{-0.05*1}$ represents the present value from seven years to six years.

Thus the value from surrendering is

$$[(0*0.5386) + (0*(1 - 0.5386))]\, e^{-0.05(1)} - (0.1611*0.9668) = -0.1557$$

option-on-an-option, this example is an instance in which an option-on-an-option is contained in another option which in turn is contained in another option, and so on (i.e., a deeply nested installment option).

[11]It is important to note that the option values of 0 (cells I6 and I8 of Table 9.3) already embed the probability that the policyholder lives for seven years.

where the number 0.1611 refers to the GMAB rider fees when the net account value is 32.0 (see Tables 9.2b and 9.2c) and the value of 0.9668 refers the number of people living at the 6-year point (see cell H4 in Table 9.4).

From the above, it can be seen that the option value in cell H7 of Table 9.4 (when the net account value is 32.05) is given by the expression $\max(-0.1557, 0) = 0$.

One has to apply this idea for all the other nodes at this time and all earlier times. Doing this yields the option tree in Table 9.4.

The result of $0.67 (that is given by cell B13 of Table 9.4) refers to the value of the early-surrender option when the policyholder is allowed to lapse only the GMAB rider. Since the annual rider fee is 50 basis points, from the policyholder's perspective paying a total amount of $0.26 (which is the probability weighted present value of the fees paid until the time of surrender) so as to receive an option that is worth $0.66 shows a great proposition from a consumer perspective. This also shows that for the annual rider fee of 50 basis points, the insurance company has underpriced the risk, assuming all the other inputs (e.g., volatility, 50-year-old annuitant, etc.) are reasonable. For a greater accuracy, one can generate the binomial tree with a weekly time step while still allowing an annual exercise frequency to arrive at an accurate value of $0.63.

Given the above illustration, I would like to point out the following interesting observations to the reader:

- In the event that this early-exercise privilege is not accorded to the policyholder (so that the policyholder cannot lapse the rider), using weekly time steps, it can be shown that the present value of the GMAB benefit turns out to be $0.58 which can be obtained by paying a total present value of $0.32 in fees—a lower return on investment than the one associated with the ability to surrender the rider early.[12]
- In doing the above analysis, I assumed that the policyholder used the mortality table as part of the decision making process to decide if he/should surrender the rider or continue paying the GMAB rider fee. In practice, it is not unreasonable for the policyholder to make the decision to surrender without paying any heed to the mortality table (i.e., simply assume that the annuitant will live for seven years). Using a weekly time step with no mortality rates (i.e., the annuitant will live past the GMAB

[12]Using the simulation used to produce Tables 9.1a and 9.1b, it can be shown that the present value of the rider is $0.55 when the annuitant is 50 years old, no lapses are allowed, constant risk-free rate is 5 percent, and volatility rate is 20 percent.

rider maturity date with a 100 percent certainty), increases the value of the early exercise option to $0.67 while the value of the option when no lapses are allowed increases to $0.61.

- It is also important for the reader to note that when the policyholder is only allowed to surrender the entire contract (i.e., both GMAB rider and GMDB contract simultaneously), the setup of the problem becomes quite different since, in addition to comparing the continuation payoff with the rider fees (as was done to derive the option values in Table 9.4), one needs to include the MER fees in the comparison (as the policyholder would only continue if the value by continuing exceeds the sum of the MER and GMAB rider fees paid). In addition to this, the death benefit also needs to be factored into the analysis (something that was not done when deriving the values in Table 9.4).

Modeling Noneconomic Rational Behavior

Examples of this assumption were used to derive Figures 9.2a, 9.2b, and 9.2c when I used deterministic annual lapse rates to value the options embedded in a GMAB rider. In addition to such static lapse rates, insurance companies often also use dynamic lapse rates to try to forecast how policyholders behave in the presence of market conditions. Since dynamic lapse rates tend to be a function of the in-the-moneyness of the option, one example of a dynamic lapse rate applied at time u (where $u > t$) is the function $\max[\frac{S_t - S_u}{S_t}, 0.1]$, where S_u is the fund value at time u and the lapse rate is capped at 10 percent. Whatever the form of these dynamic lapse rates, one can easily implement them using simulations shown in Table 9.1b. Furthermore, it is imperative for the reader to note that none of these forms of lapse rates will be as optimal (from the perspective of policyholder) as those that were derived using the economic rational behavior approach.

Hybrid of Economical and Noneconomic Rational Behavior

It is not uncommon for insurance companies to sometimes assume that only a certain percentage of the policyholders behave in an economically rational manner. However modeling this percentage of economic rationality is a tricky exercise since if it was economically rational to surrender, an economically rational policyholder would and should surrender 100 percent of the time. As a consequence, trying to use the binomial method to reduce this 100 percent to a lesser amount can be a complicating task. Fortunately, one can get around this problem by combining the binomial method with the simulation technique. More precisely, one has to first quantify the optimal-surrender boundary, derived from the binomial method. Once this has been identified, one can then easily use simulations to implement partial rational surrendering when this boundary is crossed. In the context of the example discussed in Table 9.4, the cells with 0 values indicate regions when the rider is surrendered. Thus from Table 9.4 (in conjunction with Table 9.2d), one can see that as long as the fund value exceeds \$17.86 in year 3, or \$21.71 in year 4, or \$17.68 in year 5, or \$14.40 in year 6, it is optimal for the policyholder to surrender.[13] Using this criteria, one can now simulate and appropriately decrement the population by the proportion of economically rational lapses using the method outlined in Table 9.1b.

ADDING SERVERS IN A QUEUE

The purpose of this section is to illustrate the use of real options in the field of queuing. Unlike traditional discussion of real options where the focus tended to be on the use of real options to understand the impact of expanding or contracting a project, I will use real options in this section to quantify the impact of expanding a queuing operation—although the impact here is on the bottom line as opposed to the value of optionality. In Chapter 4, I discussed queuing briefly and how simulations can be used to quantify metrics of a queue. In the discussion, I also touched on the convention (proposed by Kendall in 1953) that is in the form of A/B/k/S/N/P to help classify and group different types of queuing problems. To illustrate the use of real options in queuing, I will start with the M/M/1 queue and discuss standard queuing metrics (e.g., probability of having 0/1/2/3... people in the queuing system, expected waiting time experienced by any new arrival into the queuing system until the moment the service is completed). I then expand my discussion to include the M/M/2 queue following which I discuss the M/M/k queue. Since most of the results developed are asymptotic in nature, I investigate the effectiveness of these results when the queue is operational only in finite time (as most queues are in practice). I conclude the illustration with a discussion on the issue of optimally managing the queue when there are costs involved.

M/M/1 Queue

In Chapter 4, I discussed the simulation of an M/M/1 queue. In this section, I will discuss the use of analytical methods to obtain some interesting

[13]The reason for the optimal boundary not being montone is simply due to the fact that the tree is not fine enough (i.e., Δt is not small enough). Once Δt is made small enough, the optimal exercise would become a well-behaved monotonically decreasing function of time.

metrics associated with the queue (that was computed in Chapter 4 using simulations).

As before, I first assume that customers enter a queuing system as according to an exponential distribution with a rate of λ and get served by a server (where the service time follows an exponential distribution with rate μ). To keep my illustration simple, I further assume that the maximum number of customers served and the calling population size from which customers arrive are infinite, and whoever enters the queue first is served first (i.e., FIFO).

Probability of Having *n* Customers in the Queue Letting $P_n(t)$ represent the probability of there being n people in the queuing system at time t (including the person being served) where $n = 0, 1, 2, 3, \ldots$, and $t > 0$, by considering the possible events that can happen over a infinitesimal time Δt, one has

$$P_0(t+\Delta t) = P_0(t)(1-\lambda\Delta t) + P_1(t)(1-\lambda\Delta t)(\mu\Delta t) + \textit{higher order terms in } \Delta t \tag{9.3a}$$

$$\begin{aligned} P_n(t+\Delta t) &= P_{n-1}(t)(\lambda\Delta t)(1-\mu\Delta t) \\ &\quad + P_n(t)(1-\lambda\Delta t)(1-\mu\Delta t) \\ &\quad + P_{n+1}(t)(1-\lambda\Delta t)(\mu\Delta t) \\ &\quad + \textit{higher order terms in } \Delta t \\ &\text{for } n = 1, 2, 3, \ldots \end{aligned} \tag{9.3b}$$

Taking limits as $\Delta t \to 0$, equations (9.3a) and (9.3b) simplify to

$$\frac{dP_0(t)}{dt} = -\lambda P_0(t) + \mu P_1(t) \tag{9.4a}$$

$$\frac{dP_n(t)}{dt} = \lambda P_{n-1}(t) - (\lambda+\mu) P_n(t) + \mu P_{n+1}(t) \quad \text{for } n = 1, 2, 3, \ldots \tag{9.4b}$$

For the queue to reach stationarity conditions (i.e., be time independent and stabilize), one would want that $\frac{dP_n(t)}{dt} = 0$ (for $n = 0, 1, 2, 3, \ldots$). Doing this allows equations (9.4a) and (9.4b) to yield $P_n = \rho^n P_0$ for $n = 1, 2, 3, \ldots$, where $= \frac{\lambda}{\mu}$.[14]

Using the identity $\sum_{n=0}^{\infty} P_n = 1$, it follows that for $n = 0, 1, 2, 3, \ldots P_n = (1-\rho)\rho^n$.

[14] ρ is sometimes also called *queue intensity* where $\rho < 1$. This condition on ρ is needed for the infinite series to converge and arrive at the expression $P_n = (1-\rho)\rho^n$.

Expected Waiting Time To find the expression for the expected waiting time (the time until service is completed), one needs a waiting-time distribution. To get this, let W represent the time taken for a new arrival into the queue to finish receiving the service and $f(w)$ be the probability density function (pdf) of W (where $w > 0$). Then:[15]

$$\begin{aligned} f(w) &= \sum_{n=0}^{\infty} [P_n * \Pr((n+1)\, st\ service\ is\ completed\ at\ time\ t)] \\ &= \sum_{n=0}^{\infty} [(1-\rho)\rho^n * \frac{\mu(\mu w)^n}{\Gamma(n+1)} e^{-\mu w}] \\ &= (1-\rho)\,\mu e^{-(1-\rho)\mu w} \end{aligned}$$

Thus, the waiting time pdf is exponentially distributed with parameter $(1-\rho)\,\mu = \mu - \lambda$. As a consequence the expected waiting time is $\frac{1}{\mu-\lambda}$.

Percentage of Downtime To calculate this quantity, it is important to first observe that the server would have nothing to do if there is no one in the queue. Hence the percentage of downtime is simply given by the expression $P_0 = (1-\rho)$.

As a consequence, the percentage of time the server would be busy is simply $1 - P_0 = \rho$.

M/M/2 Queue

Unlike the M/M/1 queue where there was only one server, in this variation, there are two servers serving in the queue.

Probability of Having n Customers in the Queue As before, letting $P_n(t)$ represent the probability that there are n people in the queue at time t

[15] Since the time for each service has an exponential pdf with rate μ, the service time for $n+1$ independent services is simply the sum of $n+1$ independent exponential pdfs. As the moment-generating function of an exponential pdf with rate μ is $M(t) = \frac{\mu}{\mu+t}$, the moment-generating function of the sum of $n+1$ independent identically distributed exponential pdf is $\left(\frac{\mu}{\mu+t}\right)^{n+1}$—which is the moment-generating function of a gamma pdf with parameters $n+1$ and μ (if X is a gamma variate with parameters $n+1$ and μ, then the pdf of X has the form $\frac{\mu}{\Gamma(n+1)}(\mu x)^n e^{-\mu x}$ for $x > 0$).

(including the person being served) where $n = 1, 2, 3, \ldots$, equations (9.3a) and (9.3b) become

$$\begin{aligned}
P_0(t+\Delta t) &= P_0(t)(1-\lambda\Delta t) + P_1(t)(1-\lambda\Delta t)(\mu\Delta t) \\
&\quad + \textit{higher order terms in } \Delta t && (9.5a) \\
P_1(t+\Delta t) &= P_0(t)(\lambda\Delta t) + P_1(t)(1-\lambda\Delta t)(1-\mu\Delta t) \\
&\quad + P_2(t)(1-\lambda\Delta t)(2\mu\Delta t) \\
&\quad + \textit{higher order terms in } \Delta t && (9.5b) \\
P_2(t+\Delta t) &= P_1(t)(\lambda\Delta t)(1-\mu\Delta t) \\
&\quad + P_2(t)(1-\lambda\Delta t)(1-2\mu\Delta t) \\
&\quad + P_3(t)(1-\lambda\Delta t)(2\mu\Delta t) \\
&\quad + \textit{higher order terms in } \Delta t && (9.5c) \\
P_n(t+\Delta t) &= P_{n-1}(t)(\lambda\Delta t)(1-2\mu\Delta t) \\
&\quad + P_n(t)(1-\lambda\Delta t)(1-2\mu\Delta t) \\
&\quad + P_{n+1}(t)(1-\lambda\Delta t)(2\mu\Delta t) \\
&\quad + \textit{higher order terms in} \\
&\text{for } n = 3, 4, \ldots && (9.5d)
\end{aligned}$$

Taking limits as $\Delta t \to 0$, one can arrive at the following analogs for equations (9.4a) and (9.4b):

$$\begin{aligned}
\frac{dP_0(t)}{dt} &= -\lambda P_0(t) + \mu P_1(t) && (9.6a) \\
\frac{dP_1(t)}{dt} &= \lambda P_0(t) - (\lambda+\mu) P_1(t) + 2\mu P_2(t) && (9.6b) \\
\frac{dP_n(t)}{dt} &= \lambda P_{n-1}(t) - (\lambda+2\mu) P_n(t) + 2\mu P_{n+1}(t) \\
&\text{for } n = 2, 3, \ldots && (9.6c)
\end{aligned}$$

For the queue to reach stationarity conditions (i.e., be time independent and stabilize), one has that $\frac{dP_n(t)}{dt} = 0$ (for $n = 0, 1, 2, 3, \ldots$). Doing this allows one to use equations (9.6a) to (9.6c) to obtain $P_n = 2\theta^n P_0$ for $n = 1, 2, 3, \ldots$, where $\theta = \frac{\lambda}{2\mu}$. Using the identity $\sum_{n=0}^{\infty} P_n = 1$, it follows that

$$\begin{aligned}
P_0 &= \frac{1-\theta}{1+\theta} \\
P_n &= \frac{2(1-\theta)}{1+\theta}\theta^n \quad \text{for } n = 1, 2, 3, \ldots
\end{aligned}$$

Expected Waiting Time To find the expression for the expected waiting time (i.e., the time taken for an arriving customer to get his service completed), one needs a waiting-time distribution. As before, letting W represent the waiting time and $f(w)$ the pdf of W (where $w > 0$), it readily follows that

$$\begin{aligned}
f(w) &= \sum_{n=0}^{\infty}[P_n * \Pr((n+1)\text{ st service is completed at time } t)] \\
&= \left[\frac{1-\theta}{1+\theta} * \mu e^{-\mu w}\right] + \left[\frac{2(1-\theta)}{1+\theta}\theta * \mu e^{-\mu w}\right] \\
&\quad + \left\{\frac{2(1-\theta)}{1+\theta}\theta^2 * 2\mu\left[e^{-\mu w} - e^{-2\mu w}\right]\right\} \\
&\quad + \left\{\frac{2(1-\theta)}{1+\theta}\theta^3 * 4\mu\left[e^{-\mu w} - e^{-2\mu w}\left(1 + \frac{\mu w}{1!}\right)\right]\right\} \\
&\quad + \left\{\frac{2(1-\theta)}{1+\theta}\theta^4 * 8\mu\left[e^{-\mu w} - e^{-2\mu w}\left(1 + \frac{\mu w}{1!} + \frac{(\mu w)^2}{2!}\right)\right]\right\} \\
&\quad + \left\{\frac{2(1-\theta)}{1+\theta}\theta^5 * 16\mu * \left[e^{-\mu w} - e^{-2\mu w}\left(1 + \frac{\mu w}{1!} + \frac{(\mu w)^2}{2!} + \frac{(\mu w)^3}{3!}\right)\right]\right\} \\
&\quad + \cdots \\
&= \frac{\mu(1-\theta)}{(1+\theta)(1-2\theta)}e^{-\mu w} - \frac{4\mu\theta^2(1-\theta)}{(1+\theta)(1-2\theta)}e^{-2\mu(1-\theta)w}
\end{aligned}$$

From the above, it follows that the expected waiting time for such a queue is given by the expression $\int_0^\infty wf(w)\,dw$, which simplifies to $\frac{1}{\mu(1-\theta)(1+\theta)}$.

Little's Formula to Compute Expected Waiting Time As can be seen from the discussion presented thus far, in increasing the number of servers from one to two, the problem associated with finding the expected waiting time quickly gets more complicated. Despite the complexity associated with the derivation of $f(w)$, one can extend the problem to entertain more servers and calculate the expected waiting time until the completion of service using Little's formula (1961). Little's formula simply states that

$$E\left(\textit{number in system}\right) = \lambda * E(\textit{waiting time}) \tag{9.7a}$$

where

$E\,(waiting\ time)$ refers to the expected time taken for a newly arriving customer get his service completed.

$E\,(number\ in\ system)$ refers to the expected number of customers in the queuing system.

A related variation of the formula that is given in equation (9.7a) is

$$E\,(number\ in\ \text{queue}) = \lambda * E(waiting\ time\ until\ start\ of\ service) \quad (9.7b)$$

where

$E\,(waiting\ time\ until\ start\ of\ service)$ refers to the expected time taken for a newly arriving customer to get his service started.

$E\,(number\ in\ queue)$ refers to the expected number of customers in the queue waiting to get their service started.

Another formula that is useful in connecting equation (9.7a) with equation (9.7b) is

$$E\,(waiting\ time) = E\,(waiting\ time\ until\ start\ of\ service) + \frac{1}{\mu} \quad (9.7c)$$

To apply equation (9.7a), consider the M/M/1 queue. For this type of queue, it readily follows that

$$\begin{aligned} E\,(number\ in\ system) &= \sum_{n=0}^{\infty} n * (1-\rho)\rho^n \\ &= (1-\rho)\sum_{n=0}^{\infty} n * \rho^n \\ &= \frac{\rho}{1-\rho} \end{aligned}$$

Hence the $E\,(waiting\ time) = \frac{\rho}{\lambda(1-\rho)} = \frac{1}{\mu-\lambda}$ (which agrees with the result obtained for the M/M/1 queue).

To apply equations (9.7b) and (9.7c) to the M/M/2 queue, first consider the size of the queue that is waiting to be served. Then it is easy to see that

$$
\begin{aligned}
E\left(number\ in\ queue\right) &= \sum_{n=3}^{\infty}(n-2)*\frac{2(1-\theta)}{1+\theta}\theta^{n} \\
&= \frac{2(1-\theta)}{1+\theta}\sum_{n=1}^{\infty} n*\theta^{n+2} \\
&= \frac{\lambda\theta^{2}}{\mu\left(1-\theta\right)\left(1+\theta\right)}
\end{aligned}
$$

Hence, using equation (9.7c), one gets $E\left(waiting\ time\right) = \frac{\theta^2}{\mu(1-\theta)(1+\theta)} + \frac{1}{\mu} = \frac{1}{\mu(1-\theta)(1+\theta)}$ (which again agrees with the result obtained for the M/M/2 queue).

Percentage of Downtime To calculate this quantity, it is important to first observe that both the servers would have nothing to do if no one is in the queue. Thus, the percentage of downtime is simply given by the expression $P_0 = \frac{1-\theta}{1+\theta}$. Furthermore, the percentage of time that both the servers would both be busy is given by the expression

$$1 - P_0 - P_1 = \frac{2\theta^2}{1+\theta}$$

M/M/*k* Queue

In this section, I will generalize the discussions for the M/M/1 and M/M/2 queue by considering the instance when there are k (where $k = 1, 2, 3, \ldots$) servers to attend to the queue.

Probability of Having *n* Customers in the Queue Using similar notations, one can arrive at the following analogs of equations (9.5a) to (9.5c).

$$
\begin{aligned}
P_0\left(t+\Delta t\right) &= P_0\left(t\right)\left(1-\lambda\Delta t\right) + P_1\left(t\right)\left(1-\lambda\Delta t\right)\left(\mu\Delta t\right) \\
&\quad + higher\ order\ terms\ in\ \Delta t \qquad (9.8a) \\
P_n\left(t+\Delta t\right) &= P_{n-1}\left(t\right)\left(\lambda\Delta t\right)\left(1-\mu\left(n-1\right)\Delta t\right) \\
&\quad + P_n\left(t\right)\left(1-\lambda\Delta t\right)\left(1-\mu n\Delta t\right) \\
&\quad + P_{n+1}\left(t\right)\left(1-\lambda\Delta t\right)\left(\mu(n+1)\Delta t\right) \\
&\quad + higher\ order\ terms\ in\ \Delta t \\
&\text{for } n = 1,\ 2,\ \ldots k-1 \qquad (9.8b)
\end{aligned}
$$

$$\begin{aligned}P_k(t+\Delta t) &= P_{k-1}(t)(\lambda\Delta t)\left(1-\mu\left(k-1\right)\Delta t\right)\\&\quad + P_k(t)(1-\lambda\Delta t)\left(1-\mu k\Delta t\right)\\&\quad + P_{k+1}(t)(1-\lambda\Delta t)\left(\mu k\Delta t\right)\\&\quad + \textit{higher order terms in } \Delta t \end{aligned} \tag{9.8c}$$

$$\begin{aligned}P_n(t+\Delta t) &= P_{n-1}(t)(\lambda\Delta t)\left(1-\mu k\Delta t\right)\\&\quad + P_n(t)(1-\lambda\Delta t)\left(1-\mu k\Delta t\right)\\&\quad + P_{n+1}(t)(1-\lambda\Delta t)\left(\mu k\Delta t\right)\\&\quad + \textit{higher order terms in } \Delta t\\ &\text{for } n = k+1, k+2, \ldots\end{aligned} \tag{9.8d}$$

Taking limits as $\Delta t \to 0$, one can arrive at the following analogs of equations (9.6a) to (9.6c).

$$\frac{dP_0(t)}{dt} = -\lambda P_0(t) + \mu P_1(t) \tag{9.9a}$$

$$\begin{aligned}\frac{dP_n(t)}{dt} &= \lambda P_{n-1}(t) - (\lambda + \mu n)P_n(t) + \mu(n+1)P_{n+1}(t)\\ &\text{for } n = 1,\ 2,\ \ldots, k-1\end{aligned} \tag{9.9b}$$

$$\begin{aligned}\frac{dP_n(t)}{dt} &= \lambda P_{n-1}(t) - \left(\lambda + \mu k\right)P_n(t) + \mu k P_{n+1}(t)\\ &\text{for } n = k, k+1, \ldots\end{aligned} \tag{9.9c}$$

As earlier, for the queue to reach stationarity conditions (i.e., be time independent and stabilize), one needs to set equations (9.9a) to (9.9c) to 0. Doing this yields

$$P_n = \begin{cases} \dfrac{\rho^n}{n!}P_0 & n = 1,2,3,\ldots,k \\ \dfrac{\rho^n}{k!k^{n-k}}P_0 & n = k+1, k+2, \ldots \end{cases} \tag{9.10}$$

where ρ was defined as for the M/M/1 queue and[16]

$$P_0 = \left[1 + \sum_{n=1}^{k}\frac{\rho^n}{n!} + \sum_{n=k+1}^{\infty}\frac{\rho^n}{k!k^{n-k}}\right]^{-1}$$

[16]It is important to note that in obtaining the expression for P_0, since the infinite series has not been collapsed to an analytic function, no assumption was made about ρ.

Expected Waiting Time To find the expression for the expected waiting time, I will, as in the M/M/2 queue, first find the expected number of customers in the queue waiting to be served. To do this, observe that

$$E\left(number\ in\ queue\right) = \sum_{n=k+1}^{\infty} (n-k) * \frac{1}{k!k^{n-k}}\rho^n P_0$$
$$= \frac{\rho^k}{k!(1-\frac{\rho}{k})^2}\frac{\rho}{k}P_0$$

Applying equation (9.7c), it readily follows that the

$$E\left(waiting\ time\right) = \frac{\rho^k}{k!\left(1-\frac{\rho}{k}\right)^2}\frac{\rho}{\lambda k}P_0 + \frac{1}{\mu} \tag{9.11}$$

Percentage of Downtime To calculate this quantity, it is important to first observe that the servers would have nothing to do if there is no one in the queue. The percentage of downtime is simply given by the expression P_0. Furthermore, the percentage of time the servers would all be busy is given by the expression $1 - P_0 - P_1 - \ldots - P_{k-1}$.

Numerical Example

To illustrate, consider the instance when the service rate of any passenger agent in an airport is 8 passengers/hour, while the arrival rate of the passengers is 6 passengers/hour. Using equation (9.11), one can obtain the expected waiting time in Table 9.5 for a varying number of passenger agents.

As can be seen from Table 9.5, the waiting time for a newly arriving passenger drops drastically from 30 minutes to about 9 minutes by making two passenger agents available to serve the queue. Furthermore, the relative

TABLE 9.5 Impact of the Number of Servers on Waiting Time

Number of Passenger Agents	Expected Waiting Time (minutes)
1	30.00
2	8.73
3	7.65
4	7.52
5	7.50

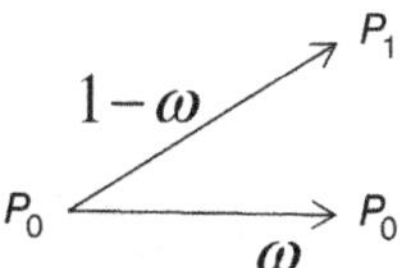

FIGURE 9.4A
Probability of Moving from State 0 to State 1

value gained by adding a subsequent passenger agent is very small compared to that gained by moving from one to two passenger agents. In addition to this, it can be shown that when there is one passenger agent the percentage of downtime is about 25 percent, and when there are two passenger agents downtime is about 45 percent.[17]

Since there are costs associated with the deployment of passenger agents, the airline has to decide if it is worthwhile to have passenger agents possibly idly waiting for passengers (a common scene in the airport when there is very little traffic) and incurring unnecessary overhead costs or if it is more worthwhile to reduce the costs by bringing more agents in only if they can be put to work immediately upon arrival.

It is in this space where the notion of real options becomes useful, as the airline needs to decide how to optimally expand the operation to bring in more passenger agents so as to minimize the cost of the operations, while ensuring that any waiting time constraints are satisfied.

As outlined in equations (9.3a) and (9.3b) for the M/M/1 queue, the probabilities associated with jumps to different states over a time interval Δt are given in Figures 9.4a and 9.4b.

Figure 9.4a shows the generation of states (with the appropriate probabilities) starting with 0 passengers in the queuing system, while Figure 9.4b shows the generation of states (with the appropriate probabilities) starting with an arbitrary state i (where $i = 1, 2, 3, \ldots$) when the expressions for $\omega, \pi,$ andα are given as follows:[18]

$$\omega = \lambda \Delta t \tag{9.12a}$$

$$\pi = \lambda \Delta t * (1 - \mu \Delta t) \tag{9.12b}$$

$$\alpha = (1 - \lambda \Delta t) * \mu \Delta t \tag{9.12c}$$

---

[17]These are simply the values of P_0 in equation (9.10) in the instance when $k = 1$ and 2.

[18]The state transition probabilities provided in equations (9.12a) to (9.12c) are all accurate for a very small Δt.

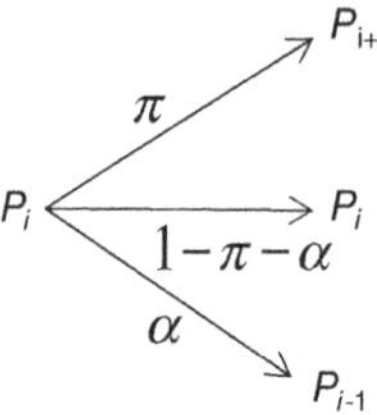

FIGURE 9.4B Probability of Moving from State i to State $i + 1$

Using the transition probabilities in equations (9.12a) to (9.12c), one can now construct the states that the tree transverses, as shown in Figure 9.5.

To apply the notion of optionality, one has to first create the state tree for the period of time the queue is operational. Once that is done, one can create a payoff tree (as in the GMAB rider) to rollback to obtain the present value of the decision. While the above approach seems theoretically feasible, implementing this in practice may not be as straightforward, due to the complication introduced by the path dependency, especially when the number of servers in the queue keeps increasing. Given this backdrop, I will instead try to put bounds on the value of the exercise rather than try to implicitly value this option.

Before the advent of fast computers, queuing theory, like many other disciplines, caught the attention of operational researchers and probabilists who spent their time and energy deriving asymptotics based on queue stationarity so as to obtain analytic solutions to compute the metrics of interest. Clearly, if the queue is only operational for a finite time (in which case the arrival rate can be higher than the service rate), the formulae derived earlier

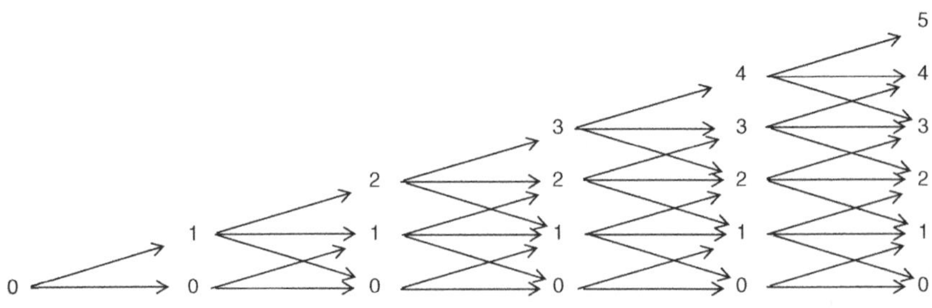

FIGURE 9.5 Transition of States in a Queue

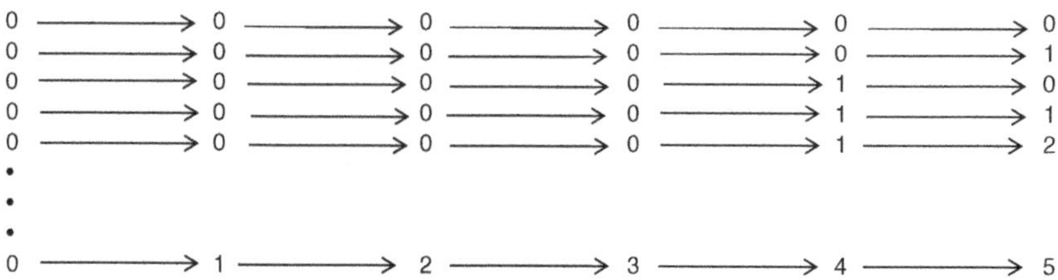

FIGURE 9.6 Transition of States in a Queue (Unlinked)

may not be a great approximation to the problem at hand. As a consequence, it is important to first question the validity of the results obtained for the M/M/k queue in finite time. Once this question is answered,[19] one needs to incorporate the notion of optionality into the managing of the operation (i.e., bringing on an additional passenger agent as and when required so as to minimize the cost and keep the expected waiting time within predefined constraints).

To answer the question of validity in finite time, it may be easier to first revisit Figure 9.5. Due to the nature of the path dependency associated with state tree in Figure 9.5, it is best (for the purposes of illustration) to unlink the branches of the tree to more clearly exhibit how the states evolve during the time the queue is operational. Figure 9.6 illustrates how the state tree above looks when unlinked.

Figure 9.6 gives a better sense of how the states (number of people in the queuing system) evolve in practice so as to be able to implicitly calculate the waiting time among other things. It is much easier to use a simulated queue (like that discussed in Chapter 4) to entertain the properties outlined in Figure 9.6—including the consideration of having more than one passenger agent. In fact, it is even possible to simulate this queue in finite time when the service rate is slower than the arrival rate (an assumption that is NOT used for queue stationarity). Table 9.6 shows the absolute value of the relative error when approximating the expected waiting time in a queue that is only operational for 30 minutes, using equation (9.11) as compared to using the simulation algorithm in Chapter 4 to simulate this queue for a period of 30 minutes after which no arrivals are allowed (i.e., the queue is closed) for an M/M/1 queue.

[19]The reason for this stems from that fact that if the asymptotic results are indeed accurate, in quantifying the optionality associated with bringing on the additional server, one can resort to the use of existing expressions related to expected waiting time.

TABLE 9.6 Relative Error When Estimating the Expected Waiting Time for an M/M/1 Queue

		Mu (μ)									
		2	4	6	8	10	12	14	16	18	20
Lamda (λ)	1.5	20.44%	2.87%	1.82%	1.24%	0.86%	0.63%	0.46%	0.37%	0.32%	0.28%
	3	1633.25%	11.35%	2.43%	1.68%	1.32%	1.08%	0.89%	0.76%	0.66%	0.57%
	4.5	3767.28%	956.70%	9.22%	3.59%	2.56%	2.05%	1.77%	1.54%	1.35%	1.22%
	5.99	5969.89%	3115.13%	99.91%	7.58%	3.32%	2.17%	1.70%	1.41%	1.26%	1.12%
	7.5	8193.99%	5277.72%	2518.42%	53.97%	6.98%	3.52%	2.37%	1.81%	1.49%	1.31%
	9	10427.94%	7481.48%	4598.37%	1615.02%	29.93%	6.15%	3.20%	2.20%	1.69%	1.38%
	10.5	12675.73%	9713.16%	6782.75%	3948.89%	148.37%	18.92%	4.85%	2.62%	1.77%	1.37%
	11.99	14910.05%	11937.83%	8985.37%	6079.02%	3268.53%	99.97%	13.02%	4.05%	2.39%	1.66%
	13.5	17171.07%	14193.70%	11229.48%	8291.20%	5418.24%	2251.95%	70.75%	10.02%	3.81%	2.46%
	15	19411.41%	16431.15%	13460.51%	10506.87%	7587.90%	4745.73%	712.94%	43.62%	8.17%	3.57%

As can be seen from Table 9.6, the higher the arrival rate relative to the service rate, the greater the relative error. Clearly, the greater the operational time of the queue the better the convergence to equation (9.11). It is also interesting to see how robust equation (9.11) is for well-behaved queue characteristics (i.e., where the service rate is higher than the arrival rate). While Table 9.6 shows the absolute value of the relative error associated with the analytical expected waiting time expression for a finite queue operating time, the results tend to be consistent across different metrics (e.g., expected number of people served).

Assume that the queue in the airport is run for a finite time, only the first 100 passengers are given a discounted price on the flight, provided they come within the hour. It can be shown that the costs for running the ticketing operation when the airline is forced to hire one, two, three, or four passenger agents at the start of the queue for a period of 60 minutes are $103, $82, $89, and $102 respectively, where I have used the following assumptions:

- The cost associated with hiring a passenger agent is a base rate of $20/hour.
- Passenger agents need to be hired for an hour.
- The airline is charged $100/hour for the time the ticketing desk is opened.
- The arrival rate of the passengers is 10 per minute.
- The service rate is two per minute.

Hence, it is more cost efficient to hire two passenger agents up front. If the airline only hired one passenger agent for the entire hour and then brought on an additional agent as needed (i.e., no additional holding time) so that the queue is not jammed up and costs are managed, it can be shown that the cost associated with operating the queue when there are one, two, three, and four passenger agents now become $103, $70, $60, and $54 respectively. These results are captured in Figure 9.7.

Figure 9.7 also contains the results associated with a 10-minute holding time that were run for the purposes of comparisons. The results associated with a 60-minute holding time and 0-minute holding time do not contain any form of optionality. The reason is that in the instance of the 60-minute holding time, servers are hired at the start of the queue and kept for a duration of the entire 60 minutes, whereas in the instance of 0-minute holding time, the servers are only brought and used when necessary—in the process demonstrating the upper and lower bounds associated with the flexibility options. To obtain the results associated with a 10-minute holding time, I assumed that whenever the additional server is brought, the server is kept for a period of 10 minutes before being released (where the condition of release

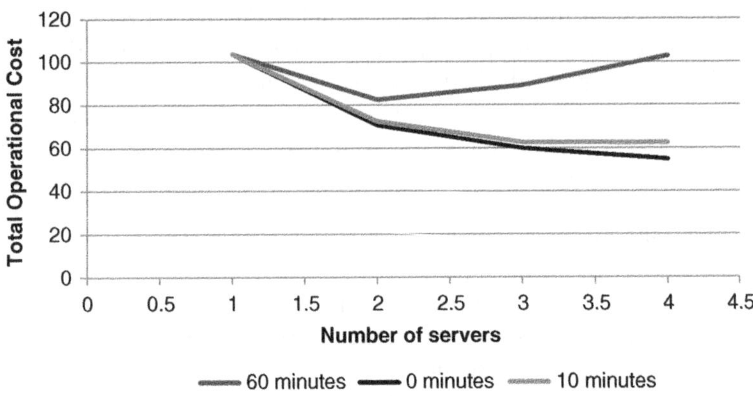

FIGURE 9.7 Impact of Server Holding Time on Operational Costs

is strictly predicated on if there is any passenger waiting to be served). As the astute reader realizes, it is more correct to implement the decision of deciding whether to bring a passenger agent onboard for 10 minutes based on the time remaining and the expected queue length over the remaining 10 minutes—something that can only be done with the aid of decision trees, like that illustrated in Table 9.4, which has been left as an exercise for the reader.

REFERENCES

Cooper, R. B. 1981. *Introduction to Queuing Theory*. 2nd ed. New York: Elsevier North/Holland.

Erlang, A. K. 1909. "The Theory of Probabilities and Telephone Conversations." *Nyt Tidsskrift for Matematik B* 20.

Hull, J. C. 2012. *Options, Futures and Other Derivatives*. 8th ed. Upper Saddle River, NJ: Prentice Hall.

Kendall, D. G. 1953. "Stochastic Processes Occurring in the Theory of Queues and Their Analysis by the Method of the Imbedded Markov Chain." *The Annals of Mathematical Statistics* 24:338–354.

Little, J. D. C. 1961. "A Proof for the Queuing Formula $l=\lambda w$." *Operations Research* 9:383–387.

Myers, S. C. 1977. "Determinants of Corporate Borrowing." *Journal of Financial Economics* 5:147–130.

Ross, S. M. 2006. *Introduction to Probability Models*. 10th ed. New York: Elsevier Science & Technology.

CHAPTER 10

Parting Thoughts

In putting this book together, I made a conscious attempt to assume that the reader is comfortable with a lot of the standard quantitative tools, like calculus, statistics, probability, numerical analysis, and so on. For those who do not have this background or need a review of such topics, I strongly encourage the consultation of the website accompanying this book–something that I will be updating regularly.

As I mentioned several times throughout this book, the use of quantitative methods in daily business and financial affairs is becoming increasingly prevalent as companies try to gain an extra edge against their competitors. Thus, the more a practitioner gets comfortable with quantitative tools (some of which were touched on in this book), the better the ability to quantify the risks associated with the impact of decisions, consumer behavior, revenues, profits, and so on. While the existence of readily available mathematical/statistical packages like Matlab and @Risk give a practitioner the necessary ammunition to tackle problems discussed without having to create the underlying infrastructure, it is important to understand that these tools are nothing but tools. Hence, a practitioner still needs to understand the assumptions, constraints, and models deployed in the respective businesses so as to be able to couch the practical problem in the context of an analytical problem (often using simplifying assumptions), which can then be solved using any known quantitative method. While this book presented the reader with examples of how a practitioner can make such simplifying assumptions to couch a practical problem into a solvable quantitative problem, it should be noted that these are just a handful of examples that are far from being exhaustive.

I was only able to scratch the surface of practical examples in this book and it is my desire to improve on the examples by supplementing them in future editions of the book. As a consequence, I would love to hear from readers about other examples and topics they would like to see discussed in future editions of this book.

About the Author

Kannoo Ravindran consults globally with financial institutions (e.g., banks, insurance companies, etc.) on all aspects of derivatives trading, modeling, and risk-management (inclusive of pricing/development/hedging of guarantees embedded in insurance and investment products). In addition, he lectures around the world (including universities) on these topics. He also runs a private equity fund trading volatility, arbitraging mispriced assets, and purchasing distressed assets. As the pioneer in applying derivatives to risk-manage market exposures relating to variable annuities, he has been involved in various aspects of implementing risk-management programs associated with these products. His unique perspective blends exotic derivatives trading and portfolio management in nearly every asset class (e.g., interest rate, currency, equity, commodity, mortality, and credit) with real-time, hands-on experience in building models/process/systems/controls/hedges relating to managing risks both as a market maker and a hedger.

About the Website

The purpose of this book's companion website is to provide materials to supplement the book so as to enhance the readability and understanding of this subject matter.

Go to www.wiley.com/go/ravindran (password: mfm14) for the following resources:

- Calculations Associated with Examples (Spreadsheet)

  This component contains 66 spreadsheets, each of which contain calculations that are used to produce the examples (i.e., tables) in the book. These spreadsheets are built using Excel functions so that readers can understand the transparency associated with the steps taken to carry out the calculations—in the process making it easier for readers to implement their version of a faster algorithm using C++, MathLab, and so on.
- Exercises to Chapters (Document and Spreadsheet)

  This component contains practice questions for Chapters 2 through 9. In addition to these exercises, data for questions in Chapters 2, 3, 6, and 8 are also given in spreadsheets.
- Supplementary Information (Document and Spreadsheet)

  This component contains documents and spreadsheets, all of which can be used by the reader to refresh on some of the basic mathematics related to matrices, calculus, differential equations, probabilities, distribution theory, Gaussian quadrature weights, calculation of bivariate cumulative normal probabilities, and impact of splining on swap rates.

Index